The

Life and Times

of

Thomas Dixon

1805 - 1871

Lead Ore Smelter, Early Railwayman,

and much more besides

Stafford M. Linsley

The Life and Times
Of Thomas Dixon
1805 – 1871

© Stafford M.Linsley

First published November 2006
by
Wagtail Press,
Gairshield,
Steel, Hexham,
Northumberland
NE47 0HS
www.wagtailpress.co.uk

All rights reserved. No part of this book may
be reproduced, reprinted, photocopied or
utilized in any form without written permission
from the author and publishers.

ISBN: 0-9538443-6-6

Designed by T.W.Kristensen

Printed by Elanders Hindson

CONTENTS

Dedication

This book is dedicated to the late Gilbert Maxwell (Jim) Budge, for many years a librarian at the University of Newcastle, and the late Vivian Fairbairn, chemistry master at Hexham, both committed and inspiring adult students of mine for many years.

Acknowledgements

The existence of Thomas Dixon's diaries was drawn to my attention by the late Eric Griffith of Sandhoe, Hexham, in 1975.

I am particularly grateful to my wife, Tessa Gray, whose research and analysis of the early diaries re-awakened my own interest in them. Hilary Kristensen has been a very helpful source of information, particularly on Thomas Dixon's daughter Jane, and a patient support throughout the preparation of this book for publication. Thanks also to Mrs L. C. White, Geoffrey Milburn, Andrew Swallow of Dukesfield, Peter Wilkinson, Raymond Fairbairn, the late Jim Budge, Dorothy Osler, Michael Smith, Dr D. C. Napier, Marjorie Dallison, the staffs of the John Rylands Library, the Northumberland County Record Office and Tyne and Wear Archives, Anthea Lang & Stuart Phipps at Gateshead Libraries. The diaries for the years 1838 and 1841 are reproduced with kind permission of Northumberland County Archives Service. All errors, whether in the text, footnotes or transcriptions are the author's.

1

INTRODUCTION

Many biographies have been written about the engineering heroes of the nineteenth century, men such as Robert Stephenson and Isambard Kingdom Brunel, and also of the 'captains' of industry such as William George Armstrong and Charles Mark Palmer; our knowledge of their works and lives is extensive, although inevitably incomplete. Within the context of the lead industry of the North Pennine Orefield, against which background much of this book is set, our knowledge of the activities of Thomas Sopwith is considerable, mainly thanks to the enormous and sometimes tedious diary which he left, likewise of Hugh Lee Pattinson and his innovative method of desilverising lead. However, we know very little of the lives of thousands of lead-industry workers whose names have come down to us only through their inclusion in ledgers and bargain books, or in nineteenth-century census returns.

This book seeks to redress that imbalance a little by presenting a study in 'history from below', a fairly recent phase in historical research which aims to illumine the lives of the 'common' people who made the wheels of history turn, but not as seen through the distorting lenses of official state documents, for these can be particularly deceptive. The 1842 *Children's Employment Commission (Mines)*, (hereafter referred to as the '1842 Report' or '1842 Commission'), provides some information on the working lives of ordinary workers in the North Pennine lead industry, of the nature of their work, the quality of their working environment, and the kinds of accidents and illnesses to which they were sometimes prone. It also tells us something of their social lives, their educational attainments, their gardening habits, their alcohol consumption, and sometimes their religious convictions. But this report, although extremely valuable, is nevertheless a flawed source, partly because the investigating commissioner often seems to have been as much concerned with the moral climate within which the men and boys worked, as with their working environments, their questions to witnesses reflecting some prevailing upper- and middle-class moral concerns, no matter how hypocritically they might sometimes have been professed. The commissioner was particularly troubled about the supposed 'moral' dangers to women and children who were required to work alongside men, but he was no doubt reassured by the answers to his questions concerning the absence of female workers from the dressing floors of the North Pennine Orefield.[1] These responses were, and perhaps remain, quite familiar - it was 'not fit work for women'. As one mill agent put it:

> *We do not think it proper to employ girls. We do not think it suitable to the modesty and delicacy of the sex to be so much associated in labour with the boys. The discontinuance of the employment of girls is all but universal in Weardale, and in all our Company's mines everywhere it is so.*

In similar vein some working men in Teesdale observed:

> *We think that in this place it is very improper that girls should be allowed to work at washing ore. It is worse than Indian slavery. It is not suitable for girls to have to work along with grown boys, and to hear what the boys may say to them.*

---

[11] Lead ore was separated from associated stone, spars and earthy materials, etc. at 'washing floors', the aim being to make the ore fit for smelting.

While it is evident that women had been commonly employed in the lead industry in the eighteenth century, their subsequent disappearance from the washing floors in the orefield was most likely due to changing economic and technological factors, rather than to efforts to protect their moral sensibilities and the supposed delicacy of their ears; no-one suggested that explanation to the commissioner, nor did he deduce it for himself. The 1842 Report does not, in its totality, present a rounded picture of ordinary life in the North Pennine lead industry and, as we shall see, it can be positively misleading. In spite of all the questions asked of the witnesses, the authentic voice of ordinary workers, telling directly or indirectly of the life which they led, is missing; the commissioner framed the questions and the witnesses were constrained to answer only what they were asked. This deficiency in the 1842 Report, common to many secondary sources, leaves us with a problem which is all too familiar to historians who seek to understand what it was like to be there, doing that job, living that life, at that time.

Fortunately, diaries for the years 1830 to 1838, and 1841, written by Thomas Dixon, an ore-hearth smelter at the Dukesfield lead smelting mill at the commencement of the diaries, do provide us with a more rounded picture of an individual worker's life than has hitherto been possible, and by inference of the lives of others at the same time and place. That story, based upon the diaries but augmented by information drawn from other contemporary sources, is presented here together with transcripts of the diaries themselves. The context for the diaries is also outlined through a brief consideration of the organisational structure of the North Pennine lead industry, the known history of Dukesfield smelt mill, and the roles of the smelters. A reflection on some technical and organisational changes being introduced into the industry at the time of Thomas Dixon's diaries is followed by some notes concerning some developments within religious and secular society. These observations lead into a commentary on Thomas Dixon's life, and thereby those of people close to him. Finally, some appendices provide a short discussion on the provenance and possible descent of the diaries; potted biographies, largely based on the diaries, of family members who feature strongly within them - inevitably these involve a degree of repetition - and of some other Dixon families in the area; lists of the known preachers who are mentioned in the diaries; a more detailed account of the workings of an ore hearth than is given in the commentary.

2

THE DIARIST AND HIS DIARIES

Thomas Dixon, (1805-71), the eldest son of Joseph Dixon, (1781-1858), and Elizabeth Bulman, (1782-1853), was born at Middle Dukesfield in the parish of Slaley, Northumberland, some 4 miles south-east of Hexham in the county of Northumberland. The parish was described in 1827-28 as:

> ... a wild romantic district lying between the Devil-Water and the Dipton bourn, and composed chiefly of sterile and black peaty moors, some portion of which has, however, been cultivated. It extends 4 miles in length from east to west, and three miles in breadth from north to south ... Its population in 1801 amounted to 585; in 1811 to 558, and in 1821 to 582 persons, consisting of 132 families, resident in 122 houses ... At Dukesfield there is an extensive establishment for smelting and refining lead ore, belonging to Thomas W. Beaumont, Esq. The ore is brought here from Wardle, [Weardale] in the county of Durham, and yields a great quantity of silver.

We know very little about Thomas' life before 1830, but as a literate and numerate person, it seems likely that he had attended school, perhaps the charity school at nearby Whitley Chapel, and that he had begun to work at the Dukesfield lead smelt mill at around the age of 18, probably to work alongside his father at an ore smelting hearth; certain other relatives also appear to have worked at the mill, and one of his brothers, Peter, would be employed there by 1832. At the commencement of the diaries Thomas, his wife Jane (Sparke), and their daughter Elizabeth born in the previous year, were living half a mile south east of the smelt mill at 'Dukesfield Hall', better seen as the generalised address of a small community, rather than as any particular building, although there was a 'hall' at Dukesfield Hall. Thomas did not remain an ore hearth smelter at Dukesfield throughout the period covered by his surviving diaries, nor did he live at Dukesfield after April 1835, but his already wide-ranging personal interests survived his promotions to new positions at Blaydon on Tyne, and subsequently at Hexham.

Thomas did not, in fact, call his record a 'Diary', but rather a 'Memorandum Book', and we can be reasonably satisfied that he began to compile it in 1830, for that year begins with the words:

> ***Thomas Dixon's Memorandum Book for the Year of our Lord 1830.***
>
> *Containing an account of most of the births, marriages, and deaths of the inhabitants of this Neighbourhood, also remarks of all the most rare occurrences [sic], weather, and every other incident within my knowledge worthy of notice or remark. Thomas Dixon. Dukesfield Hall.*

This 'preface' does not appear in subsequent years. By his own account, therefore Thomas had not set out to keep a personal diary, and at first glance, the diary does not look very promising. He never expresses a personal opinion, except in his frequent weather notes, and his diary entries are terse and often rather irritating. For example, entries such as 'Had some talk to M^r^. Emerson about something important', or 'Tweddle came down at night in distress', or 'Father with Thos Ord at the Justice', or 'Cliffan's departure clearly ascertained', provide not the slightest clue to the significance these events. But it is partly because his diary entries were essentially a record of events rather than a set of views and opinions, that an authentic story can be unravelled. This makes Thomas's diaries important in their own right, for so few diaries of this kind have come into the public domain.

One other diary, recently published under the title *A Miner's Diary of 1907*, (see Robertson in list of sources), bears some comparison with the diaries of Thomas Dixon. Amazingly, this 1907 diary was discovered in a tin box in a stream around 1960, and kept in safe hands before it was subsequently published. The 1907 diarist worked in a coal mine in East Cumbria, only some 20 miles from Dukesfield as the crow flies, and his diary offers, in the words of its editor, 'a glimpse of life in 1907'. Not the least fascinating aspect of comparisons between this diary and that kept by Thomas Dixon, is that although separated by a short distance in space, but 70 'tumultuous' years of the Industrial Revolution in time, little had changed in the lives of ordinary workers in rural industries.

The commentary, and the footnotes throughout this book are, inevitably, littered with words such as 'seemingly', 'perhaps', 'possibly' and 'probably'. This is partly because of uncertainty about the meaning of some words in the diaries, partly because the brevity of the diary entries leave much scope for speculation, and partly because of the frequency with which surnames like Bulman, Dixon, Dickenson, Forster, Spark(e), Teasdale, etc. occur. It is possible, for example, that five or six different William Ridleys are mentioned in the diaries – a genealogist's nightmare, and the obvious temptation to carry out family history on several entire communities was, therefore, easily resisted. However, if nothing else, the hesitations, doubts, suppositions and caveats expressed throughout this book demonstrate that more research could be profitably carried out on the diaries, and on the hundreds of people, (more that 800, including over 100 preachers and vicars), who are noted, often only briefly, within them; many unanswered, and some unanswerable questions remain.

Dukesfield Hall and cottages from the south-east Plate. 1

Plate. 2 Dukesfield Hall

Dukesfield Hall farm as it is today.

Plate. 3 Old Farmhouse

Granary, bothy and dovecot.

Plate. 4

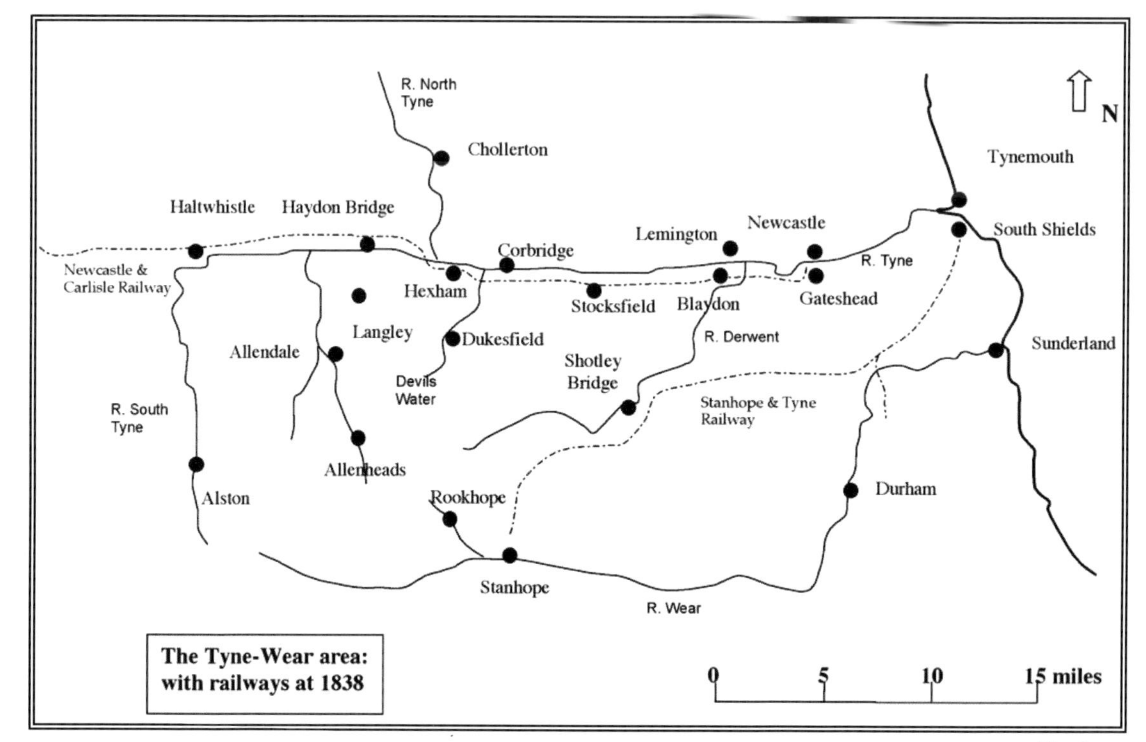

R. North Tyne
Chollerton
Tynemouth
N
Haltwhistle
Haydon Bridge
Lemington
Newcastle
South Shields
Corbridge
R. Tyne
Newcastle & Carlisle Railway
Hexham
Stocksfield
Blaydon
Gateshead
Langley
Dukesfield
R. Derwent
Allendale
Sunderland
Shotley Bridge
Devils Water
R. South Tyne
Stanhope & Tyne Railway
Allenheads
Alston
Rookhope
Durham
Stanhope
R. Wear
The Tyne-Wear area: with railways at 1838
0 5 10 15 miles

Fig. 1

Fig. 2

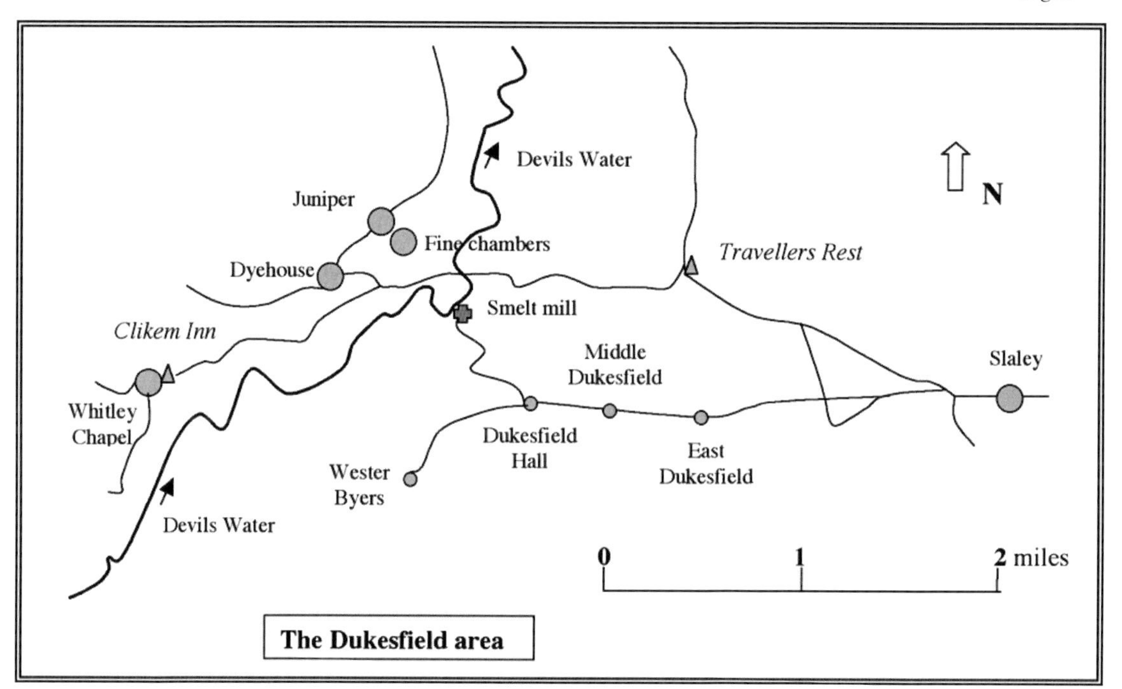

Devils Water
N
Juniper
Fine chambers
Dyehouse
Travellers Rest
Smelt mill
Clikem Inn
Middle Dukesfield
Slaley
Whitley Chapel
Dukesfield Hall
East Dukesfield
Wester Byers
Devils Water
0 1 2 miles
The Dukesfield area

THE DIARIES AND THEIR TRANSCRIPTION

The diaries from 1830 to 1837 inclusive were kept in simple notebooks, (the years 1830 to 1834 in one booklet and 1835 to 1837 in another), and were written in a continuous manner, apart from a line drawn across the page after each Saturday entry. For example, the first full week of 1830 in the original diary appears as:

> Jany 3rd At our folks' at tea - Fine day - 4th Building our hearth; had the bellows, back and workstone up - 5th Finishing our hearth - Purvis band in the country - 6th At Hexham - very strong fresh wind - 8th Ann Simpson here making Jane a gown - playing at Clickem assembly with Rowley; only 7 Ladies present - 9th A fox set off at Eshells - Seeing Jacobs children at night who have the measles -

---

A typical group of entries from May 1837 is also shown below.

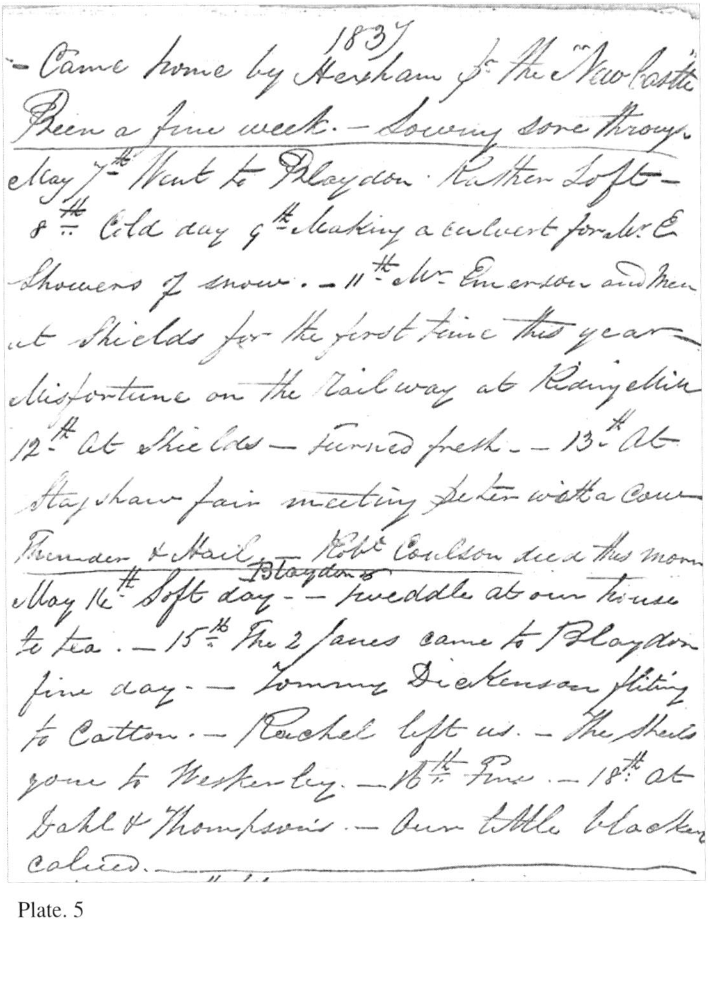
1837
- Came home by Hexham & the Newcastle
Been a fine week. – Sowing some throug.
May 7th Went to Blaydon · Rather Soft –
8th Cold day 9th Making a culvert for Mr E
Showers of snow. – 11th Mr Emerson and Men
at Shields for the first time this year –
Misfortune on the Railway at Riding Mill
12th At Shields – turned fresh. – 13th At
Stagshaw fair meeting Peter with a Cow –
Thunder & Hail – Robt Coulson died this morn
May 14th Soft day – Blaydon Tweddle at our house
to tea. – 15th The 2 Janes came to Blaydon
fine day. – Tommy Dickenson flitting
to Catton. – Rachel left us. – The Sheils
gone to Weskerley. – 16th Fine. – 18th at
Dahl & Thompsons. – Our little blacky
calved.

Plate. 5

In the transcriptions, however, individual days have been separated to aid clarity of presentation, and the months and days have been dated in a simplified manner. Thomas's division of each week to begin on a Sunday has been retained, but marked by a space rather than a line, and each Sunday of the year has been marked as such to further assist the reader. Each set of three consecutive smelting shifts at the Dukesfield smelt mill would normally begin on a Monday or a Thursday, and those days when Thomas was, or probably was on his smelting shifts, have been indented. Days when another smelter was 'on' for Thomas have been included in the indents, but not those when he was 'on' for someone else. These periods include many days for which there was no diary entry, perhaps indicating that these days were largely spent in smelting, eating and sleeping while working at the smelt mill; such days have been included in the transcripts of the Dukesfield diaries, within square brackets. Days without entries while Thomas was working at Blaydon, where the smelting shift system did not apply, have been omitted.

The 1838 diary was kept in a leather bound version of the *Newcastle Memorandum Book and Register ... 1838*, which contains much printed local and national data, with pages for an 'Account of cash' opposite pages for daily diary entries; the diarist's name does not appear, but it is Thomas Dixon. The 1841 diary was kept in a leather bound *Gentleman's Pocket daily Companion Containing an Almanack ... for 1841*, (London. Price 2s 6d.). This also contains much printed national data such as a list of bankers and MPs, assessed taxes, etc., and has pages for 'Account of cash' opposite pages for diary entries; again, the diarist's name does not appear. The personal financial accounts in the 1838 and 1841 diaries have not been reproduced in this book, but can be inspected at the Northumberland County Record Office. Illustrations from both diaries are given below.

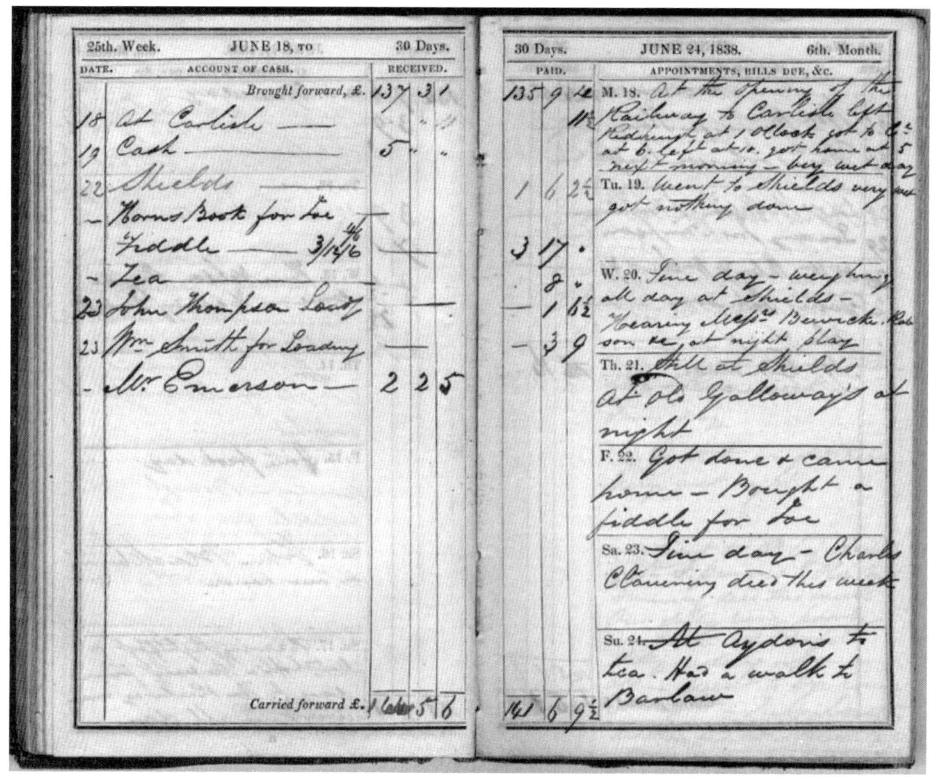

25th. Week. JUNE 18, TO 30 Days.

DATE. ACCOUNT OF CASH. RECEIVED.

Brought forward, £. 137 3 1

18 At Carlisle

19 Cash — 5 –

22 Shields

– Horns Book for Joe

Fiddle — 3/4/6

– Tea

23 John Thompson Loading

23 Wm Smith for Loading

– Mr Emerson — 2 2 5

Carried forward £.

30 Days. JUNE 24, 1838. 6th. Month.

PAID. APPOINTMENTS, BILLS DUE, &c.

135 9 4 M. 18. At the Opening of the Railway to Carlisle left Ridingmill at 1 o'clock got to C. at 6. left at 10. got home at 5 next morning – very wet day

1 6 2½ Tu. 19. Went to Shields very wet got nothing done

3 17 –

8 – W. 20. Fine day – weighing all day at Shields – Hearing Messrs Bewick Robson &c at night Play

– 1 1½

– 3 9 Th. 21. Still at Shields at old Galloway's at night

F. 22. Got done & came home – Bought a fiddle for Joe

Sa. 23. Fine day – Charles Clavering died this week

Su. 24. At Aydon's to tea. Had a walk to Barlow

141 6 9½

Plate. 6

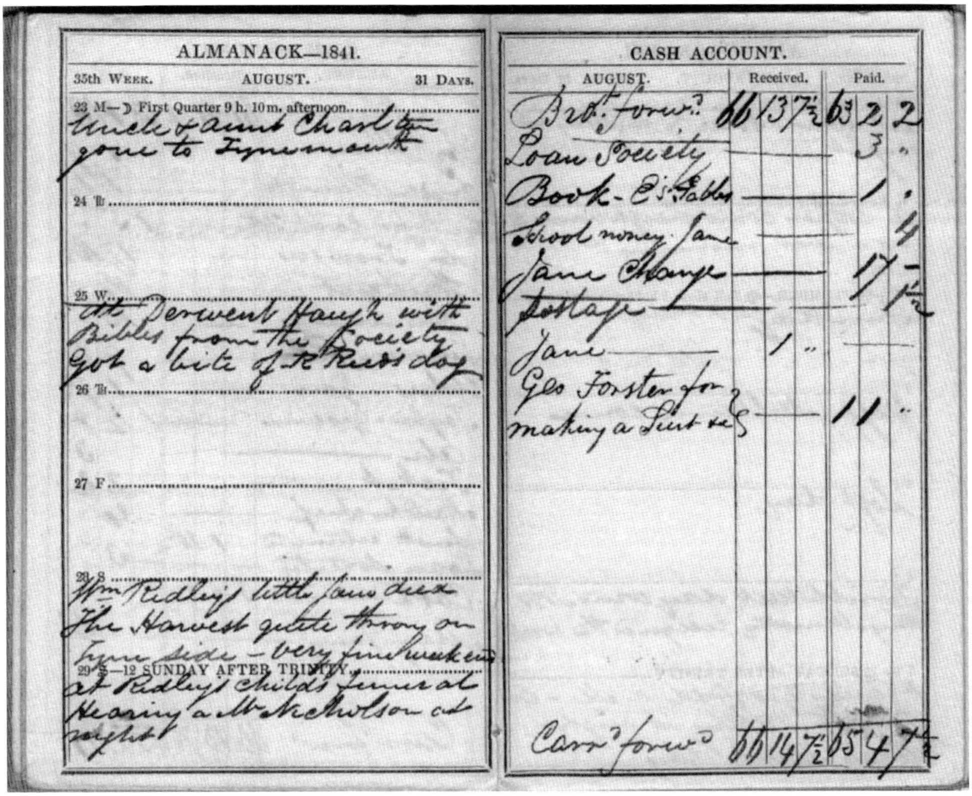

Plate. 7

Thomas's hand is fairly easy to read, although distinguishing between his capitals 'T' and 'F' can be problematic. Some of the punctuation in the diary has been altered in the transcriptions, both by omission and insertion; for example, where Thomas simply wrote 'am' to mean 'morning', and 'pm' to mean afternoon, the transcript uses 'a.m.' and 'p.m.' The original spelling has been retained in the transcriptions, (Thomas uses 'Spark' and 'Sparke' indiscriminately for example, even though his wife's family name was 'Sparke'), but editorial expansions have been added in square brackets where this was deemed helpful; the symbol [?] has been used to indicate uncertainties. Some lower-case initial letters in the originals have been capitalised, for example, 'friday' has been transcribed as 'Friday'. The names of locomotives, racehorses, and newspapers have been italicised, but the names of public houses have been left as they appear in the diaries. The footnotes are all editorial additions.

A number of words and phrases within the diaries no longer form part of common parlance, and dialect dictionaries have been used to provide some of the footnotes. In other cases, meanings become obvious as the diaries proceed. For example, the significance of 'Sally Oxley got her bed this week' is made clear by the later entry 'Babby Ellerington got her bed of a son' - childbirth. However, other terms and phrases have defeated this writer, even if he has sometimes hazarded guesses as to their meaning: 'Fooring up 'tatoes at night', 'Helping Bob to make spile shoes'.

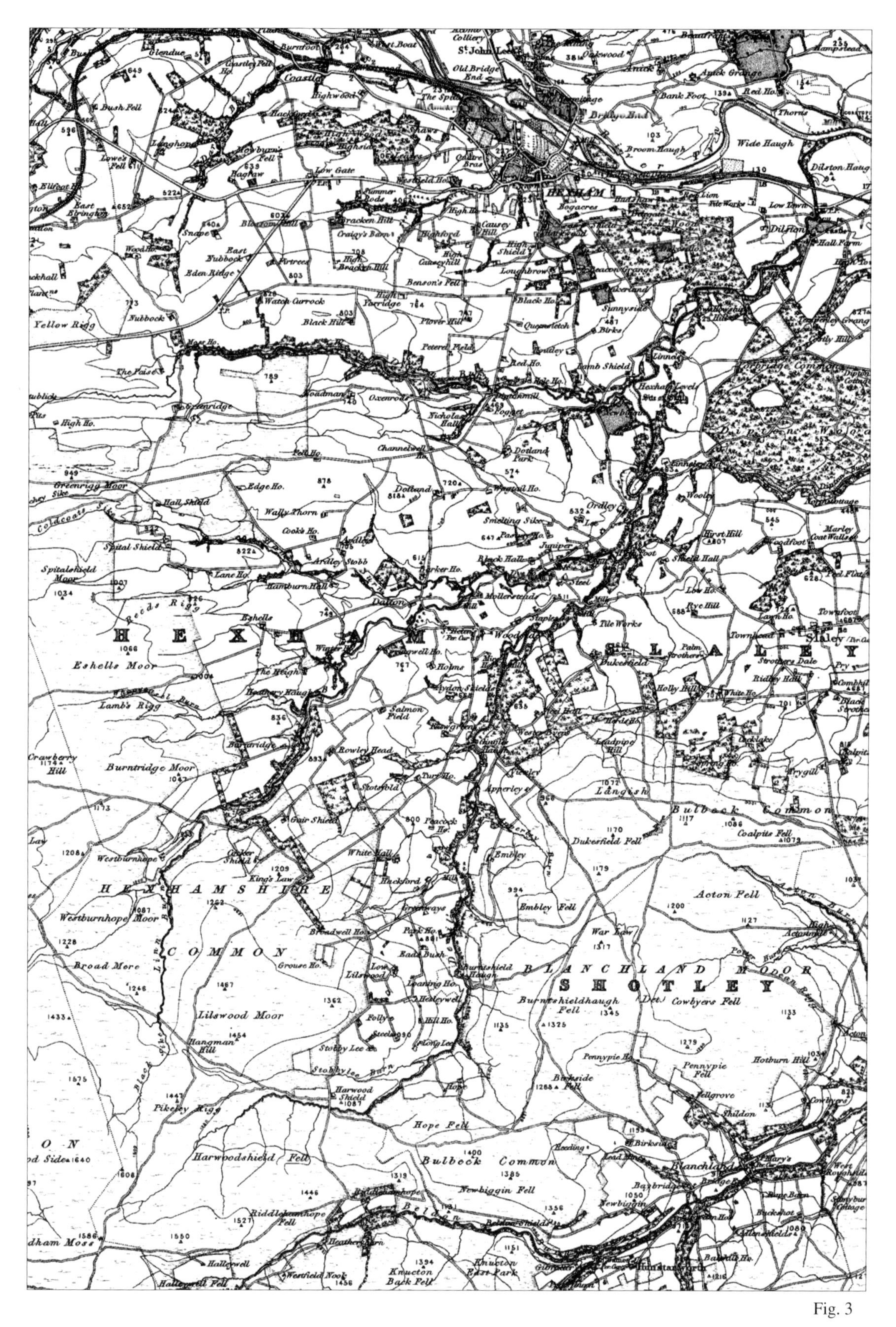

Fig. 3

1866 map showing Hexham, Hexhamshire & Slaley areas. (1 inch = 1 mile)

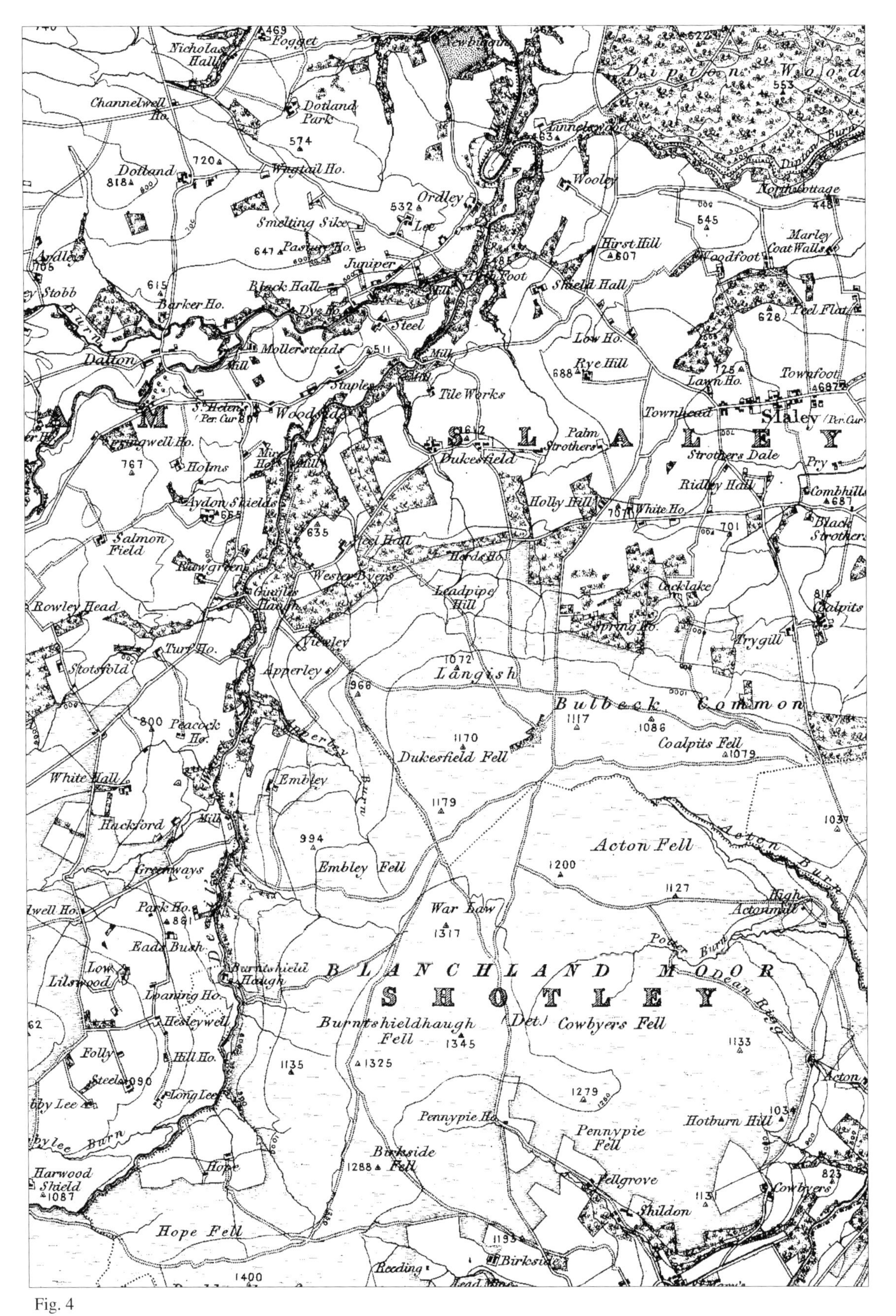

Fig. 4

1866 map showing Hexhamshire & Slaley areas in more detail (1 inch = approx. 1.5 miles)

Many alternative forenames are used throughout the diaries, some being uncommon today, for example 'Babby', meaning 'Barbara', in the quotation given above. Further examples are:

Effie for Euphemia
Bella for Isabel or Isabella
Betsy for Elizabeth
Jemmy for James
Mally for Mary
Nancy or Nanny for Ann
Peggy for Margaret
Sally for Sarah

Where forenames only are given in a diary entry, they frequently, but not always, refer to one of Thomas's relatives. The most common are:

Jane	His wife
Elizabeth	His daughter
Little Jane	His daughter
Sally	His sister Sarah
Betsy	His sister Elizabeth
Joe. Jo^s, Jos etc	His brother Joseph
Peter	His brother
Liza/Eliza	Jane's sister Elizabeth
Jemmy	Liza's husband James Ellerington
Tweddle	Jane's brother John Tweddle Spark
Jacob	Usually his uncle Jacob Bulman
Hugh	Jane's cousin Hugh Armstrong

The diaries are essentially a record of events, in some but not all of which, Dixon participated. For example, when Thomas noted 'Hexham Fair' on a particular date, it cannot be safely assumed that he was present, unlike when he wrote 'At Hexham fair with the cow'. He may or may not have attended 'Lilswood sporting', but 'Jane and I at Clickem sporting' leaves no room for doubt. Similarly, 'Leek preaching for the last time' does not necessarily imply that Thomas was present at the preaching, whereas 'Hearing Leek' does. Finally, in an age where early death was common, in adults as well as infants, Thomas's description of someone as 'old' is clearly at odds with the aspirations of the longer-living generations of today; 'Old Robert Stokoe' who died on 6 September 1832, was a mere 63 years of age.

THOMAS DIXON'S MEMORANDUM BOOK FOR THE YEAR OF OUR LORD 1830

Containing an account of most of the births, marriages, and deaths of the inhabitants of this Neighbourhood, also remarks of all the most rare occurrences, weather, and every other incident within my knowledge worthy of notice or remark. Thomas Dixon. Dukesfield Hall

January 1830.

1. Clickem and Johneys club feasts[1] *- At old Thos Dickenson's funeral - Fine frosty day.*
2. The Washing let at the Mill - Breaking up at Clickem[2] *- Bob Dixon and W^m^. Dinning fought.*

Sunday 3. At our folks' at tea - Fine day.
4. Building our hearth; had the bellows, back and workstone up.[3]
5. Finishing our hearth - Purvis band in the country.[4]
6. At Hexham - very strong fresh wind.
8. Ann Simpson here making Jane a gown[5] *- playing at Clickem assembly with Rowley;*[6] *only 7 Ladies present.*
9. A fox set off at Eshells - Seeing Jacobs children at night who have the measles.

Sunday 10. Hearing[7] *Hardcastle - The coldest day this winter - wind N with showers of snow.*
11. Sent our bacon off to Colling this morning[8] *- Filling soil - Showers of snow.*
12. Marg^t^. Burdus and Betty Teasdale here at tea - Heavy showers of snow - Wind E.
13. Jane very bad of tooth ache.
14. On with raw ore[9] *- Very stormy.*
16. Snowing - Purvis at Clickem acting.

Sunday 17. Very hard frost.
19. Mother and Jane at old Bell Dixons[10] *- Terrible hard frost.*
20. Dreadful blast at night - Wind S.E.
21. Seeing Alice Smith who has the measles - M^r^. Spark[11] *and Oxley at Bywell.*
22. An account of Jo^s^. Bulmans death.

---

[1] '*Clickem*' was the public house at Whitley Chapel, properly called the *Fox & Hounds* which closed in the 1990s; 'Johneys' is unknown, but may have been John Forster's *Fox and Hounds* at Slaley or one of the other pubs in the district; the 'club feasts' may have been associated with a savings club or friendly society.
[2] 'Breaking up' seems to imply the end of a specified period of work, or possibly the commencement of a 'break' almost as in 'holiday'.
[3] See the appendix on lead smelting.
[4] This Purvis was an entertainer, see also 16 January 1830.
[5] Jane was Thomas Dixon's wife.
[6] The function of the 'Assembly' is not obvious, but Dixon was probably 'playing a musical instrument.
[7] Dixon uses the word 'hearing' to mean listening to a preacher or priest at a religious service or gathering.
[8] The bacon from a pig which they had fattened and killed. Colling was perhaps a local butcher.
[9] Ore which had not been pre-roasted.
[10] Bell Dixon was probably the father of Percival and Bell who died at Dukesfield in 1811 (aged 32) and 1813 (aged 20) respectively. They were buried at Whitley Chapel. Bell himself died on 15 March 1831.
[11] Jonathan Sparke was the Dukesfield smelt mill agent, and also Thomas Dixon's father-in-law.

Sunday 24. At Uncle Willy Hall's at tea - A great deal of snow lying.
25. Some oats laid in our room.
26. Taking the line to Lindsey[1] *- our Jos very bad.*
27. A great twilting at Sparks.[2]
29. The severest frost this winter - Hannah Soppit buried[3] *- A thaw at night.*
30. Walton and Robson here last night - Frosty again and the wind Northerly.

Sunday 31. John Hall and Hannah here at tea.

February, 1830.

1. Coming on snow - Masons on with the furnaces - Roasters been on with soot about 6 weeks.[4]
2. Snowey day, Wind E.
3. Very hard frost.
4. Snowing.
5. Thrashing for Mr. Spark a.m.[5] *- Snowy day - Hearing Dickenson's fiddle at night.*
6. Very cold day and dreadful blast at night. Wind, S.E.

Sunday 7. Large wreaths of snow - Turned fresh at night.
8. Fresh day - At Lowes' Mill - The water in Oxleys' house.
9. Rather frosty - Hugh left Charlton yesterday.
10. Geo. Stobart here.[6]
11. Fresh day - On with part roasted [ore].
13. Fine day - Sally Oxley got her bed this week[7] *- Old Lindsey here with the web - Geo. Steevenson married lately.*[8]

Sunday 14. Geo. Barrow here at tea - Fine fresh day - Thos. Burdus hurt his eye on Friday.
15. Blaydon pay day.
16. Hard frost. Began with a severe cold.
17. Very bad.
19. Continued hard frost - Our folks leading manure - Ruddock's haystack burnt this morning - I am still very bad of a cold.

Sunday 21. Fresh snow lying this morning.
22. Charlton of Sandoe married - Stormy day.
23. Hugh gone to seek work.
24. Fine, fresh day - Dickenson the soldier here.
26. Willy Dodd taking the priest's farm.
27. Fine fresh weather - Sowing peas - Jemmy's house letting.[1]

---

[1] Lindsey was probably the weaver by the name of John Linsley, who was at Peth Row, Hexham Low Quarter, in 1827; see also 13 February 1830 and 7 April 1838.
[2] i.e. Quilting.
[3] Hannah was the daughter of Robert Dixon of Mollarsteads, and was aged 31 when she died. Robert himself died in April 1832 aged 73, while his wife Ann died in June 1837 aged 79 years; they were buried at Whitley Chapel.
[4] The 'soot' would probably be the recoverable deposits within the smelt mill chimneys which were roasted before being smelted in a slag hearth.
[5] Threshing corn, probably by hand flail.
[6] Probably Stobart the doctor.
[7] 'Got her bed' means 'gave birth'.
[8] George Stephenson married Mildred Carr at Allendale on 17 January 1830.

Sunday 28. Jane and I at meeting; a new gallery opened.[2]

March, 1830.

3. Johnson and Nixon here[3] *- Mr. Spark exchanged horses - Frosty mornings and fine days.*
4. At Hexham; got some trees; and one of Dickenson last night - A great dinner at H. Blackburns.
5. A Dance at Blackburns of Slaley.
6. Uncle Thomas here - Frosty mornings & fine days.

Sunday 7. Hearing Hardcastle - Uncle John and Nancy here at tea - Jos. Milburn here.
8. Our folks cow calved, 6 weeks before her time.
9. Sowing onions and setting 'tatoes - Mr. Spark and H. Oxley got Dickenson's farm. Babby Ellerington got her bed of a son.
12. Very windy weather - Jon. Barrow here at tea - A fresh law for begining work.
13. Robt. Smith begun a singing school - At the singing - Ellerington's house repairing.

Sunday 14. At meeting p.m. Robt. Smith preached.[4]
16. Desperate showers of snow, Wind N.W.
17. The lime all done at mill - Uncommon windy weather.
18. At Hexham; got a pair trowsers and waistcoat.
19. Joseph's looseing at Clickem.[5]
20. Very cold, windy, showery, weather.

Sunday 21. A preaching, Hardcastle preacher.
22. Setting 'tatoes on the east square of the garden. Jane at Betty Fairlambs.
23. Gardening for W Dixon, Juniper.
24. Margt. Burdus got her bed of a son - Ann Browell here - Teasdale sowing oats.
25. Hexham Fair; very low fair[6] *- old Mich. Elliot died this week.*
27. Old Thos. Simpson died - Jos Briddock cutting hedges this week - Fine day; but rather frosty. Railway begun [to be built] this week.[7]

Sunday 28. At Chapel a.m.[8] *- Meeting and T's Rest*[9] *p.m. - Jane at cakes making at Black*

---

[1] Jemmy was James Ellcrington, who would soon marry Jane Dixon's sister Elizabeth Sparke.
[2] This probably refers to a gallery within a non-conformist chapel or other meeting place. It may have been at Dukesfield where there was a Wesleyan Methodist society from at least 1826 to 1831, combining with the Finechambers Wesleyan Methodist Society in the latter year, or it might have been at Finechambers.
[3] Benjamin Johnson was a land agent for the Beaumonts, with his home at Lovaine Row, Newcastle; he would soon be made chief cashier to WB Lead; Thomas Nixon was a land agent for the Beaumonts.
[4] A Robert Smith was leader of the Dukesfield Wesleyan Society in 1826 and 1828. This Society had 17 members and 8 second class members in 1826. The Dukesfield and Finechambers WMs combined in 1831. An R Smith, Thos Smith, and R Smith junr, all of Spring House appear as a preacher on the Hexham Wesleyan Circuit in 1851; none of them were down to preach at Finechambers.
[5] Possibly the end of an apprenticeship.
[6] This was perhaps the fair established in 1741, and held fortnightly from March to November, for sheep and cattle.
[7] I.e. the Newcastle & Carlisle Railway.
[8] Meaning at the church at Whitley Chapel.
[9] The *Traveller's Rest* public house near Slaley.

Plate. 8

Above - The Clickem Inn c.1920. Also known as the Fox and Hounds and in the 19th C as Woodside farm. Now a private house.

Below – The Travellers Rest c.1905. Still open, it is situated between Whitley Chapel and Slaley.

Plate. 9

Hall Mill[1] *- Carlin Sunday,*[2] *uncommon fine day.*
29. Setting 'tatoes at night - very fine day.
30. Jane at Old Simpson's funeral - Very snowey afternoon and night.

April, 1830.

1. Cleaning a conduit at Mill.
2. Began washing - Jacob raised the timber at the Globe - Showers of snow and very cold. Wind N.E.
3. Terrible day of snow - Henry Wood here on Thursday making a pair of trousers.

Sunday 4. Hearing Leak preach a.m. All lying with snow.
5. Fresh strong rough wind.
6. On smelting for Jos. Bowman - Fresh day.
7. Went on to work at 11 Oclock to-day.[3]
8. Jo^{s}*. Bowman on for me - At Travelers Rest sporting - Hugh Nixon won the trail - Stephen Charlton and Lambert the horse courses - A terrible night of thunder and fire.*
9. Good Friday - fine day.
10. Jem. Dodd galloways sale day[4] *- Seeing the dogs run at Junipher.*

Sunday 11. Easter Sunday - At the Chapel a.m.; meeting p.m. hearing Bearpark.
12. Washing this forenoon - Jane and I at Clickem sporting - Sim won the tarrier race - Tom Todd the belt.[5]
13. The pay-day.[6]
14. At Johneys at night.
16. At Dalton sporting - Hugh Nixon won the Hounds, Mather the Whelps, Will Armstrong the Belt - fine days.
17. Setting 'tatoes. Dolly Lamb and Hutchinson married.

Sunday 18. Hearing Leek[7] *- Jane at Dalton. Old Jemmy and Hannah Richardson here.*
19. Mill on, was off last week - Setting 'tatoes at night; last row of reds small sets, last row of whites large sets.
20. Very wet day and some thunder.
21. Betty Hutchinson's sale at Hole row - Seeing Thomasin at night.
23. At Hexham buying a hat - Jane and I at Dipton sporting - The Derwent dog won the tarriers, the Cloger the belt.
24. At Bywell with Jemmy seeking license;[8] *very wet day - Old Bill Dixon the steward buried.*

---

[1] The significance of cakes making, an activity mentioned three times by Dixon, is not known to the author, but is perhaps it concerned with baptismal, marriage, or funeral occasions.
[2] Carlin Sunday was the second Sunday before Easter, Passion Sunday, when grey peas, having been steeped all the previous night in water, were then fried in butter, well peppered, and served at table by the landlords of alehouses as 'Carlins'. This offering is still made at a few public houses today.
[3] This was a Wednesday, the early start to smelting being to accommodate the Good Friday holiday.
[4] Possibly James Dodd, listed as a farmer of Long Lee in 1827/28. Galloway ponies-used as pack ponies.
[5] This may have been Tom Todd of Knarsdale, Alston, whom John Lee described in his book *Wrestling in the North Country* (Consett, 1953), as being 5 feet 10 inches tall, weighing over 12 stones, and an 'accomplished and scientific wrestler, who could buttock cleanly, hype quickly and excelled in most other chips'. He had won his first belt in about 1811, at Alston.
[6] The annual Pay at the smelt mill.
[7] Robert Leake.
[8] For Jemmy's marriage to Jane's sister Elizabeth (Eliza), see 1 May 1830.

Sunday 25. At our folks at tea. Jacob & Betty there - Droughty day.
26. Jo^s. Milburn at the Mill building a foundry house.
27. Setting the last 'tatoes.
28. At Clickem with Barrow.
29. Jemmy and Eliza setting up - Sticking peas - very droughty weather, wind S.E.
30. Very hot day - Thunder at night - Lilswood sporting.

May, 1830.

1. At Jemmy & Eliza's wedding dinner.[1] *Tom Smith and Jack Charlton fought on Monday last - Very fine day.*

Sunday 2. Hearing Hardcastle.
3. On with Westonhope, very bad stuff.[2]
4. Jane at Hexham.
5. Returned the bed, which we got last Thursday. Tythe rent day.
6. Henry Wood making Jo^s. a coat - Warm day.
8. At Turf-house sale - very cold day, and wet night.

Sunday 9. Large floods this morning - very wet day.

10. On for W^m. Ridley who is at Longhope sale[3] *- very cold E wind.*
11. Hiring day.[4]
12. The Staples folk shifting to Mollarsteads.
14. Old Peggy Smith of Spring house buried.
15. John Bownas married[5] *- John Dickenson's sale - fine day Wind W.*

Sunday 16. Hearing Leek a.m. Rich^d. Dinning and us at our folks' at tea - a severe frost on Friday did much ill.
17. Still on with Whestonhope - Uncles seeking relief at Law.
19. Seeing John Hall who is very bad of a pluracy - Ordering a pair of clogs at Juniper.
20. Our folk and Betty Teasdale here at tea.
21. On peat Fell with father.
22. Millwrights on with cylinders this week and last[6] *- Jane Curry married on Thursday*[7] *- John Hall still bad - very cold weather, wind E.*

Sunday 23. Geo. Cox here at tea - Jane and I seeing John Hall.
24. On for W^m. Ridley - wet day wind E.

---

[1] James Ellerington of Juniper, Bachelor, of the parish of Hexham, and Elizabeth Sparke of Dukesfield, spinster in the parish of Slaley, were married on May 1st 1830 in the presence of W[?] Colling and Margt Sparke. [Slaley Parish Records.]
[2] i.e. lead ore from the Westonhope mine, located a couple of miles to the south of Westgate, County Durham.
[3] It is possible that Thomas Dixon mentions 5 or 6 different William Ridley's in his diaries, but this one is the only one that we can be fairly certain about, a lead ore smelter who moved to Langley when Dukesfield was closing. He married Mary Dickinson/Dickenson at Slaley on 2 February 1828. Their son Thomas was christened at Whitley Chapel on 29 June 1828; son John was christened at Whitley Chapel on 16 August 1829; son William christened at Whitley Chapel 6 October 1833.
[4] This would be a Hexham hiring as hirings were usually associated with either a fair or a market. Hirings were essentially about the hiring of agricultural workers on a yearly basis, but it seems likely that domestic servants were similarly contracted. Hirings were normally outdoor events, held in a market place.
[5] John Bownas married Mary Rowland at St Peters, Allenheads, 15 May 1830.
[6] This might refer to blowing cylinders to replace standard bellows. See also 'Memorandum 1838'.
[7] She married Thomas Stokoe at St Peters Allenheads.

25. Hr[y]. Wood[1] making me a waistcoat.
26. Sparks' folk had party.
29. At Whitsun fair with Peter[2] - M[r]. Spark got a bay horse - Fine morning; but rather wet at night.

Sunday 30. At Allen Town with Jane, James, Eliza, and Mary - Very fine day - Betty Dinning got her bed. Very showery day.

June, 1830.

1. Mill laid off by the level running in.
2. Men on cleaning the level - Fine day - Catherine Armstrong buried.
3. Went at night to finish our week's work.[3] Very wet night.
4. Nanny Harrison got her bed on Tuesday - Large floods this morning. Willy Brown of Sheel-hall died suddenly this morning.
5. Jane and Eliz[th]. at Elizas - Thos Cliffan married[4] - Fine day.

Sunday 6. Seeking Eliz[th]. from Juniper a.m. At Jacob's at afternoon.
7. Showery day.
8. At Hexham, got an ax - Very soft day,[5] Wind N.
9. Seeing the drainers (Jack Nicholson and Mark).
10. The farmers seeking metal from Weardale[6] - John Dixon took bad on the road.
11. Jane at Smith's of Slaley - Fooring up 'tatoes at night[7] - A draughtier day.
12. Geo. Woodman died this week - John Thouburn married about a month since.[8] A very cold, wet season this so far, the wind very much to the north and east - A pigeon shooting at Clickem tonight - The quality off to the County of Durham.[9]

Sunday 13. Hearing Leek a.m. - John Hall & Jos. Smith here at tea.
14. Wet and thunder - wind N and E.
15. Very wet day, wind NW.
16. Same as yesterday - Eliza here at tea.
18. Jane at old Bells at tea.
19. Still wet weather as ever - Wind N.W. - John Dickenson's goods marked - I am ill of the toothache.
Sunday 20. At Chapel a.m. - Jacob, Tho[s]. Cliffan and wives here at tea.
21. Cold and wet - Wind northerly.
23. John Dickenson's furniture taken away - Fine day.

---

[1] Harry Wood the tailor - see 29 July and 14 August 1830.
[2] The Whitsun Fair, mainly for the sale of cattle, sheep and horses was held on a piece of open moor at Stagshaw Bank, some 2 miles north of Corbridge, and was a smaller version of the main fair held there annually on 4 July, one of the largest cattle and sheep fairs in the north of England which also provided a great spectacle and festival for all who attended.
[3] That is, he went in on the Wednesday because work had been interrupted by part of the mill race collapsing.
[4] Thomas was Uncle Jacob's brother-in-law.
[5] 'Soft' might mean drizzling.
[6] Seeking ore.
[7] Possibly Furrowing.
[8] John Thorburn married Ann Smith, probably at Whitley Chapel, on 15 May 1830.
[9] Possibly meaning a group of upper-class people.

Plate. 10

An old engraving of the east side of Hexham Market Place with the 17th C White Horse Inn in the foreground with the Moot Hall beyond. The White Horse was demolished in 1859.

24. Dull day, wind E.
25. Dickenson's things sold - Very wet afternoon and night.
26. Some rain and thunder - Jane Richardson here at tea - At Travellers Rest at night seeing dog trails.

Sunday 27. Hearing Hardcastle a.m. At Salmon Field at tea - Some thunder and rain.
28. Much thunder - Sent some wool away - Teasdale cliping his sheep.
30. Very warm day - Nanny Dickenson got her bed.

July, 1830.

1. Dressing up the garden - Jane at Hexham with Mary getting a tooth drawn.
2. Thunder and rain - Jane twilting.
3. His Majesty King George 4th died last Saturday morning 15 minutes past 3. Thunder and rain - At old Hannah's meeting hearing John Bell exhort.

Sunday 4. At Slaley Church hearing Mr. Harrison - At meeting p.m. Jemmys at tea, and Johneys at night.
5. On smelting for Cant[1] - At Travrs Rest at night - Refiners start this week, Pter Dixon comes on - Only 8 roasters on - Fine day, heavy shower near night.
6. At Hexham; saw the King proclaimed - Saw Dickenson's land sale - Mother very bad.
7. Very showery day.
8. Very droughty day.
9. Very wet - George Nevens' sporting day.
10. Mr. Sparks new mare died - Very wet day.

Sunday 11. Hearing Leek a.m. - At Slaley hearing Mr. Hall - Colling, Jemmy and Eliza here at tea - wet night.
12. Very wet morning.
13. Very fine day.
14. Mary Robson here at tea.
15. Jane and Sally at Jacobs twilting - Father and I making a barraw.
16. Railing the apple trees - Laid a blister on at night for my teeth.
17. The King was buried on Thursday - Liddell declined coming forward this week - The weather more favourable this week than it has been.

Sunday 18. Jane at Slaley Church - At Mr. Sparkes to dinner and tea; Sarah Armstrong.[2]
19. Mother and Jane at Traveller's Rest - Footing peats[3] - Mr. Sparke got a mare and foal of Jno. Lowes[4] - Old Parke casting metal at mill.
20. Peter on washing with me.
22. Peats begun coming in to-day - Mrs and Miss Longridge come.
24. Been a very warm week - Uncles John and Jacob settled to-day.

Sunday 25. At Cliffan's at tea - Hearing Hardcastle a.m. - Very warm day.

---

[1] John Cant was listed as a lead ore smelter, living at Ridley Hall, in the 1841 census.
[2] Jane Dixon's cousin.
[3] Presumably digging peat.
[4] There were two (and possibly three) men by the name of John Lowes in the area. One had married Margaret Davison and was a corn miller and perpetual overseer living at Finechambers mill in 1827/28. Another was a lead ore smelter who married an Elizabeth and may have lived both at the Lee and at Oxenrods in the period c1827-34. A John Lowes, possibly one of the above, was a member of the Dukesfield Wesleyan Methodists in 1826.

Plate. 11

The west side of Hexham Market Place with a row of shops, houses and inns in front of the Abbey. These were demolished in the mid 19th C.

26, 27, 28. Extremely hot.
29. Jane and Eliz[th]. at Jemmys - Harry Wood making Peter a new suit - Our folk and M[r]. Sparke begun mowing (Michael and Billy Purvis).
30. Helping our folk at hay - Much Thun[der] and some rain at night.
31. At Hexham - Buying a new coat - Working at hay p.m. - Fine day - Parliament was disolved last Friday - The water scarce this back end of the week, the first time.

August, 1830.

Sunday 1. Wet a.m. - Jane and I at meeting hearing J. Hunter - at Sparks at Tea - Slaley meeting p.m.
2. Helping both folks with hay - Very windy and rather wet.
3. Helping Sparks folk with hay - Very windy day.
4. At hay a.m. - Went to mill p.m.; the water still light[1] - Rather wet at night.
5. The farmers set off this morning to Alnwick - Jane at Hexham geting a tooth drawn.
6. Hexham fair day[2] - The Election at Alnwick - Got done work this night.
7. Peter and I stacking peats - John Hunter here preaching - Been a very fine week upon the whole.

Sunday 8. Hearing Leek a.m. At Jemmys at tea; an Alston man and women there. Fine day.
9. Mother and Jane at Ridleys of Steel - Rather wet.
11. Rather wet - Wind S.
12, 13. Helping Sparks folk with hay - got it all up - 12 pikes in high field 10 pikes low.[3]

14. Harry Wood here making me a frigate[4] - Sowing Cabbage seed - Our folk gone to Chatts - The assizes this week at Newcastle.

Sunday 15. At Chapel – Edw[d]. Corbet and Jane and Richey here at tea - Rather wet at afternoon.
16. Leading hay, (M[r]. Spark), came on wet and laid us off - Mally Barrow and 2 lads here.
17. Dull day but fair - Thos Dickenson of Lee removing his goods off his premises.
18. Finishing Spark's stack - Fine day.
19. Went to work this forenoon - Fine day.
20. Moody seeing the silver taken off at Mill[5] - A Lamb feast at Johneys.[6]
21. Leading our folk's hay at afternoon. Very fine day - Lowes' land sale day.

Sunday 22. Hearing Leek - Jemmy and Eliza here at tea - W[m]. Maughan and Betty at this place - Jos[a]. Smith, Dixon and others at our folks.
23. Went to work at 1 Oclock this morning; water still light.

---

[1] The 'lightness' of the water probably explains why he went to work on the Wednesday.
[2] The August Fair was for cattle, horses and sheep, chiefly lambs from the vicinity of Langholm in Scotland, when Bailey & Culley (1794; 1805) was published.
[3] A 'pike' of hay was a small stack, perhaps containing half a ton of hay; several pikes would later be added to the main stack.
[4] A 'frigate' was obviously an article of clothing since Wood was a tailor. Possibly a type of frock coat.
[5] W B Lead sent their silver to a London goldsmithing concern, selling it at the Hatton Garden market price for silver on the day of its arrival in London.
[6] Lamb Feasts are normally associated with Spring (Easter) but this one was possibly just an organised meal at a local pub.

24. Jane at Coalpits.
25. Got done work this morning.
26. Mrs Peter Dixon died.[1]
28. Very wet day - Wind NE.

Sunday 29. At Meeting hearing little Thompson - At Airdley Meeting at night - Mrs Dixon buried - Very fine day.
30. Helping Jane to wash.
31. At Hill-House leading - At Bill Paddisons' all night.

September, 1830.

1. Came home from Hill-House p.m. - Went to work at night[2] *- Plenty of water 2 days (last) but failed today - Showery - Brother George Forster here.*[3]
2. Very wet morn soon on - Jane and Elizth*. at Jemmys.*
3. Went to Allen Races - Ralph Smith's dog won the cup - W^{m}*. Bell the wrestling cup - at Jo*^{s}*. Milburn's all night.*
4. Races continued - Fine day - John Teasdale of Slaley married this week[4] *- W*^{m}*. Ridley on for me yesterday - Our gooseberrys gone this week. Plenty of water.*

Sunday 5. Came home from Allen town - Jemmy and Liza here at tea - Uncle Jemmy and Isaac Lee here at night.
6, 7. Plenty of water - Rather wet, Wind E - Tom Hutchinson removed from Dyehouse.[5]
9. Very wet day; wind southerly.
10. Seeing Jo^{s}*. Blackburn - Fine day but wet at night.*
11. Dickenson's corn sold - Fine day - Old Polly Johnson died[6] *- Plenty of water all this week at Mill.*

Sunday 12. Fine day - At meeting and Liza's at tea - Rich^{d}*. Dinning asked in church.*[7]
13. Building our hearth; Barrow drunk - Filling manure at Oxleys.
14. At Oxleys again - Fine days - Very ill at night of sickness.
16. Very wet morning.
17. Peggy Milburn and Bessy Barrow come - Henry Oxley begun shearing wheat, Teasdale also.
18. Very fine day - Chris^{r}*. Roddam and wife here at night - Plenty of water at mill all this week - Slater's crops sold at Clickem inn.*

Sunday 19. At meeting and love feast - John Hall here at tea - Jane and I at Mollarsteads at night - Very Windy day.

---

[1] Isabella Dixon died 26 August 1830 aged 46 years. Her husband Peter, formerly of Tyne Mills, died 28 March 1841 at Staples. They were both buried at Whitley Chapel.
[2] This was a Wednesday, the early start enabled him to go to the Allen Races.
[3] 'Brother George Forster occurs occasionally in the diaries and was presumably a relative, but it has not been possible to place him. The 1841 census gives a George Forster living at Redlead Mill.
[4] John Teasdale married Ann Bell at Slaley on 2 September 1830.
[5] A Thomas Hutchinson was a lead ore smelter, living at Coalpits at the time of the 1841 census.
[6] This was Mary Johnson of White Hall who died aged 74, the widow of Thomas who had died 16 June 1828 aged 70; both were buried at Whitley Chapel, (Kristensen, 2003). A Mary Johnson was a member of the Dukesfield Wesleyan Methodists in 1826. Their son John died at Berwick a few weeks later, see 9 October 1830.
[7] This may have had something to do with his intended marriage, see 2 October 1830.

20. 'Liza got her bed of a son; Jane with her all night[1] - M^{r}. Husskisson killed last week.[2]
21. Peggy Scott buried yesterday - Very windy day.
22. Fine Harvest day.
23. Elizth. unwell of her throat.
24. Both boisterous days.
25. Jane, Mother and Nanny at 'Lizas - Jo^{s}. Hutchinson here - Went to Johneys at night; Newbeggin churn there[3] - Pulling onions this week.

Sunday 26. At Chapel - Fishers meeting at night.
27. Transplanting cabbage - very windy day.
28, 29. Shearing for Teasdale.
30. Fine day.

October, 1830.

1. A heavy shower @ night.
2. Richey Dinning married[4] - Old Nancy Dixon of Lee died - Very fine harvest weather - Plenty of water to do on with at mill.

Sunday 3. At meeting hearing old Wright - Dull day - Aunt Peggy Nichol came here last Thursday very bad.
4, 5. Uncommon fine harvest days.
6. Duller day - Been scant for water, for both sides this fore end.
7. Lying idle for want of shearing - Time divided this backend - Silver taken off today 10 Sto 8lb - Geo Wilson and some ladies here - Crawhalls here yesterday shooting - Jane at Lowes' seeking apples.
8. Leading our peats - Aunt Betty Bulman got her bed of a son[5] - Jane up seeing her.
9. Fine day - Teasdale done leading wheat today - John Johnson of Berwick died this week.

Sunday 10. The new beer act takes place today - At Chapel a.m. meeting p.m. hearing Wat^{n}. Forster.
11. At Teasdales at afternoon shearing; got the corn supper; but not done shearing - Dull fine day.
13. Went to work at afternoon[6] - Dull fine days yet, Wind SE.
14, 15. Weather broken out very hot, clear and frosty.
16. Aunt Hannah, Thos. and Jane Stokoe here - Dryer weather than ever this Summer - Time divided all this week.

Sunday 17. Thos. and Jane and others here at breakfast - At Tra^{s}. Rest forenoon, got some 4d. ale. At Sparks at dinner - Setting Thos. and Jane at afternoon.
18. Went on 12 at noon to smelt Westonhope.
20. Got done work at 9 at night - Jane at Burdus' churn.
21. Taking up 'tatoes - Rather showery - At Blackburn's churn.

---

[1] Presumably referring to Jemmy and Eliza, since Jane was there.
[2] William Huskisson M.P. died in an accident at the formal opening of the Liverpool & Manchester Railway, Monday 15 September 1830; it was Huskisson who had introduced the Bill which reduced duties on imported lead in 1825, thereby initiating the economic difficulties in the orefield in the late 1820s and early 30s.
[3] The 'churn' or 'kern' was a harvest supper celebration.
[4] He married Jane Corbett, probably at Whitley Chapel, but see also 29 April 1831, 5 August 1831, 29 November 1832.
[5] Christened Thomas Bulman at Whitley Chapel, 1 November 1830.
[6] A Wednesday, because time was being divided that week.

22. Wet morning - Jem Dodd opened his house to sell ale.
23. Setting cabbage plants - At Staples at night.

Sunday 24. George Forster here standing for Jemmys child[1] *- At W^{m}. Ridleys at tea - Very Fine day.*
25. On smelting for Ridley, went on at 12 at noon.
26. At Hexham - At Richey's house for the first time - At Jo^{s}. Blackburns at night.[2]
27. Writing tunes out of W^{m}. Ridleys book - The peat pay.
28. Went to work at 10 this morning - Betty Smith got her bed.
29. Robt. Smith got himself lamed.
30. West hearth belly brunt[3] *- Simpson, Maughan and mother here - Father measuring turnips for Dixon's folk - Time divided on the fore end; but plenty of water on the backend of the week - Parliament met on Tuesday.*

Sunday 31. Uncle Thomas came last night, went home today.

November, 1830.

1. Wet - Our Jo^{s}. working in Allendale all this time.
2. Jane Richardson married[4] *- Fine day.*
3. Strong S wind.
4. Taking up 'tatoes - very showery day - My father unwell.
5. On gardening - Very wet day.
6. Uncommon wet day from 10 Oclock - Elizabeth unwell at night.

Sunday 7. At Staples with Jemmy at afternoon. Very dirty day.
8. Very Fine day.
9. Peter on washing with me.
10. Mary Richardson of Riding Mill died - Digging the garden - Very wet afternoon. Wind S.
11. On with Craawlaw[5] *- Very showery day.*
12. Walker's wife got her bed of a son.
13. Very much smoked at Mill - Jane at Ridleys of Steel - Very wet afternoon - Magic puped a week last Thursday.

Sunday 14. Hearing Leek a.m. - Thomasin died this morning - W^{m}., Mary, and Peggy Ridley here at tea.
15. Jane at cakes making - very wet at times.
16. Hiring day; uncommon wet - At Thomasin's funeral - Jack Corbett married.[6]
18. Killing swine at afternoon - Sparks 21sto. our folks 20 Stone[7] *- very fine day.*
19. Parted and salted the swine. Jem Dodd's sporting.
20. Ralph Blackburn gone to live at Blaydon last Saturday.

---

[1] This seems to imply that Forster was standing witness at a christening or perhaps agreeing to be a god-parent.
[2] This Joseph Blackburn was probably a smelter and the person of that name who was a member of the Dukesfield Wesleyan Methodists in 1826. He was still classed as a smelter in 1841 when he was living at Holly Hill.
[3] West hearth bellows burnt.
[4] Jane married William Havelock Blackburn at Bywell St Andrew.
[5] This must refer to a lead ore, but the location of the 'Craalaw' mine is not known.
[6] He married Mary Heslop of Haydon Bridge.
[7] Piglets were normally bought between February and June, fed through to the following Autumn, and then, usually killed in November. The killing was followed by cleaning, butchering, salting etc.

Sunday 21. At Chapel hearing Thomasins funeral sermon a.m.; At Slaley hearing Jon^{n}. Scurr p.m.
22. Helping Wm Dixon to hing a door for gig house.
23. Peter washing with me.
24. Jane at Dodds at tea - Planting some mint.
25. Sore smoked at mill.
26. Barrasford Jacks looseing at Richeys.
27. A Foul Mart hunt at Mill[1] - The millwrights at Mill - At Mathers at night with Jemmy &c - Robt. Dixon opened his ale house - Pruddah & W^{m}. Hall of Hexham both married lately.[2]

Sunday 28. Rather unwell - A very wet day, Wind E.
29, 30: December 1. All dull wet days Wind SE.

December, 1830.

2. Taking physic - Jane at Hexham; got me a plaid.[3]
3. Manuring the bushes - Weather the same.
4. A fine day - Geo. Blackburn got the dog on Wednesday.[4]
Sunday 5. At meeting hearing Morton - John Hall and others at our folks - very cold day.
6. Helping Bill Dixon to make a house - very wet & cold; Wind E.
7. Still the same weather.
8. Pruning W^{m}. Halls bushes - very wet - The last corn in the Shire lea in a fortnight since this day.
10. Wind got to N.W.
11. Finishing the Westonhope this week - At Clickem goose-feast at night; 14 got supper[5] - Fine day, Wind W - Cliffan taken the Blackmoor.

Sunday 12. Showers of snow from NW - At our Joseph's birthday.[6]
13. Hard frost.
14. Turn'd fresh.
16. Helping my father to wash.
17. Geting my metal roasted - Very cold, frosty, day; some snow at night.
18. Very cold day - The roasters cleaning their pipes[7] - Mally Simpson, Thos. and Peggy Dickenson at our folks'.[8]

Sunday 19. Hearing Loraine preach - Very cold day.
20. Old Peggy Nicol gone home.
21. Slag hearth men working my metal - At Bobs with Tommy Dickenson and Chatt.

---

[1] This was a local name for a polecat, referring to its habit of producing a very powerful smell when afraid or injured. British Polecats were almost hunted to extinction during the nineteenth century, but have since made a considerable recovery.
[2] Hall married Isabella Barwick, probably at Whitley Chapel, on 25 November 1830.
[3] A length of twilled plaid cloth.
[4] Possibly the George Blackburn who was a member of the Dukesfield Wesleyan Methodists in 1826, and also later a grocer & draper in Slaley.
[5] Perhaps the goose equivalent of the 'lamb feast', an organised meal at a local pub, but here, no doubt, a pre-Christmas meal.
[6] This is one of only two references to a person's birthday in the diaries, the other being that of Tweddle, his brother in law; both were their 21st birthdays and these seem to be the only birthdays ever celebrated.
[7] The implication of this procedure is not known.
[8] A Thomas and a Margaret Dickinson/Dickenson were members of the Dukesfield Wesleyan Methodists, 1826-8.

22. Went on to work this morning with hearth ends.
23. Cliffann gone to Hexham this week - Very hard frost set in this night.
24. Richeys house warming to day - Old Jenny Bells nights work - Got done our work this night.
25. Our folks here at tea.

Sunday 26. At Mr. Sparks at dinner and tea - Very hard frost.
27. Water much frozen off - Much smoked.
28. John Hall and Jos. Dickenson here to bed time.
29. Got done work this morning.
30. Jane & Elizth. at aunt Peggy's at tea; went to them at night; a very stormy night - Robson of Rests[1] geese stolen last week.
31. A kind of thaw - Wm. Armstrong here - Johneys club feast - Hannah Blackburn's dance.

Remarks on the Year 1830.
The year just ended is remarkable for its wetness, although in this County we had a good harvest. It is also to be noticed for the many Revolutions, in France, Belgium, and other Nations[2]: The overthrow of the Wellington Administration, and the appointment of Earl Grey to the premiership - Also for the disturbed state of the country, the burning of corn, breaking of machines, and the general distress throughout the Kingdom.[3]

---

[1] 'Rests' may mean *Travellers Rest*.
[2] King Charles X of France was deposed and replaced by the Duc d'Orleans; Belgium became independent of Dutch control.
[3] It was threshing machines that were being broken, but only in some southern counties, as a protest by daywage workers whose winter work on the hand-threshing floors was imperilled by the machines; no such discontent manifested itself in north east England.

MEMORANDUM FOR 1831

January, 1831.

1. Clickem Club feast, all nothing but ice, turn'd fresh at night.

Sunday 2. At our folks at tea - old Jo^{s}. and Fanny, Jacob and Betty there - M^{r}. Smith's New Curate (Armstrong) preached at Slaley for the first time.[1]
4. At Hexham - Bobs at night with my Father and Jo^{s}. Dixon - Very dirty.
5. Jane and Elizth. at Dinnings at tea, went to them at night.
7. Building our hearth from the bottom, got a new one - The Dinnings here at tea - Frosty day.
8. Finishing our hearth - At the breaking up at night - 23 men were there - Doctor Charlton died this week.

Sunday 9. At Jemmys at tea - Fresh day.
10. The Hutchinson's here viewing Teasdale's Farm - Old Mally Barrow came yesterday.
11. The Bailiff here siezeing Teasdale.
12. The taylor here making me a pair of trousers - A change of partners for our paper this week[2] *- Uncommon fine day.*
13. Bownas taken Dukesfield Farm - Barrow begun Allen Mill this week - Rather frosty.
15. The Mill been off a fortnight - Masons (Smith, Bowman, Purvis, Bulman,) crowning the furnaces - The millwrights (Birtley & Dodd) cuting our wheel - Bowman covering the west end bellows - A very hard frost - Persons seeking money for the church. Jane at Peggy Dickensons this afternoon.

Sunday 16. Andrew Graham at our folks' - Very hard frost.
17. Teasdales sale today - Robsons folk here with drink - Cold day and rather mistley, Wind E. Mill begun work today.
18. Thos. & John Teasdale taken off to Goal - Weather turned very hazy and soft.
20. Began the Mill today.
21. Playing at Bobs house-warming; Jane there at tea - a very soft day, wind still E - Went to sleep at Jemmys.
22. W^{m}. Ridley on working for me; clear with him now[3] *- Harry Surtes and Nancy Curry married today.*[4]

Sunday 23. Mary Blackburn and Tom Lamb married[5] *- At Bob Dixons, afternoon.*
24. Doing a job at our hearth.
25. Hard frost, Wind NW. Mrs Cook of Wooley was buried on Monday - Hannah Dixon & Aunt Peggy here yesterday.
27. At Slaley with Jacob - Very cold day.

---

[1] See also 6 February 1831.
[2] It has not been possible to determine which newspaper Thomas took.
[3] Presumably meaning that Dixon had balanced the numbers of shifts that he and Ridley had swopped between them.
[4] Henry Surtees married Ann Currey at Bywell St Peters.
[5] At Slaley. The 1841 census for the Slaley area has a Tom Lamb, farmer, and his wife Mary, living at Combhills.

Dye House chapel and cottages 1908. The original chapel was completed in 1832 but was later rebuilt in 1865.
Before 1832 meetings were held at the Dye House as well as other houses in the area.

Plate. 12

Plate. 13

28. Joseph gone off to Lementon[1] *- Very hard frost Wind NW.*[2]
29. Cocklake sale.

Sunday 30. Hearing Wat^{n}*. Forster - Jemmy & Liza here at tea - Jo*^{s}*. come home - Very fine day.*
31. Rather snowey day.

February, 1831.

1. A dreadful blast of snow - Wind E.
2. Blast continued all night - A woman of the name of Appleby been upon the fell all night - Calmer during this afternoon.
3. Blast very ill all last night; and morning - Fairer all day.
4. Been snowing all last night - Coming on all day today; rather softer - Wind turn'd to NE and N. - Sally Dodd got her bed this morn of a daughter.
5. Bad walking to work - Blast terrible; wind N or NW - Snow very sad and deep - At Dye house at night hearing Leek - Mat^{h}*. Pears of Allendale lost last night.*

Sunday 6. Fine day; but hard frost - The Rev. M^{r}*. Smith of Slaley died p.m.*[3]
7. Turn'd fresh rather.
8. A current fresh day - Roads nearly impassible - Martin Adamson of Witley Mill drowned.[4]
9. The snow nearly all gone.
10. Fine fresh day - Begun washing today - Old priest buried - Adamson's lad found beside Dalton (fell into the water at Hoods Crag) - A Game keeper of Matfen was lost last week.

12. At Letch seeking bushes - At T's Rest at night seeking Jane & Elizth *along with Tweddle - Very fine day - On smelting for John Cant.*

Sunday 13. Jane at church a.m. - At Meeting house at afternoon & Dyehouse at night, myself - very fine day.
14. Blaydon pay - At Jo^{s}*. Blackburn's at night; Ralph's wife died yesterday.*
15. Sowing peas.
16. Uncle John & Nancy here (our folks).
18. Messrs Johnson & Nixon here - Robt Nixon and W^{m}*. Dodd on draining about this time in Ox pasture.*
19. W^{m}*. Dinning and Peggy Ellerington married*[5] *- Jane very bad of toothache - A week of fine open weather.*

Sunday 20. At the meeting hearing old Wright.
22. Bownas' father died on Saturday; buried today - The appeal day at Hexham - Peggy Johnson at Teasdales very bad.

---

[1] Lemington on Tyne.
[2] This was the commencement of a period of quite severe weather in the North East, which culminated in 3 feet of snow. Coaches got stuck, carriers likewise, more than 20 ships wrecked between Shields and Blyth, and some people died, including presumably the two mentioned by Dixon on 5 and 8 February, the latter after the thaw of 7 February which was followed by some flooding of the Tyne and its tributaries.
[3] The Revd. Joseph Smith, incumbent of Slaley was aged 75. His wife Elizabeth died on 5 April 1835 aged 65. Both were buried at Slaley.
[4] See also 2 December 1833.
[5] This William Dinning was a lead ore smelter and he married Margaret [Peggy] Ellerington, probably at Whitley Chapel, and they were living at Steel in 1841, but see also 27 October 1838 for a different William Dinning.

23. Very hard frost.
24. Cleaning the privy[1] *- At Jemmys at night*
25. Very cold & heavy showers of snow, Wind W - Jane at Jo^s*. Forsters - Uncle John here singing.*
26. Snowey forenoon - At Slaley meeting and clubing for the Malitia (4/0 each) at night.

Sunday 27. At meeting hearing Lee - Very showery day - Albany Crawhall died yesterday[2] *- My father taken very ill.*
28. Very frosty morning - Writeing Todd a gamut.[3]

March, 1831.

1. At Hexham - Methodists here at night singing.
2. Very wet forenoon - Writing Jemson's tunes.
4. Thomasin Johnson buried - Very fine day.
5. M^r*. Nixon here giving us notice to remove*[4] *- At Slaley singing school - Fine day; but soft.*

Sunday 6. Hearing Leek forenoon - Bill Adamson afternoon - Very soft day.
9. Jane at Slaley (Smiths) twilting - Very fine day - Very smokey day yesterday at mill.
11. The Eshells sale - The singers here at night.
12. Teasdales second sale - Nancy Heslop, Sally Bolam &c here at tea - very wet day.

Sunday 13. At meeting hearing a young man from Shotley Bridge - Soft day.
14. Jane & Sally at Dyehouse; went to them at night.
15. Old Bell died last night - At father Sparks at tea; Jane Smith there.
16. On smelting for Jo^s*. Dixon.*
17. Went on sooner this morning - At old Bell's funeral.
19. The equinoctial gales very desperate this week - Dressing W^m*. Ridleys bushes - Jane Charlton at our folks' - Tho*^{s}*. Teasdale come home from goal.*

Sunday 20. Hearing old Wright a.m. Carlin Sunday - At Travellers [Rest] with Jane, Mary, Jemmy &c.
21. Cribb begun the foundry - Nixon here ordering us to remove - Fine day.
22. Helping my father to sow onion seed. Hannah Bell's girl died last weekend.
23. Bownas' plouging day (3 ploughs) - Took possession of Teasdales Garden[5] *- Caty Forster & Sally Bulman here at tea, singers here at night.*
24. Setting cabbage and sowing onion. The silver taken off yesterday.
25. Hexham fair - Our folk sold the cow - Very cold day and the fells covered with snow.
26. Digging - Oxleys bull beef sold out - At Slaley singing at night with Jo^s*. and Tweddle.*

Sunday 27. At meeting hearing M^{tt}*. Wilson.*
28. Digging - Fine day - Jos. Blackburn married.
29. Gardening for W^m*. Burdus - Malitia drawn (G. Lowes for Slaley) - Cold E wind.*
30. Went on to work this forenoon.

---

[1] Ash closet.
[2] Presumably a member of the Crawhall dynasty of lead agents.
[3] Possibly meaning a musical scale performed as a fingering exercise.
[4] The Teasdales losing their farm, perhaps because of rent arrears, and Bownas taking it, plus Nixon giving Thomas Dixon notice to move, etc., all seem to be related.
[5] This reference to taking the garden is rather confusing, but it seems likely that it was Thomas rather than Bownas who took it.

31. T's Rest Races; John Lee won: Jane and I there - John Cant on for me - Miss Charlton late of Intake buried yesterday.

April, 1831.

1. Good Friday - Mill off.
2. John Bell here removing our bushes - Setting 'tatoes, W^{m}. Ridley on with me - Father bought a Cow of Chatt - The Dinnings parted, the slaggys smelting this week.[1]

Sunday 3. Easter day - At Chapel - At our folks at tea; Jemmy & Liza there - Very fine day.
4. Jane and I at Clickem sporting - Thinly attended.
5. Jo^{s}. Dixon on this forenoon for me.
6. Taking 'tatoes out of the holes.
7. Setting 'tatoes - John Bell here sowing carrots.
8. Gardening at Burdus' this forenoon - At Dalton sporting - Jerry Carr won the belt - wet forenoon, but fine aft.
9. Setting 'tatoes - Some thunder at night.

Sunday 10. Showery - At meeting hearing J^{o}. Bell.
11. W^{m}. Dixon & Bowman cutting some trees in calf close - Very fine day.
12. Washing - Fine day - Tommy Hornsby drawn for Malitia.
13. Bownas' ploughing day; very wet, wind E.
14. Droughty day.
15. Setting 'tatoes at night (7 rows: 1st below, 2nd above, 3 next below, 2 last above).
16. At uncle Willy's ploughing day - Fine day - Sarah Armstrong here - Stewards gone off to the pays.[2]

Sunday 17. Hearing old Wright a.m. - Old Mary Taylor & John Lowes' eldest girl buried.
18. Fine day - On washing.[3]
19. Pay day at Hexham - John Barrow here at breakfast - Dull morning; but a fine day - The pay at White Hart for first time[4].

20. At J Dodds p.m.[5] *- Johneys at night.*
21. Jane at Miss Angus' sale; got a feather bed - Building our hearth - Jane Curry got her bed on Sunday or Monday.
22. Jane and I at Dipton sport - Dull day and soft at night.
23. At Sally Dixon's sale at Lee - Cold day.

Sunday 24. Jemmy & Liza here at tea - At Jem Dodds afternoon - Parliament was dissolved on Friday.
25. Begun the mill today; was off last week - Oxleys ploughing day.
26. Jane very unwell of a sore throat.
28. Marg^{t}. washing for us - Very wet betimes - Bownas leading stones.
29. A great meeting at Hexham; M^{r}. Beaumont there - Rich^{d}. Dinning's wife died yesterday - John Hulls sale today.

---

[1] 'Slaggys' are slag hearth smelters.
[2] 'Stewards' are the WB agents.
[3] The usual smelting shifts seem not to have been worked this week, possibly because of hearth rebuilding, and the Pays being made.
[4] The White Hart Inn was in Fore Street, Hexham
[5] Probably Joseph Dodds, a lead ore smelter.

30. Very wet day - wind SE - Brown's sale of Shield Hall - Canvassing commenced this week - pitmen off work.[1]

May, 1831.

Sunday 1. At Slaley Church; hearing Armstrong for the first time - At Dyehouse meeting at night - seeing John Dryden who is very ill.
2. Father on for Wm. Ridley.
3. Heavy showers - Rowells the gardeners here.
5. Showery day.
6. Very frosty day - Allendale hiring & fair.[2]
7. Uncommon frost; much ice - At Slaley seeking club money.

Sunday 8. Our folk and us at uncle Jacobs - Fine day.
9. On setting 'tatoes at night - Mr. Beaumont & Lord Howick elected for this County - Fine day.
11. Thomas Teasdale shifting to Dukesfield - The Hornsbys preparing our house.[3]
12. Removals; M Richardson from Dukesf., - Josh. Smith to Houghtley, Geo. Barrow from here - Fine day.
13. C Nevin come here - Cleaning the house and removing part furniture - Dull day.
14. Removing every-thing today - Removals this week - Ridley to Shield Hall, Young to Rye hill, Hutchinson to Lamb Shield, Betty from Sparks - At J Dodds at night - Very fine day.

Sunday 15. Hearing Wright - At Trygal this afternoon, Old Bill Robson of Slaley buried.
16. The Joiners come to Lodge.
17. At Hexham hiring - Very warm day.
18. Working in garden - John Carr, Thos. Makepeace, Jem Burdus married yesterday this week[4] *- Thos Charlton come.*
19. Mr. Nixon here - Very droughty day. Wind E. Robson leading us the first coals - Came here on Monday.

---

[1] A mass meeting of pitmen from local collieries had been held on 12 March 1831, and the meeting determined to seek better payments at the next ensuing binding. This was followed by another mass meeting, estimated at 20,000 men, with representatives of some 47 collieries, where the expressed grievances focused on aspects of the miners' Bond which enabled the owners to lay men off for three days without pay whenever there was the slightest hitch to smooth working, allowed the colliery managers to turn miners and their families out of their houses when disagreements over the Bond remained in dispute; and required young boys to spend up to 17 hours per day underground to the detriment of their education. Thousands of miners refused to accept new binding arrangements on 5 April 1831, and violence followed. The military were called in, and a detachment of marines set sail from Portsmouth. Another mass meeting of miners on 21 April decided to continue their strike peaceably, but gradually some miners began returning to work under the protection of the military and squads of cavalry; the strike collapsed around the middle of June, with no gains to the miners.

[2] This fair was for cattle when Bailey & Culley (1794; 1805) was published.

[3] Many of the Hornsbys were stonemasons and some were Wesleyan Methodists while others were Primitive Methodists.

[4] Thomas Makepeace, a farm labourer, married Ann Johnson, probably at Whitley Chapel. Their daughters Martha and Ann were baptised on 13 July 1834 while Thomas was working at Ordley, but daughter Ann must have died young for another Ann was baptised on 24 June 1836 when Thomas was at Mirehouse. The 1841 census for the Slaley area has them living at Whinney Hill. A tombstone in Slaley churchyard indicates that Thomas Makepeace of East Dukesfield, died 4 March 1872 aged 67; Ann his wife died 29 March 1872 aged 62; Mary their daughter died at Tynemouth 'when visiting that place with the Teachers and Scholars of the Haltwhistle Sunday School', on 11 July 1873 aged 41; Hannah their daughter died at Red Hemmels, 14 May 1880 aged 46; Dorothy their daughter died at Hermitage 24 November ? aged 42 Joseph Gill their Grandson died at East Dukesfield, 18 March 1872 aged 5.

21. Stagshaw fair, Bownas got 2 horses - Fine dull day, Wind E.

Sunday 22. At Slaley Church a.m. Meeting house afternoon - Thos. Charlton here at tea - Very warm.
23. Thos. Charlton gone home - Thunder & lightning at night.
24. Jack Scott & Peggy Johnson married; also Jo^{s}. Dickenson the soldier.[1]
25. Jane and I at Trygal at tea - Very fine day.
27. Allendale Band come to Tra^{s}. Rest.
28. Liza & Nancy Codlin here at tea - Aunt Peggy Charlton come to our folks' - A very strong drought wind mostly E. - The masons laying the foundations for the back building of Bownas' house this week - The smelters parting time this weekend for the first time this year.

Sunday 29. Hearing Leek - At our folks' at tea - Charlton & Peggy there
31. Mother and Jane at Hexham; got a new gown and hat.

June, 1831.

1. Helping M^{r}. Sparks' folk to sow turnips.
2. Went to work at 3 this morning - Some rain and thunder at afternoon.
3. Harry Wood at our folks' making Jo^{s}. a new suit.
4. Jane, Elizth. and Betsy[2] *at Liza's - Men on pareing the park - A Lad of the name of Stobbs drowned in Tyne this week - The water still to part this week.*

Sunday 5. At Lawslaw hill camp meeting; got ourselves very wet.
6. Went to work at 12 at noon.
8. Aunt Nancy & Mary Ridley here making Jane gown & curtains.
9. Casting peats - Mother & Jane seeing old Han^{h}. Carr.
10. Fine rain this morning - Wind W.
11. A heavy rain from the east - Seeing Frank Purvis bass fiddle[3] *- The water still to part.*

Sunday 12. Hearing old Wright - At Bobs and Jemmys at afternoon.
13. The smelters on with bad Scraith Head.
14. At Hexham; got a new hat.
15. Some thunder and rain - Went to work at midnight.
18. Jane at Hexham seeking Marg^{t}. who has got her arm hurt - Old Richard Muse of Hackford buried.

Sunday 19. At Slaley Church - Jemmy & Liza here to tea - Went to work at midnight - Peggy Dinning got her bed last week of a son.
20. Newcastle races begin today.
22. The Joiners come - Begun making a new garden.
23. Setting Jane & Elizth. to Hexham - With the Joiners at Todds, singing.
24. Playing at Bob Dixon's sporting - Some good showers.
25. Seeking Jane & Elizth. from Hexham - The King's speech was delivered on Tuesday to the new parliament - Wm Ridley married to Mary Phipps.[4]

---

[1] John Scott married Margaret Johnson at Whitley Chapel; Dickenson the soldier married Jane Foster at Slaley.
[2] Betsy was Thomas Dixon's sister.
[3] This may have been Francis Purvis, a millwright of Blackhall Mill, who seems to have subsequently moved to Blaydon with his wife Hannah (1841 census).
[4] At Chollerton.

Sunday 26. At Chapel; Thos. Charlton gave out singing[1] *- John Harrison here at tea.*
27. Soft betimes - Jo^{s}. working for Alex last week and this.
28. With the Joiners at Todds again.
29. Joiners raising the timber.
30. The Sessions at Hexham.

July, 1831.

1. The singers here at night.
2. Jane & Elizth. at Ridleys of Steel - Burdus' child of Coalpits was buried on Wednesday.

Sunday 3. Fine rain this morning - Playing the violon cello for the first time at the meeting house.
4. Stagshaw fair day[2] *- Went to work at 12 O clock at noon.*
5. Jane & Miss Dryden at Travellers.
6. Mother gone to Haltwhistle.
8. At Hexham Races.
9. The Mason on slating Bownas' house - John Ridley of Mill died - A very warm week.

Sunday 10. At the meeting hearing old Wright - Dryden of Kennel at Sparkes.
12. Washing slags for my father, who is off to the Doctor for Sally - At John Ridleys Funeral - Old John Carr of Park buried.
13. Went to work at 5 O clock tonight.
14. A very wet morning - Wind E.
15. Got done work at 7 O clock this evening - Some heavy showers today - Water for all today.
16. Fine day - at uncle John's at night singing - Some men taken on Monday for uttering base coin at Steel, Staples, &c.

Sunday 17. At Slaley Church; Priest Atkinson reading himself in - Fine day.
18. All on together today.
19. Water to part today again - At Peggy Andersons funeral.
20. At Hexham buying a new gown for Jane - and a bass fiddle.
21. On mowing for our folk - Some heavy showers - Wind W.
22. On washing - Miss Dryden of Kennel at Sparke's - Tommy and I playing in Sparke's parlour.[3]
23. The joiners finished Bownas's house this week - Setting the Joiners to Slaley - A new bridge laid on at Path foot this week.

Sunday 24. At meeting house hearing Leek - A love Feast held - At Jemmys at tea - A very warm day.
25. Mowing all day for our folk.
26. Finished the mowing this morn.
27. Helping our folk with the hay, got it all into pike & kiles[4] *- Aunt Nancy and Betty Todd*

---

[1] 'Gave out singing', can mean that the singer could not read music.
[2] This was the main Stagshaw Fair, sometimes called the 'Midsummer fair' to distinguish it from the Stagshaw Whitsun fair.
[3] Tommy may have been Thomas Oxley.
[4] Several 'kiles' of hay were assembled to make a 'pike'; several pikes made a stack. It was a method of progressive drying of the hay.

here making Jane a gown.
29. Mary Blackburn here at tea.
30. Wm Dawson married[1] *- An uncommon warm week been - The water all on for 4 hearths - At Slaley with Jemmy & Tweddle hearing the new singing master.* [2]

Sunday 31. At Slaley Church morning - Chapel afternoon with my fiddle - Miss Reader here at dinner - Thunder & rain - Jemmy and Liza here at tea.

August, 1831.

1. Water for us all today.
2. Water parted.
3. A mistley rain.
4. A wet day - Pulling berries to preserve - Dreadful thunder at night.
5. Much thunder – Ric^{d}. Dinnings child died.
6. Hexham fair; Bownas' folk gone to the new house - Some thunder and rain at night - Thos. Charlton & H Bell married - At Bobs at night; Leek preaching for the last time.

Sunday 7. Hearing old Wright - Thunder and rain afternoon.
8. Washing slags for father who is unwell - Hannah Hall taken very ill this night.
9. Hard on with trenching.
10. Helping Sparks folk with the hay stack - Went smelt at afternoon - water turn'd scarce; been plentiful for the other men.
13. Jemmy helping me - Our folk leading hay. Aunt Hannah R came yesterday - Mrs Beaumont died this week - on Thursday[3] *- The harvest very general on Tyne side, Lambshield, and Linnels &c.*

Sunday 14. At Chapel a.m. - Jane at meeting and Liza at tea p.m.
15. Went to work at midnight this shift - Began thundering and raining at 9 or 10 o clock this morning and continued nearly all day most dredfully - The largest floods in remembrance - Our dam gone; Dye-house, Pathfoot, Dalton &c. bridges gone.
16. Off from want of water till 6 at night - More thunder & rain.
17. More thunder and rain today, worst at night.
18. Helping Chris^{r}. Simpson with the race[4] *- An inquest held on the body of a man found in the Letch wood.*
19. At mill gathering wreck - Setting a new crane at night.
20. A cold NE wind - At Dye house hearing Smith - Smelters all on together.

Sunday 21. Hearing Thompson who has come to this circuit - Hugh Armstrong[5] *here at tea.*
22, 23. Very fine warm days.
24. Jo^{s}. helping me to trench - Rather showery.
25. Very showery day.
26. Very strong wind - Rye hill crop sale (Maughans).

---

[1] He married Margaret Linsley, probably at Whitley Chapel.
[2] 'Singing masters' were usually itinerant teachers of singing who charged those who wished to learn, supplied sheet music etc.
[3] This was the Mrs Beaumont who, until her death, was heading WB Lead. She was succeeded in this position by her son, who soon instituted changes in the management of the concern.
[4] Presumably the smelt mill race. A Christopher Simpson was a miller of Blackhall Corn Mill.
[5] Jane's cousin.

Plate. 14

Above – Peth Foot bridge c.1910

Left – Steel Hall farm, south west of Dukesfield Hall c. 1950

Below – Juniper House c. 1900

Plate. 15

Plate. 16

27. Messrs Teasdale's corn sale at Dukes field & Eshells - A fine afternoon - Water very scrimp for both sides.[1]

Sunday 28. Jane and I at Slaley Church a.m. Hearing Jack Hunter p.m. - Fine day; but soft near night - Liza gone to Allendale yesterday.
29. All on together - The cropers on shearing.
30. Had to go to the dam level to seek water this morning - The Joiners came yesterday to Steel hall.
31. Very strong wind last night and today.

September, 1831.

1. Shearing for Jack Scott - Wages 3s.
2. Shering at Blackburn's - Playing at Trygal churn - Soft morning; but fine night.
3. Sheafing corn for Jack Scott - very warm day.

Sunday 4. Soft morning - At home all day - At Juniper at night seeing Jemmy who is unwell.
5. Jane and I sheafing corn by the acre for Jack Scott.
6. Ditto - Fine days.
7. Finished sheafing - Went to work at 12 at noon - Some thunder & rain.
*8. The Coronation day of W^m^. 4th*[2] *- Much rain.*
9. Water for us all today; the time parted this fore-end - Allendale races begin today - Old Johney Davison died yesterday.
10. Father helping me to trench - Masons begun the garden wall - Jane & Mary at Slaley; Tweddle & I went at night - Shearing done at Dukesfield Hall (except Jack the Wright) - On with raw ore this week; the roasters been off a fortnight or more.

Sunday 11. At Chapel a.m. - At Sparks to tea - Jemmy (who is very unwell just now) and Liza there - Fine day.
13. Very wet day.
14. Fine day.
15. Fine day; but wet at night.
16. Soft day by turns - At Young's corn supper at T Rest.
17. Fine day - The Mill dam rebuilding let to M^r^. Kile - Oliver begun a singing school at Slaley this week - Robt. Elliot of Hexham died this week - Water for all sides this week.

Sunday 18. Hearing Thompson a.m. - Jane & I at Slaley church at afternoon - Jemmy & Liza here at tea - Jane and I at Dye-house at night.
19. Fine day.
20. Fine, but wet at night - Mother at Hexham buying Jane a wheel.[3]
21. I am very unwell of a cold.
22. A very fine day.
23. Soft day and strong W wind.
24. A very wet forenoon - The Joiners got a finish, been here in all eleven weeks - Setting the Joiners to Slaley - John Harrison's infant child buried - Both sides been on together all this week.

---

[1] In short supply.
[2] There were extensive celebrations in Newcastle and elsewhere in the North East on this day, as a glance at any contemporary local newspaper will indicate.
[3] Presumably a spinning wheel.

Plate. 17 Above – West Burnside cottage, Slaley c.1900 on the Slaley to Blanchland road.

Plate. 18 Below – Cottages in Slaley village c.1905. These cottages also have heather thatched roofs which were known as "black thack".

Sunday 25. Wet forenoon - Hearing old Stobart at afternoon.
27. Mary Robson here at tea.
29. Peter Dixon & Capt. Nicholson in our house - Very wet forenoon.

October, 1831.

1. Very wet day; and has been a very wet week, the wind E - At Slaley Singing school at night.

Sunday 2. Hearing M^{r}. Norther - Uncle John & Nancy here at tea - At Dyehouse meeting at night - Fine Day.
3. On washing; had Ja^{s}. Ridley on.
4. Father, Mother and Jane at Hexham - Armstrong begun a singing school at Chapel last night.
5. Fine dry day.
6. A very wet morning.
7. Sore smoked at Mill - M^{r}. Armstrong here at tea.
8. Jon^{a}. Blackburn at Mill - Mother and Jane at Jacobs - Fine day.

Sunday 9. At the Ranters meeting hearing Bilson[1] *- John Ramsey at our folks' - Very fine day - Jane seeing Nancy Dinning at night who is very ill.*
11. Betty Smith here at tea.
12. Jane, Marg^{t}. and Mary at Dye-house - Jon^{a}. Blackburn at our folks'.
13. The masons on at the wall.
14. At old Hannah Carr's funeral.
15. Our folk gone to Uncle Thomas' - At Dyehouse hearing John Bowman preach[2] *- Very fine night - The Reform Bill was thrown out last Saturday.*

Sunday 16. At Chapel - Armstrong's pupils sung for the first time - At Slaley Church on the afternoon - Jane at Dyehouse meeting at night - A very fine day.
17, 18. Helping the masons - Very fine day.
19. Hugh Armstrong helping me to trench.
20. W^{m}. Dinning and others at Alnwick - The taylors making me a pair of trowsers.
22. Got done work at seven O clock this morning - On the peat fell - The masons finishing the garden wall - A very strong wind - Been a very fine week altogether.

Sunday 23. At Chapel a.m. - Slaley Church afternoon - At Sparks to tea, Jemmy & Liza there - Jane at Fisher's meeting at night.
24. John Dixon helping me in garden - A very soft day - W^{m}. Johnson was married last Saturday.[3]
25. Taking up 'tatoes - At Chapel singing at night.
26. Very showery.
27. Cutting fire wood - Jane at Spring House - At Slaley singing at night.
28. Jenny Bell's house warming.
29. Finished leveling the garden - Been a very soft showering week - The mill been off this week on account of the masons working at the dam.

---

[1] James Bilston.
[2] The 1841 census notes two John Bowmans in the area, one a lead ore smelter of Dukesfield Hall, the other a stonemason of Steel
[3] Possibly to Hannah Blackburn at Slaley, although the International Genealogical Index gives the marriage date as 31 October 1831.

Sunday 30. At Chapel; sung Jubilate the first time - The singing masters here - At Slaley singing at night.
31. Begun the mill this morning at 10 O clock.

November, 1831.

2. Jane at Liza's.
3. Taking [up] the last of our 'tatoes.
4. Jane and Mary gone off to Humshaugh.
5. Helping my father to mend his garden wall - Very fine day.

Sunday 6. Jane come home - Fine day.
7. A very rough showery day.
9. Hexham Fair[1] - The level run; Kiles men on cleaning it.
12. Jane at Dyehouse - At Slaley singing - A preaching at W^{m}. Dixons - A rough week altogether.

Sunday 13. At the preaching hearing Loraine a.m. - Armstrong the master here at tea - At Chapel at night.
14. A sharp frost.
15. Hexham hiring - A hard frost.
16. Snow lying this morning.
17. On smelting for W^{m}. Ridley - At Slaley at night hearing a lecturer.
19. Snow still lying and a very hard frost - At Dyehouse & Steel at night at a meeting.

Sunday 20. At Thos. Walkers at tea - Hard frost.
21. Fresh day - the snow gone.
22. At Hexham seeking bushes and trees.
23. Setting bushes and trees - At Chapel singing at night.
24. Fine fresh days.
25. Wet day, wind E.
26. Jane at Nancy Dinnings at tea.

Sunday 27. Very bad of a cold - Bessy Cox & Liza here at tea.
28. Old Peggy Dixon of Quarry-house died - John Bell in this night.
29. Dressing up stones near the garden.
30. Armstrong the master here at dinner and tea - Our folk killing the swine.

December, 1831.

1, 2. Fine days - On washing.
3. At Hexham seeking cabbage plants, rhubarb - Fine day fresh week.

Sunday 4. Jane & I at preaching hearing Hopper.[2]
6. Setting more plants - Showery.
7. On smelting for W^{m}. Ridley who has been ill 7 weeks - Old Tommy Johnson of White-hall buried aged about 95.

---

[1] The November fair was mainly for cattle.
[2] This was not Christopher Hopper, the famous Methodist preacher, as he was born in 1722 and died in 1802.

10. Bill Purvis of Steel died - At Slaley singing at night - Been fresh weather all this week - A great deal of illness in the country.

Sunday 11. Jane & I hearing Thompson - At Chapel singing this afternoon - John Hall here at tea.
12. Willm. Purvis buried - Wet day, wind S.
13. Wet day.
15. Jane at Peggy Dixons to tea.
16. Jane at Betty Todds to tea - Uncle John widening the fold door.
17. Uncle John here at tea - At Uncle Willy's at night singing - The Stell people[1] *very bad yet - Remarkable open weather; wind strong and southerly.*

Sunday 18. At Fine-Chambers meeting afternoon - Fishers at night.
19. Geting the garden door hung.
20. On washing for my father - Cold S Wind.
21. Charlton on mending the machine[2] *- At Chapel singing.*
22. Sadly smoked at the mill.
24. Fine weather still - The Cholera Morbus at Newcastle.[3]

Sunday 25. Christmas day - At Chapel; the shire-head singers there - An uncommon fine day.
26. On smelting hearth ends.
27. A slight frost.
28. On smelting hearth ends and Olck[?] work this fore end.
29. Mally Dixon here at tea.
30. Johny's club feast - At Jemmy's at night.
31. Still open fine weather.

Remarks on the year 1831.

The year just ended is remarkable amongst other things for the following occurrences - For the failure of Thomas Teasdale the farmer of this place - his three several sales - his imprisonment - and his removal to Middle Dukesfield. - Also for Bownas taking and entering to this farm. - Also for our removal to the farmhouse in order to make way for Bownas a new farmhouse. - It is also very remarkable by the rejection of the reform bill - a dissolution of parliament, and a general Election - by the second rejection of the reform bill by the house of Lords. - Also for the war between Russia and the Poles, and the defeat of the latter nation. - Also for a very sultry summer and an uncommon great deal of thunder - for a storm of thunder and rain unprecedented in my life time, which took away our mill dam, several bridges, and did a great deal of mischief.

---

[1] See also 28 April 1832.
[2] Quite what this 'machine' was remains unknown, but it was presumably something used at the smelt mill and seems to have been dismantled and moved elsewhere in February 1833. See also 18 January 1836, 27 & 29 March 1837 for other references to a 'machine'.
[3] The *Cholera Morbus* had begun in Sunderland on 26 October 1831 and it had struck in Newcastle by 7 December, in North Shields by 10 December and in Gateshead by 25 December; at least 700 people died as a result in those towns.

Plate. 19

The Dukesfield Smelt Mill arches c.1900 - the only part of the mill not demolished.

6

MEMORANDUM FOR THE YEAR 1832.

January, 1832.

Sunday 1. At preaching hearing John Bell - A Jemmy's to tea all of us - Rather frosty.
2. Pailing up apple trees - Hard frost.
3. Thomas Dickenson & Peggy here at night.
4. At M^{r}. Sparke's to dinner & tea; a great party there - Very hard frost.
5, 6. The slaggys on with my metal - At Bobs at night - still frosty, wind got to E.
7. The last shift for the year 1831 - A hazy day; the ground turn'd soft - At the meeting house concerning a singing school - Billy Roddam was here on Monday.

Sunday 8. John Dixon of Heads in our house[1] *- Soft day - At Slaley singing at night.*
9. Pulling down a part of our hearth.
10. Flaging the garden door way, and putting up a seat at our door.
11. Purging with pills - At Chapel singing at night.
13. Thos. Dickenson here at tea - Began the singing at the meeting house.
14. Building our hearth this forenoon - Bowman been mending the bellow. At School at night.

Sunday 15. At Chapel a.m. - Meeting p.m. - Fine day.
16. Begun the mill today; the New Mill not on yet.
18. Fine fresh weather - Jane, Mar^{gt}. Burdus &c. at Liza's.
19. Thos. Teasdales removed to Hexham - Armstrong singing master here to tea - At Chapel singing at night; the last night for the master.
20. Liza & Jemmy here viewing Teasdales house - Teaching singing at night.
21. Writeing tunes for the scholars - The pay night (the first) - The most remarkable fine weather.

Sunday 22. Hearing Norther - Jane at J. Oxley's childs funeral - Old Jo^{s}. Renwick buried today. The Misses Burn of White Hart at this place.
23. Jem Dodd's Mildred of Staples died; and Peter Dixon of Steel.
25. At Peter's funeral - The New Mill axle tree broken today[2] *- Mather & Tom Bell began the new hearth on Monday.*[3]
26. A shower of snow this afternoon.
27. Lying white with snow this morning - A Buck set off at Allen Town.
28. Turn'd fresh, snow gone - At the singing at night.

Sunday 29. Hearing J. Hunter, Elizth. there for the first time, got tea at Liza's.
30. W^{m}. Robson turned off.[4]

---

[1] 'Heads' probably means Allenheads.
[2] The main shaft of a waterwheel was normally described as an 'axletree'.
[3] Tom Bell, a smelter, was living at Middle Dukesfield in 1841. According to Kristensen (2003) he was buried at Whitley Chapel on 28 May 1865 aged 69.
[4] This might be William Robson who was listed as a farmer at Slaley in 1827, and presumably he has been turned off his farm; see also 18 February 1832.

31. Got done our work in two days, working 20 Bings.[1]

February, 1832.

1. New mill men at our hearths.
2. Fine day.
4. Jane at Hexham with Liza - At the singing at night - A very windy weekend - Uncle John repairing Dukesfield old House for Jemmy.

Sunday 5. Hearing Thompson a.m. Teaching singing afternoon.
6. Helping Jo^s^. to set their oven - Soft day.
7. Helping Jemmy to flit[2] *- Fine day.*
8. Father and I burning Whins.
9. Sowing peas.
11. Fine day - Johnson & Nixon were here this week - The Masons done at Bownas' this week - An uncommon fine week of weather.

Sunday 12. A slight shower of snow - Hearing J Bell p.m.
15. Dressing W^m^. Hall's bushes.
16. At Jem Dodds with P Dixon - The axle tree come to the mill - At Slaley singing at night.
17. At Jonah's taking the yarn - Oliver here at tea.
18. Jemmy begun ploughing the fell - Still very fine weather - The land almost white - W^m^. Robson removed from here yesterday.

Sunday 19. Hearing old Norther a.m. - Singing afternoon - Thos. Bulman here at tea - Slaley singing at night - Fine day.
20. Helping Father lead manure - Cold.
21. Father and I leading peats - Geo. Lowes late of Cocklake buried.
23. Got our pig from Houghtly - Leading stones - Marg^t^. and her father gone to the west.
24. Burnt our bellow.
25. Got the bellow mended - The millwrights got the axletree done - Still very dry fine weather, unprecedented.

Sunday 26. Meeting at afternoon - Rather cold.
27. Blaydon pay.
29. W^m^. Ridley and Cant on helping us to smelt.

March, 1832.

1. Digging forenoon - At W^m^. Burdus' bushes aft.
3. Diging and planting rhubarb - Mother & Jane at Stobb - Still dry weather; the water all on at the mill.

Sunday 4. Hugh Armstrong here at breakfast - Hearing Thompson a.m. - very wet afternoon - At Rawgreen at night.
6. Soft day - At Hexham - The Hinds hiring.

---

[1] The 'bing' was a unit of measure used in the lead industry. It was the equivalent of 8 cwt. of clean dressed ore.
[2] To 'flit' means to move house.

7. Snowy blasty morning.
8. Fine frosty day - Jane at Jacobs - Armstrong the singer here.
9. Fine day - Aunt Nancy here to tea.
10. Jo^{s}. Bell of Corbridge buried last night. Thos. Makepeace come here to hind.

Sunday 11. At Slaley Church a.m. - Hearing W^{n}. Forster p.m. - Fine day.
12 & 13. Fine days.
14. Sowing onion seed.
15. Jo^{s}. Bownas very bad.
16. Gardening with Robt. Smith - Jane & Mary at Jemsons.
17. Very heavy cold hail showers, - with strong wind.

Sunday 18. Hearing Norther a.m. - At Liza's to tea.
19. Very wet day - Jo^{s}. & I meeting little Betsy Chatt's funeral.
20. On for Jemmy who is bad - Sowing some peas.
21. The general Fast day.
22. Old Jemmy Richardson & Hannah &c. at a private court at Hexham.
24. The mason working at Carrs - Jo^{s}. Bownas very bad this week - Jemmy setting bushes yesterday - Been a very windy week, showers of snow.

Sunday 25. At meeting hearing W^{m}. Smith at afternoon - At Burdus' to tea.
26. Hexham fair.
27. Jemmy parting with his new horse.
28. W^{m}. Ridley on for my Father who is very bad.
29. Scouring the garden dyke - Fine day - Marg^{t}. Burdus here to tea - Masons working at Dipton mill.
30. Washing slags for my Father - Jane & Mary at Park house.
31. Planting hollings &c. - Bringing 'tatoes [out] of the garden - Uncommon fine weekend.

April, 1832.

Sunday 1. Taking physic - Peter Hall at our folks'.[1]
2. Wheeling stones out of M^{r}. Sparks garden.
3. At Hexham buying a new suit of clothes - J Bulman & Dixon working in our parlour.
4. Diging in the garden. Thos. Makepeace setting up his furniture.
5. Uncle John begun roasting this week.
6. Very dry weather.
7. Been an uncommon fine week with the excepetance of this day - The water all on at the mill and full light.

Sunday 8. At Meeting hearing W^{m}. Smith preach - Dull cold day.
9. Jane and Elizth. at Dyehouse.
11. Cold day - Jane cleaning the parlour.
12. Setting 'tatoes - Very cold day with showers, wind E - Jane twilting at our folks'.

---

[1] This may have been Peter Hall of East Dukesfield who was born on 15 November 1807, baptised 28 February 1808, the second son of William Hall, a husbandman, son of John Hall, also a husbandman and a native of Bywell, and Margaret Dixon, daughter of Peter Dixon, smelter, of West Dukesfield.

Plate. 20

Above – Allendale town c.1905.

Right – St. Peter's church and Corn Mill c.1910

Below – Swinhope Mill, Allendale. c.1900

Plate. 21

Plate. 22

13. Planting box wood - Cold day.
14. Old Robt. Dixon of Mollarsteads died last night[1] *- W^m. Ridleys wife got her bed.*

Sunday 15. Hearing old Norther a.m. - Walker & wife, Jemmy and Liza here to tea.
16. Helping Burdus' folk to geld the colt - At Robt. Dixon's funeral - Fine day.
17. Jane at Hexham - Helping Bob to make spile shoes.[2]
18. Went to work this forenoon; sore smoked.
19. Aunt Nancy here making Jane's silk gown right.
20. Good Friday - At Johneys at night.
21. Stewards off to the pay - Seeking cabbage plants at Letch - The last night of the singing school.

Sunday 22. Easter Sunday - At Chapel a.m. - At meeting hearing M. Wilson p.m. - Fine day.
23. Very unwell.[3]
24. At Allen Town pay - Jane & Liza gone to peas meadows - An uncommon wet day - The first pay at the Town.
25. The Heads pay day[4] *- Very wet.*
26. Begun washing today.
28. W^m. Sheell married[5] *- Working in the garden. At Slaley singing and T Rest at night. John Barrow gone away - very cold weather.*

Sunday 29. Hearing Thompson a.m. - At Sparks to dinner - Our folks' at tea.
30. Jemmy seeking Jane and Liza from Allendale.

May, 1832.

1. Very frosty morning - A house burnt in Allendale on Sunday night.
2. A wet day.
3. Old Mary Oxley buried; Jane there.
4. Washing - Our folks stinting the haugh.[6]
5. Frosty morning; but turn'd fresh.

Sunday 6. At Chapel - Jacob & Betty here at tea - At Fishers meeting at night.
7. Setting the last potatoes.
8. Jane at Hexham.
9. Old Robson, clerk, buried today or yesterday - Colling married last week.
10, 11. Cold weather - Wind N - Very much smoked at mill.
12. Jo^s. and I went to Haltwhistle - Cold day. Jos. Dixon on for me - Barrow married on Thursday.

---

[1] Robert Dixon died aged 73 and was buried at Whitley Chapel.
[2] 'Bob' might have been Robert Stokoe the blacksmith, as 'spile shoes' were probably pointed iron shoes for the ends of timber piles or fencing uprights to enable them to be more easily driven into the ground.
[3] Dixon does not seem to have worked any smelting shifts this week; perhaps because he had been asked to help out with the Allen Mill Pay.
[4] Probably Allenheads.
[5] William married Margery Cook at Slaley. A William Shield was a member of the Dukesfield Wesleyan Methodists 1826-28
[6] Possibly sowing grass seed. A haugh normally implied flat ground by the side of a river.

Plate. 23

Left – Finechambers cottage. The first floor was used as an early meeting house until 1894 when the Finechambers chapel (below) was built.

Plate. 24

Plate. 25

Left – Finechambers Corn Mill, c.1900.

Sunday 17. At Chapel a.m. - Hearing Rob[t]. Smith p.m. - Some heavy thunders showers - Our Sally bad.
18. Thomasin Dixon here - Canvassing commenced for Beaumont & Ord.[1]
19, 20. Very warm - Hedley the piper here.
21. Jane at Walkers - Some heavy showers.
22. A very wet day, wind E.
23. Strong wine & heavy showers. Mason raiseing the timber of Simpsons house - Been plenty of water this week - Newcastle races have been this week - Very strong wind.

Sunday 24. Hearing Thompson.
25. Begun the Dispatch [news]paper lately; the first dated June 3rd.
28. Footing peats - Our folk mowing the hay - At Slaley with Jemmy & Joseph playing.
30. At Slaley singing - Came by Travellers [Rest]. Been water all this week for the smelters.

July, 1832.

Sunday 1. At Chapel - Aunt Peggy Bulman here at dinner - Very fine day.
2, 3. Washing - Very hot days.
4. Stagshaw fair - Our Jo[s]. and T. Dickenson buying a cow - A softish day - Went to work at 12 at noon.
5, 6. Foggy days.
7. Hannah Bell died - Writeing John Dixon the Jubilate - Water parted.

Sunday 8. Hearing Old Nother - Very wet day.
9. Plenty of water again.
11. Messrs Johnson & Pattison here[2] *- Ord's party here canvassing.*
13. Very wet morning - Cutting boxwood - Ord's party at Allen Town.
14. At the timber drink at Slaley - Mr Pattison gone away today - Cliffan's departure clearly ascertained - Been more rain last night.

Sunday 15. At Chapel - Uncle Jacob's folk in sorrow[3] *- Hearing Loraine afternoon - Rather cold.*
16. On washing.
17. At Hexham - Heard the Organ.
18. Painting table & form - Went to work at afternoon, the water done again.
19. John Bownas in our house - Mally Barrow & Mary Dickenson come to this place.
20. Got done work this night - M[r]. Bell at Slaley.
21. Geo Dodd & Todd mowing the back - Mather the high field Mally Barrow here at tea - The peats, lime and coal measured to us this week - At Slaley singing at night.

Sunday 22. Hearing Thompson at afternoon - A Love Feast held - A very fine day - Went to work at midnight.
24. Jane at Hexham - Messrs Beaumont & Ord there.

---

[1] For a parliamentary election.
[2] Benjamin Johnson, head cashier to WB Lead, and Hugh Lee Pattinson, recently appointed chief agent for the WB smelt mills and refinery.
[3] There is no obvious explanation for this grief.

Sunday 17. At Chapel a.m. - Hearing Rob[t]. Smith p.m. - Some heavy thunders showers - Our Sally bad.
18. Thomasin Dixon here - Canvassing commenced for Beaumont & Ord.[1]
19, 20. Very warm - Hedley the piper here.
21. Jane at Walkers - Some heavy showers.
22. A very wet day, wind E.
23. Strong wine & heavy showers. Mason raiseing the timber of Simpsons house - Been plenty of water this week - Newcastle races have been this week - Very strong wind.

Sunday 24. Hearing Thompson.
25. Begun the Dispatch [news]paper lately; the first dated June 3rd.
28. Footing peats - Our folk mowing the hay - At Slaley with Jemmy & Joseph playing.
30. At Slaley singing - Came by Travellers [Rest]. Been water all this week for the smelters.

July, 1832.

Sunday 1. At Chapel - Aunt Peggy Bulman here at dinner - Very fine day.
2, 3. Washing - Very hot days.
4. Stagshaw fair - Our Jo[s]. and T. Dickenson buying a cow - A softish day - Went to work at 12 at noon.
5, 6. Foggy days.
7. Hannah Bell died - Writeing John Dixon the Jubilate - Water parted.

Sunday 8. Hearing Old Nother - Very wet day.
9. Plenty of water again.
11. Messrs Johnson & Pattison here[2] *- Ord's party here canvassing.*
13. Very wet morning - Cutting boxwood - Ord's party at Allen Town.
14. At the timber drink at Slaley - Mr Pattison gone away today - Cliffan's departure clearly ascertained - Been more rain last night.

Sunday 15. At Chapel - Uncle Jacob's folk in sorrow[3] *- Hearing Loraine afternoon - Rather cold.*
16. On washing.
17. At Hexham - Heard the Organ.
18. Painting table & form - Went to work at afternoon, the water done again.
19. John Bownas in our house - Mally Barrow & Mary Dickenson come to this place.
20. Got done work this night - M[r]. Bell at Slaley.
21. Geo Dodd & Todd mowing the back - Mather the high field Mally Barrow here at tea - The peats, lime and coal measured to us this week - At Slaley singing at night.

Sunday 22. Hearing Thompson at afternoon - A Love Feast held - A very fine day - Went to work at midnight.
24. Jane at Hexham - Messrs Beaumont & Ord there.

---

[1] For a parliamentary election.
[2] Benjamin Johnson, head cashier to WB Lead, and Hugh Lee Pattinson, recently appointed chief agent for the WB smelt mills and refinery.
[3] There is no obvious explanation for this grief.

25. Got done work this morning.
26. Helping father & Tommy to mow - Peter Glaudhill & wife here.
27. At Slaley morning - On for Jo^{s}. Dixon at afternoon.
28. Helping our folk with hay - Went to Acomb at night - Been an uncommon fine week.

Sunday 29. At St Johnlee Church - Came home from Acomb - A very fine day.
30. On smelting for W^{m}. Ridley 2 hours - Very warm.
31. Jane and I stacking peats.

August, 1832.

1. Jemmy got the Black Cow.
2. Spark folk making the hay stack; came on wet at 12 O'clock.
3. A very soft day - wind E.
4. Mary Ridley here to tea - Our folk leading haugh hay - A very warm day - Been on with trial roasted - The time parted all this week.

Sunday 5. Hearing Nother preach - A soft morning.
6. Hexham fair - Went to work at 12 at noon - Very fine day.
8. Sowing cabbage seed - Old Geo. Bownas died.
9. Jane at Ridley's of Steel.
11. Helping our folk to lead the hay - At Slaley at night - Billy Blackburn married this week[1] - W^{m}. Woodman died this week - Very draughty weather.

Sunday 12. At Slaley school house - At the meeting afternoon - Jo^{s}. Smith here at night.
13, 14. My father at Quartre Bras[2] - At Jos Blackburn's - A great deal of new corn in the market today.
15. Mother at Cliffs sale - Some thunder & rain in different places - Went to work at 4 this aft^{n}.
16. Thunder & rain here today.
17. Fine day - At Slaley playing at night - Peter smelting.
18. At Whitley Mill seeing the masons - Father & Jacob bargain'd.

Sunday 19. At meeting hearing Lyons a.m. – Elizth. at Walkers to tea - Very showery.
20. Went to work at midnight.
22. Jane & Mother at T's. Rest - Allen Fair day - The Architect at Slaley Church.[3]
24. Our Jo^{s}. at Blanchland fair.
25. Tom Stokoe bringing Jane and old Hannah - A very wet afternoon - Shearing begun in different places.

Sunday 26. Setting Tom Stokoe to Intake - A soft day.
27. Jane unwell of her throat - Bownas' folk begun shearing - A very fine day.
28. Came on very wet this forenoon.
29. A very wet day again, Wind NE - The waters very rough. Jane rather better.
30. Wet again - Our folks' swine bad.

---

[1] William Blackburn married Jane Lishman of Bywell St Andrew on 4 August 1832.
[2] The location of 'Quartre Bras' is not known, but it seems to have been near Steel Hall.
[3] The architect was said to be Milton Carr.

Right – Plan of Turf House 1805

Below – Whitley Corn Mill, c.1900. There was a corn mill on this site from at least 1334 and it only closed in the 1930s.

Plate. 26

Plate. 27

September, 1832.

1. My father at Hexham at the Bank - Our Jo^{s}. come home bad - Martha Spark here now - The tythers here today - Been the wetest week ever known in harvest - Old Hannah and Jane Stokoe gone home.

Sunday 2. Hearing Matt. Wilson a.m. - John Dixon at our folks'.
3. Wet day - The Slaggys building an ore hearth.
4. A fine day - Spark's folk shearing wheat.
5. At Linnel Wood & Newbeggin seeking for a swine - Very fine day.
6. Old Robt. Stokoe died.[1]

7. At Turf house - The taylors making Joseph a new suit.
8. At Oxleys shearing - with Jo^{s} & Tweddle at T Rest at night. Been a very fine week since Monday.

Sunday 9. At Slaley Church a.m. - Meeting p.m.
10. At Bownas' binding oats - came on very wet at 4 O clock.
11. Shearing at Bow$^{'s}$ - Miss Spark here at supper.
12. Fallen very unwell today - A very strong wind.
13. A wet morning; but fine after - Some dreadful fire at night with thunder.
14. Jackey Hedley & sons & Scott here at night (Sparks).
15. The Bells hung at Slaley [Church] - At Aydonshields buying a pig - A fine day and been a fine week.

Sunday 16. At Meeting hearing Pilcher - Heslop preached at Slaley [Church] the first time.
17. Went to work at 7 O clock.
19. Seeking the pig at night.
20. Shearing at Oxley's.
21. Ditto - Sparks churn today.
22. Idle - At Slaley seeing the Church - Tommy Hedley came home with us - Beaumont been expected all this week - The finest harvest weather ever known - Shearing near done.

Sunday 23. Very unwell of a cold - Jane and I hearing W^{m}. Smith preach - Young ones at Queen Cave.[2]
24. The refiners begun (Waugh & Jaques). Bownas done shearing today - Thomas Pearson came to reduce.

---

[1] According to volume 4 of the *Northumberland County History*, p29, an inscription to 'Robert Stoker', at Whitley Chapel church who died aged 63 years, reads:

> My anvil and hammers lies declin'd.
> My bellows have quite lost their wind,
> My fire's extinct, my forge decay'd,
> My vices are in the dust all laid,
> My coals are spent, my iron gone,
> My nails are drove, my work is done,
> My mortal part rests nigh this stone,
> My soul to heaven I hope is gone.

[2] In Dipton Woods.

26. Father at Hexham with Betsey at the doctor - Binding at Sparks - Got done their shearing.
27. Jemmy Parker got on to smelt.[1]
28. Aydonshields and Dotland churns today.
29. Allendale's Races yesterday and today - Burdus churn - The water parted all this week - Fine weather.

Sunday 30. Hearing old Nother a.m.

October, 1832.

1. Building our hearth; began to work at 12 - Robinson the refiner begun.
2. Beaumont & Ord at Slaley - Fine day - Markets low; wheat 12/0.
3. Liza shouting out at night[2] *- Went to work for Jemmy at 10 O'clock.*
5. Had Wm. Dixon on washing - Very wet afternoon.
6. Father taking money from Bank - At Slaley singing at night.

Sunday 7. Wet this morning - At Slaley hearing Heslop for the first time - Hearing John Bell aftn.
8. Very wet morn - Plenty of water for all - Robt. Todd & J. Dodd begun to reduce.
9. At Hexham - Father settleing with Jacob - Old Dolly Angus died.
12. A very wet day; strong W wind - Tyne high.
13. Robt Todd here with his Bass - Bill Errington the carrier died.

Sunday 14. Jane and I hearing Pilcher - Seeing Liza aft. Colling there - Dixon here at tea.
15. Nanny Roberts died - Seeking maslin at Oxley's at night.[3]
16. Pattison at the mill.
17. Aunt Peggy from Hexham come.
18. Planting cabbages - Jane Mother & Aunt at Jacobs.
19. Bob Dixon's sporting.
20. Jemmy's christening[4] *- Aunt Peggy dined here - At Slaley singing. Uncommon fine weather - Been plenty of water.*

Sunday 21. At Slaley school-house - Fine day.
22. Taking up the American potatoes[5] *- Aunt Nancy making Jane a gown.*
23. Digging in garden - Leading peat at night.
24. Jane, Mary & Martha at Mally Dixons.
26. Rather soft.
27. Dull - Old Jack Bulmans sale - Fine weather - Plenty water.

---

[1] Presumably meaning that he had been given employment at the Dukesfield Mill.
[2] This may mean that Liza had commenced her labour with her second child, Elizabeth, who was born around this date, and that Thomas worked a shift for Jemmy so that he could remain at home; sometimes the term has been used to denote a feature of religious ecstasy.
[3] Maslin was the mixed grains of wheat and rye, usually having been grown together, and thought by some to be preferable to wheat alone in the baking of bread.
[4] Presumably the christening of daughter Elizabeth, rather than Jemmy himself, although the IGI gives 27 October as the date of her christening.
[5] Sweet potatoes?

Sunday 28. Hearing Norther.
30. Jane at Hexham - A very wet day.
31. Jane, Martha & Mary at Dye house.

November, 1832.

1. Writing tune from John Thompsons book.
2. Wet day.
3 Silver taken off today - Silvertop at the Mill - John Bulman's wife of Barker-house died this week - At Slaley singing at night.

Sunday 4. At the opening of Slaley Church - Mr. Armstrong preached on the morning Heslop in the evening.
5. Helping our folk to kill their cow.
6. Mary Ridley here at tea.
7. Washing slags for my father, who is at Bates' sale - A very hard frost.
8. Begun with Whestonhope ore, the worst we ever had.
9. Hexham fair day - Martha Spark went away yesterday, been here 10 weeks - A fine day.
10. A very cold day; terrible SE wind & rain at night. Mr Ord of Ardley died this week.

Sunday 11. Hearing Lorraine a.m.
13. The hiring at Hexham - Our Peter done at the mill.
14. Uncle Jacob removed to Hexham.
15. Father seeking some drawers.
16. Frosty - Taking up 'tatoes in the window garden.
17. Digging - Tweddle gone to Humshaugh.

Sunday 18. With Jane & Elizth. at the meeting hearing old Stobart; a Love Feast held after - Fine day.
19, 20. Dull days.
21. The Barristers at Allen Town.
24. Thomas Nicol seeking furniture with old Peggy - M^{r}. Spark got a new mare of John Lowes - Very fine open weather & little frost.

Sunday 25. Hearing Nother a.m. - Soft morn.
26. Still on with Westonhope; broke down this morning.
27. Sore smoked.
28. Geo. Crawhale & Wilson here at night.[1]
29. Rich^{d}. Dinning married today for the second time.[2]
30. Mr Paddison here.[3]

December, 1832.

1. The plate taken off yesterday[4] *- Been a very showery week altogether - At Slaley singing in the vestry.*

---

1 WB Lead agents.
2 To Mary Nixon, probably at Whitley Chapel.
3 Hugh Lee Pattinson.
4 I.e. the silver.

Sunday 2. At meeting hearing Brown - A very wet afternoon.
3. The Smelters begun to measure all their fuel - Our folks killing their swine (17 Sto.) Jane at Burdus' twilting.
4. My Father at Hexham with a cart taking the silver plate; Jo^s^. & I cutting down the pigs - Tweddle been seeking Marg^t^. home from Bensham.
5. Sally Bulman here to tea.
6. The New Mill begun Whestonhope today.
8. Taking lead out of our hearths - At Juniper with Joe at night - Uncommon fine weather: Been a fine week rather between fresh and frost.

Sunday 9. With Jane at Meeting hearing Pilcher - Jane seeing Nancy Codlin afternoon.
10. Begun with Breckonsike.[1]
12. Our folk got a charge for Ben.
13. Tom Stokoe here seeking my Clarinet.
14. Killing our pig 9 (stones?)
15. Salting the pig - The joiners here yesterday - Still fine open weather.

Sunday 16. At Slaley Church with the Bass a.m.; at the meeting and John Ellerington's at afternoon.
17. At Hexham hearing the nomination of the Candidates.
18. On washing - Very cold.
19. Begun our work this afternoon.
20. At Hexham - The Election begun; Beaumont first, and Ord last on the Poll - A fine frosty day.
21. The Poll closed today in favour of Beaumont and Bell - Our wheel fast this morning.
22. Fresh day - Still fine open weather.

Sunday 23. Soft day.
24. Jane at Hexham seeing Beaumont and Bell chaired - A fine day.
25. Went to work at midnight; came off in the lightening - Very soft morn
26. Sparkes folk killing the white cow.
27. Helping to weigh the cow out - Helping my father at afternoon to wash.
28. Writing tunes for Jo^s^. Blackburn - Johneys club feast - Begun to be unwell.
29. Still unwell - Weather still very open.

Sunday 30. Still bad - A strong wind at night and some snow.
31. Tweddle seeking something from the Doctor.

Remarks on the year 1832.

The year just ended is remarkable amongst things for the following - The raging of the Cholera in many places - The resignation (of Earl Grey) and return to office - The passing of the Reform Bill - The dispute between Belgium and Holland, and the war between France and the latter at Antwerp - The war between Don Pedro and Don Miguel in Portugal - The failure of the Derwent Company[2] *- A general Election - The hard contest among Beaumont, Bell, and Ord and the defeat of the last, at Hexham (the first Election there) - The discharge of Mr Mulcaster and appointment of Paddison to Blaydon & Mr Johnson as head casher at Newcastle - The building of a new Church at Slaley.*

---

[1] I.e., ore from the Breckonsike mine at Cowshill, County Durham.
[2] The 'Derwent Company' was probably the Derwent Mining Company, succeeded by the Derwent Mining and Smelting Company in 1832, and working lead mines in the Derwent valley to the south of Blanchland.

7

MEMORANDUM FOR 1833

January, 1833.

1. Still very bad.
2. Doctor Thomas Jefferson here seeing me.
3. The pox coming out - Joseph working for me.
4. The Doctor here again.
5. The pox at the height this morning - A very hard frost a great part of this week.

Sunday 6. Still lying in bed.
7. Sat some up today.
8. Father and mother at Hexham - The Slaggys working my metal.
9. Our men building the hearth - Geting a good deal better.
10. A great dinner at Hexham today.[1]
11. Old Betty Dinning died.
12. Our Jo^sh^. working at the furnaces - Still stands frosty - Marg^t^. Sparke and the lass gone up to Allenheads.

Sunday 13. My uncle Jacob here seeing me - Fine frosty day.
14. The mill begun today; W^m^. Ridley on for me.
15. Jane begun to be unwell - My mother at Hexham seeing Robinson the assesor - John Dinning on for me.[2]
16. Jane very bad - Peggy Sheell come to wait on her - very misty frosty days - Dinning of Lilswood on for me.[3]
17. I am out for the first time - Frost not so keen.
18. A dull, soft day of soft snow & sleet.
19. My father at Hexham seeking the Doctor for Joe and Jane and geting his other business done - The Doctor here; bled both Joe & Jane[4] *- A very soft day.*

Sunday 20. The Doctor here again - I am out today.
21. Both Joe & Jane easier.
22. Jane's pox at the height.
24. W^m^. Ridley on for me - A very hard frost - Tommy Purvis married today for the third time.

---

[1] Perhaps something to do with the earlier election.
[2] This John Dinning was clearly a lead ore smelter, marrying Elizabeth Dodd before 1827, but he may have been the same John Dinning listed as a farmer of Tenterhill House in 1827/28 and as a member of the Dyehouse Primitive Methodist Society in 1845. According to Kristensen, (2003), a John Dinning of Tenter-House died on 26 May 1853 aged 59, while his wife Elizabeth died on 11 September 1880 aged 87, both being buried at Whitley Chapel.
[3] There were probably two John Dinnings of Lillswood. The one referred to here was clearly a lead ore smelter, and he probably married Marjory/Margaret Johnson before 1827; he was listed as a smelter and farmer in the 1841 census, and he died on 15 April 1879 aged 85, being buried at Whitley Chapel; his wife Marjory died 24 January 1880 aged 80 (Kristensen, 2003). A a directory of 1827/28 also lists a John Dinning of Lillswood as a grocer.
[4] 'Bleeding', blood-letting' or 'Phlebotomy' as it is technically known, was generally dying out as a medical treatment in the 1830s in Britain, and was little used after 1840, although it was occasionally practised in treating certain cases in the twentieth century.

25. Begun work today - Tweddle at Blaydon yesterday - An uncommon hard frost, the water nearly all frozen up.
26. The Young's left the Ryehill it is said - Jane a great deal better - Turned fresh today - The masons been building the old furnace.

Sunday 27. Strong wind and very cold.
28. The old furnace begun - Nixon come to make some alterations with the farms.
29. My father meeting Nixon; Peter smelting.
30. Some snow lying this morn.
31. Helping my father to lead some hay - Very hard frost; the smelters not all on for want of water.

February, 1833.

2. Turn'd fresh - Youngs sale at Ryehill - Been some very windy nights this back end of the week.

Sunday 3. At the meeting hearing Pilcher - Roads very dirty.
5. At Hexham with Joseph seeking for Nevin & signing the deed - paying the Doctor - Father and Tommy meeting Nixon & settleing for a fresh farm.
7. Smelting Sedlin,[1] but had to draw for want of lime - Mending a conduit at afternoon - Joe at the Riding - A very strong wind.
8. Old Peggy gone - Making Elizth. a bed.
9. Our folk taking possession of their new farm - Tweddle got a letter of appointment - Been some very boisterous weather this week.

Sunday 10. At Slaley Church a.m. - Tweddle, Hugh, Joseph and Peter here at tea.
11. A very wet day - Drinking tea with Tweddle.
12. Mr Paddison here - Begun the washing - Jo^{s}. Proud died yesterday of the pox.[2]
13. Tweddle gone to Allen Mill - A child of Waugh's died.
14. Begun the Mill again; been off a week for want of lime.
16. A very rough morning of sort snow - At Rob Todds at night - Been a very blowey week.

Sunday 17. Hearing Nother a.m. - Jane & Mary taking a walk for the first time.
18. On washing.
19. A fine day.
20. A very wet day and snow lying.
21. Katy Hall got her bed of a daughter - Mr Pittison[3] come tonight.
22. A meeting of the Smelters - The washing put up - Chartons [Charltons] men done pulling the machine down.[4]
23. Very wet & snowey; been so all this week end - Tweddle come home.

Sunday 24. Cold day - Hearing Henry Wilkinson p.m.
25. Old Peter Dixon of Red Lead Mill died - Elizth. unwell.
26. Soft day.
27. Carts, taking away the Machine - Taking up a conduit at our house end - Fine day.
28. At Peters funeral - Very cold.

---

[1] Lead ore from the Sedling mine at Cowshill, County Durham.
[2] A Joseph Proud was a local preacher with the Slaley Primitive Methodists in 1832.
[3] Hugh Lee Pattinson.
[4] Probably 'Charlton's men' – see 21 December 1831. It is not obvious what the machine was.

March, 1833.

1. Very wet.
2. Seeking sticks from the woodmen in far garden - Peter in Allendale with Tweddle's clothes - Been a shift of the wetest weather seldom known.

Sunday 3. Hearing Pilcher a.m.
4. Draining the garden; Peter helping me at afternoon.
5. On for John Dinning of the Cage.
6. Draining - Cold day, wind N.
7. On with Crawlaw [ore]; father bad, Peter on a part.
8. Peter on.
9. Peter on again. At Adamson's sale at afternoon - Very cold.

Sunday 10. At home all day - W^m. Charlton at our folks', very soft day.
11. Joe smelting with me; had the lead to take out - Very snowey day.
12. Nixon here setting out our folks dyke.
13. A very ill day - Joe been on all this time.
14. Our folk on twilting in our Parlour.
15. At Blaydon - A very snowy day.
16. Tweddle come down - Been a very soft week - The land very soft, gardens back.

Sunday 17. Hearing Nother a.m. – Thos. Purvis' child died.
18. Our folk leading manure to their new farm - Very soft day.
19. At Hexham with Hugh.
20. Finishing draining - Sally Bulman here.
21. Very snowey day, wind N.
22. Hugh making drawers for us - Snowey.
23. Jane at Travellers Rest - At Todds at night - Snow very on the Daleheads.

24. At the Ranters hearing Ramsey a.m. - Hearing Brown at afternoon.
25. Hexham fair - Very soft & cold. Clubby Willy died - Got a cat from Dalton.
27. Jane twilting – M^r. Sparke at Newcastle.
28. Mending the milk house.
29. Jemmy gone to Durham fair[1] *- Very heavy shower of snow at night.*
30. Jane very bad of a cough - The weather rather better - Old Jack Carr, and Mally Nevin died lately.

Sunday 31. Hearing Pilcher a.m. - A very fine day.

April, 1833.

2. At Hexham helping Peter to buy a hat, & some medicine for Jane - Soft day.
3. Went to work at 12 Oclock today.
4. T Rest races - Soft day.
5. Good Friday - Painting the chest -Fine day.
6. Old Sally Dixon hanged herself -Planting an Apple tree and some bushes beside the parlour window - Been a fine day.

---

[1] This was a great fair for horses and cattle, the horse fair lasting a week, according to Bailey's *Durham*, (1810).

Sunday 7. Easter day - At Slaley Church. Jemmy & Liza here at tea - Some thunder at a distance.
8. Jin helping Jane to wash - At Sally Dixons funeral - Jane Walker here to tea.
9. At Allen Town Pay[1] - Fine day. Jemmy lost his mare.
10. Sowing Onion seed & Peas - Fine day, but wet at night.
11. Colouring the parlour - At Dotland at night seeing a cow.
12. Father & Tommy finishing the dike - At Todds at night.
13. Cutting hedge & planting cabbage. Fine day; but frosty.

Sunday 14. At Slaley Church hearing the Shotley singers - At Jemmy's to tea.
16. Jane very unwell.
17. Very cold showery day, wind N.erly - Seeing Robt Graham's cow at night.
18. Ann Dickenson come to stop here[2] - Setting Jemmy some plants.
19. Frank Campbell here painting - Seeing Davisons cow.
20. Planting rhubarb in parlour garden - At Dotland at night.

Sunday 21. At the Chapel - Meeting at afternoon hearing Lyons.
22. Setting 'tatoes - Parting the field at Middle Dukesfield - Very fine day.
23. At Hexham; bought a Cow of Robt. Graham - Peter brought Hugh's chest.
24. Very wet forenoon - Sally very bad of the measles - Mally Nevin buried yesterday.
25. Mr Nixon here seeing about the ground.
26. Measuring the field at night.
27. Robt. Smith finishing M^r. Spark's garden - Hugh come to stop here.

Sunday 28. Hearing Pilcher a.m. - With Joe & Hugh at Jonah Egglestone's[3] - Fine day.
29. Got settled with Jemmy about the field - Jemmy seeking quicks.[4]
30. Thought the [hearth] bellow on fire; open'd her out.

May, 1833.

1. Dalton sale day - Very much smoked this week - Begun the dyke in the field.
2. Wet forenoon; Father & Peter helping me.
3. Uncle John helping me.
4. Uncle John & Peter on helping me; nearly finished the dyke. Seeking a cow from Bob Graham's.

Sunday 5. Taking some physic - Joe at Stobilee - A very warm day.
6. Peter seeking Dr. Jefferson - Jane delivered of a daughter at 8 O'clock this morning - Peter and I finishing the dyke and setting 'tatoes.
7, 8. Very hot days.
9. Some thunder - Hexham Races.
10. Allen Town fair - M^r. Sparke got a cow.
11. Setting up an old bed - Been an uncommon fine week; spring much advanced - Influenza prevailing.

---

[1] This seems to imply that the Dukesfield Pay for the 1832 smelting year was actually made at Allendale. In total it amounted to £6765 for the smelters and for ore and lead carriage.
[2] An Ann Dickinson was a member of the Dukesfield Wesleyan Methodists in 1826-8.
[3] A Jonah Eggleston was a weaver living at Fell House, Slaley,in 1827/28.
[4] 'Quicksets' i.e. Hawthorns for hedging.

Sunday 12. Hearing old Nother.
13. Ann Dickenson gone - Got our pig. Helping my father & Tommy to dyke a gap.
14. The hiring day at Hexham.
15. A dreadful hail & thunder storm[1] *- Joe & Hugh come from Haltwhistle fair.*[2]
17. Working in garden - More thunder and rain - At Graham's at night.
18. Old Tom Rowland canted[3] *- Hugh bad - Much disease raging.*

Sunday 19. At Slaley Church.
20. Seeking rails - Our Peter gone to Aydonshields.
21. At Hexham buying milk vessels - Very unwell of my limbs.
22. Jack on railing for us - John Bowman was married on Monday[4] *- Opening out the quicks.*[5]
23. Time parted for the first time at the mill this year.
25. Stagshaw fair - a good fair - today very hot droughty weather.

Sunday 26. Hearing old Nother - Cutting cabbage.
27. Sowing turnips - went to work at 12 at noon.
28. Our cow calved this morning.
30. Finishing the dressing up of the garden - Cleaning quicks.

June, 1833.

1. Finished the quicks. Uncle Skelton come - Very warm.

Sunday 2. Jemmy & Liza here to tea.
3. Casting a ditch beside the rails - Rather wet; wind E - Wt Pattinson & wife here.
4. Leading wood for a shade[6] *- J. Milburn got lamed last Saturday - Stephen Brown gone . from Ardley yesterday*
8. Seeking for pigs at Rye Hill - Laying the cow out to night. Still droughty weather; great want of rain.

Sunday 9. Hearing old Nother a.m. At Jem Dodds with Joe & Hugh.
10. Went to work at midnight - Our Joe gone to Rob[t]*. Dodds to work.*
11. A curious morning & complete wet afternoon and night.
12. A great deal of ill done by the wind - Sold our calf for 36 shilling.
13. At Slaley seeking for swine - A wet day, wind E.
14. At Turf-House buying 2 pigs - Turning soil.
15. The smelters all on together this weekend - The ground completely wet.
Sunday 16. Soft morning - At Sparks to tea; John Taylor & Tweddle there.
17. Building our hearth this morning.
18. At Hexham.
20. On smelting hearth ends; The old ore finished this week.

---

[1] Considerable damage was caused throughout the North East as this storm passed over from the west, mainly on account of the accompanying hailstones, reported as being 'upwards of 4 inches in circumference'. At least two people were killed.
[2] The Haltwhistle May fair was for cattle, chiefly cows for grazing, when Bailey & Culley (1794; 1805) was published.
[3] A 'cant' was a public auction, but here it might mean recanted.
[4] He married Hannah Johnson at Hexham.
[5] According to the Whitley Chapel Parish Records, daughter Jane was christened on this day, but see diary entry for 16 February 1834.
[6] Shed.

"A Border Fair" by J. Ritchie. This painting is of the Stagshaw Bank Fair 1865.

Plate. 28

22. On casting peats - Showery. Exchanging a pig with John Dinning for a calf - Been plenty of water this week - Been a very windy cold week.

Sunday 23. Hearing Pilcher at afternoon - A Love-feast held.
24. Shifting the cow shade - At Aydonshields with the cow at the bull - Mr Spark off to N.Castle[1] about the coals letting.
25. Nanny at Hexham with butter. The mill been off these two days to get the chimneys cleaned.
26. Begun work today.
27. Got done today - Been much rain last night.
28. Winding the rails with rice[2] - Showery. Our folks mowing the haugh.
29. Some heavy showers - At John Ellerington's at night - Been plenty of water.

Sunday 30. At Slaley Church a.m. - Fine day.

July, 1833.

1. On washing; a very cold day.
2. Cold, wind W - Got a new barrel churn.[3]
4. Stagshaw fair day: dull day.
5. Very warm close day.
6. Warm, wind SE. - Mark Potts here - M^{r}. & Mrs Anderson at Sparks - Been plenty of water.

Sunday 7. Hearing old Nother a.m. - A great deal of company at Sparks.
8. Went to work at 12 at noon.
9. Todd mowing out the three nooked close.
11. Turned the calf out at night.
12. Footing peats.
13. Very unwell; in bed all day. Todd and J Purvis mowing in Sparks high field[4] - Fine weather for hay - Water parted this week

Sunday 14. At home all day - Thomas Scott & Betsey at our folk's.
15. At the bull with the cow this morning - Soft afternoon.
16. At Hexham; got a new sythe[5]; gave our names to the overseer.[6]
17 Helping my father to lead the haugh hay - Helping Sparks folk to rake at afternoon.
18. Mich. Walton parting wood in Dog Bank - Went to work this forenoon.
20. Time parted all this week - Mowing a road up the meadow.

Sunday 21. At Coalpits with W^{m}. Hedley who came here to dinner and tea - A very wet
24. Preparing a sythe.
25. Mowing for our folk at afternoon – Went to smelt for Ridley at midnight.
26. Sparks folk making the stack - John Ramseys sporting.
27. Mowing in our pasture - Fine day - Time parted at the mill this back end.

---

1 Newcastle.
2 Making a wattle fence; 'rice' means brushwood, or hedging wood.
3 Presumably for butter making.
4 John Purvis may have been the man of that name who married Susannah Bowman at Slaley on 24 November 1838.
5 A scythe presumably, the essential tool for mowing when haymaking.
6 Perhaps regarding Statute Duty on the roads.

Sunday 28. At Slaley Church a.m. Hearing Loraine at afternoon; and tea-ing at Peggy Sheells - Uncommon warm day.
29. Warm day - Helping our folk to pike at afternoon.
30. Forster mowing for Jemmy - Laying a byre loft - Old Willy Charlton of Stobilee buried.
31. Forster here at tea.

August, 1833.

1. The water too light for the refiners and us - Robt. Stokoe the smith married.[1]
3. Begun to mow our meadow - Been a very fine droughty week - Time parted.

Sunday 4. Hearing Nother - Fine day.
5. Went to work at midnight this shift. Sally & Nanny Kyleing our hay.
6. Hexham fair - Pikeing some hay at night - Fine day.
7. Got done work early this morning - Mowing at afternoon - A meeting of Dickenson creditors at Clickem inn.
8. Forster helping me to mow - A heavy shower at afternoon - Mother gone to Tynemouth.
9. Sowing cabbage seed - Strewing hay - Rather dull day.
10. Got all our hay to Kyle - Jane seeing Nanny Robson who is very ill - Fine day. Fine weather for the corn. The water very light.

Sunday 11. At meeting hearing Ryan at afternoon.
12. Leading & pikeing our hay - Helping our folks to pike their last - Fine day - Mary Robson here at tea - Bill Walton left Bownass.
13. Soft day.
14. Railing the garden.
16. Mother come from Tynemouth - Soft.
17. At Todds at night with the Bass[2] *- Been a week of very moderate weather - Time parted.*

Sunday 18. Hearing Fairless preach - Uncle Jacob & Betty here at dinner - Dull day.
19. Went to work at 12 at noon.
20, 21. Very windy, showery days.
22. On smelting for W^{m}. Ridley.
23. At Slaley with the cow at Rowells bull.
24. Making our hay stack and our Folk's - Nanny at Blanchland fair - Fine quiet day; but wet at night - Been a very boisterous week for wind & rain - Smelters all on this back end.

Sunday 25. At Slaley church at afternoon - A very fine day.
26. Railing the hay stacks - Stinted our fog.[3]
27. At Hexham - Fine day.
28. Went to work at 4 at noon.
29. Hugh gone to seek work.
30. Bownass begun to shear wheat. Old Jemmy Roberts died.
31. Very cold wind NE - Harvest commenced at different places; Tyneside throng[4] *- Time parted all the week.*

---

[1] Robert married Ann Shield at St Peters, Allenheads; he was presumably a son of the Robert Stokoe who died on 6 September 1832.
[2] Bass violin.
[3] 'Stinted our fog' means putting stock out to graze.'Fog' means the grassland after the hay has been cut.
[4] 'Throng' meaning very busy, in this case with harvesting.

September, 1833.

Sunday 1. At the meeting hearing Short for the first time - Brother George here.
2. Went to work at 1 this morning. George here at dinner & tea.
3. George gone home - Some distant thunder, and rain.
4. Got done work this morn - Our Joseph gone to Jona. Marshall to work - past rain.
5. Shearing wheat for Mr. Sparke. Dull day.
6. Dressing our haystacks - Very warm day.
7. Dull misty day - Harvest but slow yet here - Time parted all the week - Singing at Dyehouse at night.

Sunday 8. At Slaley Church a.m. Jane and I at meeting hearing Brown.
9, 10. Warm days.
11. Wet day.
12. Put our cow to Spark's foise[1] *last night.*
14. Sore smoked: and very unwell - Water for all this back end - Thomas Dinning married last Wednesday.[2]

Sunday 15. Hearing Mr Hannah for the first time - With Jane at John Halls at tea.
16. Went to work this forenoon.
17. Soft day.
19. Stacking my peats.
20. Langhorn got the churn at Blackham, the away going - At Letch & Lee at night.
21. Fine weather - Time parted.

Sunday 22. Slaley Church - Some young men from Allen Town here with Tweddle - Fine day.
23. Shearing Oats at Sparks in the E high field - Wind S.
24. Very wet day - some distant thunder.
25. Put the cows into the flatt - Mr. Sparke got a kiloe [3] *- Fine day.*
26. Water for us all today.
27. Time parted - Wm . Dinning bled us the cow.
28. Got done work at 7 this morn - Been a fine week end for the harvest; but wet tonight.

Sunday 29. Been much rain - Hearing Mr. Short - Ordered the Harp of Zion[4] *- Our folk and us at uncle Johns at tea.*
30. All on together - Hugh come home - Henry Armstrong here; stoping all night. Mr. Sparks churn.

October, 1833.

2. Pulling onions.
3. With Hugh seeking wood in the Sandy-ford for rails.
4. Erecting a saw pit.
5. Sawing rails - Time parted this backend. Uncommon fine week of weather - Joe come home.

---

[1] Presumably a bull of some sort.
[2] To Margaret Pattison at Haltwhistle.
[3] 'Kiloes' or 'kyloes' were a Scottish breed of small cattle, usually having been driven down from the highlands and sold at one of the large cattle fairs in northern England.
[4] Presumably a piece of music.

Above – Cottages on the road to Baybridge from Blanchland, c.1905. Plate. 29

Below – Blanchland village, c.1900. Plate. 30

Sunday 6. Hearing John Bell.
7. Sawing and railing - Fine day - W^{m}. Burdus got the churn.
8. At Hexham - Rather soft - Oxleys churn.
9. Railing forenoon - Mother & Jane at Jacobs getting tea - John Dickenson of Newcastle died on Monday.
10. Very smokey day - Tommy Carr & Peter Dixon churns - Billy Bowman was married on Monday.[1]
12. Bownas' churn - At Todds at night - Been very fine weather but very frosty - A heavy shower fell this morning - Time parted.

Sunday 13. Hearing Mr Hannah.
14. Went to work at midnight or 1 this morning.
15. A heavy shower of rain & snow.
16. Got done this morning at 4. The millwrights come to Peter['s] mill this week. Some heavy showers; plenty of water.
17. Jo^{s}. Richardson married today.[2] *Mally Chatts teaparty.*
19. Went to Shotley Bridge to see Joseph - Fine day. Been a very fine week, very little corn out - Was at Dotland on Thursday.

Sunday 20. Spent the day at Shotley Bridge at the Ranters meeting &c.[3] *- Came home at night.*
22. At Hexham - very heavy showers today. Got a pair of new shoes (strong).
23. Washing a.m. - Leading peats p.m.
24. On smelting, plenty of water; time parted this fore end of the week.
25. John Carr here seeing the cow.
26. Rather smoked - At Robt Todds to tea - Fine day - Wind much to the southerly this week - Joseph Cowen & Nichol Walker died of typhus fever this week - Sparks, Marthas, our folks and Betty Nixons tea drinkings this week.

Sunday 27. Went to Slaley expecting W^{m}. Arkle[4] *- Joseph & Thos. Bulman here at tea very fine day.*
28. Soft day; wind E - Nanny at Hexham with onions.
30. Had our churn supper.
31. My father gone to see Geo. Chatt's cow - Taking up our potatoes.

November, 1833.

1. On smelting a while for Jo^{s}. Dixon who is at Hexham concerning church rates - Very strong wind - Allen Town fair.
2. Digging in the garden - Very showery & strong wind - Water plenty this week.

Sunday 3. Jane and I at the meeting hearing John Hunter.
4. Digging - Our Sally bad.
5. Soft day - Our folks killing the pig.
6. Some bitter showers of sleet - Taking up the last of our potatoes.
7. Old Peggy Nichol buried.

---

[1] Billy married Mary Ward at All Saints, Newcastle.
[2] Joseph married Esther Forster, probably at Whitley Chapel.
[3] A Primitive Methodist Society had been formed in Shotley Bridge by 1822.
[4] Probably a son of Christopher Arkle, both of them being joiners based at Bywell.

Slaley Church, 1900

Plate. 31

8. Allen Town hiring - Old Nancy Teasdale buried.[1]
9. At Hexham fair with the cow - Fine day - Geo. Forster here at night - Jo^s^. Dixon on for me - Been some very windy weather this week.

Sunday 10. Brother George here at breakfast - Hearing Mr Hannah.
12. Nanny left us - Hexham hiring day.
13. Sally come to live with us.
14. Preparing our byer - Father seeking a cow from Geo. Chatt - At Ordley at night.
15. Washing.
16. Washing, digging the garden - Todd here at night - Been a week of fine weather.

Sunday 17. At the meeting - Joe & Aaron Davison here at tea - Old Hannah Dickenson & Henry Stobb's wife died.
18. Frosty.
19. Wheeling soil - At old Hannah's funeral - Very fine day.
20. Marg^t^. Burdus got her bed of a Daughter.
22. An uncommon wet day; strong W wind.
23. Very cold day - Leading some sand from Light Pipe - At Nunbrough at night.

Sunday 24. Hearing Mr Short a.m. - Uncle John, Todd and wives here at tea.
26. Fine day.
27. Mather killing our pig - pig 9 Stone weight - Much smoked to-day.
28. Salting the bacon - Tremendous wind and rain at night - Wind SE.
29. Wheeling soil - Very wet day.
30. Wheeling soil at the low end of the field - A very decent day - Took the calf in at night. Been a very boisterous week.

December, 1833.

Sunday 1. At Slaley Church a.m. - With Jane at the meeting hearing W^m^. Lee - Mr Spark and Hugh at Sarah's - A wet night.
2. Wheeling soil - John Adamson of Whitley Mill buried (died of small pox).[2]
3. On for W^m^. Ridley - A very soft day.
4. Very wet with a strong W wind.
6. A most tremendous day of wind and rain - Mary Robson here telling Hugh about a child being born to him.
7. Very wet forenoon - Billy Purvis married last Saturday[3] *- A most uncommon week of wind & rain as ever known.*

Sunday 8. Hearing Mr Hannah - Joshua Smith & Hannah Hall here at tea - Joseph at home this weekend.
10. Jane at Hexham.
11. Cold day - Jane at Nanny Makepeace's twilting.
12. Leading soil upon a sledge - Frosty day.
13. Dikeing out the sheep[4] *- Our house on fire - At Thos Dickensons at night.*
14. Washing - Mother & Jane seeing Nanny Robson of Rest - Turned fresh last night. Betsy Todd, Geo. Brown's wife and several others died this week.

---

[1] Ann Teasdale died 5 November 1833 aged 85 years and was buried at Whitley Chapel, (Kristensen, 2003).
[2] There was perhaps an out break of smallpox at this time – see 14 December 1833.
[3] Billy married Christiana Hedley at Slaley.
[4] Presumably meaning creating a barrier to keep sheep out of his fields.

Sunday 15. At Slaley Church: a fresh priest there - Very fine day.
16. A very wet morn, but fine day - Washing.
17. Tremendous day of wind & rain.
18. Finishing the washing - Mather killing Irish.[1]
19. Very wet day - F. Campbell here slabdashing at night.[2]
20. Very strong wind - Frank finished us.
21. Got done smelting - Seeing uncle John who is very unwell - Very rough weather.

Sunday 22. Hearing Short a.m., Bill Adamson p.m. - Rather soft.
23. Taking out our bellow - Fine frosty day.
24. At Hexham - Snow lying this morn very slushey day, much aufall .
25. Christmas day - Fine day - Went to work hearth ends at night.
26. Little Henry here at afternoon.
27. Johneys club feast.
28. Our bellow put in; building our hearth - The breaking up at Johneys - Slaggys working my metal - unsettled weather.

Sunday 29. At the meeting; a prayer meeting held - A very blowey day.
30. Begun smelting for another year - Fine day; but wet at afternoon.
31. A very soft day.

Remarks on the year 1833.

The year just ended is memorable for the meeting of the first reformed parliament - For the appointment of Tweddle to Allen Mill. Our taking possession of a small farm. It is also remarkable for the birth of our Jane, for Hugh stopping with us, for my father taking possession of Quartre Bras - Our Joseph left Jacob.

[1] Killing a pig, presumably called 'Irish'.
[2] Colouring the walls of a room to imitate wallpaper.

8

MEMORANDUM FOR 1834.

January 1834.

Wednesday 1. The ground extremely soft - Wm. Dickenson in here with his violin.
2. Begun to scour quicks.
3. Speading[1] soil - Soft.
4. Thos. Oxley taking our ploughing[2] - A fine day.

Sunday 5. Hearing Mr. Hannah - Our Joseph come with Harry.
6. Scouring quicks.
7. Very fine day.
8. Very wet; wind SE.
9, 10. Both wet; wind SE.
11. Sore smoked. Thos. Oxley ploughing - At Juniper expecting a ventriloquist - Most uncommon soft season.

Sunday 12. John Hall & wife here - Still soft.
13. Thos. Oxley finishing the ploughing - Very wet at night.
15. Setting old Peter home who has been here drinking - Geo. Blackburn here with his fiddle.
16. Speading soil.
17. Very wet & strong wind.
18. At Mary Robsons wedding - A very strong wind.

Sunday 19. Jane and I at Slaley Church. The wedding people there - Fine day.
20. Spreading soil & helping my father to lead hay - Wet at night.
21. Finished the soil - Wet morn; but fine at afternoon.
22. Riddleing hay seeds - Peter's mill opened out.[3]
23. Very wet day - Thos. Makepeace's house entered.
24. Wet afternoon - Dickenson of Letch here at night - Hugh finished his violin.
25. At uncle John's till bedtime; Jane there at tea - Been an wet week and strong West Winds.

Sunday 26. Showery day - At meeting with Joe & Hugh hearing Watn. Forster.
27. Fine day - On with bad Slit.[4]
28. A very soft day of rain & snow; waters rough.
29. Very hard frost.
30. Helping our folk to fill manure - Turned fresh.
31. Scouring quicks - Father at Hexham seeing a garden wall.

---

[1] Perhaps 'spading' i.e. digging.
[2] Probably the Thomas Oxley who was a farmer at Palm Strothers, Slaley, in 1827/28.
[3] This must be a Peter Dixon; see appendix on other Dixon families.
[4] Presumably bad ore from the Slitt mine Westgate in Weardale, County Durham.

February 1834.

1. Wet day; but no wind - Johneys club money parted[1] *- Cuth*[t]*. Dryden in here - Extreme soft weather.*

Sunday 2. Hearing M[r]*. Hannah - Agnes Maughan & Betsy Dinning in here at night.*
3. Scouring quicks - Fine day.
4. At Hexham.
5. Leading some hay - Very cold day, wind S.
6. Mr Pattinson come in a gig - Fine day; but wet at night.
7. Hugh gone to Sarah's.
8. Jona. Blackburn buried this week - At Frank Purvis' with Tweddle at night. The weather rather more settled & inclined to frost.

Sunday 9. At the meeting with Jane & Eliz[th]*. hearing Rob*[t]*. Smith - Fine day.*
10. Some of the smelters begun with the bad parcel.[2]
12. Seeking some willows - Very cold with slight showers of snow.
13. Little Harry coming from Shotley for the last time - Dickenson & Geo. Blackburn here at night.
14. Finished the hedge scouring.
15. At Mollarsteds at night. Been very foggy this week end.

Sunday 16. Hearing Short a.m. - Got Jane christened at afternoon[3] *- Very fine day.*
17. Making drains in the high field.
18. Casting soil beside Bownass' - Very fine day.
19. Very unwell today - Strong wind.
20. Terrible night of wind & rain.
21. Bitter showers of snow.
22. Mrs Cowing's sale at Slaley - Very peevish weather.

Sunday 23. Soft day - At home all day.

25. Sally at Hexham.
26. Dressing the bushes - Aunt Peggy of Hexham come.
27. Setting out a new quick fence - Helping my father to lead his hay. Thomasin Dixon here; Aunt Peggy also. Rather soft all day; snow at bed time. The sweeps cleaning our chimney - Our Peter left the mill.[4]
28. Snow lying - At Todds at night.

March 1834.

1. Dikeing - Mother, Peggy & Jane at Mally Dixons. The Assizes this week - Cousin Thos. Skelton died this week, buried today.

---

[1] Divided.
[2] Bad ore.
[3] This entry contradicts the Whitley Chapel Parish Records which suggest that Dixon's daughter Jane was christened on 22 May 1833 – a Wednesday.
[4] This clearly refers to Thomas's brother, and seems to imply that he had left the smelt mill. If so, it was only a temporary departure.

Sunday 2. Hearing M^r. Hannah a.m. - At Slaley Church hearing Airey, p.m.
3. Peter & Father at Quatre Bras dikeing.
4. Peter helping me to dike.
5. Very rough night & morn been for wind; stacks blown down &c. - Showery day.
6. Very rough day.
7. Hugh gone to Matfen to seek work - Drying day.
8. A very ill day of wind & rain - Rough weather.

Sunday 9. Hearing Brown preach - Our Joe at Home with an Ass.
10. Old Close found dead last night on his way from Salmonfield.
11. Peter at Hexham with a cart seeking quicks for me - A very fine day.
12. Got done the bad ore (our share). Mary Conkleton and Nanny Robson here at tea - Leading the last of our soil - Fine day.
13. Peter helping to dike - Uncommon fine - Closes funeral.
14. Dikeing - At Josh. Blackburn's with Todd.
15. Filling up quicks, sowing onions - An uncommonly fine day.

Sunday 16. With Jane hearing Mr. Short - Fine day - Carlin Sunday.
17. Dikeing - Peter brushing in our manure.
18. Father at Hexham seeing Jacob who is unwell. Rather cold.
19. Finishing the new dike. Very fine day but very frosty.
20. On with Breckonsike [ore] - Jane with Mary Conkleton at Mollarsteads.
21. Peter gone to Lementon[1] yesterday - Uncommon hard frost.
22. Very cold day; strong W wind - Old Thos. Hall died this week - Seed time busy.

Sunday 23. Uncle Thomas here - Very showery day.
24. Peter come home; likewise Hugh from Sarah's christening.
25. Old Bill Dixon on with me: Father at Hexham fair with the cow - Cold frosty weather - wind NW.
26. Got done work early this morn - At Lowes' mill at night.
27. Got some hay led; fine morn - Setting some 'tatoes at aft^n. and sowing some turnips.
28. Good Friday - Leading some gate posts - Very rough aft^n.
29. Helping to clean the house - Showers of snow - Mary Teasdale come here on the 3^d

Sunday 30. Hearing M^r. Hannah a.m. Joe at home - Jane at Ranter meeting.
31. Cleaning quicks - M^r. Sparks folk got a new cow of one Hogg.

April 1834.

1. Casting up soil - Old John Wood buried - The Taylor[2] here for Hugh.
2. Begun work[3]; only 16 Bing this week - M^r. Spark & Hugh gone to Newcastle.
3. Got done work early - Mr Heslop's sale - Setting 'tatoeonions.
4. Our pay at the mill[4] - Ann Cox here.
5. Setting tatoes - At Johneys at night with Tweddle &c. - Dry, rather frosty weather, wind W.

---

[1] Lemington on Tyne.
[2] I.e. Tailor.
[3] This was a Wednesday; early start to shifts on account of the Pay on the Friday.
[4] The Pay for the year 1833 was clearly made at Dukesfield on this occasion; a total of £7564 paid out to the smelters and carriers.

Sunday 6. At Slaley [church] hearing Mr. Heslop.
7, 8. Allen Town pay - Jane at Hexham.
9. Hugh gone to Stokoe - Sowing some salt .
10. On Smelting for Dinning of Lillswood.
11. On for Joe Dixon.
12. Our folks' cow calved - Setting some 'tatoes - C Dryden here last night - Very cold weather - Wind NE - Edwd. Todd of Raw Green died.

Sunday 13. Hearing Mr. Short.
14. Hoeing whins - Helping Purvis to lead in a stack of corn - Leading clots off our field at night.
15. At Hexham buying clover seed.
16. Sowing seed forenoon - At Peter Dixon's sale at afternoon. Thomas Errington bought our folk's calf - Dodd of Blackhall got lamed.
17. The water all on and rather scarse.
19. Father unwell; Peter on [smelting] with me. At Kettlewell's at night seeing a quey[1] - Very dry weather; and great want of rain.

Sunday 20. Jane and I at Church hearing Mr. Scurr - Joe & Tweddle here at tea - Fine day.
21. Peter on today - The water very light - Kettlewell here at night.
22. Time parted today for the first time.
23. A slight shower - Peter wrought this week's work off.
24. At New-Ridley seeking Stobart for my father who is still very bad of his chafts.
25. Setting tatoes, dikeing & hoeing whins.
26. Laird Johnson died this week; Mary Close yesterday - Dressing the garden - Still very droughty.

Sunday 27. Looking for Stobart all day.
28. Very wet day; wind easterly - Geo. Stobart here at night.
29. Dull, cold day - Riddling hay seeds.
30. Rather wet.

May 1834.

1. Peter on again - Stobart here again - Henderson the Jobber here.
2. Jane at Flodders.
3. Billy Stokoe and John Hornsby Senr. both married[2] - Most delightful weather set in.

Sunday 4. At Slaley Church - Uncle Jacob seeing my father - Old John Leathard buried - Jane and I seeing aunt Peggy Hall who is very bad.
5. Very warm.
6. Very strong wind.[3]
7. Thomas Oxley here ploughing.
8. Thos. Oxley ploughing & harrowing.
9. Setting cabbages in the field - Washing at afternoon - Allen Town Fair & Hireing.
10. Bownass' sale at Allenheads - Thouburn's sale stopt. – Geo. Hornsby bought our folks' cow. Joseph & Hugh both come home.

---

[1] Scottish term for a young cow which has not yet calved.
[2] Billy married Ann Brown, probably at Whitley Chapel.
[3] This was daughter Jane's first birthday but Thomas does not refer to it.

Sunday 11. Hearing Mr. Short.
12. Setting 'tatoes in the field - John Bell removing to Aydonshields.
13. Geo. Stobart been here all night - At Hexham hiring.
14. Went to work today.
15. Got done our old ore; had only 16 Bing this week.
16. Smelting hearthends today.
17. Peter & I at Stagshawbank selling our cow - Very wet day.

Sunday 18. At Slaley Church - Dined at Mr. Sparks - At Jemmy's to tea - At Johneys at night.
19. Setting the last 'tatoes in field and garden - Margt. swearing her child.
20. Building our hearth - At Spring house seeing a quey.
21. Margt. delivered of a son.
22. Water parted today - Got done work only 16 [Bing] of raw.
23. Busy quickening.[1]
24. Peters pony sale - Thos. Rowell married today;[2] *Geo. Makepeace this week.*[3]

Sunday 25. With Jane hearing Mr. Hannah. At Slaley with Jemmy & Liza seeing young Walker. Very droughty cold air.
26. Got all the quickens on to the fires.
27. Helping Peter out with the calf - Mr Spark got a cow of Mr Wilson.
28. Went to work at 11 tonight - Ned Davison's wife died.
29. Jane at Spring-house.
31. Got done this morning at 5 - Peter got a pig of Lowes. Our Joseph & Hugh come - Very droughty.

June 1834.

Sunday 1. At Slaley Church - Jemmy & Liza here at tea.
2. Went to work at 12 at noon - Jane at Travellers Rest.
4. Mr. Johnson[4] *at the mill - Bought a pig - Jane bought a cow of Robt Smith.*
5. Put the cow to Blackburns pasture.
7. With Peter at the Highways near R. Thompsons[5] *- Some thunder showers this week in different places; but still very droughty - Time parted all this week.*

Sunday 8. With Jane hearing Short; a Love feast held.
9. Leading stone off the fallow.[6]
10. Laying on ashes[7] *- Father at Hexham for the first time since his illness - Scurr's people stopt with rain.*
11. Aunt Mary of Lementon come - Laid the cow out tonight.
12. Went to work at 10 this forenoon - Aunt Sally come.

---

[1] Either tending the quickset hedges or more likely pulling up couch grass – see 26 May 1834.
[2] Thomas married Hannah Blackburn at Slaley.
[3] George married Ann Linsley, probably at Whitley Chapel.
[4] Probably Benjamin Johnson, Chief Cashier to WB Lead.
[5] Possibly doing his Statute Labour on road repairs.
[6] Possibly associated with Statute Labour on road repairs.
[7] Possibly laying the 'ashes' from an ash midden onto land before ploughing

The Halliwell Spa

Away to the picnic at Halliwell Spa
The water is pure and the best of them a',
The tea has a flavour there's naught can excel
When brewed with the water at the Halliwell

The walks they are neat, the trees evergreen
Bespangle the place with a silvery scene,
The banks they are blooming with flowers so rare
And rivals the garden where nature is there.

The De'ils water purling its sweet little stream
Awakens the thought like an enchanted dream,
Where trout they are jumping like a magic spell
Refreshed with the stream as it comes from
Halliwell.

The Pic Nic again I would wish to report
Where lads and young lasses they often resort,
Where hearts full of love their stories may tell
As they rove on the banks of the Halliwell.

You talk of the grandeur of Starwood Le Peel
Where warriors have fought with the glittering
steel,
But to talk of these heroes their deeds for to tell
They still would come short of the old Halliwell.

O could I find language to flow at my will
The old Halliwell I would advocate still,
I would tell of its flowers there's naught can excel
The wonderful cures made by the famed well.

O could I but sound it to the East and the West
Of all the spa waters I'm sure it's the best,
The wonderful cures I'm glad for to tell
So many's been made by the old Halliwell.

O could I entreat you to give it a try
When health it is wanting no one can it buy
But when it is wanting and you want a cure
At Halliwell Spa you will find it I'm sure.

This poem was dedicated to Miss Mary Bell, Mollersteads, on August 17th, 1873, writer unknown.

Fig. 5

The reputation of the Holy-well /Halliwell Spa (see entry for 14th June) seems to have inspired more than just this poem. A picnic was held beside the spa's source between Dukesfield smelt mill and Red Lead Mill, beside the Devil's Water. The Spar was popular with the smelters as it apparently was charged with sulphuretted hydrogen.

Halliwell Picnic c.1910

Plate. 32

13. Aunt Mally gone.
14. Mill men repairing the Holy-well - At Slaley with Peter & the cow - Some heavy showers. Time parted all this week.

Sunday 15. At Slaley church a.m. - Aunt Sally & Jos. Smith here to tea.
16. Went first [to work] this week (our side) - Davison brought the last of our lime today.[1]
18. Some rain - Got done this morning early.
19. Aunt Sally gone - Laying on lime.
21. Dixon & Thomasin married today - Mother and Jane at Hexham - Leading manure - At Clickem Inn with Joe, Tweddle, Hugh &c. - Still very droughty.

Sunday 22. Hearing Mr Hannah.
23. Joe at Hexham; the taylors making him a suit - Thomas Oxley ploughing in our lime.
24. The ploughing finished - Very droughty.
25. Sally here washing - Went to work at afternoon; the water very light - Some rain fell at night.
27. Got done this evening.
28. Mowing commenced at this place - Gathering quickens at afternoon - Very droughty weather, the slag hearth clean laid off.

Sunday 29. At Slaley Church a.m. - Jane at meeting hearing J. Hunter.
30. Went to work at 12 O'clock at noon.

July 1834.

1. Peter unwell: Father on for the [first] time since his illness.
2. On as late 11 Oclock at night.
3. Helping Purvis to lead hay.
4. At Stagshaw fair with Peter; saw Wombwell's collection[2] *- An uncommon fine warm day.*
5. Burning quickens - Brought the cow from Blackburns - At Slaley at night singing - Uncommon droughty weather - Mill very scanty of water. Langley Mill taken this week.[3]

Sunday 6. Hearing J. Ryan a.m. - Jane at Ranter meeting; Thomas Baty came home with her.
7. Helping in with all the seed hay - Rakeing at afternoon - Came on very wet.
8. Sowing my seeds this forenoon. Mr Pattinson here yesterday proclaiming Langley mill.
9. Bill Dixon here laying the wood on our pig house - Some wet this morning.
10. Some rain - Went to work at 11 a.m. - John Dickenson of Allendale died.
11. The masons here slating our pig house.
12. Got done at 6 p.m. - Elizth*. at Scurrs.*

Sunday 13. At Slaley Church a.m. - Thomas Hedley & Mary Teasdale here at tea - John Dickenson's funeral today.
14. Went on at midnight, the water so light as to make the refiners give up.

---

[1] For Dixon's smallholding, rather than for the smelt mill.
[2] George Wombwell formed his first collection of animals in 1805 and it was so successful with the public that he formed two more menageries, all three of them touring throughout Britain. After George's death in 1850, his number 2 menagerie was taken over by his niece until 1884 when she sold it to the Bostock family, James Bostock having joined her business in 1839. Thereafter it continued travelling as Bostock's & Wombwell's Menagerie until December 1931, when its last show was held at the Old Sheep Market, Newcastle.
[3] Dixon means that WB Lead had taken the Blagill smelt mill at Langley.

15, 16. Got done this 12 Oclock; Peter on all this week.
17. Todd mowing in Spark's high field - Very droughty.
18. Very wet morning with thunder - Jane at Todds; Billy's wife there.
19. Uncommon wet day, all day wind E. Mr. Spark at Newcastle - Betsey Rowel married.[1]

Sunday 20. Hearing Mr. Hannah a.m.
21. Mally Barrow gone home.
22. At Hexham - Got the cow bulled on Sunday.
23. Engaged hoppleing the cow[2] *- Very hot days.*
24. Put the cow in Sparks field.
25. Billy Bowmans wife at our folks' - Very droughty.
26. Joe come home from Satley - Smokey forenoon; very wet afternoon - Been plenty of water for both sides all this week.

Sunday 27. Very wet morning - Old John Teasdale of Slaley buried.[3]
28. Billy Bowman & Joe gone off to Satley.
29. Very foggy days.
30. Betty Todd & Billy's wife here at tea - Very warm.
31. Jane at Thomas Dixons.

August 1834.

1. Shearing grass. Jane at John Elleringtons - Put Spark's calves in our high field.
2. Begun to mow - Helping Todd to mow - At Slaley at night buying rakes - Been a hot week end, but plenty of water all the week.

Sunday 3. Hearing Ryan a.m.
4. Father & Peter begun to mow - Mr. Spark got the last of their hay.
5. Martha Spark & Miss Kirkley gone to Hexham; been here a faw days. A heavy shower at night.
6. Hexham fair day - Taking a walk at night to Dyehouse.
7. Went to work at midnight this shift.
8. Went to work at 10 last night - A very wet morning - Got the cow bled & bull'd.
9. Went this morn at the usual time - Plenty of water today - Time parted 5 shifts. Mowing at afternoon - Todd mowing Jemmy - Shearing very throng. Linnels, Lambshields &c.

Sunday 10. At the Chapel with Jane hearing Mr. Nanne preach his first sermon[4] *- Warm day - Jane unwell at night.*
11. Went on at 12 at noon.
12. Very warm smelting day; smoked at night - Thos. Forster's sale at Trygal.
14. Mowing all day; Father helping at afternoon.
15. Peter and Sally gone to shear at Dilston - Strewing hay forenoon; Robt. Todd helping me to mow at afternoon.

---

[1] Betsy married Edward Rowell at Slaley.
[2] Tying two of its legs together to prevent it from straying.
[3] John, the son of Thomas and Mary Teasdale, died on 24 July 1834 at the age of 69. He was buried at Slaley.
[4] H Nanney was the new incumbent at St Helen's, Whitley Chapel.

16. Making hay - Father and Mother shearing Sparks wheat in our high field. At John Forster's land sale at Juniper.[1] *Uncommon warm weather this week.*

Sunday 17. Hearing Mr. Hannah - Very hot.
18. Very wet day, wind E.
19. Got the last of our hay into kile.
20. Breaking out the hay - Father & Mother got done the wheat.
21. Went to work at 12 at noon - Father on - Wet at night.
22. Very showery - Plenty of water today.
23. Went on at 5 this morning - The harvest very general; but the weather only moderate this week - Mr. Spark got 2 cows at the fair yesterday.

Sunday 24. With Jane at Slaley Church - Billy Roddam at Mr Sparks. Fine day.
25. Went to work at 5 - A wet morn, and continued all day.
26. Soft again.
27. Pikeing the last of our hay - A heavy rain at night.
28. Helping my father to lead their hay - Fine day.
29. Leading some hay into the loft - Allendale races begin today - Wet at aftn. and night.
30. Leading our hay with Oxley's horse - Helping Jemmy at afternoon - Thos. Dickenson set up at Middle Dukesfield lately - Been plenty of water all this week - A great deal of corn cut in this country.

Sunday 31. Hearing Mr. Short.

September 1834.

1. At Blackburns binding; had some ale.
2. Mrs Nicholson of Slaley died[2] *- Jemmy making me some water furrows.*
3. A fine leading day - Spark's folk shear out - Wet at night.
4. Soft forenoon - Kirsopp of Shield Hall sold off.
5. Droughty.
6. Very wet day - Old Peggy Purvis of Steel died - Plenty water all this week.

Sunday 7. At Chapel meeting the Shire Head singers - Jane, Mary, and Hugh at Sarah's - Fine day.
8, 9, 10. Very wet days.
11. Fine day.
12. Leading soil Very wet forenoon came on - Bowness churn stopt.
13. Finished the soil - Helping Spark folk to lead clover hay and oats - Very frosty morn and fine day - Our Joe come home - Ned Steel at Sparks - Bownass churn and dance.

---

[1] Several John Forsters lived in the area at the time of Thomas Dixon's diaries. John Forster was a member of the Finechambers Wesleyan Methodists in 1820. John Foster/Forster of Greenways was a lead ore smelter who married Ann Hornsby before c1827. John Forster of Pasture House was a lead ore smelter who married Elizabeth Lindsley before c1827. John Forster was a victualler at the *Fox and Hounds* at Slaley in 1827/28. John Forster was a farmer at Steel in 1827/28. John Forster was a member of the Dyehouse Primitive Methodists in 1832 and a class leader in 1837-43. The 1841 census for Slaley area notes John Forster of Lee, a lead ore smelter, and John Forster of Ryehill, farmer.
[2] Possibly Ann Nicholson who had been victualler of the *Red Lion*, Slaley, in 1827/28.

Above – Middle Dukesfield, c.1915. Plate. 33

Below – Dukesfield Corn Mill House, c.1930,
also known as the Low Mill. Demolished c.1970 Plate. 34

Sunday 14. Hearing Coghill for the first time - At our folks' at tea. Tweddle & Mary there.
15. Father helping me to finish the hay stack - Joe gone to Satley again - Very fine day.
16. Casting up soil in the lane - Helping Jemmy to lead his corn.
17. Wet at afternoon.
18. M^r^. Pattinson at the Mill - Very warm day.
20. Took the lead out of the hearth - Very warm day - Purvis mowing the second crop of old land - Oxley's churn; had a dance at this place - Plenty of water - Ore gone to Langley this week - Shearing near done. Lancelot Robson married lately.

Sunday 21. At Slaley Church - Very wet.
22. Begun with the bad ore; only 20 Bing - Very unwell at night.
24. John Purvis seeking hay from Parkhouse.
25. Taking physic.
26. Washing - The quey bulled at night - Soft day.
27. Joe Millburn's mother died - Mary and Tweddle gone to Hunstonworth[1] *- Fine day - Been only a soft week.*

Sunday 28. Hearing M^r^. Short a.m.
29. Peter helping me to wash - Dull day.
30. At Hexham; Father & Peter at Quatrebras - Fine day.

***October 1834**.*

1. The Barristers at Hexham - The corn almost all in.
2. Harry [Armstrong] begun a singing school at the Chapel.
3. Peter on with me; Father and Betsey gone to Uncle Thomas' - Fine.
4. Peter on - At Johney's with a Fiddler's company at night - Very fine weather - Plenty of water this week.

Sunday 5. At Slaley Church - Rather soft.
6. Father come home.
7. Strong wind & rather soft - Our cow bulled.
8. Peter been on all this weeks work.
9. At Unthank coals the first time in my life[2] *- Very wet at afternoon - Harry Armstrong here at tea.*
10. Cleaning quicks. Hearing Harry's singers at night.
11. Casting up soil - Very fine day. Been water plenty - Fine seed time.

Sunday 12. Hearing Coghill a.m.
13. Taking up 'tatoes in the field.
14. Wet forenoon - Helping Jane to wash.
15. Taking up american 'tatoes in garden.
17. Very strong wind.
18. Misstress Cox come - John Teasdale's fiddle raffled for - At the Chapel singing - Carr the Attorney gone off lately - Fine airey weather.

---

[1] Hunstanworth, a lead mining and smelting area just a mile or so SW of Blanchland.
[2] This was probably Unthank near Kiln Pit Hill, some 6 miles NSW of Dukesfield. There was certainly a coal mine at nearby Greymare Hill.

Sunday 19. At Slaley Church - Nanny Pig here at Dinner & tea - Mrs Cox here at night again.
20. Rather scanty this morning - Came on wet this forenoon - Mrs Cox gone home.
21. Been a very wet night; the water past riding this morning. The parliament houses burnt down last Thursday night.[1]
22. Weaned little Jane today.
23. Taking up 'tatoes in the field - Strong N wind - Harry here at tea.
24. On smelting for W^m^. Ridley - Very hard frost - Todd & I at the singing school.
25. Joe and Jo^sh^. Burn come; at the singing with them at night - Very cold day.

Sunday 26. At Slaley Church, a great many of us; at Ranters at aft. - At Sparks to tea.
27. Joe & Burn gone - Taking up 'tatoes - A fine day - Pattinson come.
28. Balloting for Blagill taken place[2] *- Got our folks' quey.*
29. Sparks folk killing 2 cows.
30. Father taken ill of his back.
31. Strong wind.

November 1834.

1. Nailling the apple trees[3] *- Been a fine week of fresh weather; but windy.*
Sunday 2. At Slaley Church; with Jane hearing W^m^. Hornsby at aft.
5. Made a bargain with Jos^h^. Blackburn.[4] *Tremendous wet day.*
7. Wet day, wind E - Tuning John Teasdale's dulcimer.
8. Some of the smelters at Blagill - Taking Jameson's book home at night - Took our cow in.

Sunday 9. Hearing Coghill - Uncle John & Nancy at our folk's.
10. At Hexham fair - Forster here at night.
11. At Jos. Blackburn's settleing with him about the change.
12. Digging in the garden - Hiring yesterday.
14. A Missionary meeting at Chambers.[5]
15. The work tools gone from our Mill to Langley[6] *- The roasters been on at Langley this week - At Slaley seeing M^r^. Scurr at night - Been a week of fine weather.*

Sunday 16. At Slaley Church - Smelters off with wallets today.[7]
17. Old Tommy Dixon begun in our mill.[8] *Mr Nanney in our house.*[9]
18. Mather killing our pig & our folks' - Very fine day.

---

[1] The Palace of Westminster was so severely damaged in this fire that it was almost completely rebuilt by 1852. It was again partially rebuilt after the bombing raids of the Second World War.
[2] Deciding which smelters should be transferred to the Blagill smelt mill.
[3] Perhaps for a cordon.
[4] There was a smelter of this name, so the bargain may have been work related; see also 11 November 1834.
[5] Presumably Finechambers.
[6] Blagill at Langley.
[7] As with the lead miners known as wallet men; presumably the former-Dukesfield smelters were going to lodge at Blagill smelt mill.
[8] It is unlikely that 'Old Tommy' was an uncle of the diarist, for he is never referred to as such. The 1841 census recorded that probable brothers Thomas and Joseph Dixon, both lead ore smelters in their 60s, were living together at Steel, while another Thomas Dixon aged about 25, also a lead ore smelter, was living at Juniper.
[9] The curate at Whitley Chapel.

19. At Mrs Armstrong's sale at Ryehill.
20. Brushing a dike.
21. Tho[s]. Oxley leading our folk's muck.
22. Peter helping me to hing a gate - At Slaley Church at night - Betty Brown of Lightside died this week - Wilson Bell chosen master of Whitley Chapel school[1] - Duke of Wellington took office last week end. [2]

Sunday 23. Hearing M[r]. Short a.m.
24. With Peter at Dotland buying 2 pigs.
25. Mother & Jane at Hexham.
26. At M[r]. Scurr's at afternoon.
27. Carr the Attorney's sale going on this week.
28. Nanny Robson here making Jane a cloak.
29. Very rough at night.

Sunday 30. At Slaley Church - Fine day.

December 1834.

1. Very rough morn - Liza got her bed of another daughter.[3]
2. Our tub thrown from the stair head.[4]
3. Rob[t]. Curry's sale at Bush - Betty Forster at our house to tea.[5]
4. Old Tommy Killing Sparks swine - Jos. Bowman very ill at Langley.
5. Bowman died last night at _ past 7 O'clock - Hugh come home and off again to Sarah's - At Slaley with J. Teasdale and Peter at night.
6. At Bowman's funeral - Fine day.

Sunday 7. Soft morn; but fine aft. - Geo. Barrow here at tea.
8. Cold morning, the hills covered with snow - Took in the queys.
9. Had Joe Ridley washing.
10. Hanging up the bacon - Peter helping me a little at afternoon to wash.
11. Jane unwell at night.
12. At Liza's at night tasteing bread and cheese.
13. A Carriage full of gentlemen came up the Railway yesterday to Hexham[6] *– Father at Hexham today - John Teasdale at Lillswood raffleing his violin - Still continues fine open weather.*

Sunday 14. Tho[s]. Bulman and Sally at our folks.
15. Jemmy at Bywell.
16. The farmers meeting Nixon about their farms.
17. Desperately bad of a cold - Done smelting to-day for this year.

---

[1] Whitley Chapel has had a school of some sorts since the seventeenth century, associated with the church of St Helen's, and it was probably this school to which Dixon's father was appointed master in 1836.
[2] As Foreign Secretary in Peel's minority government.
[3] This daughter was named Mary.
[4] There is no obvious explanation for this happening.
[5] A Betty Forster was the victualler at the *Fox and Lamb* at Dipton mill in 1827/28.
[6] The Newcastle & Carlisle Railway had opened for horse-drawn goods between Hexham and Blaydon on 26 November 1834.

18. Slaggys working my metal - At Todds at night seeing his new Bass.
19. Leading rails at aft.
20. Joe the Taylor here making a shag waistcoat - Smelters all break up today - Still fine open weather - W^m^. Burdus bad.

Sunday 21. Jane and I at meeting hearing Short.
22. Building our hearth; had the workstone up.
23. At Hexham with Jemmy.
24. Hugh gone to Newton to break up.
25. Christmas day - Joe come home.
27. The silver taken off; and the Refiners done - At the breaking up at John Taylors at night.

Sunday 28. At Slaley Church with John Skelton & Robt. who came here on Friday - Jane and I standing up for Liza's little Mary - Very cold day.
29. With Joe and Hugh at Farnley Tunnel.[1]
31. Helping Mr Spark with his accounts. Sally Bulman here makeing Jane a gown - I have a bad nose. A very wet night.

Plate. 35

Dye House cottages c.1890.

[1] Farnley tunnel on the Newcastle & Carlisle Railway, was just opposite Corbridge. It was originally built for single-track working before being doubled in 1846-47, but was by-passed with a cutting in 1962.

9

MEMORANDUM FOR 1835

January 1835.

Thursday 1. Helping Mr Sparke to make up the acct^{s}.
2. M^{r}. Spark at Allen Mill helping Tweddle.
3. Hard frost this weekend.

Sunday 4. Hearing Coghill.
5. M^{r}. Sparke at Hexham meeting Johnson - Thos. Steel placed for Allen Mill[1] *- At Todds with Joe at night.*
6, 7. Helping M^{r}. Sparke to finish the acct^{s}. Jane & Maria Smith at Sparks.
8. Begun to smelt for another year.
9. Terrible wet and strong west wind.
10. The Refiners taking their work tools to Blagill - The weather very uncertain - Newcastle Election this week.[2]

Sunday 11. Snow lying this morning. Coming on snow at night.
12. Beaumont & Bell elected without opposition at Hexham - Very snowey morning; turn'd half fresh.
13. Wind S.
14. Fine fresh day; the snow all gone - Joe gone away.
15. Dressing rails.
16. Tweddle and his father gone to Newcastle to seek the money[3] *- Lying white with snow this morning and snowing all day.*
17. Leading some hay - Fine frosty day - At Dilstone at night meeting the Stewards.

Sunday 18. Hearing Mr Short.
19. Our Pay-day at Dukesfield Mill[4] *- Much fighting at the low Mill - The Stewards gone off to Allendale - Very blasty night.*
21. Very frosty and cold - At Mollarsteads at night.
22. Turn'd to a thaw.
23. On smelting, have only 2 shifts this week - The snow almost all gone.
24. Marg^{t}. and Jane gone to Newcastle - Very windy day.

---

[1] Thomas Steel began working in smelt mills in 1799, aged about 15 years, and he was a smelter at Dukesfield for 19 years, then Rookhope for 17 years, first as a smelter, then as clerk, and then as sub-agent for 7 years. He then went to Allen mill as agent, where he amongst other things he oversaw the building of long horizontal chimneys, and by 1860 he had been there 25 years, (Hunt, 117, quoting Sopwith's diary for 30 April 1860). Plate. 39
A tablet in Allendale church notes 'Thomas Steel of Podsbank in this parish, upwards of 30 years manager of the smelt mills, connected with the W B Lead Mines … his sound judgement and integrity in the discharge of his duties gained him the confidence of his employers and the esteem of many friends. Died 10 May 1864 aged 80 years.'
[2] Parliament had been dissolved on 29 December 1834. The Newcastle seats were won by William Ord and Sir M. W. Ridley and the latter 'was most brutally assailed with missiles of all descriptions' as he left the hustings.
[3] For the Pay.
[4] This Pay for the year 1834 at Dukesfield amounted to £3105 for the smelters, £2493 for the ore carriage, and £596 for the lead carriage, in total of £6193 paid out.

Above – Whitley St. Helen's church at Whitley Chapel, Hexhamshire, as it looked in the 19th C. The small upper story window was in the west gallery area where musicians would play.

Plate. 3

Below – With the advent of the church organ the gallery was no longer used and had been removed by the 1920s, by which time a vestry had been added and window positions altered.

Plate. 3

Sunday 25. With Tweddle at John Willy's - Jane at Lementon to-day.
27, 28. Jane come home; came to Hexham last night.
29. Helping Purvis to lead some thorns to our field - At Mollarsteads at night.
30. Dressing some rails a.m. - Mather killing our pigs p.m.
31. Salting the pigs - Peter helping me to rail - Been a fine week of fresh weather.

February 1835.

Sunday 1. Hearing old Stobart.
2. Finished the rails - Peter at Glendew.
3. Thos. Steel fliting to Allendale, Tweddle to Blagill - Got our cow bulled.
4. Bownas fliting to Rookhope - At Burdus' garden at E. D [East Dukesfield].
5. Terrible day of wind, showers of rain hail and snow.
6. Frosty.
7. Fresh again - Been a terrible week of wind.

Sunday 8. Lying with snow this morn.
9. Cold day - Jane at Slaley seeing Marg^ts^. child who is ill.
10. Very frosty - Leading thorns at night.
11. Old Jenny Taylor buried.
12. Bell Graham and Rowley Rowlands wife buried - Our folk twilting in our room - Jane and Ann at Slaley at night.
13. On smelting for J. Forster - At Lowes' and Todds at night.
14. Peter and me taking in a garth for 'tatoes - Fine day - Been a fine weekend.

Sunday 15. Hearing Mr Short.
16. Dikeing and leading hay - Fine day.
17. M^r^. Spark gone to Morpeth.
18. At Wally Thorn and Stobb - M^r^. Nixon here today - Some showers of snow.
19. Meeting of Parliament today - Showers of snow.
20. Jemmys old Stobart cow calved[1] - Very ill showers of snow.
21. Mary Dixon of Juniper got her bed last night or this morn - Got done work by daylight this morning - Joseph come home.

Sunday 22. With Joe, Peter and Hugh at Shire Chapel - Dreadful night of wind and rain.
23. Most dreadful day of rain and wind.
24. Joe gone off.
25. Thos. Rowland here with straw.
26, 27. Very showery days of snow and rain.
28. Frosty morning - Peter seeking hay at Literage - At a Temperance meeting at Dyehouse at night.

March 1835.

Sunday 1. Hearing Coghill a.m. Thomas Charlton of Lemington married lately.
2.. Leading manure on to the seeds - Peter on for Forster.[2]

---

[1] Presumably a cow which Jemmy obtained from old Stobart.
[2] The 1841 census list two John Forsters, one of Lee, the other of Mollersteads, both lead ore smelters.

Plate. 38

"The Depot at Hexham", 1836.

3. On for Forster - Snowey morning.
4. Showers of rain and snow.
5. Newcastle Assizes.
7. Much snow lying this morn - Heavy showers of snow to-day - Rob[t]. Smith here at tea - Little Jane very unwell - A week of uncommon rough weather.

Sunday 8. Writeing a letter to Joe.
9. Forster on for me - At Hexham seeing the opening of the Rail-Way.[1]
10. A heavy storm of snow lying this morning.
11. Fresh again.
12. Spreading manure - Martha got a cow.
13. Marg[t]. Spark gone to Geo. Forster's wife's funeral at Newcastle.
14. Diging with Peter in the high field. Been 3 fine days; only some wreaths of snow left. W[m]. Ridley at Sparks at night.

Sunday 15. Hearing Short - Jona. Barrow here with Tweddell this weekend.
16. Finishing the diging in the field - Old Betty Fairlamb died this morning.
17. Peggy Sheell here washing - A very soft day.
18. Jane at old Betty's funeral - Rather soft day. The Taylors making Peter a suit.
21. Father on for Peter, who is at Thomas Bulman's wedding - Jane and I skaleing[2] *- Tweddell and Clare wounded - Agnes Maughan here.*

Sunday 22. Tho[s]. John and George Charlton here at dinner.
24. Sowing onion seed at night.
25. Went to work early this morning - At Hexham fair.
26. Cleaning the slime pits[3] *- Jane at Todds to tea - Hearing M[r]. Boyd on temperance at night.*
27. Old Bill Dixon of Dukesfield died this forenoon.
28. Setting cabbage and sowing peas - A fine dry seed time. Peter at John Halls.

Sunday 29. Hearing Coghill a.m. - At old Bill's funeral at afternoon.
30. Purvis ploughing our rig - Nanny and Mary Robson here clearing off about the child.[4]
31. Marg[t]. come from George's and little Sam with her - At Ridleys of Steel at night.

April 1835.

1. Forster on for me; have only 2 shifts each this week. Jack sowing oats and tares[5] *for us - Some heavy showers.*

---

[1] This was the formal opening of the Newcastle & Carlisle Railway between Blaydon and Hexham, with locomotives. The line had been opened for horse-drawn goods carriage, including lead, from 26 November 1834.
[2] Probably meaning spreading manure.
[3] Slime pits were usually large wooden boxes, typically 3 feet wide by 30 feet long and up to 3 feet deep, set out in the open, at ground level. They formed a final catchment for all the water used in washing, where any lead or ore left in the water would settle out as 'slime' in the pit from where it could be recovered and reprocessed.
[4] The meaning of 'clearing off' is not known.
[5] 'Tares' usually implies vetches.

Plate. 39

Above- Peasemeadows farm, near Allendale. The family home of Jonathan Sparke,
Thomas's father-in-law

Below- A 1859 map of the Allendale area with the Allen Smelt Mill shown at the top left.

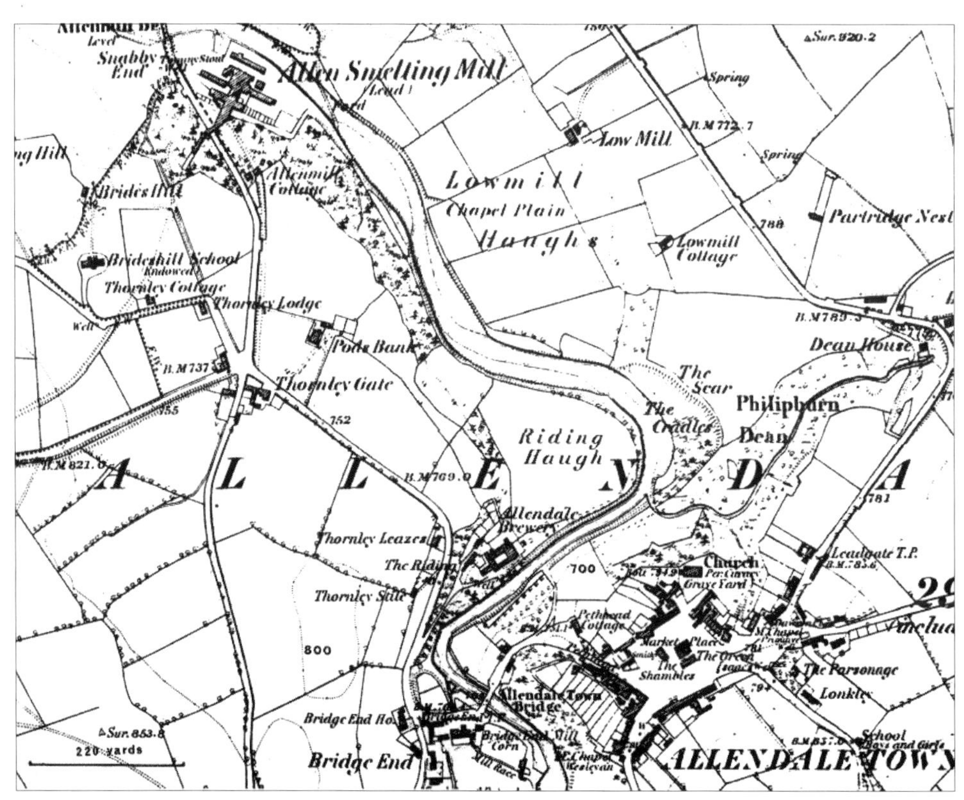

Fig. 6

2. Finishing the Breckonsike [ore] today - At Dyehouse at night - Fine spring day - Father at Tommy Steels.
3. Soft day, cold E wind.
4. Carr gone to start at Blagill - Seeing Bill Dixon at night - Our folks cow calved on Tuesday morning.

Sunday 5. Hearing H Wilkinson at afternoon - Old Mrs Smith of Slaley died this morn.[1]
6. Begun with Scraith Head;[2] *making the pigs 12 Stone*[3] *- Father weighing the ore - Peter got his foot lamed.*
7. Forster on with me - John & W^{m}. Dinning left this mill.
8. Leading some manure to the 'tatoes - At Nunbrough seeking for a dog.
9. Johney Johnson's sale at Ordley - Peter got the cur bitch at J Halls.
10. Will. Colling here at night.
11. Setting 'tatoes - Cleaning the Roasters ore pits.[4] *- Very fine dry weather.*

Sunday 12. Hearing M^{r}. Short.
13. M^{r}. Steel and M^{r}. Walton at the mill - Settled with them to go to Allen Heads.[5]
14. At Hexham at afternoon - Finished my washing this forenoon.
15. Went to work this forenoon - Got a letter from M^{r}. [Benjamin] Johnson to go to Blaydon.
16. At Blaydon with Mr Spark - Very frosty and snowey.
17. At Allen Mill and Peas Meadows.
18. Working our last shift of ore - Only 12 Bing left - Jack Woodman and Betty Bell of Slaley died this week.

Sunday 19. At M^{r}. Sparks at Dinner - Easter day - Our folks' at tea.
20. Went off to Blaydon to my [new] situation - Begun to lodge at Matt^{w}. Stobbs'.
25. Spent the whole week at Blaydon.

Sunday 26. At Lementon all day.
27. Jim Jemson brought me a parcel.
29. Jack the Wright begun carrying Kettlewell's sale - Finished the week at Blaydon.

May 1835.

Sunday 3. At Winlaton Church at aft^{n}. At Thomas Pearsons to tea.
4. M^{r}. Emerson[6] *gone west - Our Lucy calved on Sunday.*

---

[1] Elizabeth Smith, aged 65, was the widow of the Revd Joseph Smith of Slaley who had died 6 February 1831.
[2] Lead ore from the Scraith Head mine at Burnhope Seat just west of Ireshopeburn in Weardale, County Durham.
[3] The 'pigs' or ingots of lead were in various weights, but were commonly 1 cwt (8 stone) if the lead was deemed to be worth refining, or 1.5 cwt (12 stone) if it was not.
[4] The significance of this activity is unclear. Presumably the ores to be roasted were stored in what would normally be called 'bingsteads', and the roasted ores placed in 'pits', and since the mill was effectively being closed down, Thomas was removing the last remaining roasted ore in the pits in order to smelt it.
[5] Presumably Thomas Steel, agent at Allendale smelt mill, and William Walton, agent at Allenheads smelt mill. Dixon agreed with them that he should move to Allenheads smelt mill.
[6] Thomas Emmerson, agent at the Blaydon Refinery.

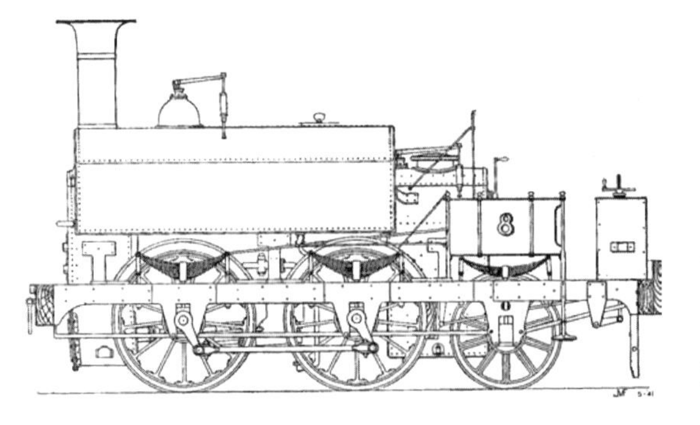

The "Tyne" engine 1836

Fig. 7

NEWCASTLE AND CARLISLE Railway.

Notice is hereby Given,

THAT all Persons trespassing on the Railway, or the Works thereof, are liable *to a considerable Penalty* for each Offence. And that the Punishment for doing any Injury or Damage to the said Railway is

Transportation for 7 Years.

THE DIRECTORS GIVE THIS PUBLIC

WARNING,

that they are determined to Prosecute with the utmost Rigour, all Persons who may do any such Injury or Damage to the Railway; and that positive Orders are given to all the Servants of the Company, to give Information against any Persons trespassing thereon.

JOHN ADAMSON,
Clerk to the Company.

Railway Office, Newcastle upon Tyne,
21st August, 1835.

Plate. 40

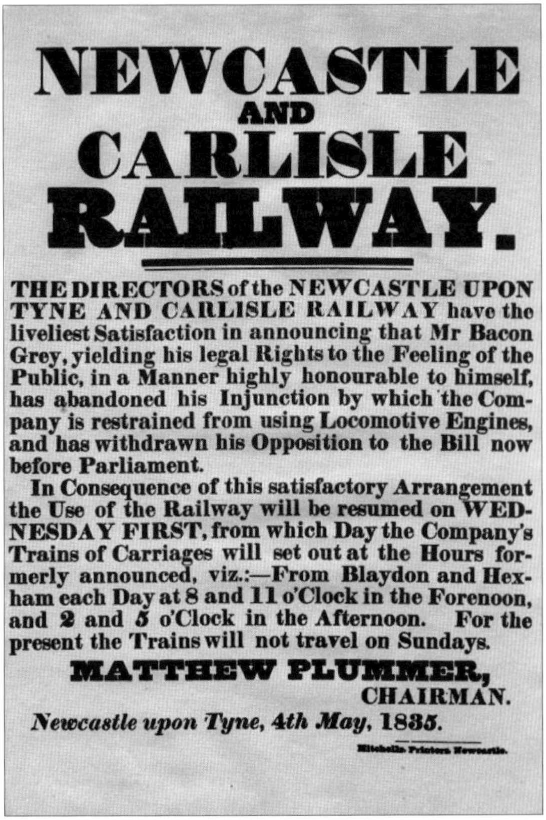

NEWCASTLE AND CARLISLE RAILWAY.

THE DIRECTORS of the NEWCASTLE UPON TYNE AND CARLISLE RAILWAY have the liveliest Satisfaction in announcing that Mr Bacon Grey, yielding his legal Rights to the Feeling of the Public, in a Manner highly honourable to himself, has abandoned his Injunction by which the Company is restrained from using Locomotive Engines, and has withdrawn his Opposition to the Bill now before Parliament.

In Consequence of this satisfactory Arrangement the Use of the Railway will be resumed on WEDNESDAY FIRST, from which Day the Company's Trains of Carriages will set out at the Hours formerly announced, viz.:—From Blaydon and Hexham each Day at 8 and 11 o'Clock in the Forenoon, and 2 and 5 o'Clock in the Afternoon. For the present the Trains will not travel on Sundays.

MATTHEW PLUMMER,
CHAIRMAN.

Newcastle upon Tyne, 4th May, 1835.

Plate. 41

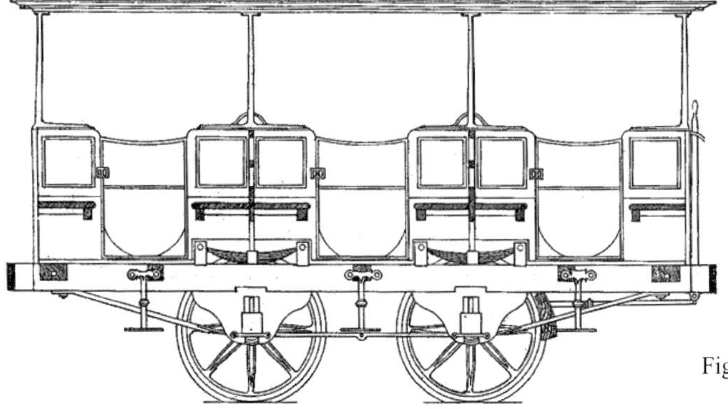

Second-class carriage
1838

Fig. 8

5. The Steam carriages begun again[1] *- A new boiler put in at Blaydon this week.*[2]
9. Came home with the steam [train].

Sunday 10. At the meeting with Jane - Bidding Thos. Dickenson and Robt. Todd farewell - Wet morning.
11. Went down to Blaydon this morning with Thos. Steel in the Steam.
12. Jane hired a girl named Smith.
16. Finished the week at Blaydon.

Sunday 17. At Stella Catholic Chapel a.m. - At Lementon at af^t^. - Anth^y^. Reay at Ma^tt^. Stobb's.
18. Bill Stobbs at Blaydon informed me of John Bownass' death - M^r^. Sparke came to Blaydon last Thursday going to Newcastle.
20. At Ben. Johnsons at night.[3]
23. Came home in the Steam. Jack at Dilston with 3 horses - A great many changes in the Country - A M^r^. Temperly came to Blackhall - H. Dickenson come to Ordley. Matt Robson gone to Blackburn - Jo^s^. Smith from Mollarsteads - Old Scott from Viewly - A. Hunter to Ryehill - Jack Charlton to Juniper - Bob Dixon to Starwood. Ralp Blackburn to Whinny-hill.[4]

Sunday 24. With Jane at the meeting a.m.
25. Went to Blaydon today.
30. Uncle John & Jane came to Blaydon to see me. At Lementon seeking Jane at night.

Sunday 31. With Jane at Newcastle seeing George who is ill.

June 1835.

1. Jane came home from Blaydon at 5 O'Clock. A very wet morning.
3. George & Marg^t^. came up - Makepeace very ill at Blaydon.
6. Came home with old Tommy Dixon - Stagshaw fair day - Very warm day. W^m^. Ridley flited from Steel to Langley this week.

Sunday 7. At the meeting with Jane, very fine day.
8. At Langley Mill and Ellerington[5] *seeking a mare - Thos. Steel & Clemetson at the Mill here.*
9. Went to Blaydon today. Very hot and much thunder here.
10. Much thunder at Blaydon.
11. Thunder again.
12. Peter & Betsey come to Blaydon.
13. Been a very hot week.

---

[1] A writ forbidding the use of steam locomotives had been served on the Newcastle & Carlisle Railway company on 28 March, at the behest of Charles Bacon Grey of Styford, but a 'storm of indignation' forced Grey to withdraw his opposition to locomotives, which commenced working the line again on 5th of May (see plate 41).
[2] The Blaydon refinery had long used water-power to drive the furnace bellows, but it was probably using steam-powered blowing cylinders when Dixon arrived there, which might explain this reference to a new boiler.
[3] If this refers to Benjamin Johnson, the WB head cashier, then Thomas was in exalted company.
[4] Possibly Winnowshill, near Blanchland.
[5] Probably Elrington.

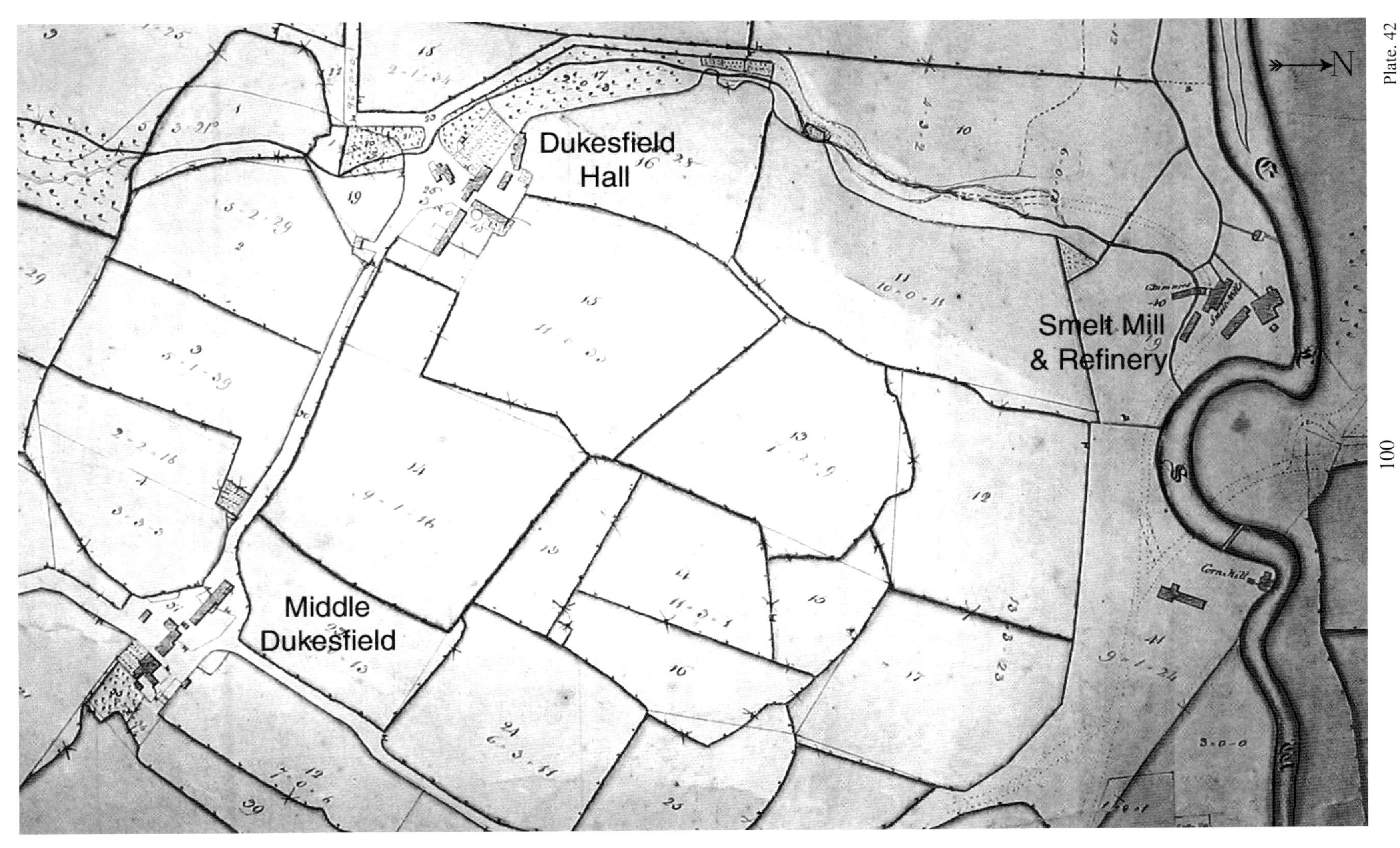

An early 19th C plan of Dukesfield showing Middle Dukesfield, Dukesfield Hall and the Smelt Mill.

Plate. 42

Sunday 14. At Lementon at afternoon.
15. Miss Mulcaster died.
16. Peter & Betsey come home.
18. A Dreadful Explosion at Wallsend.[1]
20. Came home very late on tonight - Newcastle Races this week - Isaac Wilson and 2 Shields here at Mr. Sparks.

Sunday 21. Spent the day at home and Mr. Sparks - A wet night. Tweddle & Geo. Sheell came back from Dalton.
22. Went off to Blaydon, took the Steam at Stocksfield - Very wet.
27. Went to meet Jane and Sally at Newhouse tonight[2] *- Been a very cold week.*

Sunday 28. Spent the day at Uncle Thomas's.
29. Went to Blaydon.
30. Our Lucy bull'd.

July 1835.

4. Came up to the fair,[3] *and home to Dukesfield - Our Joe there also - A fine day.*

Sunday 5. At our folks' to tea - About 17 or 18 weeks since I saw Joe.
6. Went to Blaydon today - Weighing Litharge.
11. At Emerson's hay this week sometimes. Our black quey calved on Wednesday. Old Johney Chatt died yesterday.

Sunday 12. Spent the Sunday at Blaydon and seeing the spa well.[4]
13. Some rain.
14, 15. Working at Emerson's hay. Mr Emerson gone west - Busy with our hay at home - Jack Purvis and Peter mowed it last week.
17. Mr. Emerson gone to Shields & Sunderland.
18. Came home to night. Have 5 large pikes of hay up. Robt. Todd & Betty been through at our house.

Sunday 19. With Jane at a love feast.
20. Went to Blaydon.
21. Came home by Hexham - Jane and Mother bought me a new black coat at Hexham today.
23. Mowing out our seeds and helping Jack to mow out the back field.
24. Making our hay stack; and pikeing the last of our hay.
25. Matt. Stobbs here seeking me to go away to Blaydon - Mr. Spark got all the back field into pike.

Sunday 26. Very warm day - A Ranter camp meeting in brick Kiln field. Went off to Blaydon at night.

---

[1] An explosion at the Church Pit, Wallsend, resulted in the deaths of 26 men and 75 boys.
[2] The location of Newhouse is unknown, but could be the farm called Newhouse near Lilswood.
[3] This would be Stagshaw Fair.
[4] According to J Maughan in an undated (but post 1909) and un-named news cutting relating to Blaydon, people continued to use the Spa Well after a water supply was laid on to two fountains, because of its excellence for making tea, and when the villagers had their large tea meetings, formerly called *soirees*, the water was always drawn from the spa well.

27. Our folk begun to mow.
28. Mr. Emerson gone to the west - Mulcaster's folk leading their hay.[1]
30. Mr. Spark leading their hay.

August 1835.

1. Came home at two O'Clock - Leading the last of our hay into the byer - Our folk got theirs all to pike.

Sunday 2. At Home all day.
3. Went to Blaydon this morn.
6. Hexham fair day; Jane and Peter there selling our cow, got 7 Guineas for her.
7. Mr Emerson at Shields - A very windy day.
8. Peter and Old Tommy gone to Tynemouth - Very droughty weather. Our black quey bulled on the fair day.

Sunday 9. At Lementon at tea - Jane Barrow died yesterday morning - John Charlton married today.
10. Our white quey bulled today.
15. Old Jemmy and Hannah came up from Tynemouth - Jane met me at Hexham at Harry's concert, Dukesfield [Smelt] Mill finished this week.

Sunday 16. Matt. Stobbs come to seek me - Went to Blaydon at night.
17. Our folk gone to Tynemouth.
20. Jane come to Blaydon.
22. Went to Tynemouth with Jane. Rather wet - Been a fine week - Harvest very throng on Tyne Side.

Sunday 23. Came up in a Steam Boat from Tynemouth - Got tea at Peter Glaidhills.
24. Our folk and Jane came home.
25. Very wet - Mr. Emerson & Anderson gone to Allen pays.[2]
27. Jane bought a quey of her father. Been two or three days of wet.
29. Came home from Blaydon with J Lowes. Our Joe at Home.

Sunday 30. At Home all day.
31. Went to Blaydon - Joe & his Mother at Hexham. The Harvest very throng.

September 1835.

3. Jane & Mother shearing the few oats in our field.
5. Blind Jack died - Billy Purvis been at Blaydon this week.

Sunday 6. At Dunston at aft.
9. Mr. Spark called at Blaydon.
12. Came home with the 'Meteor' - Most of the wheat shorn in this neighbourhood.

---

[1] Clearly there were still Mulcasters living at Blaydon, perhaps John Mulcaster, the former mill agent who had lived at Blaydon House, or possibly John Peter Mulcaster, probably a son who was a barrister living at Blaydon House in 1851.
[2] Anderson was probably Robert Anderson, who seems to have been an assistant to Benjamin Johnson.

Sunday 13. Uncle Jacob and Betty here all day.
14. Pulling onions this morning - Went to Blaydon at 10 O'Clock.
17. Father in Allendale.

Sunday 20. Nancy Dinning buried today.[1] *Thos. Charlton and wife here last night - At Lementon to tea.*
22. Father gone to Allen Mill to work.
23. Peter gone to Allen Mill to the smelting furnace.
24. W^m. Walton & Bownass at Blaydon.
26. Came home in the 3rd Train. Fine day - Joe come.

Sunday 27. At Slaley Church - Uncle Thomas here at tea.
28. Went to Blaydon in the 2nd Train.
30. At Hexham seeing after lead.

October 1835.

1. At Shields.
2. M^r. Steel at Blaydon.
3. Got my quarters pay.

Sunday 4. Came home today - A very wet morning - Went to Blaydon at night.
5, 6, 7. Wet days.
8. M^r. Spark at Blaydon.
10. Came home with Betty Purvis & Thos. Dixon - A good deal of corn out yet - The separators left Blaydon.[2]

Sunday 11. At meeting with Jane hearing the new preacher Mitchell - Very blowey day.
12. Went to Dilston with Hugh this morn.
17. Came home in the last train. Been a week of fine weather - Corn all in here now. Jemmy gone to Allen Mill this week.

Sunday 18. Went to Blaydon at night - Fine day - Our Peter gone to Dickenson's at Lee's.
24. Been a very wet this week at times - Ann Robson of Flother died this week - John Forster of Dipton Mill married lately - The new market opened at Newcastle.[3]

Sunday 25. Came home from Blaydon this morning. Tweddle & T. Stainthorpe at Hunstonworth.
26. Went to Blaydon this morning, very wet - Hugh with me.
28. M^r. Spark and Mary gone to Ncastle.
29. N Castle fair day.[4]
31. Came home with Robt. Smith - Our Joe come home, been working at Ryding Mill. Betsey been in Allendale this week.

---

[1] At Whitley Chapel.
[2] 'Separators' probably worked the Pattinson Process.
[3] The Grainger Market.
[4] The October Newcastle Fair had long been one of the most important in the north with, usually, a horse fair beginning 9 or 10 days before the 29th and regarded as one of the finest horse fairs in the Kingdom, followed by the fair for cattle (mainly Kyloes) and swine on the 29th held on the Town Moor and called the 'Cow-hill fair'.

Plate. 45

The hirings at Hexham, Martinmas, 11th November 1878. There were usually two hirings a year for single servants – May Day & Martinmas. Those looking for work would often wear a token to denote their trade. Thatchers wore a token of straw or heather and carters a piece of whipcord around their hats, whilst shepherds carried crooks.

November 1835.

Sunday 1. Joe & Peter here at tea - Uncle John here at night.
2. Went down with Joe this morning.
3. Rough weather.
5[1]
6. At So. Shields.
7. Very wet day - Mally Dodd died - At W^{m}. Ellerington's at tea.

Sunday 8. At Whickham with Thos. Pearson.
9. Hexham fair day - Very wet morning.
10. Hexham hiring.
11. The Railway time changed today.
14. The separators done this week at Blaydon. Came home by 12 O'Clock Steam - W^{m}. Ridley at Blaydon - Miss Longridge here.

Sunday 15. At M^{r}. Sparks at Dinner - Our folks' at tea.
16. Went to Blaydon.
17. Jane at Hexham.
21. James Ellerington at Blaydon - Very wet.

Sunday 22. Very wet - At Blaydon meeting - Very large floods.[2]
23. Very wet - Tweddle at Newcastle.
25. At Samples meeting with Frank Purvis.
27. Old Jack Bulman died.
28. Came home - Joe at home - Jos^{h}. Dickenson married today.[3] *Mather killed our pig on Monday.*

Sunday 29. Jemmy & Eliza here at tea - Willm. Blackburn died.[4]
30. Went to Blaydon. Shield's folk gone to Sunderland - Soft day.

December 1835.

1. At No. Shields.
2. Aunt Betty Bulman got a daughter.[5]
4. At Newcastle at night.

Sunday 6. Lementon.
10. M^{r}. Emerson at Shields.
11. Came home to Tweddles Birth Day.[6]
12. Our Joe at Home unwell. Uncle & Aunt John & Nancy here at Sparks.

---

[1] Dixon does not mention an interesting event on this day on the railway between Newcastle and Hexham, when a cow, presumably alarmed by something, jumped out of a cattle wagon, rolled down an embankment, then ran after the train. It was subsequently secured in a cattle wagon with ropes.
[2] Heavy rains caused the Tyne to overflow its banks, covering the fields between Ryton and Redheugh.
[3] Dickinson had been christened on 29 October 1806 at Slaley, married Mary Nevin on 28 November 1835 at St Peters, Allendale, and died before 1871 at Allendale. Mary Nevin had been christened at St Peters, Allendale on 7 February 1813, the daughter of John Nevin and Elizabeth Ridley.
[4] William was the 17 year old son of John Blackburn, a farmer of Shield Hall/Steel Hall. John himself died aged 62 at Wooley on 27 May 1841. The family tombstone stands in Slaley churchyard.
[5] The daughter was christened Thomasin on 1 January 1836. She may have died young – see 1 July 1841.
[6] His 21st

Sunday 13. At Home all day.
14. Went to Blaydon.
16. M^r. Nixon here seeing about the Farms.
19. Very snowey day - The Mills all break up today - Baty horse came on Wednesday.

Sunday 20. Snowey day - At Blaydon all day.
24. Got all the Lead in.
25. Christmas day.
26. Sent the Machine to Langley - Came home by Hexham.

Sunday 27. At home all day - Father and Mother and John Skelton here at tea.
28. Went to Blaydon with John Skelton.
29. The weighers at Shields.
30. At So. Shields weighing the last of the Lead.
31. Weighing off today.

10

MEMORANDUM FOR 1836.

January 1836.

1. Jane & Elizabeth came to Blaydon.
2. At W^{m}. Ellerington's to tea. Weather open.

Sunday 3. With Jane and Lizth. at Anth^{y}. Reay's at Ryton.
4. Jane & Lizth. came home.
8. The Stewards gone to Newcastle.
9. Came home by Hexham with Makepeace - Joe at home. Peggy Scott died this week.

Sunday 10. At home all day.
11. Very snowey rough day - Jemmy at Hexham with the gig for the stewards.
12. Went to Allendale Town with my father early this morning - Helping Tweddle to pay - Fine frosty day.
13. Went to Blaydon today.
16. Very little employment this week at Blaydon - At Robinson's at night.

Sunday 17. Came home in 'Hercules' with J Egglestone - Jane hearing Josh. Darg at night.
18. Went to Blaydon - M^{r}. Emerson gone to Langley - The Litharge Machine begins.[1]
20. The Lead begun to come in.
23. Came home with Joe Robinson - Uncommon strong wind. Our folk giving up the Haugh. John Bell's wife of Aydonshields died this week[2] *and old Peggy Purvis of Ordley - W^{m}. Burdus & Joe Bownas fallen out.*

Sunday 24. M^{r}. Middleton come today - Josh. Leck and Jack Elliot here at this place.
25. Marg^{t}. Spark married at Slaley to John Middleton of Byker Hill - Went to Blaydon.
26. Tweddle, Mary, & Jemmy come home from the wedding.
30. Been a very rough week of wind & snow - Geo Barrow and Mary Ann Reed married.[3]

Sunday 31. At Newcastle seeing Geo Forster.

February 1836.

2. Thos. Oxley leading our manure, Josh Bownas & Geo Blackburn on fighting.
6. Came home - Father & Mother at Hexham. Hugh come home - Been a rough week. M^{r}. Spark got a letter from M^{r}. Beaumont lately.

---

[1] Litharge was a product of the lead refining process. It could be used as a source of Red Lead, or it could be reduced back to metallic lead either in an ore hearth, or more commonly at this time in a reducing furnace. However, the function of the 'Litharge Machine' remains uncertain, unless it was for breaking up any lumpy litharge before the reducing process.
[2] On 18 January at the age of 42, buried at Whitley Chapel. She was probably the Elizabeth Dixon of the parish of Shotley who married a John Bell on 21 August 1820. John Bell of Aydon Shields died 11 December 1868 aged 78 years and was also buried at Whitley Chapel.
[3] At Haydon Bridge.

Above – The Hexham fair c.1890 Plate. 44

Below – Bostock & Wombwell's menagerie. Thomas notes when they arrive in the area.

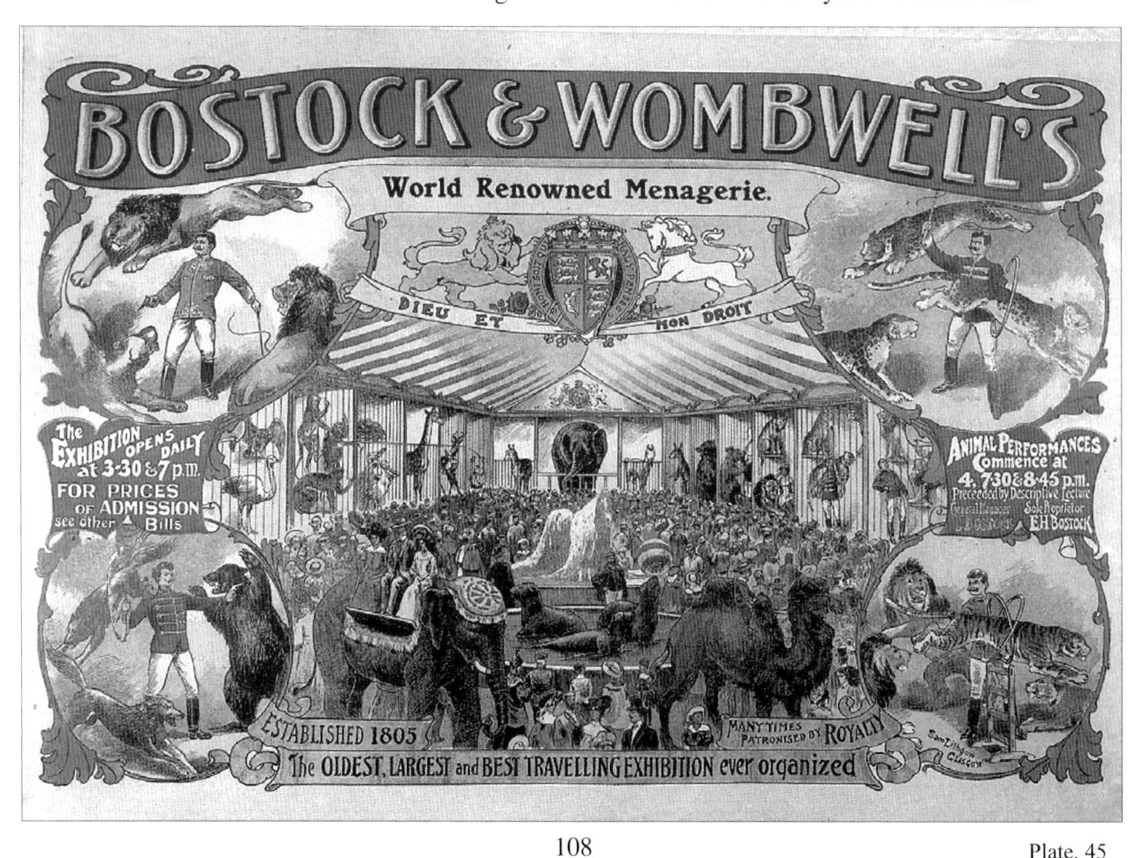

Plate. 45

Sunday 7. At Home all day.
8. Went to Blaydon - Windy weather this week.
13. At Newcastle at night with W. Ellerington.

Sunday 14. At Winlaton Church this morning. At Lementon at afternoon.
17. Terrible day of Wind & Cold - A very high tide today. M^r^. Sparke gone down to see Margaret's.
20. Came home with M^r^. Sparke - Our Joe at home - A very fine day.

Sunday 21. Fine day - At Home all day.
22. Went to Blaydon.
23. At Hexham (Jane).
26. Jane and Sally went to Allen Town.
27. Terrible day of snow & rain - M^r^. Emerson gone to the north.

Sunday 28. At Blaydon all day - Very ill day.
29. Still soft.

March 1836.

1. M^r^. Emerson went off to Rookhope Mill and retreated to Hexham.
2. Jane & Sally came home.
4. M^r^. E.[1] *come home - W^m^. Lowes got some dinner with me.*
5. Came home by way of Hexham - Very wet after landing - Joe Wilson lost his pony - Tide at six o'Clock.

Sunday 6. Old Tommy Carr Dotland died last week - At home all day.
7. Went to Blaydon with first train - Wrote a second letter to Joe.
12. At Shields with 2 men - Wombwell at Newcastle – Been a fine day.

Sunday 13. At Uncle Thomas' - Our Peter at Shotley Bridge seeing Joe who is bad.
17. Very rough day - Water much swollen.
19. Came home by 1st train - Joe at home very ill - Peter helping me to sow onions and set cabbage - M^r^. Nixon here - Old Tommy Roddam died last week.[2]

Sunday 20. At home all day - Peter at Hexham seeking oranges for Joe.
21. Went to Blaydon.
25. Came up to Hexham Fair; Father & Jane there with our Whitey and Kettleweell, sold the latter, Father sold his Jemmy Quey[3] *- Went to Blaydon at night - M^r^. Emerson at Shields - Angus appointed overseer.*
26. Come home by the 4 Oclock.

Sunday 27. At home all day - Very showery.
28. Went to Blaydon.
31. Thos. Steel taken ill at Newcastle.

---

[1] Mr Emmerson.
[2] A Thomas Rodham was a 'fallen' member of the Slaley Primitive Methodists in 1835.
[3] Whitey and Kettleweell were cows, the latter perhaps the quey which Thomas looked at in April 1834.

"Barge Day on the Tyne" at Newcastle
(see entry for May 12th)

April 1836.

2. Old Mrs Close died this morning - Daninel Teasdale died this week.

Sunday 3. Easter Sunday - At Lementon.
9. Came home the first train - Sarah Wilson here - M^{r}. Sparkes sale - Sold our white cow.

Sunday 10. Old Tommy Barrow & Mally, Geo. & Wife here at tea.
11. Went to Blaydon with little Johney - Peter & Jemmy bought us a cow at Woodman's sale.
12. At South Shields.
13. A very wet day.
16. Came home by the last train - Been two fine days.

Sunday 17. Went to Blaydon, Jane & Peter set me.
18. Mary Sparke come to Blaydon going to Byker.
19. Sent the Fan Blast away from Blaydon.[1]
23. Came home by 2^{d}. Train - Marg^{t}. Sawers died this week - Nanny Dixon married this week - Been very blowey weather.

Sunday 24. John Barrow here at dinner - At Jemmy's at tea.
25. Went to Blaydon.
26. At Newcastle at D^{r}. Frost's.
28. At South Shields - Wet morning.
29. At Sir Matthew's Bank.[2]
30. Came home by last Train - Been a week of very cold weather, wind northerly - Joe at home.

May 1836.

Sunday 1. Went to Blaydon.
2, 3, 4. Very cold weather.
6. At Hexham - Our cow calved.
7. Came home by the 11 O'Clock Train - Setting 'tatoes. Jack the Wright at Blaydon - Father removing the bees.

Sunday 8. With Jane hearing Short this morning.
9. Went to Blaydon.
10. Fumigating the house at Blaydon. Hexham hiring.
11. Gardening & Whiting the house, M^{r}. Emerson at Shields.
12. The berge [barge] day at Newcastle.[3]
13. Setting 'tatoes at B [? Blaydon].
14. Came home by the last train. Got a new servant girl (Rachael Bell) today. Bownas got possession of M^{r}. Sparks farm - Thomas Oxley left Palms - Thos. Ridley from Steel - Sheel from Rowleyhead.

---

[1] The 'Fan Blast' may have been an alternative to the standard bellows used with smelt mill hearths and furnaces.
[2] This must refer to the old-established bank of Sir Matthew White Ridley and partners, in Newcastle.
[3] 'Barge Day' was the annual survey of the boundaries of the Tyne, by the mayor, the brethren of Trinity House, the River Jury, etc., as conservators of the port of Tyne; it was a very colourful river procession of brightly decorated barges.

Sunday 15. Blackey calved this morning - Uncle Joshua here at breakfast - The Sun eclipse.[1] *Went to Blaydon at night.*
18. At Newcastle buying a bedstead.
19. Went to my new lodging room.
20. Mr. Emerson at Shields - Some Thunder and rain last night. Margt. Sparke called at Blaydon with Johney.
21. At Shields marking Lead - Stagshaw fair day - Geo. Dodd sold our cow - Been a finer week of weather.

Sunday 22. Came home this morning.
23. Helping Mr. Spark to Langley - Slept at Langley with Jane.
24. Came home by Allen Mill - Got Tea @ Henderson's. Came to see Geo. Barrow at Allen Town.
25. Went to Blaydon.
28. My father is elected clerk at the Chapel.

Sunday 29. Spent the Sunday at Blaydon, at the Spa Well.

June 1836.

4. Came home by Hexham, called of Betsy [see also 10 July 1837] - Fine weather come. Geo Wilson taken from Hexham today[2] *- Jane sold the calf this week - Our Joe & three men with him come home.*

Sunday 5. At the reopening of the Chapel, my father was clerk[3] *- Tweddle & J. & Liza here at tea.*
6. Went to Blaydon.
8. Jane & little [Jane] came to Blaydon.
10. Went to Shields all night.

11. Came home by Stanhope Railway[4] *- Been heavy rain today; Railway open'd to Derwent haugh.*[5]

Sunday 12. With Jane at Charley's well.
17. Aunt Mally through at Blaydon. Jim Routhledge buried today. Some thunder & rain.
18. Came home with the two Jane's - Been much rain here about.

Sunday 19. At the Chapel - Soft day.
20. Went to Blaydon - Newcastle Races this week.

---

[1] According to *Sykes' Local Records* the eclipse was on 15 May, and Alnwick, Northumberland, was 'the most favourably situated town in the kingdom for observing it … The day was as fine as ever shone from the heavens, not a cloud being visible, and the progress of the eclipse could be most minutely traced.'
[2] George Wilson, aged 23, a spirit merchant, was charged with forging and uttering a promissory note for £45 and later found guilty by a jury who recognised his previous good character and recommended mercy. The judge however sentenced Wilson to 6 months hard labour at the Morpeth House of Correction, to be followed by transportation for life (*Newcastle Courant* 6 August 1836) See also diary entry for 29 July 1836.
[3] At Whitley Chapel.
[4] The Stanhope & Tyne Railway had opened from South Shields to Stanhope in 1834, it passed no closer to Blaydon than 6 miles as the crow flies. However, given Dixon's clear interest in railways, perhaps he just wanted to ride part of the line and be prepared for the walk at the end.
[5] This was a short eastward extension of the Newcastle & Carlisle Railway.

22. Tweddle gone to the Races.
23. Tweddle came to lye with me at Blaydon.
24. Blackey bulled.
25. Came home by the 2 O'clock train - M^r. Spark here at tea - Went to see Dinnings Kyloe at night. Been a week of very windy withering weather.

Sunday 26. Josh. Smith at our folks' - Went to Blaydon.
27. At Shields today.
28. The Railway opened out from Hexham to Haydonbridge, - A great number of people there.[1]
30. At Haydonbridge today.

July 1836.

1. Driving Mrs Emerson in the gig to Lintzford bridge.
2. Came home by Langley - Been a week of fine weather - Father and Jane bought a Cow of F. Rowell. Ann Elrington of Ardley buried.

Sunday 3. At the Chapel with Jane.
4. Stagshaw fair day - At home all day.
5. Went to Blaydon - Terrible day of thunder.
8. Shifted to M^r. Cail's rooms.[2]
9. Came home - Joe at home.

Sunday 10. At the Chapel with Joe - Went to Blaydon at night.
11. Jane came to Blaydon.
12. M^r. Emerson at Shields, Betty Makepeace got her bed.
14. Jane at Byker.
15. Very wet at times.
16. Came home with Jane. Very windy. Mary Sparke come.

Sunday 17. At Chapel with Tweddle, Mary Jane &c. - At Liza's at tea.
18. Went to Blaydon - Old Johney Taylor died.
22. M^r. Emerson & men at Shields.
23. Went to Shotley Bridge to see Joe, went by Stocksfield & Shotley field - Been a week of very wet weather - Father & Peter Mowing for us.
Sunday 24. Spent the day with Joe at Shotley B., very dull soft day.
25. Came away from S. Bridge at past four this morning. Wet day.
26. An Election at N. Castle in room of Sir Matt. who is dead- Hodgson elected[3] *- Carlisle end of the Railway was opened last Tuesday*[4] *- M^r. Emerson & Anderson go west today.*

---

[1] A westward extension of the Newcastle & Carlisle Railway, the formal celebration of which commenced with a railway procession from Blaydon; Dixon may have witnessed this, and it seems he took a ride on the following day. The opening celebration was one of 'considerable splendour' with bunting and gun firing at points along the way. Contemporary accounts note that 'scarcely a spot on either side of the river [Tyne] which commanded a view of the procession was without its group of spectators, who, by their acclamations, testified the interest they took in the scene'.
[2] Mr Cail has not been identified, but there is no reason so far to suppose that he was Richard Cail, the noted Tyneside contractor.
[3] Sir Matthew White Ridley, MP for Newcastle, had died at Richmond, Surrey on 15 July, and John Hodgson of Elswick, Newcastle, had been elected in his place.
[4] Between Carlisle and Blenkinsopp Castle.

Plate. 47

Langley railway station c.1910.

27. A Lead carrier pay at Allen Town - Making Mr Emerson's hay stack - Old Thos. Ridley & Bess Close buried today.[1] *Our folk piked the hay.*
28. The Assises at N Castle.
29. Terrible thunder at afternoon & night with heavy rain from NW - Geo. Wilson got sentence of transportation.
30. Very high floods this morning - the water up to our quay - Pikes of hay swept away[2] *- Our Rowell*[3] *bulled at Burdus's - Came home by the 2 O'Clock.*

Sunday 31. M^r. Nanny at our folks at tea.

August 1836.

1. Went to Blaydon.
2. M^r. Emerson & men at Shields - Fine day.
3. Very wet day.
5. Fine day.
6. Hexham fair day - Came home by Hexham. Peter mowing the last of our hay.

Sunday 7. At the Camp meeting in Brick Kiln field - Our Joe at home.
8. Raking the last of our hay - Peter & Tommy begun with theirs.
9. Leading our hay.
10,11. Mowing for our folk.
12. Helping Jemmy to lead hay - Our folk got theirs all into Kile - Got a letter to go away.
13. Went to Blaydon - Johny Taylor's sale - Been a week [of] remarkable fine weather.

Sunday 14. At Uncle Thomas', went with Makepeace.
17. M^r. Emerson at Durham.
18. Mrs E. got her bed of a son.[4]
20. Came home by the last train.

Sunday 21. At the Chapel - At Jemmy's to tea at afternoon - M^r. Middleton here.
22. Went to Blaydon.
24. Mother & 2 Janes came to Blaydon.
26. Mother came home.
27. At So. Shields to-day, very wet morning - Shearing busy on Tyneside.

Sunday 28. Spent the day at Blaydon.
29. M^r. Spark called to see us.
30. Wet day.
31. John Hawdon buried.

September 1836.

1. Jane at Heslop's - very wet forenoon.

---

[1] Thomas Ridley of Row Green died at Juniper 24 April 1836 aged 61 years and was buried at Whitley Chapel, (Kristensen, 2003).
[2] According to *Sykes' Local Records* the flood 'had not been equalled for many years' and many sheep and other farming stock were swept away as well as a great quantity of hay.
[3] I.e. the cow which Jane bought from F Rowell on 2 July 1836.
[4] Elizabeth Emmerson, wife of the Blaydon agent Thomas, gave birth to James Mulcaster Emmerson; both of them would die within 12 months.

Plate. 48

NEWCASTLE AND CARLISLE RAILWAY.

No. o'Clock, 1836.

From Carlisle to Hexham.

1st Class—Paid 6s. 6d.

This Ticket will be required on your Arrival at your Destination.
NOTICE.—No Fees allowed to be taken by any Guard, Porter, or other Servant of the Company.

Plate. 49

3. Came home with the 2 Janes - Rather wet.

Sunday 4. Soft day - Got Rowell bulled - Old Matt Martin died.
5. Went to Blaydon.
8. Johnson entered to Allen Mill.
9. At Shields.
10. Came home by the last train - Shearing not commenced at Dukesfield yet.

Sunday 11. Mary Sparke here at tea - Went to Blaydon at night - Very bad of a cold.
13. Our folk got Blackey [their cow] to their fog.
14. Elizth. gone to Langley.
17. Came home by the 2 O'Clock - Joe & Hugh at home - Been a week of bad harvest weather - Bownas not begun yet - Father been off the School this week.

Sunday 18. Setting Joe down the Lead Road.[1]
19. Went with John Teasdale to Eltringham.
23. At Shields, dined at the Laird's.
24. Jane & Elizth. come from Langley.

Sunday 25. At Brunswick Chapel a.m. - Bethesda p.m., came by Lementon. Uncle Skelton called to see me - Very fine day.

October 1836.

1. Came home by 2 O'Clock Train. Wet day - Been very changeable weather.

Sunday 2. With Jane at Chapel hearing M^{r}. Airey.
3. Went to Blaydon - Very unwell at afternoon.
7. At Shields.
8. Father at School this week.

Sunday 9. At Ryton Church a.m. - Lemington at afternoon.
11. Very wet day.
13. M^{r}. Steel at Blaydon - The 'Tyne' Engine come to Blaydon.[2]
14. Fine day (frosty).
15. Came home by the 2Oclock - Met James going to Byker. Liza got her bed on Thursday morning[3] *- A good deal of corn to cut at Dukes^{d} yet.*

Sunday 16. Went to the Chapel with Jane, came away without a priest - Jon^{a}. Barrow & Johnson here to tea.
17. Went to Blaydon.

18, 19, 20. Fine days.
22. Jane come to Blaydon. Was at J. Teasdales all night - Went to N Castle at night.

---

[1] Most lead from Dukesfield was either taken across the Tyne at Corbridge and then to Newburn via Newton and Newburn, where it was carried across the river to Blaydon, or via Riding Mill and Prudhoe along the south bank of the Tyne to Blaydon. The 'Lead Road', however, was a long distance route from the Allendales to Whitley Chapel, and then on to Blaydon via Scales Cross, Apperley Dene, Hedley on the Hill, Leadgate, and Greenside. Joe was presumably going to Shotley Bridge.
[2] Instead of the usual steam whistle provided on most of the company's locomotives, the *Tyne* was seemingly fitted with a small steam pipe-organ at the suggestion of the Vicar of Ovingham.
[3] This was Jemmy and Liza's third daughter, named Margaret.

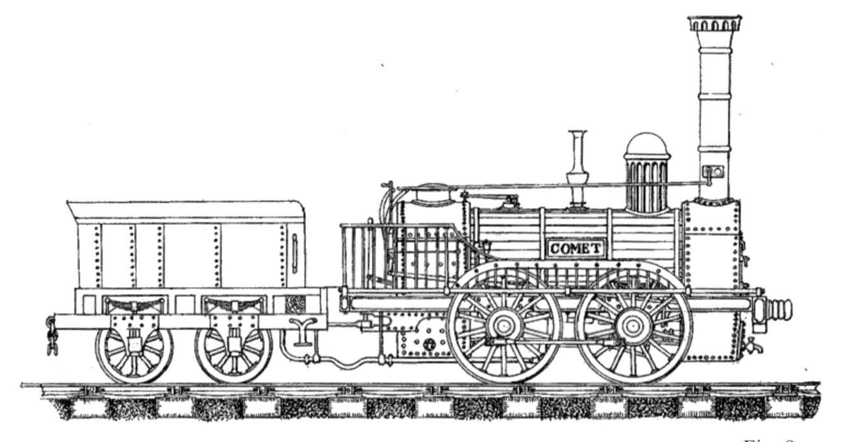

Fig. 9

The "Comet" 1835

The "Lightning" 1837

Fig. 10

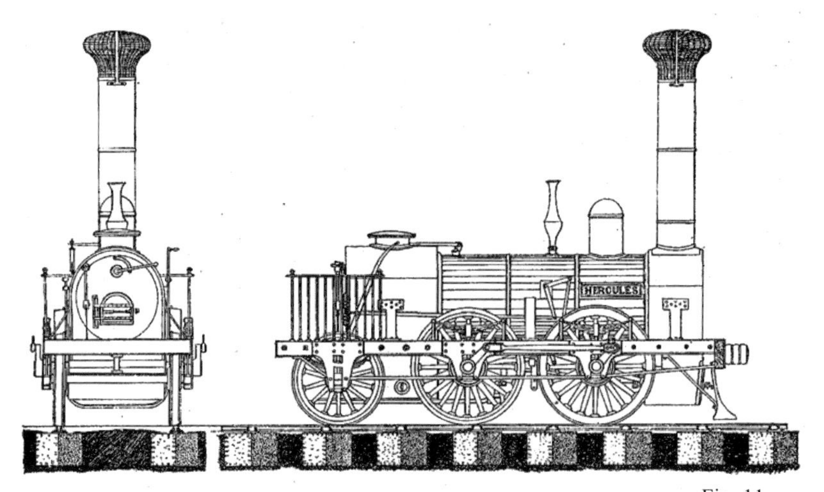

Fig. 11

The "Hercules" 1836

Sunday 23. At Blaydon all day.
24. At Shields, came home by Byker Hill to call of Jane.
27. Terrible cold day.
28. Hard frost. Aunt Mally & Hannah Charlton drinking tea with Jane.
29. Lying white with snow ancle deep - Came on last night to snow - Newcastle Fair - Came home with Jane, snowing part of the way - Corn to cut at Duk^{d}. yet.

Sunday 30. Tweddle at Jemmy's.
31. Went to Blaydon with P^{r}. Purvis.

November 1836.

1. Elizabeth begun to write.
4. M^{r}. E. & Men at Shields. John Dickenson poney put in our field.
5. Bownass shear out - snow gone.

Sunday 6. Up the Waggon way.
9. Hexham Fair, M^{r}. E. got a cow.
11. Hexham hiring today for the first time on a Friday. New Engine 'Eden' started yesterday.
12. Sally Purvis married[1] - Bownass, Ned, Peter, & Jim gone this term - Came home by the [?] past 3 train.

Sunday 13. Joe come home this forenoon.
14. Went to Blaydon. Peter set me.
19. Hannah Hall got her bed of a son lately, the child buried this week - Tweddle taking poss^{n} of old Matts. Shop.

Sunday 20. At Blaydon all day.
22. John Dickenson gone to an Attorney.
23. M^{ssrs}. Steel & Anderson gone west - Terrible day of rain, snow westward.
26. Came home with Jane Burdus.

Sunday 27. Jane went with me to Blaydon - Fine day.
28. M^{r}. E. & men at Shields.
30. H. Oxley's churn.

December 1836.

3. At N. Castle with Jane. Very unwell.

Sunday 4. Taking pills; in my room all day. A man and 2 Boys killed yesterday at Corby.[2]
5. Jane staying with me all the week.

---

[1] Thomas Dodd and Sarah Purvis were married on 12 November 1836 at Slaley in the presence of Thomas Dixon and Mary Purvis.
[2] This quite horrific accident was blamed on the negligence of a pointsmen at the Corby coal depot who had left the main line switched to the coal cells, such that the locomotive *Samson*, travelling with a mixed train from Newcastle, was 'precipitated' over the cells, dragging with it the tender and two waggons laden with grain. The engine driver and fireman were able to jump to safety, but a man working at the coal cells was fatally injured while two boys who had hidden under the cover of one of the grain waggons, to avoid paying their fares, were killed on the spot. No-one in the passenger carriages towards the rear was hurt. (*Newcastle Journal*, 10 December 1836.)

10. Came home by the first train - Been changeable weather this fortnight.

Sunday 11. At the Chapel - Jemmy & Liza here at tea - Tweddle here at night.
12. Went to Blaydon by the 1st Train with J. Smith. Came on very snowey.
13. Got a letter from America for Mr. Spark.
17. The Mills cease this day for this year.

Sunday 18. Sent a letter to Tweddle by Jos. Makepeace. Old Jos. Smith & Peggy at Lementon - Taking physic - At Lemn at night.
19. Old Tommy Dixon killed our pig.
21. Our Peter come to Blaydon to see me.
22. Mr. Emerson at Shields finishing the Lead weighing for this year - Got all the Haydonbridge Lead in on Monday.
23. Peter went to Lemn. - Came on a snowey day.[1]
24. Came home by the first train. Peter went to New house - Very stormy day.

Sunday 25. Very stormy day. Mr. Spark & J. Smith here to tea.
26. Prevented from getting away by the weather.
27. Went to Blaydon. Very stormy day.
28, 29, 30. Very stormy days - The Tyne frozen.
31. Came home by the last Train. Our Joe at home (came on Thursday) - A child of Dodds killed at Dotland - Margt. Burdus got her bed this week.

[1] According to *Sykes' Local Records* a 'prodigious quantity' of snow accumulated, and the roads were impassable.

11

<u>*MEMORANDUM FOR 1837.*</u>

January 1837.

Sunday 1. At Chapel with Joe Peter &c. - Very sharp frost.
2. Went to Blaydon with Jane & Elizth. - Fine frosty day.
3. Elizth. & Jane went Byker Hill.
6. At N Castle meeting Jane & E.
7. The ice all broken up in the Tyne - Jane unwell.

Sunday 8. M^{r}. Sparke at Byker standing for Marg$^{t's}$. child.
9. A fine fresh day.
10. A very great fresh out at Blaydon - The water up to the sixth tier in our yard.[1]
11. A sharp frost.
13. The Stewards down seeking the money.
14. Came home with Jane & Lizth. by 2^{d} train. Old Thomas Errington buried this week.

Sunday 15. At home all day - Joe at home.
16. Leading soil with Oxley's horse - Joe helping; but went away at afternoon.
17. At Allen Town Pay helping Tweddle. Got my dinner at Holmes'. Came home with W^{m}. Dinning.
18. At home all.
19. Went to Blaydon. Fine.
20. Josh. Smith gone to B. Hall.
21. Been a fine week - 'Lightening' Steamer come.

Sunday 22. At School House Church service. Soft day.
24. Joseph Oxley almost dead.[2]
26. Tweddle at NewCastle.
28. Came home - Stormy day - Old Betty Teasdale died this week - Old Mally Stokoe of Chapel died today.[3] *The greatest number of deaths ever remembered. Influenza prevailing. Very harsh weather.*

Sunday 29. Snowing all day. Marg^{t} Bulman here.
30. Went to Blaydon by the 1st Train and right off to N. Castle. Mrs Emerson died this night.[4]

---

[1] According to *Sykes' Local Records* a very rapid thaw coinciding with rain resulted in the water in the Tyne rising by 5 feet.
[2] A Joseph Oxley was a farmer at Dukesfield in 1827/28, and a member of the Dukesfield Wesleyan Methodists in 1826-8.
[3] Mary Stokoe was the widow of Robert the smith who died on 6 September 1832.
[4] This was Thomas Emmerson's first wife, Elizabeth, who died aged 37; he was to marry again, but he also outlived his second wife, Hannah, who died in 1864. Emmerson himself died at Peepy, Stocksfield on Tyne, on 31 August 1885 aged 87. All three, plus two children of the first marriage, were buried at Ryton.

Plate. 50

"Newcastle-on-Tyne from Redheugh station", 1836.

February 1837.

3. At Mrs E's funeral.
4. Fine days this week.

5, 6, 7, 8, 9. Fine days - The Directors[1] down to Redheugh with an Engine both last week & this.
11. Came home by 2nd Train - Very wet day. Peter & Jemmy working labourage.

Sunday 12. Peter gone to stand for Chatts child.
13. Jane went with me to Blaydon.
18. With Jane at N. Castle - Father leading the manure into our field.

Sunday 19. At Blaydon all day.
24. The Judges came down from Carlisle - Tweddle & Johnson came up from the North.
25. Sent a letter to my father - Considered to stay at Blaydon.

Sunday 26. With Jane hearing Mr. Weardale.
27. Got a letter from my father.

March 1837.

1. The Railway opened to Redheugh.[2]
4. Jane left Blaydon - Got some straw this week.

Sunday 5. Hearing Mr Forsyth & the Curate.
7. Making a road to Townley's.
8. Stoke [possibly Stokoe - see 6/2/38] looking at the Mill - Setting off the ground with N. Sanderson.
9. Mr Bell setting of house steads.
10. Wet day.
11. Lying with snow. Came home by 2d train - Mr Nixon been here this week - John Lowe's sale.

Sunday 12. Setting Joe to Whinny Hill, M. Elsdon went off with him.
13. Went to Blaydon, leading stones to the new road.
18. Sent a letter by John Blackburn - Been a week of cold weather - Hugh & another at the Bone Mill.[3] At N. Castle seeking a new book.

Sunday 19. At Blaydon all day.
21. The Lead begun coming again.[4]
22, 23. Terrible cold weather with snow.
24. Old Steel at Blaydon.

---

[1] The Newcastle & Carlisle Railway directors.
[2] Prior to this date, the Newcastle & Carlisle Railway had terminated at Blaydon from 1834 to 1836, then at Derwenthaugh for a short while until it reached Redheugh in 1837. The celebrations seem to have been quite muted, although the banks of the Tyne were said to have been lined with people. It was not until 1839 that the line was taken across the river at Scotswood to a temporary station near the Shot Tower at Elswick; the Forth was reached in 1847, and Newcastle Central Station in 1851.
[3] Bone ash was needed in the refining process, and bones had to be ground before they were calcined (burnt). The bone grinding mill at Blaydon seems to have been powered by a windmill at this time, but see later.
[4] The lead carriage by road having been stopped over winter.

25. Hexham fair - Came home by the 2 Oclock - Railway Company begun to run 4 Trains on Monday - W^{m}. Ridleys wife died on Thursday - very snowey night.

Sunday 26. At the Chapel - Hugh here at night - Easter day.
27. Went to Blaydon with Hugh - M^{r}. Emerson seeking the Machine from Blagill.[1]
28. Old Steel &c. at Lemington.
29. Burnett's men putting up the Machine.
30. Jane came to Blaydon with Jemmy & Liza.

April 1837.

1. Been a week of bad weather. Wind NE with no intimation of a change.

Sunday 2. J. & Liza with Marg^{t}. & children came up.
3. Peter & Jemmy came to Blaydon to temse litharge[2] *- Very ill day.*
4. At Dunlop's.
5. Our folk's cow calved.
8. At N Castle with Peter - Been a week of very snowey weather.

Sunday 9. Spent the day at Blaydon with Peter.
10. Alex Davison taking down the old windmill.[3] *At a missionary meeting at N Castle.*
11, 12, 13. Cold snowey frosty days.
15. Came home with the 2 Janes, Peter & Jemmy very wet day before coming off - Old Tommy Burdus died this week - Robt Walton .

Sunday 16. A very stormy day - Joe at home.
17. Went to Blaydon by 2nd train with M^{r}. Nixon.
18. Very unwell.
19, 20, 21. Josh Makepeace working for us.
22. Working labourage.

Sunday 23. Lay all the forenoon; at Lementon at afternoon. John Charlton come to Lem^{n} - Tho$^{s's}$ wife got her bed a month since - Hearing Cook at night.
24. The Masons, Joiners & Millwrights come to Blaydon.[4]
26. Very fine day. The weather sore taken up.
29. Been working labourage all this week - A week of fine weather - Came home by 2 O' Clock - Father with Thos Ord at the Justice - Closes sale at Mollersteads.

Sunday 30. At Chapel at afternoon.

---

[1] The 'Machine' may have been an alternative to the windmill used in bone grinding, and was perhaps bought by WB Lead for use at the Blagill smelt mill, but having abandoned Blagill, could now use it at Blaydon. See also 29 March 1837.

[2] To 'temse' meant to sieve. Litharge, the lead oxide produced in the refining process, could easily be converted into 'red lead'. The litharge cooled as it fell from the refining furnace and concreted into lumps. As they cooled, these lumps partly fell to 'scales', called 'flake litharge', but the outer parts of the lump, which cooled much more quickly, did not, and were termed 'coarse litharge'. The flake litharge and the less valuable coarse litharge could be separated by sifting on a screen; I am grateful to Peter Wilkinson for this information. Brother Peter's and brother-in-law Jemmy's arrival at Blaydon was clearly not a permanent switch, and they only remained there a few weeks.

[3] This was probably the Alex Davison who was listed as a stonemason, living at Bywell, in 1827; he was presumably dismantling the windmill formerly used to power the bone mill.

[4] Possibly to build a new bone mill, perhaps steam-powered.

May 1837.

1. Went to Blaydon with Hugh who is working there - Showery morning.
2, 3. Fine days.
4. The Barge day - Thunder showers.
6. Been working all this week - Came home by Hexham pr the 'Newcastle'. Been a fine week - Sowing sore through.

Sunday 7. Went to Blaydon. Rather soft.
8. Cold day.
9. Making a culvert for M^r. E. Showers of snow.
11. Mr Emerson and men at Shields for the first time this year - Misfortune on the railway at Riding Mill.[1]
12. At Shields - Turned fresh.
13. At Stagshaw fair meeting Peter with a cow - Thunder & Hail - Robt Coulson died this morn.

Sunday 14. Soft day - Blaydon - Tweddle at our house to tea.
15. The 2 Janes came to Blaydon - Fine day - Tommy Dickenson fliting to Catton - Rachel left us[2] *- The Sheels gone to Weskerly.*[3]
16. Fine.
18. At Dahl & Thompson's - Our little blackey calved.

Sunday 21. Hearing old Hales - Geo Forster here at tea - Very cold.
22. Winlaton Hopping & Races.
23. At Winlaton getting measured for a coat.
24. At Archbold's, N Castle - Mr Spark here been at Margt's who is ill.
26. At Swalwell with 2 Janes.
27. Went to D^d[4] *- Joe at home - 2 Janes and Tweddle at Byker - Joe Errington married lately & Tom Forster*[5] *- Father had our Black Cow at Hexham on Tuesday. Sarah Skelton at D^d - Cows turned out at night.*

Sunday 28. At Chapel with Joe.
29. Came to Blaydon - Taylors making Joe a suite - M^r. E & Hall gone to Cumberland.

June 1837.

2. Sleeping at M^r. E's this week.[6]
3. M^r. Emerson come home - Had both Masons, Joiners, Plumbers & Slaters &c. Hugh working here all this time.

Sunday 4. Hugh and us walking on the Summer house Hill -Fine day, cold a.m.
6. M^r. Emerson's child died.[7]

---

[1] The cause and result of this 'misfortune' has not been determined.
[2] No-one succeeded Rachel as house servant at Dukesfield, for Jane was about to join Thomas at Blaydon.
[3] Presumably Waskerley.
[4] Dukesfield.
[5] Joseph Errington married Mary Bell, and Thomas Forster married Mary Elliott, probably at Whitley Chapel.
[6] Presumably Thomas was looking after Emmerson's house while he was away.
[7] Thomas Emmerson's son James Mulcaster Emmerson was only 11 months old when he died, his mother having died just over 4 months earlier.

7. Davison's masons left this morning.
8. Marg[t]. Burdus here at tea.
9. At Shields - The Bone Mill begun - The 'Carlisle' Engine come.
10. Weather taken a change today for the better.

Sunday 11. Went to Duk[d]. Chapel at afternoon. Father sold the black Cow to the Miller on the 29th ult.
12. Came to Blaydon.
13. Geo. Carr here at tea.
17. Very busy with the bones this week - Been a week of fine weather every day - Hugh's child drowned this week.

Sunday 18. At meeting on the morning - Thunder & rain at afternoon.
19. Newcastle Races commenced today.
20. Still fine weather - King W[m]. the fourth died this day.
22. At the Races seeing the Cup won by "Bees Wing".[1]
24. Went to D[d]. with Hugh and 2 Janes - Called at A. Davison's - Joe at home - Isaac Walton drowned in Langley Dam - Been a fortnight of excellent wether.

Sunday 25. At Chapel with Joe: sung the "Heavenly Vision" & "Lift up your heads".
26. Came to Blaydon with the 2 Janes.
27, 28. Warm days.
29. M[r]. Emerson at Tynemouth seeking lodgings - M[r]. Anderson at Bretton Hall this week.[2]

July 1837.

1. Had some talk to M[r]. Emerson about something important. Been a week of fine weather - Mowing commenced this week

Sunday 2. At the old connexion meeting in the morning - At the Spa well at afternoon - Hearing M[r]. Allen at night.
3. M[r]. Emerson at Newcastle.
4. Stagshaw fair day - 1,060 passengers on the train this morning - Saw Peggy Dickenson on the train today.
6. Saw W[m]. Martin's Royal Mail.
7. Marg[t] . Middleton & Bessy Barrow came down.
8. M[r]. E begun mowing - Very droughty weather.

Sunday 9. Went to Dukesfield - At the Chapel at aft[n] hearing John Scurr.
10. Came to Blaydon with Sally - Betsy gone to Hexham to finish her apprenticeship today - Rob[t] Walton lost his place lately.
11. Mary Aydon here at tea.
12. Jane & Sally at Lemington - Dull day.
13. Some thunder & rain.
14. M[r]. E & family gone to Tynemouth - Terrible thunder & rain.
15. Sally went home - Much thunder & rain - Edw[d]. Steel died the 1st of this month.[3]

---

[1] See also 24 June 1841
[2] The Beaumonts owned the Bretton Hall estate in West Yorkshire. Anderson was presumably one of their agents.
[3] Edward, son of Edward and May Steele died at the age of 28 and was buried at Whitley Chapel, (Kristensen, 2003)

Sunday 16. Fine morning; but Thunder & rain afterward - The weather quite broken.
17. M^{r}. E up at Blaydon - Making some hay into Kiles for M^{r}. E.
18. Soft day & some thunder.
19. Had a letter from M^{r}. E - Sent W^{m}. Stobbs off to Sh^{ds}.[1]
20. Went to Shields & Tynemouth. Got tea with the Nurse.
21. At N. Castle at Robt. Watsons.
22. At Shields with the Men weighing Litharge. M^{r}. E at Edinburgh - Sleeping at M^{r}. E's.

Sunday 23. M^{r}. E come from Edin^{gh}. - Wet morning - Tweddle came down for the purpose of proceeding to Edin^{gh}.
24. M^{r}. E's hay all piked today.
25. N Castle election. Ord & Hodgson returned.
26. The family come from Tynemouth.
27. Jane went to D^{d}. Thunder & rain. N. Shields & So. Shields Election, also Gateshead this week.

Sunday 30. Tweddel come from Ed^{gh}. - Went up home. Thunder & rain.
31. Jane come to Blaydon.

August 1837.

1. Wet morning.
2. Expected Mother & Betsey going to the sea - Very wet aft^{n}.
3. Most terrible Thunder & rain - Uncle Jacob here at tea - Saw M^{r}. Steel at night.
5. Been a very wet week - Stopping here this week end - Josh Makepeace come from west.

Sunday 6. At the old conexion meeting - Walking at afternoon.
7. Mary Spark here all day - Gone off to Byker at night. Hexham fair day.
8. Making M^{r}. E's hay stack - Been two fine days.
9. Dull day - M^{r}. Anderson here.
10. M^{r}. E & Men at Shields - Got a letter from father saying that Betsey & him are unwell.
11. At Shields myself.
12. Went to D^{d}. with 2 Janes - Thunder and heavy rain to the west - Got tea at Uncle Jacob's - Fine night; some corn cut at Corbridge.

Sunday 13. At the Chapel - Fine day - Hugh at D^{d} at aft^{n}.
14. Peter & R Nixon mowing - Helping our folk with the hay, got the Cow bulled at Bownas'
15. On with hay - Peter & Robt. got done mowing.
16. Got the hay all to Kile - Peter gone to the Mill.
17. Got the hay all piked. Got a letter from M^{r}. Emerson.
19. Leading our hay with Jemmy's mare - Very fine day - Our Joe and Aaron came to D^{d}. - Been a fine week.

Sunday 20. At the Chapel with Joe & Aaron - Terrible morning for thunder & rain to the west. Tweddle and us at our folks' to tea - Fine day.
21. Got notice to come to Blaydon - Very windy day - At my fathers school.
22. Came to Blaydon.

---

[1] Probably South Shields.

22. Came to Blaydon.
24. At Shields - Fine day.
26. Very windy - The Heads band went up from Tynemouth - John Dickenson of Lead Birks died & buried this week.

Sunday 27. At the Old connexion meeting hearing Mitchell - Fine day - Our Betsey come to see us.
29. Betsey & Jane at N. Castle.
30. Hearing Sample.
31. Robt. Dixon & J. Oxley called on their way to Tynemouth.

September 1837.

2. Betsey & 2 Janes off to Newhouse - Very dull cold day - Sent a letter to D^{d}.

Sunday 3. Wet day - Went at night to meet Jane & Betsey.
4. M^{r}. Sparke here - Betsey went to Lemington.
5. M^{r}. Sparke called on his return.
6. Betsey making Jane a gown.
7. A very windy day.
9. Went to D^{d}. with J. Oxley & Betsey - Harvest very throng on Tyne side. Benson has 24 stacks in No corn cut at Dukesfield.

Sunday 10. At the Chapel - Very windy night.
11. Came to Blaydon with Elizabeth by the first train.
12. Went to Shields to the Men - fine day.
13. Wet day.
14. Came from Shields - Jane and the Children been at Marg^{ts}. who was here on Sunday with M. Smith.
16. Very wet day.

Sunday 17. Hearing M^{r}. Rickaby - Walking round by Swalwell.
18. Painting an old sail - Got a letter from D^{d}. by Wm Johnson - The Cows bulled the day after I left.
19, 20. Dull days.
21, 22. Fine Harvest days.
23. Went to D^{d}. - The last train altered from [?] past 6 to 5 O' Clock - The Harvest general at D^{d}. now - Betsey in Allendale at Chatt's - Father broken up the school for Harvest.

Sunday 24. At the Chapel - Setting Peter at aft^{n}.
25. Came to Blaydon by the 1st Train - Taylor the Guard killed last night.
27. Our lead commenced coming today, been stopt since 12 Aug^{t}.
28. Went to Shields with 2 Pruddahs, very dull morning.
29. Been at Shields all night. Came home.
30. Elizabeth wrote a letter to her Grandfather at D^{d}.

October 1837.

Sunday 1. Preaching house forenoon. Hearing M^{r}. Adams at night.
2. The Club Feasts at Blaydon - M^{r}. E. shearing out.
3, 4. Fine harvest days.

5. My father come to Blaydon.
6. Seeing the new Bridge[1] with father.
7. Father & Elizabeth gone home. 2 Janes to Langley - Fine day - A good deal of Corn out.

Sunday 8. At Newhouse, a preaching there. 2 Janes came from Langley in Jemmy's Cart.
9. Father begun the School again.
10, 11. Jane staying at D^{d}.
12. Came here (Jane).
14. M^{r}. Emerson got his ribs broke - Been a week of fine weather. The Small pox prevailing in Hexhamshire at this time.

Sunday 15. With Jane at the preaching house. At Winlaton at afternoon - Methodist (old) at night.
16. At N. Castle with M^{r}. E's boys.
17. Hearing Lewis preach.
18. M^{r}. E got out again, been confined to his room.
21. Intended to go to Shotley Bridge but did not - Fine day - Sent a letter to our folks by Jno Blackburn, who says they are done shearing at Steel Hall.

Sunday 22. At meeting - Jane at Swalwell at aft. At the old Methodist at night.
23. M^{r}. E and the Pruddahs at Shields - Rather soft.
24. Went to Shields with M Stobbs in the Gig - A soft day. Seeing a fiddle maker - Molyneux at Newcastle.[2]
25. Marg^{t}. and bairns been here all night.
26. Cold.
27. Very rough showers, and heavy fresh - M. Makepeace here with a horse.
28. Fine day - Horse fair at N. Castle - Begun a [singing] school at Blaydon.

Sunday 29. At the meeting.
30. NewCastle fair day. Very rough day.
31. A fight between Renwick of Winlaton & Molyneux the black at Cambo.[3]

November 1837.

1, 2, 3. Inclined to frost.
4. Very fine day - Went by Hexham and bought a coat on my way to Dukesfield. Billy Dixon died lately[4] - Little Wm Robson died at Coalcleugh.

Sunday 5. At Chapel (Shire) - Uncle John at our folks' at tea.

---

[1] Scotswood railway bridge.
[2] The first two American professional boxers, both blacks, made their names in England. The second of these was Tom Molineaux (or Molyneaux) who had been a slave on a Virginia plantation. He came to England in 1809 and twice fought Tom Cribb, the English boxing champion in 1810. It was widely agreed that Molineaux had won this fight but had been denied an official victory by skulduggery. He gained a return match, suffered a broken jaw in the 10th round and was knocked out in the 11th.
[3] The quite illegal bare-knuckle match between Molineaux and Will Renwick held near Cambo (actually at Middleton Bridge), for a purse of £25 each, lasted for 87 rounds, with a half-minute break between each round, and it went on until dark ending in defeat for Renwick. The Laing Art Gallery in Newcastle has a print illustrating the fight.
[4] This was probably the William Dixon, son of John and Hannah, of Juniper, who died 15 October aged 20 years, and was buried at Whitley Chapel.

Plate. 51

Scotswood railway bridge, 1836.

6. Came home by 1st train. Fine frosty morning - Brought the fiddle with me.
7. Uncle Skelton called.
8. Tweddle called, been at Newcastle to see Mrs. Martinson's friends, who died this morning.
9. Hexham Fair day. Father sold our Quey for 3£. H. Oxley intended shearing out yesterday - Very fine day.
10. Fine day - Got up windy.
11. Got my coat from Forster the Taylor - Sent a letter to enquire after Hugh's health - At the singing school at night, some Swalwell men there - Very sharp and frosty.

Sunday 12. At the meeting with the singers - Taking a walk to see the bridge at afternoon.[1]
13. Fine day.
14. Very wet.
15. Mr. E and men at Shields - Old Ridley the smith called to see.
16. At Shields, took my fiddle with me. Got done weighing by 12 O'Clock.
17. Got a letter informing us of Hugh's death which took place yesterday.
18. Jane gone off to Dunkirk[2] *- Still open weather. Got a letter from our folk by Carrier.*

Sunday 19. Hugh's funeral today.
20. Jane come from Hugh's funeral. Came on a terrible sleety rain at afternoon.
23. Geo. Forster here at tea - A heavy fresh being the 2nd this week - Got a letter from our folk informing us of Nixon's austerity.
24. Mr. E and Men at Shields.
25. Sent a letter by F. Purvis to my Father - At the singing school at night - Been some rough weather this week - Our Betsey unwell.

Sunday 26. At the meeting twice - Fine day.
28. Jane at Mr. E about the house, his displeasure &c.
29. Makepeace gets orders to quit room.
30. Makepeace shifts the beds.

December 1837.

1. Fine day - R & B Ellerington in house at night.
2. 2 Janes gone to Dd. by Hexham. Fine day - Men taking down our new yard wall for the Railway by Scotswood.[3]

Sunday 3. At the meeting twice.
4, 5. Frosty. Geo Nixon here seeking a job for Joe - Robt. Bell of Embly died last week - Jane Anderson poisoned herself last week.
6. Went to Shields today.
7. 2 Janes & Peter come down, brought a bed with them.
8. Very wet day, Mr. E came to see us at Shields.
9. Came from Shields at 4 OClock - brought the Fiddle up from old Galloway - Found Peter here on my return.

---

[1] Scotswood railway bridge.
[2] Near Chollerton, Northumberland.
[3] An additional section of line was needed to link up with the new railway bridge at Scotswood.

Sunday 10. At meeting with Peter twice.
11. Peter gone home - Fine day.
13. Thos. Dickenson called on his way to NewCastle.
14. Very hoary frost - Jim Charlton at our Mill.
15. Chipping lead with candle light. [1]
16. At Swalwell. Fresh open weather - Little Burdon at our singing.

Sunday 17. At the Meeting twice.
19. Uncle John of Dyehouse: Janes and him went on to the other side of the water[2] *- Very wet night M^{rs}. Cox called - Uncle at the singing with me.*
20. Uncle gone home - Very wet day.
21. M^{r}. E, Matt, Willy &c. at Shields, Coopering Casks. M^{r}. E & Pruddah were there on Monday weighing up the Lead - The Lead ceased coming today here.
23. Weighed up the Lead - Went home by the last Train. Went by Hexham, got company home by T. Brown - The Mills broke up last week.

Sunday 24. Spent the day at D^{d}. Very wet forenoon. Setting Peter & Jemmy to work.
25. Came to Blaydon.
27. Our Joe come to see us.
29. Joe Davison come. Dull Fine day.
30. At N. Castle with the 2 Joes - Fine day. At the singing at night.

31. Setting the 2 Joes who are gone home. Jane very unwell.

Remarks on the year 1837.

The beginning was remarkable for harsh Stormy weather; for a cold spring (indeed there was no spring) The Summer was excellent for growth, it commenced on the 9th June, there was an uncommon great deal of Thunder & rain. A fine harvest. A mild back end - and concluded without any snow - It has been remarkable by our leaving Dukesfield, in a great measure for T Dickenson leaving also for Wm Blackburn coming - At Blaydon it has been so by the death of M^{r}. Emerson's wife - By the building of a new bone mill &c. By the commencement of a new Bridge at Scotswood for the Railway - By the Death of poor cousin Hugh Armstrong.

[1] Precisely why Dixon was chipping lead is uncertain, although it is known that a skilled person could tell whether a piece of lead had been refined or not merely by cutting a chip from its corner.
[2] The Devils Water presumably.

THOMAS DIXON'S DIARY FOR 1838

January 1838.

1. Monday. A great meeting at N. Castle concerning the poor Law[1] *- Weighing off Lead to finish the orders.*
2. Clemitson in our office.
3. Got 2 Letters and a parcel from Langley[2] *- Seeking M*r *E from Winlaton at night. Fine fresh weather.*
*4. M*r *E's Kyloe calved last night.*
*5. Mr E sold his Kyloe - M*r *A up. Mr E & him at Locke Blacketts office*[3] *- At Robinsons at night.*
6. At Stocksfield chipping Lead - Very misty - Sent letter to my father by the Hedley Carrier.

Sunday 7. At the Meeting twice. Dull misty frost.
*8. A thin portion of snow lying this morning - M*r *E taking his boys to school - The Railway labourers striking for wages.*
*9. M*rs *Reay of Ryton died - Very stormy day, Wind E.*
10. At Angus' paying Cess, very snowey day - Collecting rents. Got a Glass with A Hall. Saw R H Smith.
11. Still snowing all day. Jack the Wright called - Got some Flour of Patterson. The Keelmen's binding at Stella.
12. Still snowing a little. The waters fast with snow.[4] *Willy & Nancy lying in our house to night.*
13. Still stormy. At the singing at night. Hearing Calcutta. A Ellerington sleeping with Jane to night - Got some butter by the Carrier.[5]
*Sunday 14. Hearing T Harrison preach morning. M*r *Moxon at night, very sharp frost.*
*15. Very intense frost. The water hard frozen - Got the 4*th *Set of Fawcett.*[6]
16. People walking cross the Tyne.

---

[1] According to the *Newcastle Courant* of 5 January 1838, between 1,000 and 3,000 people were said to have attended this meeting, which began with a procession from St Nicholas' Square, and went via Pilgrim Street and Northumberland Street to the 'Parade Ground' with 'flags, union colours, banners, placards &c' A 'working man' took the chair, and one of the speakers was J. P. Cobbett, the son of William Cobbett. In general, the meeting sought to have the 'hateful, illegal, unnatural poor law' repealed. The meeting was followed by an 'excellent plain dinner' for about 300 in the Blackett Street Music Hall, where a band played 'appropriate' tunes, while ladies sat in the gallery and 'considerably enhanced the interest of the scene by their presence'.
[2] Presumably from Jane's parents.
[3] Locke Blackett's lead works was established at Gallowgate in 1799 and continued until c.1933.
[4] *Sykes' Local Records* for 6 January notes that a 'frost of an extreme intensity prevailed throughout the northern counties … All passage on the river Tyne was stopped, it being frozen for upwards of five miles below Newcastle, and crowds of skaters appeared upon it … loaded carts crossed the Tyne, the Coquet, the Tweed, and other rivers in the north, upon the ice at various points'.
[5] Perhaps some home-produced butter from Dukesfield.
[6] This may relate to the purchase of sheet music as he had bought the '4th Set' for 5s. 0d. to send to his brother Joe (8 February 1838) who was also a fiddle player.

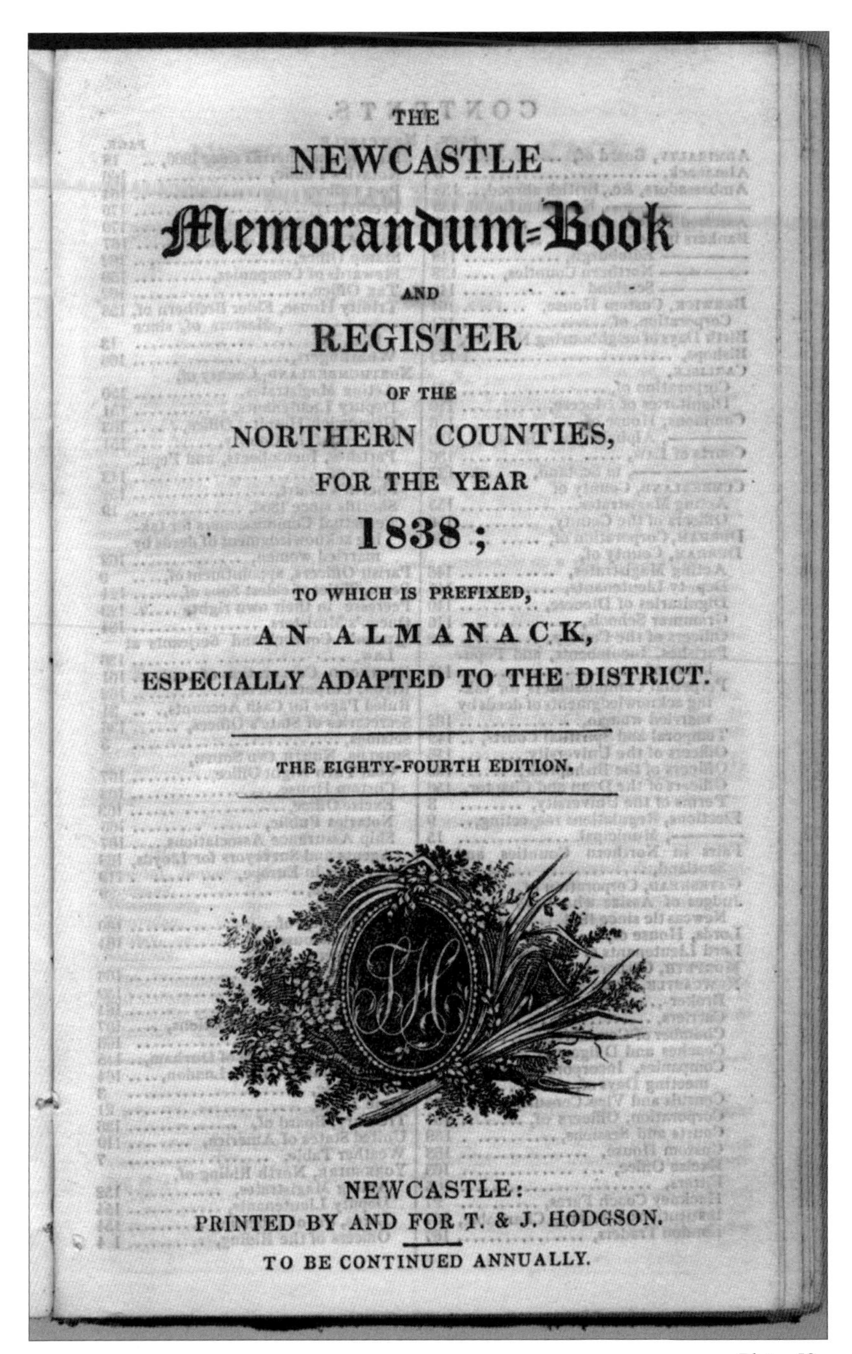
THE
NEWCASTLE
Memorandum-Book
AND
REGISTER
OF THE
NORTHERN COUNTIES,
FOR THE YEAR
1838;
TO WHICH IS PREFIXED,
AN ALMANACK,
ESPECIALLY ADAPTED TO THE DISTRICT.
THE EIGHTY-FOURTH EDITION.
NEWCASTLE:
PRINTED BY AND FOR T. & J. HODGSON.
TO BE CONTINUED ANNUALLY.

Plate. 52

17. Snowing on the morning. Mary Aydon & Edwd. got tea with us. Attended Sample's meeting with the singers.
18. Desperate Showers of Snow - Walked across Tyne with Cail.
19. The Agents come down. Uncle Jacob Mr Spark & T Bulman here at dinner - Snowing all day - Sent a letter to Father.
20. Very frosty - Mr Frost[1] at little T Emerson's Eyes.

Sunday 21. At the meeting - At Lementon at aft - Very blasty day to the west.
22. Went to Haydonbridge and Langley. A sort of Thaw. Tea'd Sup'd and slept at the Hill Top.[2]
23. At A[llen] Town Pay - Came home to D^{d}. with Peter & Jemmy - Very misty.
24. At Lee & Dyehouse seeing friends - Very sharp frost again & snow. Removed the Kitchen bed.
25. Setting Father & Lizth. to School. Called to see old Peter. Got dinner at Liza's - Joe come home.
26. Came to Blaydon, Peter & Joe set me - Snowing hard.
27. Sent a parcel by Carrier for Eth. - Ann Dixon late of R L Mill[3] married lately.

Sunday 28. Confined all day of a severe cold & hoarseness.
29. In the Assay office - Coming on soft snow all day. A child named Walton burnt to death yesterday at H. bridge.[4]
30. Dull day. W^{m}. Bell late of Stublick killed today.[5]
31. Assaying alone all day. Misty dull weather neither frost nor fresh - W^{m}. Hudspeth and Mrs Harrison married.[6]

February 1838.

2. At Winlaton at J Johnsons.
3. W^{m}. Bell buried - At N. Castle, very sharp frost. The water open to Redheugh.

Sunday 4. Snowing a little. At the Meeting twice. Thos Dickenson found dead having been lost in going to Weardale Friday week.[7]
5. Sent a Letter to Father by old J Bowman.
6. Stokoe here looking at the Mill - Mary Aydon here at tea.
7. Mr Steel here gave an intimation of a pow-ful nature.
8. Sent 4th of Fawcett to Joe - Mr Anderson here at night, sung a good deal. - A kind of thaw.
9. Mr Spark here - Mr A[nderson?] gone west - The ice partly broke up.
10. Mr Spark here all day - Got supper at Mr Hall's - Very hard frost.

Sunday 11. At the Meeting twice - M^{r}. Spark went off by the [?] past three - Frost very intense.

---

[1] Doctor Frost.
[2] Jonathan Sparke's residence.
[3] Probably Red Lead Mill.
[4] Haydon Bridge.
[5] This must have been the William Bell, aged 26, a son of Joseph Bell, one of the lessees of North Elswick Colliery, who fell from a cradle while working on the pump in the pit shaft. He fell 20 fathoms and 'was dashed to pieces'. (Coroners inquest report, *Newcastle Courant*, 2 February 1838).
[6] William married Isabella Harrison at All Saints, Newcastle.
[7] No information has been found relating to this sad event, Dickenson may have been a WB agent.

12. Very sharp frost. Got an intimation to stay at Blaydon for some time. T. Dickinson appointed to his fathers work.[1]
13. Desperate frost
14. Frost extreme - Attended Sample's meeting with the singers.
15. 2 Janes at Fewsters - Making out decimal tables for Mr A.
16. Strong E wind - Cold.
17. Jane went to D^d.

Sunday 18. At the meeting with little Jane.
19. Jane returned. My mother poorly.
20. At Dunlop's Cooperage. Signing a will at M^r. Hall's. Hannah Burn very ill. Sent a letter to M^r. Spark.
21. Marking Lead with Letters.
23. Hannah Burn died.
24. A most terrible day of snow and blow from E - The worst this winter.[2]

Sunday 25. At the meeting a.m. Very soft underfoot - some rain.
26. Still stormy.
28. Water open to the Railway Bridge.

March 1838.

1. Sent an order to Cox for shoes - very soft day, wind E not right fresh.
2. The Ice partly broken but still rem's - Open at L^n.[3]
3. Sent a letter to D^d. and one to Joe - Dull heavy weather little fresh or frost here. Snow nearly all gone here but much lying to west.

Sunday 4. Hearing J^n Hall a.m., Ranters aft.
5. Got a letter informing of my Mother's illness.
6. The river open this morn. Fresh day, wind W.
7. Got a letter from Byker informing of Wylam's illness.[4]
8. Jane at Byker. Frosty fine day.
9. Assaying. M^r E at Bywell.
10. Went to D^d. to see Mother who is poorly. Old Peggy Robson died this week (of T. Rest).

Sunday 11. T Ord & R Fairlamb at D^d. Set Peter & Janes off to the Mills.
12. Came down this morn. W^m. Ridley came to weigh Lead. Little Wylam died last night. Railway begun 4 Trains again.
13. M^r. Spark & Mary gone to Byker.
14. At Samples Meeting.
16. Arkles sons got tea here. Tweddle came at night.
17. Some snow to-day. Tweddle came from Byker, went to the singing.

Sunday 18. At meeting morn & night. - At Zion at aft. Tweddle gone home.

---

[1] Presumably the son of the man who got lost on his way to Weardale.
[2] According to *Sykes' Local Records*, the snow drifted up to 10 or 12 feet deep in many places, several main roads being blocked; shipping was also effected, some vessels being lost, others driven on shore, 'many of the crews being drowned'.
[3] Presumably Lemington.
[4] Wylam was the young son of Thomas's sister-in-law.

19. John Skelton gone to Gateshead - J Charlton here - Saw Forster & H Dixon. Sent a letter to Joe.
20. Mary Spark come from Byker - wet at aft.
21. Desperate weather from N - Sent a letter to D^{d}.
22. Snowing all day. Robinson &c in at night.
23. Mary Sparke gone home - Very snowey.
24. Fine Frosty day. Sent a pan to D^{d}. W^{m}. Johnson gone to Canada.[1]

Sunday 25. At Swalwell meeting. Hearing Mitchell at night.
26. Fine day. Hexham Fair.
27. Fine day. Some wild Beasts here.[2]
28. At Winlaton singing. Two Janes at Aydons to tea.
29. Jane at New Castle - Taking a letter to peth Head at night.
30. Got some Flour of W^{m}. Burn.
31. Got some 'tatoes from D^{d}. and a letter.

April 1838.

Sunday 1. Hearing J Nixon & J Innes. Cold day, showers of snow.
2. Desperate cold day, strong W wind.
3. Sally Bulman here at Dinner.
4. Aunt Peggy Bulman & Sally called.
5. Got a letter from D^{d}. p^{r}. N Guy.
6. In the assay office all day - Mild weather.
7. Very soft day - Old John Linsey died this morn'g.[3]

Sunday 8. Been a rough night.
9. Great number of Cattle come down Railway.
10. Got a letter & book from Tweddle.
11,12. Windy.
13. Went to Dukesfield with the 2 Janes. Fine day.
14. Setting our garden with tatoes, father & Peter helping.

Sunday 15. Easter day - At Chapel Hearing Irwin. Left D^{d}. after tea. Josh Smith there at tea, he married lately[4] *- Also Charton Todd to E Errington lately.*
16. Went to Shields the first time this year, very cold. Visited Groves theatre.
17. Got done and came home, extreme cold, called and saw Mr Anderson. Millwright here at Bone Mill.
18. Still cold - Wind N.
19. Cold.
20. Lying with snow.
21. Mr Emerson gives me know of a change in my situation. John Skelton came at night.

Sunday 22. At Lementon with John Skelton at aft^{n}. Weather turned milder.
23. Mr A. here telling me of my change. Got a letter from Joe & sent one.
24. Desperate cold.

---

[1] It is not clear who William Johnson was, but many people travelled from the North Pennines to seek work in Canada.
[2] Presumably a menagerie.
[3] Perhaps John Linsley the weaver.
[4] Josh had married Hannah Nixon, probably at Whitley Chapel.

25. At Scotswood paper mill - At Burdons singing at night.
26. Got a Letter from M^r. Spark.
27. At Shields seeing after the Lead. At Ouse-burn seeing T. Stokoe.
28. Went to Shotley Bridge with A Davidson. Very Cold.

Sunday 29. Lying with snow - Spent the day at Shotley Bridge. Visited a new well.[1]
30. Came home from Shotley Bridge at [?] past 4. Got a letter of the death of cousin Betsy Bulman[2] *- Coming on snow and rain all day.*

May 1838.

1. At Tyne-mouth last night. Came home to day.
2. Very soft day.
3. The first fine day this year. Sent a letter to Joe & a bottle.
4. At Simpson's rent day.
5. Fine day - Sent a letter to Dukesfield.

Sunday 6. At Zion Chapel with the 2 Janes - Fine day. Hearing Mitchell at night.
7. Very warm day.
8. Excessively hot. At Winlaton Missionary. Got a letter from D^d. with bad news - Old Cowen buried.
9. Weather colder - At Samples meeting.
12. At Whickham, Swalwell & Derwent Haugh.

Sunday 13. Hearing Oley a.m., W^m. Greener at night - Very showery day. Wind cold N.
14. Hexham Hiring day. W^m. Ridley removed to Blaydon.
15. Went to Shields - Very Cold weather, at Marsden rocks at night.
16. At Tynemouth at night with W^m. Ridley.
17. Came home.
18. Tweddle called.
19. Went to Dukesfield by Hexham with Elias Sheele[3] *- Very wet.*

Sunday 20. At Dukesf^d all day. M Linsey and S Skelton at our folks'.
21. Came to Blaydon. Very wet morning.
22. Raining all day. Aunt Mary gone west. A fight - Brown & Forbister near Hedley. Brown killed.[4]
23. Water up.
24. The Barges up - Aunt Mary returned from D^d. The 'Wellington' Engine come.
26. Still continues cold.

---

[1] Shotley Bridge Spa was the bright idea of Jonathan Richardson, the Quaker banker and backer of the Consett ironworks who, having acquired land in the area, found a mineral spring on it and decided to develop Shotley Spa as a major attraction. Pathways were laid to the spa well which was situated in the centre of ornamental gardens, and a bath room with shower-bath and changing rooms was provided. It was predicted, in 1841, that 'Shotley Bridge will emulate the celebrity of Harrogate, Cheltenham, and Leamington', but it never did.
[2] This would be Uncle Jacob and aunt Betty Bulman's daughter Elizabeth.
[3] See also 6 September 1841.
[4] According to *Sykes' Local Records*, 'One of those disgusting and demoralising scenes, a prize fight, took place on Hedley Common, near the village of Ryton, in the County of Durham, between Robert Forbister, an engine wright, and John Brown, a white smith, both of Newcastle. They fought for £20, and their encounter ended in the death of Brown. Forbister was convicted at the Durham Assizes of the manslaughter, and was sentenced … to four month's hard labour. Considerable excitement was caused in Newcastle by the Rev. W. Dodd, incumbent of St Andrew's, refusing to allow Brown's body to be interred in the churchyard.'

Sunday 27. At Winlaton Zion Chapel. Hearing T Burn at night.
28. Masons building Kiln for paint.
29. Tweddle married to Bessy Martinson. Some Thunder this morn at 6 O'clock.
30. Went to Shields. Dull day - Seeing old Galloway.
31. Came home from So. Shd^{s}.

June 1838.

2. Fine Day - At Swalwell Gate[1] sending a Letter to Joe. Stagshaw fair. The first fine day.

Sunday 3. Thunder & Rain. Fine grow day. Hearing W^{m}. Ridley preach.
4. Blaydon Hopping - Thunder & rain - Beautiful day.
5. Thunder & rain.
6. Thunder & rain. Hearing M^{r}. Adams. M^{r}. Beaumont at Bywell.
7. Carrier brought some butter - Got a letter from D^{d}. by W^{m}. Winter.
9. Got a letter from Joe. Jane gone to Dukesfield. The 'Victoria' Engine come. Went to Wylam with her.

Sunday 10. Hearing J Dodd & Cawthorn preach. Jane come back.
11. Fine day.
13. The 'Nelson' Engine come - Hearing Forsyth.
15. Fine fresh day.
16. John Blackburn in our house.

Sunday 17. Hearing Lightfoot & Mitchell - Avery fine day - The Railway men working all day.
18. At the opening of the Railway to Carlisle, left Redheugh at 1 o'Clock got to C[2] at 6. Left at 10, got home at 5 next morning - Very wet day.[3]
19. Went to Shields, very wet, got nothing done.
20. Fine day - weighing all day at Shields - Hearing Messrs Bewick, Robson &c at night play.
21. Still at Shields. At old Galloway's at night.
22. Got done & came home - Bought a fiddle for Joe.
23. Fine day - Charles Clavering died this week.[4]

Sunday 24. At Aydons to tea. Had a walk to Barlaw.
25. Mr Spark and Liza here - Emerson gone to Colourcoats.
27. Frank Purvis in our house - Sally Bulman here at tea.
28. The Queen's Coronation day - Race Week - Fine day.

---

[1] The toll house at the east end of Swalwell bridge.
[2] Carlisle.
[3] By June 1838, the only major gap in the Newcastle & Carlisle Railway was between Haydon Bridge and Haltwhistle, and this was closed, and the whole line between Redheugh to the canal basin at Carlisle ready to open, on 18 June 1838. There had been celebrations of varying kinds as each new part of the line was opened, but the June 1838 opening throughout was the most spectacular. See introductory text.
[4] Charles John Clavering died at home at Axwell Park aged 77 years. He had been the senior magistrate for Northumberland, and a High Sheriff for County Durham.

"The River Wall at Wylam Scars", 1836. Plate. 53

Plate. 54

"Scotswood Bridge, over the Tyne", 1832.

29. Jack the wright here - Very wet night.
30. Went to D[d]. by Hexham with F Purvis - Old Ann Dinning died this week.[1] Our Sally very poorly.

July 1838.

Sunday 1. At the Chapel. Sally riding upon an ass - Went to Dyehouse at night. J [or T] Mulcaster discharged at Allen Mill.
2. Came to Blaydon with F Purvis - Very dull day - Very unwell at night.
3. Warm day.
4. Stagshaw fair - Remarkable fine day.
5. Very warm. Got 7 Stone Flour of W[m]. Burn.
6. Some thunder. Rob[t] & Tho[s] Smith in our house with paint samples.[2]

Sunday 8. Fine day. Hearing Cowen's man & W[m]. Greener. Walking round by Swalwell - Mary Aydon married.
9. Fine fresh day - Saw Billy Blackburn pass. Got all the Lead in. Robinson in seeing the new fiddle.
10. Marg[t] Middleton came from Dukesfield.
11. Went to Shields - at Cullercoats at night - M[r]. Dunn the Chemist at Blaydon.
12. Fine day.
13. Came from Shields. Got all the Lead weighed for the half year. Geo: Forster here & little Sam.
14. Wet at noon.

Sunday 15. [Blank]
16. Mr E come from Cullercoats. Fine hay day and much doing with it.
17. Very Soft day. Uncle Thomas here seeking a hound.
18. At the Chain Bridge[3] at night with little Jane.
19. Soft morning - fine aft. At Winlaton at Angus' at night - At Massey's forge.[4] Mr E begun mowing.
20. Boisterous winds.
21. Joe come to see us and seek his fiddle - Fine day. Got a Coat from Hexham.

Sunday 22. Hearing T Burn & W[m]. Ridley.
23. Joe went off at 3 this morning - Fine hay day until night and rain then.
24. Cold N wind.
26. New Wylam Coals come down - Helping to get up the hay - Came on rain at 4 oClock.
27. Kileing hay - Hearing Mr Mitchell at night.
28. Went to D[d]. with Frank Purvis and J. Forster. The Assizes finished today - Both rain & thunder.

Sunday 29. Hearing old Pearson for the last time at Chambers [Finechambers?] - Very soft day - Mary Sparke at Jemmy's - At Ryehill with Peter & the Cows. A very great Winlaton Flood.

---

[1] This Ann Dinning, who died on 26 June 1838 aged 71, the widow of the William Dinning of Steel who died on 9 September 1825 aged 63, was probably the woman of that name who was listed as a grocer of Steel in 1827/28; both were buried at Whitley Chapel, (Kristensen, 2003).
[2] Robert and Thomas Smith of Spring House were recorded as 'House Carpenters' in the 1841 census.
[3] Presumably the Scotswood Chain Bridge.
[4] Massey's Iron Forge was at Blaydon.

30. Came to Blaydon with Frank - W^{m}. Bownas going to Mary Lambs funeral - Very wet. In the Assay office all day. A tea held in the[Methodist] Chapel.
31. Drawing a plan for Mr E's houses - Got out a fine day.

August 1838.

1. Making hay in Mr E field.
2. Been a very wet night.
3. Pikeing the last of Mr Emmersons hay - Got a letter from Mr Johnson.
4. The 2 Janes gone to Langley.

Sunday 5. At St Nicholas' Church. Looking about the Town with Josh. Makepeace[1] - Visited the Redheugh Gardens. Uncle Thomas & wife called at night.
6. Hexham fair - F Purvis gone to Howden - Stella Hall sale.
8. Been very wet through the night - At Stella Hall.
10. Tweddle came down at night in distress.
11. Been a fine day. Tweddle got tea with me.

Sunday 12. Went to [Shotley] Bridge and Shotleyfield meeting.
13. Came from Shotley Bridge this Morning - Fine day. Our folks' old Cow calved on 3rd inst.
15. Helping to make Mr E^{s}' hay stack - got a letter from Duke^{d}.
16. At N. Castle at night.
17. Been a frosty night - a fine day. Mr Steel gone up from N. Castle.
18. Dull day but fair. Our folk have all the hay mown.

Sunday 19. Went to Dukesfield on foot to Wylam.[2] Sally very weak - Some rain - Came back to Blaydon.
20. At NewCastle, had an interview with Mr Johnson. The British Association meeting begins.[3]
21. James Nixon of Winlaton buried. Fine day excepting a shower.
22. Sent a letter p^{r}. Mr Simpson to D^{d}.
23. Very Cold day - Seeing E Aydon at night - Uncle & Aunt John Bulman going from Tynemouth.
24. A Balloon went from N. Castle.[4]
25. Fine dull day - Old T Dixon & others going from Tynemouth.

Sun 26. Hearing Neal for the first time. At Winlaton at aft. 2 Janes came at night. A Love feast held here.
27. Delivering bones from Sunderland.
28. Went to Shields - At Tynemouth at night - Saw R Smith & J Ellerington &c.
29. Came from Shields with T Maughan &c. - Hearing Sample at night.

---

[1] This may have been has Joseph Makepeace, a Newsagent at Blaydon, from whom Thomas was certainly buying his newspapers in 1841 - see Whellan (1856) p 919.
[2] Perhaps meaning that he walked to Wylam station and then caught a train.
[3] The eighth annual meeting of the British Association for the Advancement of Science. The meeting lasted 7 days.
[4] "Mr Brown, the aëronant,of Sheffield, made an ascent from the enclosure in Green-court, Newcastle, in his splendid balloon 'The North Star'. The gas was supplied from Clayton-street and Newgate-street. The process of inflation was completed soon after three o'clock, and the cords loosened which restrained its aërial flight. The balloon cleared the houses beautifully on rising, and then proceeded in a south-easterly direction, in full view of thousands of spectators, who watched its progress with intense interest." (*Sykes' Local Records)*

30. Sister Sarah departed this life at 1/2 past nine at night with a full assurance of the blessed Eternity.[1]
31. Got a letter from D[d]*. Sent Joe one & Uncle George.*

September 1838.

1. Went to Dukesf[d]*. with the 2 Janes - The Cakes made.*

Sunday 2. Sarah's funeral today. J Dixon, J Teasdale, H Hall, & Bulman servers - Interred at Slaley by Mr Scurr - A heavy showery rain.
3. Leading the hay with 2 carts - Fine quiet day.
4. Setting Joe to Branch end. Jane & Betsy at Hexham. Came to Blaydon - Very dull day.
5. Very wet forenoon. Mr E bought Browns houses this week.
6. Wet day. Mr Spark called on going home from N. Castle.
7. Desperate wet cold day - Wind N - Writing Circular for Mr E['s] *buildings.*
8. Old Nancy Carr died this week. W[m] *Johnson of Allen Mill's fathar killed very lately.*

Sunday 9. Hearing old Ingham and young Brooks - Got a letter from Dukesf[d] *by Tho*[s] *Bowman.*
10. At NewCastle seeing M[r] *Johnson who made a form of application - G. Blackburn & W Errington seeking work. Very fine day.*
12. Writing an application to the Railway - Uncle Thomas called and got tea.
13. Fine Harvest weather - some corn cut.
14. Fine.
15. Beautiful day - Tweddle come down.

Sunday 16. Tweddle here all day. 2 Janes & Eliz[th]*. came at night.*
17. Tweddle left. Eliz[th]*. ill of the Jaundice.*
18. At NewCastle delivering applications - Mark Carr got lamed.
19. In the Assay Office. M[r]*. Challoner appointed me to the Railway.*[2]
20. Entered to the Railway. Fine weather.
22. Sent a letter to Joe & Duk[d]*.*

Sunday 23. With the Children at the meeting - Wet at afternoon.
24. Uncle Jacob here at Dinner.
25. Very wet day.
26. Fine day - Hearing Sample at night.
27. Fine dull day.
28, 29 Fine.

Sunday 30. Attending the Office. Hearing W[m]*. Dawson [or Davison] at the N R Chapel.*

October 1838.

2. Wet dull day.
3. Fine frosty day.
4. Heavy fog.
6. Very dull day. Went to Dukesfield.

---

[1] Sarah, Thomas Dixon's sister, died aged 26 years.
[2] Dixon was appointed as '2nd Clerk' at Blaydon Station, for the Newcastle & Carlisle Railway. John Challenor was chief agent to the railway company.

Sunday 7. At Chapel - Uncle John & Nancy at our folks. Came by the train at night. Killed a cow at Stocksfd.
9. The prince of Oude here[1] *- The Directors up.*
10. Mary Hall here at tea. Margt. Middleton come from the west - Very fine day.
11. Mr. Scott at Carlisle.[2] *Very windy. 'Hercules' broke down.*
12. Very strong wind.[3]
13. Snowing very much. Been a desperate frost.

Sunday 14. Very showery - attending the office.
15. Heard of Peter having the Jaundice - Middleton gone to the west.
16. Very wet to the west.
17. Showery.
18,19. Unsettled weather.
20. Willy Ellerington got a piano.

Sunday 21. October 1838 Went to Langley with Elizth. - Saw Tweddle's wife for the first time.
22. Came from Langley - Fine day. Mr Sample got a watch given.
23. Fine day. Mr. Spark came down.
24. Hearing Mr Sample. The 'Bedlington' Engine come.[4]
25. Mr. Sparke come to stay all night.
26. Mr. Spark went home by the new NewCastle. The Train arrived at 11 at night.
27. Wm. Dinning married very lately.[5]

Sunday 28. At the opening of Blenheim Chapel hearing Mr Lessy. Hearing Wm. Charlton at night.
29. Tommy Lighhouse in our house at night. NewCastle fair, very wet morning.
30. Showery weather.
31. Been a very frosty night.

November 1838.

2. Went to Bywell to see Nixon - disappointed. Saw the Bridge - the arches all turned.[6]

Sunday 4. Hearing Wm. Ridley a.m. F Purvis here at tea - Hearing Brooks at night - Very wet.
6. The Directors here.
7. At Bywell this morn, saw Nixon - Very wet.
8. Jane gone to Dukd.

---

[1] According to the *Newcastle Courant*, Friday 12 October 'His Royal Highness the Prince of Oude, accompanied by two servants in their native costume, arrived at the Queens Head Inn, in this town [Newcastle], on Tuesday evening, and after inspecting the town, and the glass-houses of Messrs Cookson, proceeded by the railway to Carlisle'.
[2] John Scott, station master at Blaydon.
[3] Considerable damage to property was caused by this gale, and at least one person lost his life.
[4] Either a locomotive made at the Bedlington Ironworks, or one named *Bedlington*, but probably the former.
[5] To Mary Nicholson at Bywell St Andrew.
[6] A stone-built road bridge of 1836-8. Pearson (1838), noted 'a handsome bridge by Mr. Beaumont, the remains of the old bridge were blown up by Mr. Beaumont. Now I think that a man who blows up any vestige or memorial of that fine people [the Romans] ought to be blown up himself for it: and if he has a wife I hope she did it for him'.

9. Hexham fair. Jane came back. Fine day.

Sunday 11. Trains changed today. Hearing Forster & W. Greener.
12. Cold frosty foggy weather - The Train run over the sheep.
13. Marg^t Middleton & H Eggleston here.
14. Still cold foggy weather.
16. Marg^t & Hannah Eggleston been here all night. Jane at Mary Hall's.
17. Very wet day. The' Victoria' off the line at Allerwash.

Sunday 18. Went Duk^d. this morn. The fells all covered with snow.
19. Came down this morn. M. Carr gone to Redheugh.
20. Bownas has much corn out yet - Burdus not done shearing.
21. A Horse killed at Ridley Hall by the Train.
22. A Cow killed at Stella.
23. Aunt Peggy come to stay all night.
24. J Charlton here at tea. Tom Bowman of Steel married.

Sunday 25. At Meeting twice. Attending the Office.
27. Mr Emmerson & J S [John Scott the Blaydon station master?] at variance about Coals. The Directors up. Came from H Bridge in 65m to R H.[1]
28. Wet day, desperate at night.
29. Train broken at H Whistle Dining with Jno: Scott.
30. High waters.

December 1838.

Sunday 2. Hearing W^m. Charlton, Morning - M^r. Bond at night.
3. Saw Susan Bowman go down, she has been married lately.[2]
6. 2 Janes at Hexham. M^r. Challoner here talking about my going to N Castle.[3]
7. A Murder discovered in the Savings Bank at N Castle.[4] *Tommy Lighthouse in our house.*
8. 2 Letters from M^r. Challoner about my going to N Castle.

Sunday 9. Attending the Office. Very fine weather.
10. Saw Marg^t Nixon. F Purvis come here to live.
11. The Directors here. Got intimation to stay.[5]
12,13. Sharp frost.
14. The inquest on Millie concluded. Bolam committed.
15. Got a letter from Uncle Robt. informing of Sarah's death.[6]

Sunday 16. Went to Uncle Thomas' and Ebchester Church - Sarah [Bulman] came to Blaydon with us.
17. Sarah Bulman making Janes Cloak. Very sharp frost.
18. Jane and S. Bulman gone to Haltwhistle.

---

[1] Redheugh?
[2] Susannah Bowman married John Purvis at Slaley on 24 November 1838.
[3] Possibly to be station master or assistant station master at the proposed temporary N&CR station at Forth Banks, Newcastle, near the Lead Shot Tower. The Scotswood railway bridge was completed during 1838, and the line was officially opened to the temporary station on 21 May 1839. In the event Thomas remained at Blaydon.
[4] See 7 December. Joseph Millie was assistant clerk at the Savings Bank, and it was alleged that he had been murdered by Archibald Bolam. Bolam was found guilty of manslaughter at his trial on 30 July 1839, and he was sentenced to transportation for 7 years.
[5] I.e., not to move from his present position to one at Newcastle.
[6] Thomas's cousin, Sarah Skelton.

19. Jane came home.
20. John Teasdale & Tweddle got tea here.
21. Frost given way. A boy's leg taken off at B.[Bardon?] Mill.

Sunday 23. At the meeting twice. Very dirty day.
24. Very dull soft day.
25. Went to S. Bridge this morn - Attended the tea & concert there. Slight showers of snow.
26. Came home this morn. Father come with the Clock Glass. J Bownass married yesterday.
27. Father gone home, called at Bywell as he went.
28. Jane very unwell.

Sunday 30. Hearing Davison & Neal.
31. The weather changeable. Been no snow yet to lie.

Memorandum, 1838.
The year just gone has been very particular for the following reasons. Viz, Long frost and snow, Tyne frozen several weeks, late Spring, Cold Summer, Very late Harvest, deficient crops, dear Corn (Flour now 3/2 p^r^ stone) - by the death of my Sister Sarah & Cousin Sarah Skelton, Tweddle's marriage, by my leaving Mr Beaumont's employ & getting into the Railway - by the opening of the Railway thro' to Carlisle, by the coronation of "Victoria", by the taking the Cylinders from Dukesfield and setting at Allen Mill.

13

THOMAS DIXON'S DIARY FOR 1841

January 1841.

Friday 1. Cousin Jacob Bulman of M W [or 'WW'] Burn died.[1] *Complete holiday.*
2. Fine fresh day - Peter Hall come to enter to dinn. At J. Unwin who has been buying furniture.

Sunday 3. Been very wet during the night. Frosty morning. Thos Colbeck of Denton died.[2]
4. At Cousin Jacob's funeral. Very stormy day - T: Unwin married to S. Burn.
5. A stormy day. Snow 6 or 8 inches at H Bridge[3] *- Jane at the Brides house. Tyne fast.*[4]
6. Very intense frost.
7. Desperate frost - Tyne hard frozen. Mr Scott got a pony. People walking across Tyne.
8. Still very keen frost. The Engine set in Cowran Cut[5] *- Betsy making girls frocks.*
9. Frost continues - Jane very unwell,

Sunday 10. Been a blow during the night. T Urwin & wife here at tea.
11. A kind of thaw at night. Got a letter from D^d^.
12. Turned to keen frost again. M^r^. Scotts pony bad - His Cousin gone to Ireland.
13. Very hard frost again. At Mr Samples revival meeting.
14. Got a Cart of Coals out of Stella Staith.
15. M^r^. Spark come down to the pays[6] *- C Arkle here at tea.*[7] *John Teasdale here.*
16. Very ill day of snow - Wind E, turned fresh at night.

Sunday 17. Fresh day. M^r^. Spark came at Dinner. The Ice removed.[8] *Very wet night.*
18. Tweddle came from N Castle this morning - The agents gone up[9] *- Turned frosty again - The 'Venus' Engine come on to the line.*
19. Very frosty & part snow at night. Mr Beaumont's pay at Allen Town.
20. Some heavy showers of snow, went to Shotley Bridge at aftn. The water fast again, part snow lying.
21. Went with Joe to Dukesf^d^. Very tiresome journey. Peters fiddle finished.

---

[1] This cousin might have been a son of Uncle Jacob and Aunt Nancy Bulman, but no such evidence has been found.
[2] Presumably Denton near Brampton, Cumbria, where the Colbecks had lived for generations.
[3] Haydon Bridge.
[4] Iced up.
[5] Cowran Cut on the N&CR, near Gelt. Presumably Thomas meant that the locomotive got stuck in snow or ice.
[6] Presumably he came to Newcastle so that he and the other principal agents could travel out with the money to make the pays.
[7] Parson & White's *Directory* of 1827/28 has Christopher Arkle, Joiner, Bywell St. Andrew.
[8] Quite disastrous results ensued from this sudden thaw, especially on the river Wear, as ice sheets flowing down river firstly piled up, effectively forming a dam, and then yielded under the weight of river water behind them, rushing headlong into the shipping near the river mouth. The result was described as 'a chaos of horror enough to appal the stoutest heart'. Some ships were swept out to sea, while others were sunk within the harbour; hardly any ships and keels on the river escaped damage; one boy was drowned.
[9] To make the Pays.

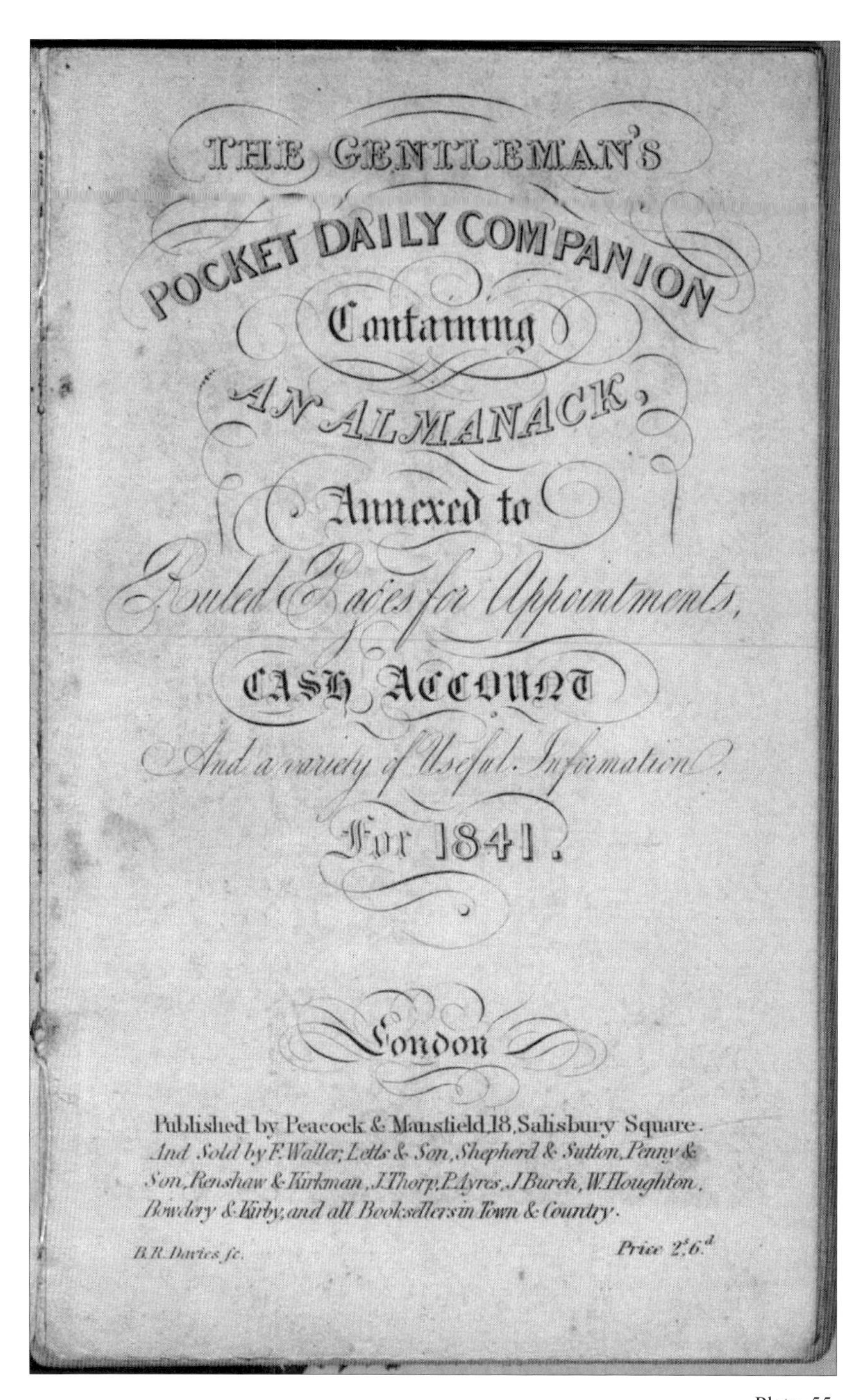

THE GENTLEMAN'S
POCKET DAILY COMPANION
Containing
AN ALMANACK,
Annexed to
Ruled Pages for Appointments,
CASH ACCOUNT
And a variety of Useful Information
For 1841.

London

Published by Peacock & Mansfield, 18, Salisbury Square.
And Sold by F. Waller; Letts & Son, Shepherd & Sutton, Penny & Son, Renshaw & Kirkman, J. Thorp, P. Ayres, J. Burch, W. Houghton, Bowdery & Kirby; and all Booksellers in Town & Country.

B. R. Davies sc.

Price 2s. 6d.

Plate. 55

22. At Dukesf[d] all day - Saw J Burdus. Uncle John and others there at night - Very rough day.
23. Came home by Hexham. Very frosty again.

Sunday 24. Hearing M[rs] Darley preach twice. Very frosty cold day.
25. The water fast the 3rd time in 8 or 9 days.
26. Tom Henderson [or Hesterson?] taking the fiddle Belly off.
27. The water open again.
28. Got the fiddle glewed on. John Forster of H Bridge in our house.
29. Some fine days this week.
30. Peter Hall removing - wet day.

Sunday 31. At T Urwins at tea. Heavy showers of snow from the east. Hearing M[r] Johns & W Ridley.

February 1841.

1. Very stormy day. Wind E. M[r]. Scott at N Castle seeking some lost load.
2. Desperate day of snow, W[d] E. A sale at Peggy Reay's.
3. Another desperate day of snow. At T Urwins at night with drawers.
4. Desperate cold day.
5. Got a letter from Dukesf[d]. Extremely cold. Wind E. At Bywell at night.
6. Old M[rs] Tate, Stella buried. J Smith gone to Hex: Shire.

Sunday 7. Hearing E Hall A.M. - At Winlaton at aft with the singers hearing M[rs] Darley - Jupiter off the line at night.
8. Hearing M[r]. Fisher at night - A report of M[r]. Pow leaving the railway.
9. Still dull frosty weather, wind continuing Easterly. People walking on the Ice.
10. Got no sleep last night for Toothache - R Newton at N. Castle - The princess Royal christened.
11. A kind of fresh at night.
12. Very fine day.
13 Fresh day - Snow got out of the Tyne at night.

Sunday 14. Taking physic - Very unwell all day - Very wet at night.
15. Fine fresh morning - Wet aft; M[r]. Scott & mother at N. Castle.
16. Fine day.
17. Very fine day.
18. Got some coals from Stella. Jane very unwell at night.
19. Remarkable fine day.
20. Stobart bleeding Jane. J Bulman & Sarah got tea here - Very fine day

Sunday 21. Uncle George here at aft. Hearing old Ingham and Pattinson - R Blackman.
22. M[r] Scott very poorly.
23. Dull mild day.
24. The Judges come from Carlisle.
25. The assizes going on at N Castle
27. Uncle Jacob returned.

Sunday 28. Hearing Jennings & Eltringham, very fine day - Jos Smith here at tea. On for Mr Scott.

Plate. 56

Dukesfield Corn Mill, c.1900, to the north of Dukesfield Hall, often referred to as the low mill.
Above – The Mill House Below – The Corn Mill

Plate. 57

March 1841.

1. *Taken very ill of a cold.*
2. *Still very poorly.*
3. *Cold soft day - Saw Isaac Knott*[1] *- Young W*^{m} *Carr of Slaley died lately.*
4. *At Axwell park well.*
5. *Got a letter from D*^{d}*. At Axwell again.*

Sunday 7. Kept [in] the house except at train times - Very strong wind.
9. Very fine day.
10. Uncommon fine - Along with T Urwin and the pony taking a walk - Miss Gill and a lady here.
12. Brother Peter came, very fine day.
13. Dull cold day - Got a Tooth drawn at night. Jno Dinning here at Dinner.

Sunday 14. At Meeting forenoon - At Josh's with Peter at Tea.
15. Peter at Lemington - Cousin George better - Very fine day.
16. Peter gone home. Little Jane with him - Very fine day. Mr *Whitfield here.*
17. Whitfield here again - A very heavy shower at aft. Jenny Forster buried yesterday.
18. Weather turned colder.
19. Sarah Burn here at tea.
20. Some Thunder and heavy rain. E Pruddah put himself into Tyne.[2]

Sunday 21. Hearing old Kimpster - At Swalwell at aft. - heard Bell there and Blaydon.
22. Preparing the Garden for cabbages - Showery weather.
24. At Swalwell with W E & J D hearing the singers.
25. Sally Nixon here this morning early.
26. Very soft wet day.
27. Little Robin the master died this week.

Sunday 28. Hearing Johns & Snowball at Dunstan at Aft^{n}*.*[3] *Old P Dixon died.*[4]
29. Went to Dukesf^{d} *at 12 o clock. Fine day, old J Forster died this morning.*
30. Old P Dixon of Staples buried. Came home at night. Helping Peter to set potatoes.
31. Very wet day westward. Mr Scott of Winlaton ann^{l}*. meeting.*

April 1841.

1. *Mally Ridley got her bed of a daughter.*
2. *Aunt Peggy & little Joseph called. Showers of Hail.*
3. *Cold clear day.*

Sunday 4. Hearing Eltringham & Lumley at Ranters Chapel, Winlaton. Hearing Mrs Darly at aft.
5. Betsy Middleton & the child come.
6. At Hexham taking Elizth *and bringing Jane - Saw Uncle Skelton. Fine day.*
7. Jane Bowman going to N. Castle to see her Brother Thomas who died last night from a fall.
8. B Middleton gone home - Rain, a fiddler, in our house at night.

---

[1] An Isaac Knott was listed as a shoemaker of Dotland in 1827/28.
[2] Drowned himself?
[3] According to Whellan (1856) Dunstan had Wesleyan Methodist, Primitive Methodist, and New Connexion Methodist chapels.
[4] The *Newcastle Courant* for 2 April 1841 has 'Peter Dixon, formerly of Tyne Mills, died 28 March 41 at Staples, Hexhamshire, aged 70.'

9. [Good Friday] [Blank]
10. Very fine day - A great festival at Dyehouse - Men setting our potatoes.[1]

Sunday 11. Hearing Ste[?] Hall a.m., at Greenside at aft. Hearing Kimpster at night. Very cold day. Little Jane bad at night.
12. Lying white with Snow - Very cold day - A great day at Corbridge with Rechabites.
13. Mally Ord died[2] *- Mary Dixon at D [Dotland] park died*[3] *- Lowrey at N castle getting appoint^d^.*
14. Eliz^th^. come from Dukesf^d^ - Very fine day - Got all our 'tatoes set.
15. At Swalwell hearing Mr Casson at night.
16. Hearing Mr Barker at night.
17. Fine day - Sent a letter by Phoebe Richardson.

Sun 18. Hearing Mr Barker a.m. - Pierson at night - Very cold windy day.
19. Cold & windy.
20. Heavy showers with thunder.
21. Got a letter from Langley stating M^r^. Sparks ill health.
23. Went to Langley to see M^r^. Spark - Got some Churn milk from T Burns.
24. Came from Langley to D^d^. with James & Eliza - Very wet & windy.

Sun 25. At Chapel with Peters fiddle - Park folk there - Very wet aft - Got tea at Liza's.
26. Came home - Brother Joe here at night having been at N Castle with Billy Rooks.
27. Very fine day - At Swalwell at night - Seeing little Miss Errington.
29. Thomas Teesdale died this week.[4]
30. At Swalwell at night with T Stobbs.

May 1841.

1. Very warm day - Got some Timber for a fiddle Belly.
Sunday 2. Hearing J Davison & G Makepeace - Very cold soft day.
3. Hills covered with snow.
4. Very cold day.
5. Old Tommy Dickenson of Catton died - Dull morning but fine day.
6. Got our Books away.
7. T Unwin flitting to Mitfords - Heavy thunder showers.
8. Very wet day - Saw J Teesdale & Mary.

Sunday 9. Jane had bad night - Hearing T. Burn - In Ranters school at aft. Very fine - W^m^. Charlton called.
10. Very fine day - Got a drive with M^r^. Scott in the Gig.
12. Beaumont's new Engine started. Hearing Mr Barker at night. At Crawcrook Mill with Mr Scott.
13 At Hexham with Extra pass^r^ Train. Hexham Hiring - Very fine day.
15. Very fine day. In Peter Halls taking Bread & Cheese.

---

[1] At Blaydon presumably.
[2] According to Kristensen, (2003), Ann Ord, wife of Richard of Dotland died 12 April 1841 aged 60 years and was buried at Whitley Chapel.
[3] Mary was the 20 year old daughter of a Thomas Dixon who had died in 1823, when agent at Dukesfield mill and living in Dukesfield Hall.
[4] Many people with the surname Teasdale/Teesdale lived in the Slaley area. It has not always been possible to distinguish between them.; another Thomas Teasdale died on 19 June 1841.

Sun 16. Hearing Lucas a.m. also at Swalwell aft[n] - Old Kimpster at night - Very dusty day. Winlaton Hopping.
17. At Winlaton at night.
19. At Swalwell at night with the Clarinet.
20. The Barges up today - Eliz[th] taken ill - Jane very unwell at night.
21. Very fine day - Got doctor Simpson at night.
22. The Lodgers leaving us.

Sunday 23 Hearing Mr John a.m. - At Ranters at aft - Hearing Ethrington at night.
24. Very warm day - M[r]. Scott at Lintzford.
25. Colder day.
26. At N. Castle - Very droughty - Ann Dixon of Staples died[1] - Hearing Sturges last.
27. Got the ashes lead away yesterday.
28. Jane been very bad all night - Very warm day.
29. Stagshaw Fair day - W[m] Martin of Litharge & Jno Blackburn died this week.

Whitsun 30. Hearing Butterwell a.m. - S Hall at night.
31. Sunday Scholars at N Castle - Got tea with at night. Jane got herself bled - Very fine day.

June 1841.

1. Got tea with the Ranters.
2. Very droughty dusty weather.
3. M[r] Sparke here at night.
4. Weather turned colder.
5. Jane delivered of a Daughter at [?] past 1 this afternoon attended by D[r] Simpson.

Sunday 6. Hearing W[m] Ridley at night - A very cold day - M Spark come.[2]
7. Very cold day.
8. Cold very .
9. Eliza come down.
10. Warmer day - The Child taken very ill.
11. Very cold again - M[r] Wardle[3] Baptizing the child Sarah - Sarah died at 8 o clock p.m.
12. At Winlaton this morning. The Infant Sarah buried.[4]

Sunday 13. At meeting a.m. - Mary and Liza gone to Byker.
14. Mary Blackburn going to her Sister's funeral - Liza gone home.
15. Still dull cold weather wind Northerly and great want of rain.
16. John Daglish engaged to C W Campion[5] - Mr Scott at Tynemouth.

---

[1] Ann was the 20 year old daughter of Isabella and Peter Dixon who died in August 1830 and March 1841 respectively. Another daughter, Isabella, was to die on 7 November 1859 aged 34 years. They were all buried at Whitley Chapel.
[2] Probably Jane's sister Mary Sparke.
[3] Henry Wardell, the curate of Winlaton Church and a friend of Walter Scott the novelist; one of his sons, Charles Clavering Wardell, a soldier turned actor, was Ellen Terry's second husband.
[4] There is no known monumental inscription relating to Sarah (Thomas's and Jane's daughter).
[5] The 1841 Census for Blaydon suggest that a John Daglish, a wood turner aged about 20, and Euphenia Daglish aged around 65, presumably his mother, may have lived next door to Thomas Dixon. Thomas refers to Euphenia as Effy.

Plate. 58

Hexham town with the railway station in the foreground, c.1840.

18. Mary Spark gone home.
19. Old T: Teasdale of Slaley died.[1]

Sunday 20. Uncle Willy Hall died - Hearing Mr John & J Davison - Very droughty day.
21. John Daglish gone to Hexham - N Castle races begun - Some rain last night but droughty today - Got a Cart of Coals from the yard.
22. Went to Dukesf^d today, came home at night by Hexham - Pulling berries at Low Garden - Seeing father at School - Mother poorly.
23. Some rain in various places.
24. Extraordinary number at the races. Beeswing won the Cup.[2]
25. A good deal of rain. Mr Scott at Carlisle.
26. Much thunder & rain.

Sunday 27. Hearing Snowball & Todd. Very fine day.
28. Beaumonts folk begun making Red lead.
29. Some thunder today.

July 1841.

1. Aunt Betty got her bed of a daughter.[3]
2. Very fine day - Jane at the meeting getting churched.[4]
3. Fine warm day - Very wet at night - Sent our Books off.

Sunday 4. Hearing Mr Jennings a.m. - at Greenside at aft^n with Singers - Fine day but wet at night.
5. Stagshaw Fair. Hexham Election - Bell & Ogle elected - Very wet afternoon.
6. Very bad of my eyes - Nomination day at Alnwick.
7. Joseph Angus died, the Relf [Relief?] officer.
8. East Cumberland Election.
9. Brother Joseph here. He went to Dukesf^d at aft - Viewing Cowens projected Railway.[5]

Sunday 11. [Blank]
12. Very soft day - Jos: Angus buried.
13. Brother Joseph here again - at D Haugh - Cowen's, Laycock's, &c.
14. A Special Train of Teetotalers from H Bridge. Very wet day - At M^r. Ramsey's at night
15. Joseph went away this morn^g.
16. Dull morn^g but fine after.
17. Fine day.

Sunday 18. Hearing John & Eltringham - Taking a walk with Jane - Very fine day. Jno Daglish at Dukesfield.
19. Much rain round about and Thunder - Old R Clemitson of A [Allendale?] Town died.
21. Dull day but not much rain. Hearing the Ranters sing at night.
22. Wm Ellerington got his shoulder lamed.

---

[1] This was Thomas son of Thomas and Mary Teasdale of Slaley, who died 18 June 1841 aged 73. His brother John had died on 24 July 1834 aged 69, and brother William was to die on 3 August 1841 aged 70.
[2] *Beeswing* belonged to a Mr Orde, and this was the 18th cup she had won. Seemingly 'the north country friends of the mare backed large stakes on the occasion'.
[3] The daughter was christened Thomasin Elizabeth on 28 July 1841.
[4] To give thanks for the delivery of a child.
[5] Perhaps along the Blaydon Burn.

23. Putting up some spouts.
24. The weather got out at aft. Jno Daglish at home. Thos Ord married.

Sunday 25. Hearing Bagshaw a.m. W Ridley at night - Very fine day.
26. At Langley with 2 Janes - Very fine day - A young woman drowned herself at Eshells yesterday.
27. Henderson appointed as Relieving officer for Winlaton.[1]
28. Very windy weather.
29. Still windy and cold.
31. Went to Langley at night.

August 1841.

Sunday 1. Went from Langley to Dukes^{fd} - Dull day - At Lee & J Halls at night - Mally Stobbs of Mollarsteads buried.
2. Came down with Peter and Bell Dixon.[2] *Fine day.*
4. W^m. Ellerington begun working at Mr Beaumonts.
5. Very fine fresh day - Wind S - A Lamb fair at N Castle.
6. Old Humble of Prudhoe buried.
7. Mary Charlton of Lemington died - Janes come from Langley to D^d.

Sunday 9. Very fine day - Ranters at Blyth in a steam boat - Wm Ellerington gone to Hexham.
10. At Mary Charltons funeral - Very fine day.
11. Old Effy Daglish removing to Hexham - Very wet day.
12. Fine day.
13. M^r. Scott gone to Tynemouth - very wet afternoon.
14. Very wet day.

Sunday 15. Went to Dukes^{fd}. The fares of the Railway raised.
16. Came from Duks^{fd} in James' cart - F Purvis gone from here to N Castle - Easton into Franks house.
17. Joseph Blackburn of Holly Hill died - At the Bible Society Meeting at night - Very fine day.
19. Wm Ridley of Ordley very bad at Crooks.
20. Aunt Sally and little Mary Jane came at night from Tynemouth.
21. Terrible morning of Thunder & rain. Aunt Mally here - Aunt Sally gone away.

Sunday 22. Hearing S Hall a.m. Adshead [Allenheads?] p.m. Camp Meeting at afternoon.
23. Uncle & Aunt Charlton gone to Tynemouth.
25. At Derwent Haugh with Bibles from the Society. Got a bite of R. Reed's dog.
28. W^m. Ridley's little Jane died.[3] *- The Harvest quite throng on Tyneside - Very fine weekend.*

Sunday 29. At Ridley's child's funeral - Hearing a Mr Nicholson at night.[4]
30. At Loan Society meeting at night.
31. A cooper come neighbour to us - Wet morning & dull day.

---

[1] Presumably to replace Joseph Angus.
[2] Probably a relation of the Bell Dixon who died in March 1831.
[3] Probably the child born on 1 April 1841.
[4] A Sunday excursion was run between Newcastle and Carlisle on this day.

September 1841.

1. Fine day.
2. Peggy Milburn come.
3. Soft day.
4. Terrible wet day, wind NW. Whig Ministry resigned this week.[1]

Sunday 5. Hearing Geo Todd a.m. – A prayer Meeting at night - Very sweet day.
6. Elias Shield was killed yesterday in a Steam Boat.[2] *Jane at N Castle.*
7. Mr Scott at Shotley Bridge. Resumed our singing at night.
8. Got a Bundle from Joe for D^d^. - Dull morning but fine after. Got a cart of Coals from the yard.
9. Thos Gardner died last night.
10. Gardner buried - Very fine day - Hearing Mackintosh for the first time. Peggy Milburn here at night.
11. Very fine day.

Sunday 12. Hearing M^r^. John a.m. - at Lemington aft - Hearing Davison at night - Most beautiful day.
13. Beautiful day - M^r^. Scott gone to Gilsland.
14. Very dull day - A man killed by fighting at Dunston.[3] *'Satirist' won the St. Leger.*[4]
15. Father come to see us - having been at S. Bridge.
16. Father gone home - Some Thunder - Harvest at the throngest in Hexhamshire. Davison of Shields married.
17. Sunderland Election yesterday - Howick returned.
18. Been an uncommon fine week for the Harvest - a good deal got in - The Wellington off the line by some cows nr Dilston.

Sunday 19. John Chatt called to see us - Hearing Kimpster a.m. At Winlaton hearing Mr Reed & Wm Ridley at night - Very fine day.
20. Dull morning & rather wet - Pearson & Jane Bulman in our house - Some rain.
21. M^r^. Scott at Gilsland again.
22. Dull cold day.
23. Great agricultural Show at N Castle[5] *- Very fine day.*

---

[1] Lord Melbourne resigned as Prime Minister on 28 August, and Robert Peel became Prime Minister again on 30 August.

[2] As reported in the *Newcastle Courant* for 10 September 1841, Elisha Shield, aged 22 years, was fireman on board the *Comet* steamboat of Newcastle. With his boat moored to another by a quay, he had just about finished cleaning one of the boat's two engines when he somehow accidentally started the engine and became trapped within it. Although the engineman was able to stop the engine, and extricate his fireman, he had been fatally injured and died soon after.

[3] Dixon seems to have mistaken the location of this death, for local newspapers say that it took place at Elswick Haugh. The fight had been between two fellow-workers at Abbots and Co. of Gateshead, one a blacksmith, the other a moulder. Seemingly they had spent one day drinking together and then fighting each other, only to repeat both activities on the following day. They then decided to settle their differences by means of a fair stand-up fight on the third day on Elswick Haugh. Again they were both drunk, but somehow fought for about 40 rounds, watched by some 100 people, before the blacksmith fell to the ground unconscious and never recovered.

[4] According to the *Newcastle Courant*, Lord Westminster's *Satirist*, running at 6 to 1 against, beat the 2 to 1 on favourite *Coronation*, by half a neck at the Doncaster St Leger.

[5] This was a show put on by the Northumberland Agricultural Society in the Bull Park at the north entrance to Newcastle, with exhibitions of prize stock, implements of husbandry, plants, etc.

24. Very wet day. First wet day for a long time.
25. Wet again - John Daglish here at night.

Sunday 26. Hearing Davison a.m. - At Swalwell at aft with J Daglish - Hearing W Bell at night. Very fine day.
27. John Daglish gone home. A Special Train from N Castle & Shields only thinly attended.
28. The Directors gone up to Carlisle.
29. Been a desperate rain west last night. Tyne much flooded today.

October 1841.

2. Uncle Jacob in - Peter been at the Doctor - A very fine week end.

Sunday 3. Hearing T Elliott a.m. - A Love feast at aft. - Hearing Pattison at night. J Day here at tea - Some rain at night.
5. Very wet day wind E.
6. Got a letter fr. D^{d} - Bownas's child died a week since. Still wet.
7. Tremendous rain - Tyne high water touching the rails at Reays Boat.[1]
8. Been much damage done in Derwent by the water yesterday.
9. A fine day - M^{r}. Scott cousin James died - Been an awful week for the late Harvest.

Sunday 10. Went to Dukesfield - Joe & S Rooks there - Soft day - Great deal of corn out at D^{d} very much grown.
11. Came home by Lee & Hexham. Saw J Dodds fiddle - Very fine day. Miss Patty & A Lilly in our house to tea.
12. Mr Scotts cousin buried.
14. A Fine airy day.
15. Very soft day - The investigating Directors here.[2]
16. Very wet morning - At N Castle recovering my Book.

Sunday 17. Hearing old Ingham a.m. At Ranters at aft hearing the Children. Hearing Snowball at night.
19. Very frosty: some Ice formed.
20. Showery day - Hearing Mr Fisher at night - Got my fiddle wood glued.
21 Very frosty morning - T Urwins wife got a daughter.
22. Jane been sleeping at Sarah's. Got tea at their house. Wm Ellerington in our house.
23. Very wet day. Got our potatoes up yesterday.

Sunday 24. Hearing Wm Kimster - The Sunday Scholars & Eltringham.
25. Very soft.
26. Still soft weather.

---

[1] 'Reay's Boat' was probably a ferryboat, and the 'rails' were probably on a landing. Many of the cellars on the Newcastle quayside were flooded.
[2] This may well refer to the investigation which resulted in the ledger now held by National Archives (RAIL 509/58) as referred to in the section of text dealing with Thomas Dixon's work on the railway.

27. Took ill of a bowel complaint. Very soft cold day - Grand Bazaar at N Castle.[1] A man killed at Rose Hill.[2]
28. In the house all day - Very cold. Old Effy came at night.
29. In the office again - N Castle Fair - Dull fine day.
30. Fine morn but wet aft. Old Effy gone home. Mary Sparke married.[3] Uncle Thomas got tea.

Sunday 31. In house all forenoon - Sally Dodd at Peth head - Hearing a Mr Niele of Swalwell at night. Very dull day. Mary only married today.

November 1841.

1. Very dull soft day - Got 12 St flour and 8 Maslin from J Dixon.
2. A very bright day - Sent a letter by S Dodd to Dukesfd.
3. Fine Day.
4. Fine Day.
5. At Hexham taking the fiddle. Jane gone to Langley - Very fine day.
6. J Smith gone to the Shire. Very fine day.

Sunday 7. Hearing Mr. John a.m. - at N Castle Nelson St. Chapel aftn[4] - Hearing Kears at night. Very fine day.
8. Desperate bad of a cold - Fine dry day.
9. The Queen delivered of a prince.[5]
10. Jane came from Langley to Hexham.
12. Very soft cold day.
13. Jane come from the west, brought a piana with her - Cold showery day.

Sunday 14. Hearing Todd a.m. Howe at night.
15. A very sharp frost - At the [Loan] Society at night - Bought a share.
16. Very frosty.
17. Mr Scott poorly - Joe Greener's sale - Got a new Bed of Finnigan - A [or N] Johnson here at tea.
18. Terrible frost - the water frozen to Lemington.
19. Very frosty - Joe began a Singing School at Broomley.

Sunday 21. Hearing Kimster & Joe Stobbs. Very wet afternoon.
22. Fine fresh day.
23. Very ill of my inside - In house all day.

---

[1] The bazaar was in aid of the funds of the Northern Asylum for the Blind and the Deaf and Dumb, and was held in the Newcastle Music Hall; the proceeds exceeded £900.
[2] Rose Hill was the N&CR railway station at Gilsland. According to the *Newcastle Courant* of 5 November 1841, Thomas Wilson, the keeper of the 'Denton School Gate, near Rosehill on the Newcastle & Carlisle Railway' was opening the gate which must have been across the line, to allow the steam locomotive *Hercules* to proceed on its way to Newcastle, but he was struck by the locomotive and thrown onto the rails, the locomotive then passing over him. He was carried to his home, but died from his injuries within half an hour.
[3] Mary Sparke, daughter of Jonathan, married Samuel Walton in the parish of Warden on 31 October 1841. Her sister, Thomas's wife, seems not to have been present.
[4] This is given as a Primitive Methodist Chapel in *Wards Directory* (1851). Thomas spent 6d. at the chapel, presumably put in the collection.
[5] Edward 7, second child and eldest son of Victoria.

24. Joe Ridley here at breakfast. Mr Dunn married. Wm Dixon of D [Dotland?] park buried.[1]
25. Very sharp frost again.
26. Got a pair of Trousers from James Lilly.[2]
27. Very soft uncomfortable day.

Sunday 28. Very wet morning - Hearing Butterwell at night - Uncle George here at night.
29. Fine fresh day. Jas Glendining died. Biyboard[?] killed at Shields.
30. Been a desperate rain last night. High floods today.

December 1841.

1. Mr Scott very poorly.
2. Doctor at Mr Scott who is suffering from salivation.
3. Very wet day - Wind E.

Sunday 5. Hearing Mr Hillaby & Mr Mackintosh - Seeing old Aydon at aftn.
6. Mr. Scott a good deal better. An account of Lady Durham's death.[3]
7. Berwick Bank stopped payg.[4] *Got a letter from Duksfd. Sent Peter the strings &c. The directors here stating the reduction of wages.*[5]
8. Young Wm Charlton ill.
9. Fine frosty clear morning. Got some offall fr. Dd.
11. Mark Potts here giving Elizth a lesson.[6]

Sun 12. Hearing Rowell & G Makepeace. Very fine day. Walking past Hedgefield - Got tea at Josh's.
13. Mr. Scott got into the office again - Fine day. Hudspeth ceased being guard.
15. Very windy day. Hearing Sample at night.
18. Very sharp frost.

Sunday 19. Went to Dukesfield. Very sharp day.
20. At Dyehouse & Lee. Got tea at Dodds.
21. Came home by Hexham - At the singing at night. Tickets given out for the tea.
23. Sister Betsey & Mary Bulman here seeing us.
24. Females at N Castle. Betsey got some chairs.
25. Had our grand festival at the Chapel - A very fine day - J Daglish here.

Sunday 26. Hearing Mr White & Mr Stanley a.m. Lilly here at tea. J Daglish went home.
27. Fine frosty morng. Betsey & Mary gone home. Elizth with them - G Tate in our house. Old T Crawford buried.
28. Janes at J Smith's.
30. Nancy Ellerington here packing up the furniture. Dull soft day. Wm Pruddah killed.
31. Nancy flitting to Hexham. A great number of men discharged from the Company's employment.[7]

---

[1] William was the 24 year old son of Thomas, and sister of the Mary who died in April 1841.
[2] Lilley was a tailor in Blaydon.
[3] According to *Sykes' Local Records* Louisa Elizabeth, Countess of Durham, relict of John George Lambton, earl of Durham, died in Genoa on 26 November, her remains being buried in the family vault at Chester le Street on 28 December.
[4] The Tweed Bank stopped paying on 29 November 1841.
[5] The Newcastle & Carlisle Railway Ledger held by National Archives RAIL 509/58 details the proposed wage reductions.
[6] Possibly on the piano.
[7] See page 211.

14

THE MAJOR NORTH PENNINE OREFIELD, LEAD MINING AND SMELTING CONCERNS

When Thomas Dixon began his diaries in 1830, Dukesfield smelt mill belonged, and may always have belonged, to 'WB Lead', one of the most important lead mining and smelting concerns in the North Pennine Orefield. WB Lead had been established by Sir William Blackett after he acquired the Allendale Estate in 1694, its object being the mining and smelting of lead ore won from that estate, although the concern would later lease mines on other estates, notably in Weardale. Successive generations of the family ran the concern's lead interests until they were abandoned in 1899.

The other major players in the North Pennine lead industry in the nineteenth century were the Commissioners of the Greenwich Hospital for Seamen, (henceforth the 'Greenwich Hospital' or the 'Hospital'), and the London Lead Company (henceforth the 'LLCo' or 'the Company'). The Greenwich Hospital had been a major landowner in Alston Moor since 1735, when it acquired the mineral rich lands of the former earls of Derwentwater, while its dominant lessee was the LLCo., a concern which had been active in the area from the last decade of the seventeenth century, initially from a base at their smelt mill and refinery at Blaydon on Tyne. The rent paid by the Company for its Greenwich Hospital leases took the form of a 'duty ore', in other words a percentage of all of the ore raised at every mine, but these duty ores were then sold back to the Company to be smelted at their Nenthead mill. In 1768, however, the Hospital commissioners were persuaded of the financial gains to be accrued by operating their own duty-ore smelt mill and, as it happened, a near-ideal site for such a mill was readily available to them at Langley on Tyne near Haydon Bridge.

The Hospital, the LLCo., and WB Lead, together dominated the lead industry of the North Pennine Orefield from the mid-eighteenth century until its demise around 1900, but there were some lesser outfits, one of which played a small part in this story. A concern entitled Jobling & Co. also held mining leases from the Greenwich Hospital, especially around Blagill in the Nent valley near Alston, where there was a smelt mill, possibly built by the Greenwich Hospital. But around 1784, anxious to secure dedicated smelting facilities for their ores, Jobling & Co. persuaded the Hospital to erect a new smelt mill and refinery adjacent to its own Langley Mill, which Jobling & Co. would then lease. Confusingly, the new mill was called 'Blagill' after the principal mine worked by Jobling & Co., some 10 miles to the south west of Langley.

The Dukesfield smelt mill

The main functions of a lead smelt mill were firstly the conversion of lead ore into metallic lead by smelting, although the ore might first be 'roasted' as a preliminary to smelting. Secondly, but only when economically viable, silver might be extracted from the metallic lead by 'refining'; a frequent and usually inevitable sequel to the refining process, which

Plate. 59

Above – The "new" dam dating from the the early 19th C, with the Halliwell bridge over the Devil's Water.

Below – All that remains of the smelt mill.

Plate. 60

produced litharge (lead oxide) as well as silver, was the re-conversion of the litharge back to 'refined' lead - a process known as 'reducing'. While the production of silver was not an end in itself, refining did provide the market with litharge, and the much-prized refined lead. Consequently, as well as providing Hatton Garden with silver, refining offered a way of preserving a balance between the separate market demands for refined and un-refined lead, while supplying the paint industry with litharge. Even so, the refining of lead was only carried out if the value of the silver, refined lead and litharge so produced, exceeded the cost of producing them, and that cost included wastage, in terms of lead lost, plus the expenses involved in either selling the litharge or reducing it back to refined lead. All the above smelting procedures, except roasting, produced slags which contained some lead, and from late in the eighteenth century, these would be processed in a slag hearth.

Two further points of interest regarding smelting need be made. Firstly, the basic smelting process was performed in an ore hearth, and the slag hearth was essentially a modified ore hearth. The other main processes, of roasting, refining and reducing, were carried out in 'reverberatory furnaces' often referred to as 'cupola furnaces'. Secondly, ore hearths, slag hearths and refining furnaces, all depended upon water-powered bellows, while peat, coal and lime were also needed for some of the smelting processes.[1]

WB Lead certainly owned the Dukesfield smelt mill by 1729, although it was in operation before 1725. At the same time they also operated the Blaydon refinery and wharf and had smelt mills at Rookhope in Weardale, and Allenheads; they subsequently acquired Allen mill, at Catton near Allendale, at some time between 1786 and 1795. Dukesfield was the only WB mill to be located some distance off the main orefield, the nearest WB mines being some 7 or 8 miles away in the upper Allen valleys, but it was handily placed to receive ores from various mines within the orefield, including those leased in Weardale, and to forward the lead pieces and silver bullion for export from the wharf at Blaydon. Consequently, Dukesfield had historically smelted Weardale ores which Rookhope could not handle, plus some of the Allenheads and Coalcleugh ores.

The Blaydon refinery was on a fairly convenient but constricted site on the south bank of the Tyne, having little room for expansion and, by the 1760s, it may have been have been less than adequate for WB's total refining needs, which could explain why a refinery was added at the Dukesfield mill in 1765, and another at Allen mill in 1795. Dukesfield mill was always the largest of WB Lead's smelt mills during the second half of the eighteenth century, capable of handling some 8000 bings of ore per annum (3,200 tons[2]) after 1780, and although the establishment of a refinery there must have made economic sense at the time, it was closed down in 1806, 'on account of their making a bad produce, or over great waste of the lead in the operation of Refining and Reducing' according to Jno Mulcaster, the then chief smelting agent. Lead markets, and therefore lead prices, have always been volatile however, and Dukesfield's refinery was re-commissioned only 2 years later to meet increased demands for refined lead. This required some shuffling of personnel in the concern, a mason sent from Blaydon to superintend the rebuilding of Dukesfield's reducing furnace, and the temporary transferral of reducers from Allen mill to Dukesfield to train men there in the art of reducing.

Dukesfield was also chosen for an evaluation of the usefulness or otherwise of roasting different ores, and as Mulcaster noted in 1808:

---

[1] Further details of ore hearth smelting are given in an appendix, and standard works on the industry provide details of the other smelting processes.
[2] 1 bing = 8 cwt.

If it should be found beneficial to employ the Roasting Furnace constantly at this place it will be necessary to erect a new one in a larger house, as the confined situation of the present place, renders it unpleasant & probably injurious to the health of the Workman.

These experiments at Dukesfield showed that if 12 tons of ore were roasted before smelting, then 8 tons 1 cwt. of lead was produced in the ore hearth, as opposed to 7 tons 14 cwt. when un-roasted ore was smelted, and that the extra cost in roasting was outweighed by the net profit from the additional lead produced; roasting subsequently became general at the WB Lead mills.

By 1821, Dukesfield mill comprised two roasting furnaces, five ore hearths, two refining furnaces, one reducing furnace and two slag hearths, and its complement would probably be similar, if not identical, at the beginning of Thomas Dixon's diaries. Nine of its twelve hearths and furnaces needed water-powered bellows and the adjacent Devils Water was usually, but not always, a reliable source of water. The mill probably employed about 36 men at the hearths and furnaces, plus 8 others ranging from the mill agent to labourers, and the available evidence suggests that almost all of these employees lived within 1 mile of the smelt mill, mainly to the west of the Devils Water around Juniper and Dyehouse, but also at Dukesfield on the east; few if any smelters seem to have lived in Slaley village.

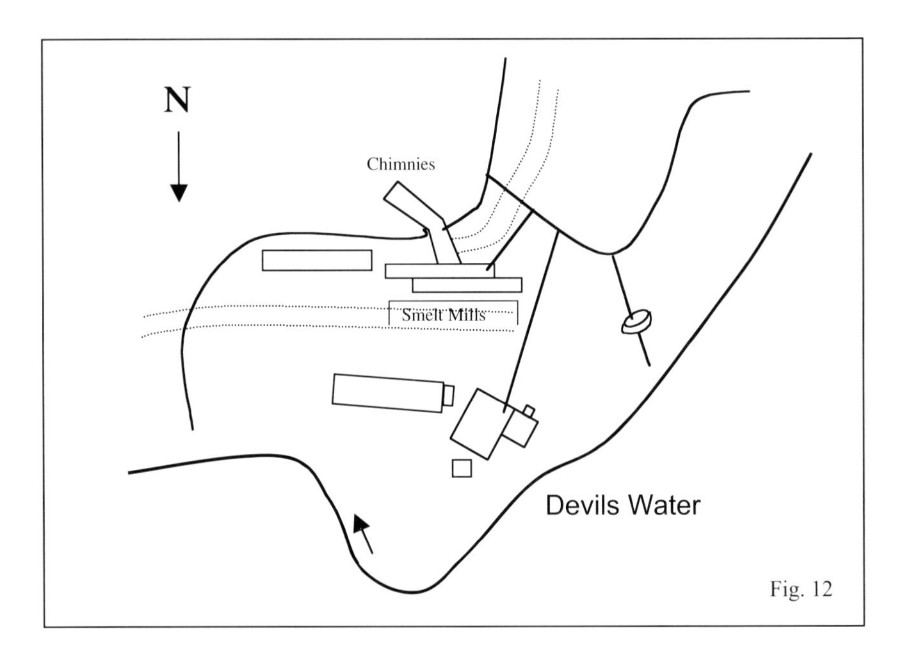

Dukesfield smelt mill layout c1835, based on an undated map in the possession of Andrew Swallow of Dukesfield Hall, which is probably a copy of an extract from an estate map.

Smelting at the ore hearth was demanding, unpleasant and heavy work, but all smelting procedures required highly skilled personnel, especially in the refining process. All was done through experience, and consequently it is not surprising that sons would join their fathers at the ore hearths to learn the intricacies of smelting on the job, once they were deemed old enough at about 18 years of age.[1] For the smelter there were good ores and bad ores, clean and dirty ones, and each might require a slightly different treatment in the ore hearth, where the strength of the air blast and the fuel to ore ratio might have to be adjusted to suit. There were no temperature-indicating instruments nor gauges to measure the bellow's blast, so that experienced and skilled combinations of hand and eye were the essential requirements of a good smelter. The quality of the end product was vitally important, for the pigs of lead would be sold as such unless they were to be subsequently refined, and smelters were therefore often the last in the line of quality control. A good smelter was worth keeping, and sometimes worth poaching, and they were generally well looked after by the major concerns, for example through the provision of houses, even in the eighteenth century; some smelters were also provided with, or encouraged to take, smallholdings. None of this meant that smelters were immune from criticism if things went wrong. For example, in 1730, when an unfortunate smelter had put lumps of slag in the pig mould, whether by accident or design, the chief agent observed that 'Hanging is too good for him'.

Smelting was regarded as a full-time occupation and, like lead mining but unlike the washing and dressing of lead ores, it was not seasonal in the nineteenth century, although there were some planned and many unplanned shut-downs and periods of short working. Consequently, although ore-hearth smelters were required to work long shifts, and although such shifts were usually specified or at least generally understood, it will be seen that the actual hours worked by smelters could be quite irregular. Any system of payments to smelters for their work would have to accommodate such vagaries, but our understanding of the mechanisms by which the appropriate payments were determined is sketchy to say the least; the historical record offers only a few clues and, unfortunately, Thomas's diary offers little assistance towards a better understanding.

Some relevant information arises from the circumstances surrounding an 1809 strike of the Rookhope smelters who claimed to be unable to make sufficient wages to maintain their families at the rate which had been set, on account of the poor quality of the ore that they were being required to smelt. John Mulcaster, chief smelting agent for WB Lead at the time, (on a salary of £120 per year), argued that the main problem lay in the Rookhope smelters' practice of having three men to each ore hearth at all times, such that when they shared the proceeds, each man received only about 10s. 9d. per week.[2] If, on the other hand, the Rookhope smelters could be persuaded to work with two men per hearth, as they did at the Allen Mill, each would earn about 14s. 6d. per week. At Dukesfield mill, he added, smelters' earnings had been about 9s. 8d. per week, but again with three men employed at each ore hearth, whereas using only two men would have provided each with about 13s. 6d. per week. All the mills, he believed, should be encouraged to use only two men at a hearth at any one time, but even so, given the high cost of living, Mulcaster believed that an advance in wages was appropriate at that time, to 8s. per fother when hand picked ore was

[1] There are no records of women or boys ever performing smelting duties.
[2] Pre-decimal coinage values are used throughout, but for guidance, 6s. = 30p.

Above – Men working at the hearths at Rookhope Smelt Mill, c.1900. Plate. 61

Below – Nenthead Smelt Mill with the Pattinson Silver Refining process, c.1900.

Plate. 62

being smelted, and 9s. 4d. per fother for ores obtained after crushing. Then, provided that only two men worked at the ore hearth at any one time, each should earn between 16s. and 17s. per week. It is apparent then, that these ore hearth smelters were paid according to the amount of lead produced from the hearth in a week, at a rate determined largely by the quality of the ore but, no doubt, underpinned by the agent's notion of an appropriate, or perhaps a sufficient weekly wage for a smelter, with due attention being paid to the current costs of living. But there was clearly an upper limit to the amount of pig lead which could conceivably be produced in a normal working week at the ore hearth, a limit imposed by the very nature of the ore hearth smelting process rather than by the men operating it. So it seems likely that while smelters were ostensibly paid by results, this was in reality a fiction, the rates being set to maintain generally agreed income levels for a generally agreed output, with the possibility of adjustments should the general economic circumstances warrant them.

None of the above explains how the smelters actually received their money, but given that Thomas recorded the holding of annual 'Pays' at or near the mills, and this is confirmed by extant WB Lead ledgers, it is implied that smelters, like lead miners, received subsistence payments throughout the year, the difference between those payments and their yearly earnings based on output being made over at the Pays. Roasters, refiners and reducers must similarly have had set rates, with the refiners probably being paid a little more than the ore hearth smelters, and the roasters and reducers probably a little less.

One curious aspect of Dukesfield mill in the nineteenth century was the absence of a 'horizontal chimney', a feature common to most North Pennine smelt mills. In reality, these structures are neither horizontal nor chimneys in the usual sense of those words, for chimneys are generally designed to create draught and to disperse fumes at altitude; the taller the chimney the greater the draught and the more diluted the fumes in the atmosphere. But the 'horizontal chimney' in the lead industry, whilst in part being concerned with fume dispersal, had a much more important economic function, that of the recovery of lead and silver that would otherwise be lost to the atmosphere. Ore hearths in particular, but the other mill furnaces to a lesser extent, produced a 'fume' or 'smoke' which consisted of fine particles of ores, fluxes, etc., swept through the hearth or furnace by the air currents before smelting had occurred, plus vapours of the oxides of lead and zinc in particular which yielded a powder on cooling. Before the introduction of horizontal chimneys, this 'smelters' fume' passed out of the stubby chimneys of the hearth and furnace houses, together with the sulphur dioxide produced in smelting, all of which eventually fell onto the surrounding land, often as acid and toxic rain, causing local environmental devastation.

The economic situation in the Napoleonic War period, when lead prices reached an all-time high, clearly encouraged the local smelting concerns to enthusiastically adopt the horizontal chimney at almost every mill, and with good reason. Four horizontal chimneys had been built at the Greenwich Hospital's smelt mill at Langley by 1805, perhaps the first in the area, and these had yielded an income equal to 70% of the costs of their construction in only one year. WB Lead began building a horizontal chimney at their Allen mill before 1808, and started one at their Rookhope mill in 1809. These early horizontal chimneys seem to have been about 100 yards long but, over the following decades, much longer horizontal chimneys were built, in the well-founded belief that an increased length improved the efficiency of recovery. By 1865 the WB Lead had a combined total of some 8.5 miles

Plate. 63

Above – A group of miners and smelt mill workers at Rookhope, c.1900.

Below – Smelters outside Rookhope smelt mill with a slag-ladle.

Plate. 64

of horizontal chimney at their Allen, Allenheads and Rookhope mills, generating some £10,000 p.a. to the concern.

The remains of these chimneys are striking features in the North Pennine Orefield, a century or more after they were last used, but none were ever provided at Dukesfield, for no very obvious reason. Their absence not only disadvantaged Dukesfield mill's economic prospects, but it also made life more difficult and unpleasant for its smelters, for it was generally agreed that horizontal chimneys ameliorated the worst effects of working at a smelt mill by carrying much of the fume away. One witness before the 1842 Commission noted of one mill that 'the men suffered very much ... there not being proper flues to take the smoke away'. The frequency with which Thomas refers to having been 'Sore smoked at Mill' is testimony to the accuracy of that observation.

Some Changes in the lead industry and society in the years covered by the Diary.

The trade in lead was very slack when Thomas began his diaries, the entire industry being in the midst of a depression. The market price of lead had fallen from its Napoleonic War highs of £40 per ton in 1805 and 1809, to only £13.5 per ton by 1830, and it remained at that level until 1834 when it rose to £17; it reached £26 in 1836 but fell back to £19.5 in 1837. Work in the lead mines was scarce as a consequence of this trade depression, perhaps explaining why some lead miners were persuaded to move into coal mining on Tyneside in 1832 where, wittingly or not, they were to act as 'strike-breakers'.

The difficulties in the lead districts in part reflected a more general post-Napoleonic War depression, but the deteriorating situation in the industry throughout the country was worsened by two pieces of legislation, one enacted in Britain, the other in Spain. Firstly, an Act of Parliament of 1825 lowered the duties on imported lead and lead ore, and secondly, but more or less simultaneously, Spanish mines were freely opened to both Spanish and foreign adventurers. Some 3,000 new lead mines were opened in Spain within a year, and Spanish ore and lead production was thereby dramatically increased, much of the output being exported to England where it sold below the price of indigenous supplies. Some North Pennine mines were forced to close under the impact of these changes, and a degree of depopulation followed, through emigration to Canada and America for example. The ongoing depression also enforced a streamlining of the affairs of the major lead concerns. The 'old guard' of agents such as the dynastic Walton, Mulcaster and Crawhall families would be replaced by new men, specifically brought in to run affairs more economically. Men like Hugh Lee Pattinson, John Grey of Dilston and Thomas Sopwith.

There had been some recovery in the local lead industry by the 1840s, partly as a result of technological improvements such as the Pattinson desilverising process, of which more later, which meant that almost all of WB's lead became worth desilverising, not only giving greater outputs of silver but also, and more importantly, enabling increased amounts of the highly desirable refined lead to be produced. Some external factors also assisted the local lead industry at this period, notably the impact of railways in cutting transport costs within the industry, especially the Newcastle & Carlisle and the Stanhope & Tyne railways. The opening of these two lines was to cause a re-evaluation of the optimum location for the WB smelt mills.

Some important political and social changes also occurred at this period. Firstly, the Reform Act of 1832, gave the vote to all male landholders, and £10 householders in the boroughs; this undoubted extension of the franchise still left all women and 5 out of every 6 men without a vote, but it was a start. Secondly, a Methodist revival within the lead dales was being spurred on by the secession of the Primitive Methodists (the 'Ranters') from the Wesleyan Methodists. All these matters are reflected in Thomas's diaries for, either directly or indirectly, they impacted upon him, his family, workmates and friends.

Plate. 65

Langley Smelt Mill, c.1880.

15

THOMAS'S WORKING LIFE AT DUKESFIELD SMELT MILL

The working year at Dukesfield.

A successful working year at the Dukesfield smelt mill was certainly dependent upon its personnel, but also on the mining and dressing of the lead ore at mines as far south as Weardale, and on the carriage of that ore, plus peat, coal and lime to the mill. Lead mining was carried out throughout the year, although often with a pause at harvest time, but for accounting purposes, the mining year usually ended on 30 September. The miners would subsequently be paid for the ore which they had won in the year up to that date, less the subsistence money which they had received during the year, at a general Pay in the following spring; that time gap would, hopefully, enable the ores to be washed, dressed and weighed, for the miners were not paid according to the quantity of minerals won from the mine but on the weight of clean, dressed ore extracted from the mined materials by 'washing and dressing', a necessary preparation for its smelting. It took some time to get the ore washed and carried to the smelt mills, and the year's ore output up to 30 September might not reach the smelt mills until the second week of the following January. Moreover, the washing and dressing of the ores at the mines was totally dependent on water for power and for washing, and was, therefore, seasonal; water would not separate the ore from the dirt efficiently in frosty weather and there was no water flow at all in icy weather. Hence most washing floors would normally close down for 2 or 3 winter months.

Carriage of dressed ore to the smelt mill was also generally seasonal, having to be suspended over the winter months when carriage was usually difficult and often impossible. But smelting was not seasonal, and hence sufficient ore and other raw materials had to reach the mill, preferably before late December or at the worst by early January, to ensure that smelting could continue through the winter months. Thus it was important that the mill had at least 4 months' stock of ore by early January, for the next ore deliveries might not be made to the mill until May or June; as Thomas recorded in his diary on 10 June 1830, 'Farmers seeking metal [ore] in Weardale.'[1] Most of the ores mentioned by Thomas were from mines at a crows'-flight distance of about 11 miles from Dukesfield, but Scraith Head mine was some 16 miles away - a very full day's pack-horse journey in very good weather with firm conditions underfoot. Dukesfield mill was capable of smelting some 8,000 bings (about 3,200 tons) of ore per year, which was almost one-tenth of the total ore production of the North Pennine Orefield in 1831, and if all that ore was carried by pack horse, as it might well have been, with each horse carrying 2 cwt of ore, Dukesfield would witness almost 11,000 individual pack-horse arrivals in order that a necessary 2,700 bings of ore should be in hand by early January.

Although Thomas tended only to mention his work at the smelt mill when something unusual happened, such as a change in shift times, or some problem with the ores or the equipment, some annual and weekly patterns of work can be discerned. The smelters' year was programmed, at least in theory, and the early years of the diary indicate that the smelting year began around the second week of January after a maintenance shutdown. The washing of slags was let early in the year and the smelters' annual Pays were made in April, usually at the mill. Quite large sums of money could change hands at the Pays, and these

[1] From 1796 some Blackett-Beaumont farm leases had included an obligation to carry.

could obviously be a times of overexcitement. After a Dukesfield Pay was made on 19 January 1835, when over £6,000 was paid out to smelters and carriers, Thomas noted that there was 'Much fighting at the low mill'.

The process of ore hearth smelting always resulted in an accumulation of particles of unreduced and semi-reduced ore, intermixed with fragments of fuel and lime, on and around the masonry which supported and buttressed the hearth. Collectively known as 'hearth ends', these accretions were periodically removed from the hearth area to be later washed, roasted, and smelted in an ore hearth, at 6-month or yearly intervals. The Dukesfield mill hearth ends were smelted in May-June, when some of the hearths and furnaces would normally be subject to some maintenance and re-building, and then again in December. Refiners seem to have been drafted in to carry out their specialist work in the second half of the year, although the evidence is not strong, while slag-hearth men seem to have been brought in to process the smelters' slags in December or January.

The smelting year usually ended late in December, and was followed by a two-week lay-off while the hearths and furnaces were partly dismantled, cleaned, repaired and rebuilt, in January. The ore hearth smelters cleaned and repaired their own hearths, but specialists saw to the bellows and stonemasons were contracted to do any necessary work on the cupola furnaces; the new smelting year could now begin around 14 January. A typical shut-down period was summed up by Thomas on 15 January 1831: 'The Mill been off a fortnight - Masons (Smith, Bowman, Purvis, Bulman,) crowning the furnaces - The millwrights (Birtley & Dodd) cuting our wheel - Bowman covering the west end bellows'. The above yearly cycle changed slightly towards the end of 1833, the hearth and furnace repairs being carried out in late December and the new smelting year beginning on the day before new year's eve; the last smelting year at Dukesfield began on 8 January 1835 but lasted only a few months.

As Dukesfield mill did not have the long horizontal chimneys common to other mills, it may be that its short flues and vertical chimneys were only cleaned out, and their deposits recovered for re-smelting, every 3 years or so. An early entry in the 1830 diary noted that the roasters had been on with 'soot' for about 6 weeks, and this almost certainly alluded to the fine deposits recovered from Dukesfield's flues and chimneys which would be first sintered in a roasting furnace and then processed in a slag hearth. The only other diary reference to the recovery of flue deposits occurs in June 1833, when Thomas noted that the mill had been closed down for a couple of days while the chimneys were being cleaned.

But many happenings could and did interrupt the annual patterns of work. Some interruptions were relatively minor matters such as when the hearth bellows caught fire, or the waterwheel axle broke, or when the mill ran out of lime. Other stoppages were more frequent and occasionally dramatic. In particular, the water supply needed to power the mill's bellows could be erratic on a river like the Devils Water, where problems could arise from insufficiency or excess, as the events of 1831 show. There had been plenty of water during the first 5 months of 1831, but dry spell followed and only some of the hearths could be fully utilised. Some heavy showers in July allowed Thomas to note 'water for us all today', but just 9 days later he wrote 'Went smelt this afternoon - water turned scarce; been plentiful for the other men,' and 5 days after that there were 'The largest floods in remembrance - our dam gone'. There then followed a period of intermittent working while repairs went on until the last day of October.[1]

[1] This was not the first occasion that the Devils Water in flood had caused mayhem at the mill. The Dukesfield, Allenheads and Rookhope smelt mill dams had been washed away on 29 August 1792, and the Dukesfield mill dam was again destroyed in flood in 1809.

This flood seems to have destroyed much more than Dukesfield's dam, for the diaries contain several references to a 'New Mill' in early 1832, suggesting that some of the ore-hearth houses may have been lost, their re-commissioning being held up by the failure of a waterwheel axle. The unpredictability of the Devils Water may have been one reason why Dukesfield was soon to close, although the ready availability of another mill, together with the opening of the Newcastle & Carlisle Railway, were also significant factors.

The working week at Dukesfield.

Most ore hearth smelters in the North Pennine Orefield worked in pairs on shifts of 12 or 15 hours, the hearth being allowed to cool down for a few hours between each shift. The precise patterns of shift work varied over the orefield, perhaps according to the practices of the different concerns, but the shift pattern at Dukesfield, as evidenced by Thomas's diary, was typical. A pair of ore hearth smelters would normally carry out their smelting duties at a particular hearth between a Thursday and the following Wednesday, but in two sets of three shifts with the intervening Sunday off, for no-one worked on Sundays. Each smelting shift would normally last some 15 hours, theoretically beginning at 4 o'clock in the morning and ending at 7 o'clock in the evening, and each pair of smelters would be expected to smelt about 6 or 7 bings of clean dressed ore per shift, that is between 18 and 20 bings over three shifts to produce around 60 pigs of lead, dependent upon the quality of the ore being smelted. Once their Wednesday shift had been concluded that pair of smelters would not normally be required to return to the mill until the Thursday of the following week. In short, ore hearth smelters had 6 days on in 7, followed by 7 days off, giving 45 hours worked in each week, quite a short working week when compared with many contemporaries in other industries. When any pair of smelters finished their two sets of shifts on a Wednesday, another pair would work at the same ore hearth for two sets of shifts beginning on the Thursday. Although the mill was not worked on Sundays, Good Friday appears to have been the only official holiday in the year, not even Christmas Day being entirely exempted from work.

These unusual shift arrangements may have arisen from the tendency for the ore hearth to heat up as a shift progressed, until eventually it would no longer function satisfactorily and had to be left for a period to cool down - a 12 or 15 hour shift was presumably deemed to be the optimum length for smelting before the hearth became too hot to work. It is noteworthy in this context that Thomas recorded his hearth bellows to be on fire on three occasions, presumably near the end of a shift when everything was overheating. It would follow from this that the shift patterns peculiar to ore-heath smelting were as old as that method of smelting, and while various suggested modifications to the hearth were made over time, with the aim of lessening its tendency to get too hot, none were known to have been implemented during Thomas Dixon's time at Dukesfield mill. On the other hand, Hugh Lee Pattinson noted that 'some intelligent smelters' had made their hearths deeper than was usual, with the twofold advantage of increasing the quantity of lead retained in the hearth while at the same time lessening its tendency to get too hot during the smelting shift.

The more closely Thomas Dixon's work patterns are examined however, the more apparent it becomes that the neat and simple shift system described above was, and had to be, capable of great flexibility. For example, for whatever reasons, be they technical or arising out of personal preference, Thomas quite frequently began his Monday shift at noon. Also, the required week's work could sometimes be accomplished in only two shifts; as Thomas wrote on Tuesday 31 January 1832, 'Got done our work in 2 days, working 20 Bings [8 tons of ore].'

Although no smelting took place on Good Fridays, smelters would compensate for that by beginning their three shifts on a Wednesday, have Friday off, and return to work for a short shift on the Saturday. Similar arrangements were made if an annual Pay was scheduled to take place on a Friday, as when Thomas and his partner began a smelting shift on Wednesday 2 April 1834.

It is not always easy to determine the precise reasons for departures from the standard shift system, but it seems certain that the flexibility built into the system suited the smelters as well as the mill agent On Wednesday 25 March 1835, Thomas began his shift early and was consequently able to attend Hexham fair in the afternoon: he also appears to have made a conscious choice to begin a set of shifts on a Wednesday rather than the normal Thursday in September 1830 so that he could spend a couple of days at the Allendale races. It is also apparent that smelters could opt to work two long shifts in order to have most of Wednesday or Saturday free for activities such as harvesting for example, and they might sometimes have worked very long and even double shifts. Thus, Thomas began a set of shifts on Monday 14 October 1833 at about 1 o'clock in the morning, and was able to finish at 4 o'clock on the Wednesday morning. Quite how this affected the over-heating of the hearth is not clear, unless he worked at two different hearths on such occasions.

Just to make matters even more complicated, there were numerous occasions when smelters exchanged shifts with one another, often when one of them wished to attend a special event, or was ill. Thomas was 'on for' Joseph Bowman one Tuesday, so that Bowman could reciprocate on the following Thursday when Thomas wished to attend a 'sporting' at the *Travellers Rest* at Whitley Chapel. There were occasions, when Thomas was 'on' for some other smelter, that he must have worked four or even five shifts in the same week, and no doubt other smelters did likewise. Early in 1833, when Thomas had 'pox' and was ill for a few weeks, Wm Ridley, John Dinning and Dinning of Lilswood all deputised for him. This regular exchange of shifts may have been one reason for keeping a diary - 'W^{m}. Ridley on working for me; clear with him now'. The complications of the shift system as practised, with its seeming ability to be infinitely accommodating, can be seen in Thomas's diary entries around Easter 1831:

> *Wednesday 30 March 1831, Went on to work this forenoon.*
> *Thursday 31 March 1831, T's [Travellers] Rest Races; Jane and I there - John Cant on for me.*
> *Friday 1 April 1831, Good Friday - Mill off.*
> *Saturday 2 April 1831, W^{m}. Ridley on with me.*
> *Sunday 3 April 1831, Easter day - At Chapel.*
> *Monday 4 April 1831, Jane and I at Clickem sporting.*
> *Tuesday 5 April 1831, Jo^{s}. Dixon on this forenoon for me.*

But it was the vagaries of the weather, and therefore of the water flows in the Devils Water, which had the greatest influence on the shift patterns, for water shortages frequently meant that only some of the hearths could be worked - 'Time divided', 'Time parted' or 'Water parted' being the expressions which Thomas used for such occurrences, meaning that there was insufficient water to keep all the necessary mill bellows going all the time. Adjustments to the shift times were the inevitable result, Thomas recording, for example, that he had sometimes commenced work at midnight, at 1 a.m., 3 a.m., 10 a.m., noon, 2 p.m., and even 4 p.m., and accordingly had finished at such times as 9 p.m., 11 p.m., or 7 a.m. Water shortages usually began late in May, and thereafter they played havoc with the shifts, especially when the refiners were also at work. The month of August 1833 offers a good illustration of the adjustments which had to be made to the shifts on account of low water flows:

Thursday 1 August, The water too light for the refiners and us.
Saturday 3 August, Time parted.
Monday 5 August, Went to work at midnight this shift.
Wednesday 7 August, Got done work early this morning.
Saturday 10 August, The water very light.
Saturday 17 August, Time parted.
Monday 19 August, Went to work at 12 at noon.
Saturday 24 August, Smelters all on this back end.
Wednesday 28 August, Went to work at 4 at noon.
Saturday 31 August, Time parted all the week.

Thomas also occasionally worked at the mill on his days off from smelting, usually at 'washing', almost certainly referring to the washing of slags in preparation for re-smelting, rather than that of dirty ore. It appears that the smelters were not obliged to carry out this washing processes, but rather that they could bid for the job early in each year. Thus the washing was 'let' on 2 January 1830, and was 'put up' on 22 February 1833. Thomas only carried out the washing outside of his designated smelting shifts, but at almost any time of the year. Like ore-hearth smelting, this washing of slags may have been a two-person job, or at any rate made easier if two people did it together, for Thomas, his father, and his brother Peter, and sometimes other smelters, all helped each other with the washing. It could be quite a pleasant job in the summer, but not so in the winter, for it was almost certainly performed in the open air. Hence:

2, 3 July 1832, Washing - Very hot days.
18 December 1832, On washing - Very cold.

While it cannot be totally discounted that women did some washing at the mill, it seems more likely that diary entries such as the following refer to the washing of clothes or, conceivably, to whitewashing:

28 April 1831, Marg^t^. washing for us.
25 June 1834, Sally here washing.
14 October 1834, Helping Jane to wash.
17 March 1835, Peggy Sheell here washing.

Finally, in the context of working life at the Dukesfield mill, it should be noted that there are very few known instances of industrial disputes concerned with the lead industry of the North Pennine Orefield. There were occasional strikes at certain mines and at washing and dressing floors, one at the Rookhope smelt mill already referred to, and the well-known strike of miners in the Allenheads area in 1849; these disputes were always localised occurrences, and were usually prompted by periods of economic depression. No Trade Unions were ever formed within the lead industry, and the flexibility inherent in the employment of lead ore smelters may go a long way towards explaining an apparent lack of enthusiasm for unionism on their part. Thomas did note a 'meeting of the Smelters' on 22 February 1833, but it seems just as likely that this concerned their role in organising work at the mill, than an attempt to bring about changes in their favour or to express a grievance.

Changes in the WB Organisation.

Mrs Diana Beaumont had been in effective charge of WB Lead for 35 years when Thomas began his diaries, and in absolute control after the death of her husband, Col. Thomas Richard Beaumont, in 1829. Her business acumen, her resultant wealth and extravagant lifestyle combined with her fearful temper, aroused hostility in many less capable contemporaries. She, of course, depended heavily on her head cashier, auditor and agents, and she obviously favoured some familiar dynasties for such positions. John Mulcaster had succeeded his father Robert as chief agent for the WB Lead's Blaydon Refinery and smelt mills by 1808. Robert's brothers, James and Peter, had been joint agents at the Greenwich Hospital's Langley Smelt mill, and were succeeded there by James' son, also James. A Mr Crawhall was head cashier for WB Lead at their Newcastle head office, other members of his family having worked as agents to the concern for generations. Benjamin Johnson was chief land steward for the Beaumonts, and the auditor since 1828 had been James Losh. On Mrs Beaumont's death in August 1831, her son Thomas Wentworth Beaumont took over as head of the concern and he immediately embarked on wide-ranging changes to the administrative hierarchy. Basically, he sought to dismiss the Crawhalls and the Mulcasters and all of the other senior agents except Benjamin Johnson, and to make James Losh's son, also James, his new auditor. These changes reflected the new mood in the country when, under Earl Grey with his promise of 'Peace, Reform, Retrenchment', the Whig government was advocating a sense of real politics to the nation, and consequently a more economic management of its affairs.

Some of these proposed changes were effected immediately. Firstly Crawhall was replaced by Benjamin Johnson as head cashier, and he was to be based at WB Lead's head office in the Royal Arcade, Newcastle upon Tyne, recently completed to the design of John Dobson. Secondly, on the recommendation of James Losh, Hugh Lee Pattinson took over from John Mulcaster as chief agent for the refinery and smelt mills, on a salary of £300 per year plus £30 per year 'Allowance for keep of house'. William Crawhall remained agent at Allenheads however, and George Crawhall kept a similar position in Weardale. Thomas included these changes amongst his listing of the remarkable events of 1832, along with the local cholera epidemic, and the passing of the Reform Bill.

The new appointments at WB Lead were to bring many changes and, although he did not hold his position very long, the innovations introduced by Hugh Lee Pattinson not only affected Dukesfield mill, and therefore Thomas Dixon, but also radically advanced the prosperity of WB Lead. Neither Johnson nor Pattinson were office-bound, and they soon saw fit to make an immediate inspection of the WB smelt mills. Thomas noted they had visited Dukesfield mill on 11 July 1832, and that Pattinson then spent 2 or 3 days there, probably staying in the hall at Dukesfield Hall with Jonathan Sparke, the Dukesfield mill agent. Pattinson was critical of several aspects of the smelting operations at Dukesfield, particularly with respect to ore-roasting. Indeed, he blamed the poor quality of the WB Lead's common (i.e. unrefined) lead on inadequate roasting, and he immediately sought to remedy the problem at Dukesfield; thus Thomas noted on 4 August 1832 that he had 'Been on with trial roasted.' Pattinson was back at Dukesfield on four more occasions before June 1833, and he concluded that smelting operations at Rookhope should be expanded, while those at Dukesfield should be reduced. Johnson was more cautious however, and recommended that such decisions should be deferred until the Newcastle & Carlisle and the Stanhope & Tyne railways had opened; that time was not far off.

The potential significance of the railways to WB Lead were obvious to all, for in reducing the costs of lead carriage from just under 7d. per ton per mile by road to about 2.7d. per ton per mile by rail, WB Lead would save, according to Johnson's conservative estimates, £1000 p.a. on lead carried from the Allen and Allenheads mills when the railway reached Hexham, and £1200 p.a. when it reached Haydon Bridge. The annual saving on the carriage of Dukesfield's output of some 3,000 tons per year, by taking it 5 miles by road to Dilston, and then by railway to Blaydon, would be £750; it was currently costing 12s. 9d. per ton by road to Blaydon, but would be only 7s. 9d. by a combination of road and rail. Johnson did not include the WB's Rookhope mill in these calculations, but carriage from that mill would clearly benefit by the railway then being built between South Shields, at the mouth of the Tyne, and Stanhope in Weardale, the Rookhope mill being just 4 miles from the Stanhope railhead.

The taking of Blagill Mill and the closure of Dukesfield Mill.

Blagill smelt mill at Langley was occupied by John Wilson's Hudgill Burn Mining Co. by c.1819, and Wilson seems to have purchased that mill from the Hospital by 1832, for he smelted and refined some WB ores at Blagill in that year. The Greenwich Hospital then ceased to carry out their own smelting and refining at Langley and leased that mill to Wilson's company in 1833. Wilson then agreed to lease Blagill to WB Lead, and it is clear that, having taken Blagill, WB Lead had no further need for Dukesfield. Thus, Pattinson was at Dukesfield on 7 July 1834 'proclaiming Langley [Blagill] mill.'

Although Blagill mill was only 7 miles north-west of Dukesfield, its location offered several advantages. The adjacent Stublick coalfield gave easy access to coal, and the mill had a much more certain water supply, unaffected by drought or flood, for it was mainly drawn from the colliery. Moreover, Blagill had direct turnpike communication with WB Lead's mining areas whereas ore carriage to Dukesfield necessitated the use of some moorland tracks and parish roads. Blagill also had direct turnpike links with Tyneside for its lead carriage whereas only parish roads connected Dukesfield with the turnpikes.[1] More importantly, the impending opening of the Newcastle & Carlisle Railway would further cement Blagill's transport advantages, being only about 2.5 miles from Haydon Bridge station. The first part of the railway to open for goods, in November 1834, was between Hexham and Blaydon, and WB Lead made immediate use of it - some 491.5 tons of lead were carried in horse-drawn wagons from Hexham between 26 November 1834 and 1 January 1835, and 115.5 tons from Stocksfield, all to the WB refinery at Blaydon. A phased closure of Dukesfield mill was now put in place, as Thomas noted in his diary:

> *20 September 1834, Ore gone to Langley this week.*[2]
> *28 October 1834, Balloting for Blagill taken place.*
> *8 November 1834, Some of the smelters at Blagill.*
> *15 November 1834, The work tools gone from our Mill to Langley - The roasters been on at Langley this week.*

Most of the Dukesfield smelters were dispersed either to the Allen mill or the newly taken Blagill mill, some deciding to completely relocate their families to their new place of work, others preferring to maintain their home base near Dukesfield and use alternative

---

[1] Blagill mill was 3 miles by turnpike from Haydon Bridge, and 8 miles by turnpike from Hexham; Dukesfield mill was 3 miles by parish roads from the turnpike at Corbridge, and 8 miles by parish roads from the turnpike at Stocksfield.

[2] Although Dixon refers to Langley, we can take it that he means the Blagill smelt mill at Langley,

accommodation when at work, a decision made somewhat easier by the shift patterns of the ore hearth smelters and the fact that lodging barracks almost certainly existed at the Allen and Blagill mills. Thus, although Thomas's father, brother Peter and brother-in-law Jemmy were all transferred to the Allen mill, they all retained their homes at Dukesfield.

Thomas and a few others were kept on at Dukesfield for a while, presumably to work up whatever stocks of ore and slags still remained there, but on new year's day of 1835 and on 6-7 January, he was 'Helping Mr Sparke to make up the accts.' As already noted, Jonathan Sparke was the Dukesfield mill agent, but he was also Thomas's father-in-law. Thomas then returned to his smelting work while more mill workers were transferred to the Blagill, Rookhope and Allendale mills. Thomas then agreed to go to the Allenheads mill,[1] but he received a letter from Benjamin Johnson just 2 days later, asking him to take a position at the Blaydon refinery. Thomas visited Blaydon with Jonathan Sparke on the following day, and Allenheads on the day after that, perhaps to get a clearer insight into his options, but he was in lodgings at Blaydon by 20 April, having worked up his last 12 bings of ore at Dukesfield mill. It had been quite a week.

There seems to have been just one permanent employee at the Dukesfield mill by the middle of 1835, one Joseph Clemitson, who was kept on to wash whatever ores, slags and wastes still remained on site, so that occasional smelting still took place, presumably carried out by some of those smelters who had retained a home base near Dukesfield; Clemitson continued his lonely vigil until at least the end of 1840. Jonathan Sparke was also eventually relocated to Langley/Blagill, in 1836, and with the hall at Dukesfield Hall now vacant, it seems likely that Thomas Dixon's father, by then a schoolmaster, moved in; certainly the 1841 census, for which Joseph was the enumerator, seems to record him as living in the hall.

[1] His wife's family were from the St Peters area, and some of her family probably still lived there.

16

THOMAS AND JANE DIXON'S LEISURE HOURS AT DUKESFIELD.

When commissioner Dr James Mitchell interviewed an ore-hearth smelter for the 1842 Report, coincidentally also called Thomas Dixon but employed at the Greenside smelt mill in the Lake District where the shift pattern was identical to that at Dukesfield, he was told:

> *I work three days in a week. I go on Thursday and work to Saturday night. I come back again on Monday morning, and work to Wednesday night. There are two hearths at work, and there are two men for each hearth. We work 17 hours generally, but on Wednesdays we work 12 at smelting; and when that is done weighing the lead which we have made in the six days, which is usually eight tons. We have a certain quantity of ore to smelt every week, and if we see that we are behind we sometimes work 21 hours a-day. At the end of Wednesday night we have a week's cessation from labour, until Thursday the following week.*
>
> *Working so many hours near the hot smelting-hearths is injurious to our health. The hours are much too many, and the work is hot. During the week of idleness we come home, and do nothing, spending the time in dozing and sleeping to recover ourselves from the exhaustion ... Other men take our places during the six days that we are not at work. The men approve of this arrangement, chiefly on account of having a week's rest.*

Commissioner Mitchell's summarised this account in his own words:

> *So long hours in so great heat at smelting cannot but be exhaustive, and the week's cessation from labour is not likely to do more than to recover the body from the effects of excessive labour.*

When presented with an alternative viewpoint, Mitchell evidently doubted its veracity:

> *Some masters lay stress on what the miners and smelters may gain on the days when they do not come to work, but the men who, by over-exertion, require to stop at home on those days to rest themselves, are not likely to do much by which they can add to their earnings.*

But it would be unfortunate if this view of the work and life of an ore hearth smelter, as expressed in the 1842 Report, was to become common understanding, for abundant evidence is presented here to indicate that the 'week of idleness', was not always spent in recovering from the undoubtedly arduous work, but might be spent in a wide range of intellectual, recreational and social activities. Certainly the smelting shifts were long, but the hours worked per week were modest when compared with contemporary coal miners or agricultural labourers for example, and some, perhaps many smelters, made full use of their 'leisure' hours.

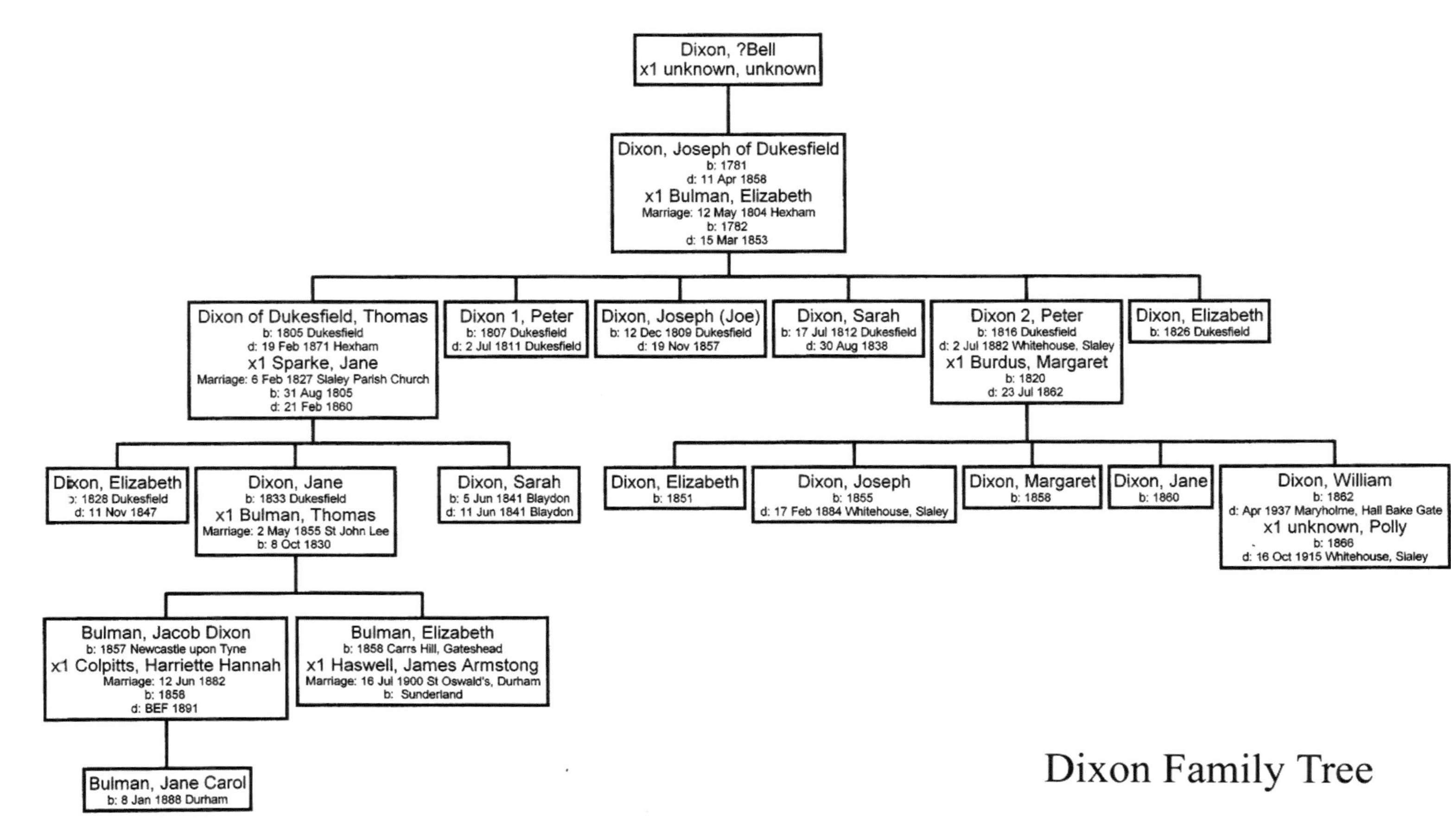
Dixon, ?Bell
x1 unknown, unknown
Dixon, Joseph of Dukesfield
b: 1781
d: 11 Apr 1858
x1 Bulman, Elizabeth
Marriage: 12 May 1804 Hexham
b: 1782
d: 15 Mar 1853
Dixon of Dukesfield, Thomas
b: 1805 Dukesfield
d: 19 Feb 1871 Hexham
x1 Sparke, Jane
Marriage: 6 Feb 1827 Slaley Parish Church
b: 31 Aug 1805
d: 21 Feb 1860
Dixon 1, Peter
b: 1807 Dukesfield
d: 2 Jul 1811 Dukesfield
Dixon, Joseph (Joe)
b: 12 Dec 1809 Dukesfield
d: 19 Nov 1857
Dixon, Sarah
b: 17 Jul 1812 Dukesfield
d: 30 Aug 1838
Dixon 2, Peter
b: 1816 Dukesfield
d: 2 Jul 1882 Whitehouse, Slaley
x1 Burdus, Margaret
b: 1820
d: 23 Jul 1862
Dixon, Elizabeth
b: 1826 Dukesfield
Dixon, Elizabeth
b: 1828 Dukesfield
d: 11 Nov 1847
Dixon, Jane
b: 1833 Dukesfield
x1 Bulman, Thomas
Marriage: 2 May 1855 St John Lee
b: 8 Oct 1830
Dixon, Sarah
b: 5 Jun 1841 Blaydon
d: 11 Jun 1841 Blaydon
Dixon, Elizabeth
b: 1851
Dixon, Joseph
b: 1855
d: 17 Feb 1884 Whitehouse, Slaley
Dixon, Margaret
b: 1858
Dixon, Jane
b: 1860
Dixon, William
b: 1862
d: Apr 1937 Maryholme, Hall Bake Gate
x1 unknown, Polly
b: 1866
d: 16 Oct 1915 Whitehouse, Slaley
Bulman, Jacob Dixon
b: 1857 Newcastle upon Tyne
x1 Colpitts, Harriette Hannah
Marriage: 12 Jun 1882
b: 1858
d: BEF 1891
Bulman, Elizabeth
b: 1858 Carrs Hill, Gateshead
x1 Haswell, James Armstong
Marriage: 16 Jul 1900 St Oswald's, Durham
b: Sunderland
Bulman, Jane Carol
b: 8 Jan 1888 Durham
Dixon Family Tree

Fig. 13

Thomas Dixon's family.

Thomas Dixon was born at Middle Dukesfield in 1805, to Joseph Dixon and Elizabeth (Bulman), and was christened on 3 February 1805 at St Helen's, Whitley Chapel. He married Jane Sparke at Slaley Church on 6 February 1827 when they were both aged about 22 years; although a native of the East Allen valley, Jane would have been living with her father, Jonathan Sparke, in the hall at Dukesfield Hall at the time of her marriage, her mother, Elizabeth (Dryden) having died in 1818 when Jane was aged about 12 years. Jonathan Sparke, as the Dukesfield smelt mill agent, was being paid £100 p.a. by 1831, and was handling some £10,000 p.a. in that capacity. Thomas's father, Joseph, was also an ore-hearth smelter at the start of the diaries, but he was later to become a full-time schoolmaster soon after having been elected 'clerk' at Whitley Chapel in May 1836. No grandparents of either Thomas or Jane are ever mentioned in the diaries which may simply imply that they were no longer alive.

Thomas and Jane's eldest daughter, Elizabeth, was born in 1828, and their second daughter, Jane, was born on 6 May 1833; Thomas recorded this latter birth in typically laconic manner, 'Jane delivered of a daughter at 8 o clock this morning - Peter and I finishing the dyke and setting quicks.' They were to have a third daughter while living at Blaydon on 5 June 1841, baptised 'Sarah' just hours before her death aged just 6 days. Such early deaths were clearly commonplace, and few people in that area at that time could have been unfamiliar with frail mortality.

Thomas gave his address as 'Dukesfield Hall' at the beginning of his 1830 diary. This does not mean that he lived in the 'Hall', for it is clear that several people lived at Dukesfield Hall; at the time of the 1841 census some twenty-eight people lived there in six buildings, two of which held two households. It is not possible to describe the dwelling occupied by Thomas and Jane Dixon in 1830, but evidently they were soon required to move to a different house at Dukesfield Hall. The sequence of events surrounding this move appears to be that Thomas and John Teasdale, who were farming the land associated with Dukesfield Hall,[1] became bankrupt in 1830, had their goods seized, and were sent to jail for a short while in January 1831, returning to take a farm at Middle Dukesfield by May. Mr Bownas, probably William, agreed to take Teasdale's farm, but he was to be provided with a new farmhouse, to be built precisely where Thomas and Jane were then living; accordingly the Dixons would shift into Teasdale's old farmhouse. They entered it in May, just days after the Teasdales had moved their remaining belongings to Middle Dukesfield. The old farmhouse, which was large enough to have a parlour, was clearly needed some modifications before the Dixons moved in, for Thomas noted 'The Hornsbys preparing our house', and most of the Hornsbys in the area were stonemasons.

Thomas' previous dwelling was presumably demolished, and joiners and masons began to build the new house for Bownas before May was out; the joiners may have lodged with Thomas and Jane for the duration of the building work. The new farmhouse was completed by late July 1831 and Bownas and family moved in on 6 August. Thomas now began to create a new garden at the old farmhouse and, having finished their work on Bownas's house, the masons provided it with new garden walls. This took until 22 October, and over the next few weeks Thomas bought bushes and trees at Hexham, followed by cabbage plants and rhubarb.

[1] Some 1,730 acres in 1849, nearly 1,400 acres of which were classified as moorland.

Various pieces of evidence, mainly maps, directories and census returns, point to the present Dukesfield Hall Cottage, which lies to the immediate south-east of the Hall, as having been the old farmhouse which Thomas and Jane entered in 1831, and also suggest that the new farmhouse built for Bownas stood immediately to the east of a row of four cottages immediately to the north of Dukesfield Hall; both house and cottages were demolished some years ago. This move into Teasdale's old farmhouse was summarised by Thomas at the end of his diary for 1831:

> *The year just ended is remarkable amongst other things for ...the failure of Thomas Teasdale the farmer of this place - his three several sales - his imprisonment - and his removal to Middle Dukesfield. - Also for Bownas taking and entering to this farm. - Also for our removal to the farmhouse in order to make way for Bownas a new farmhouse.*

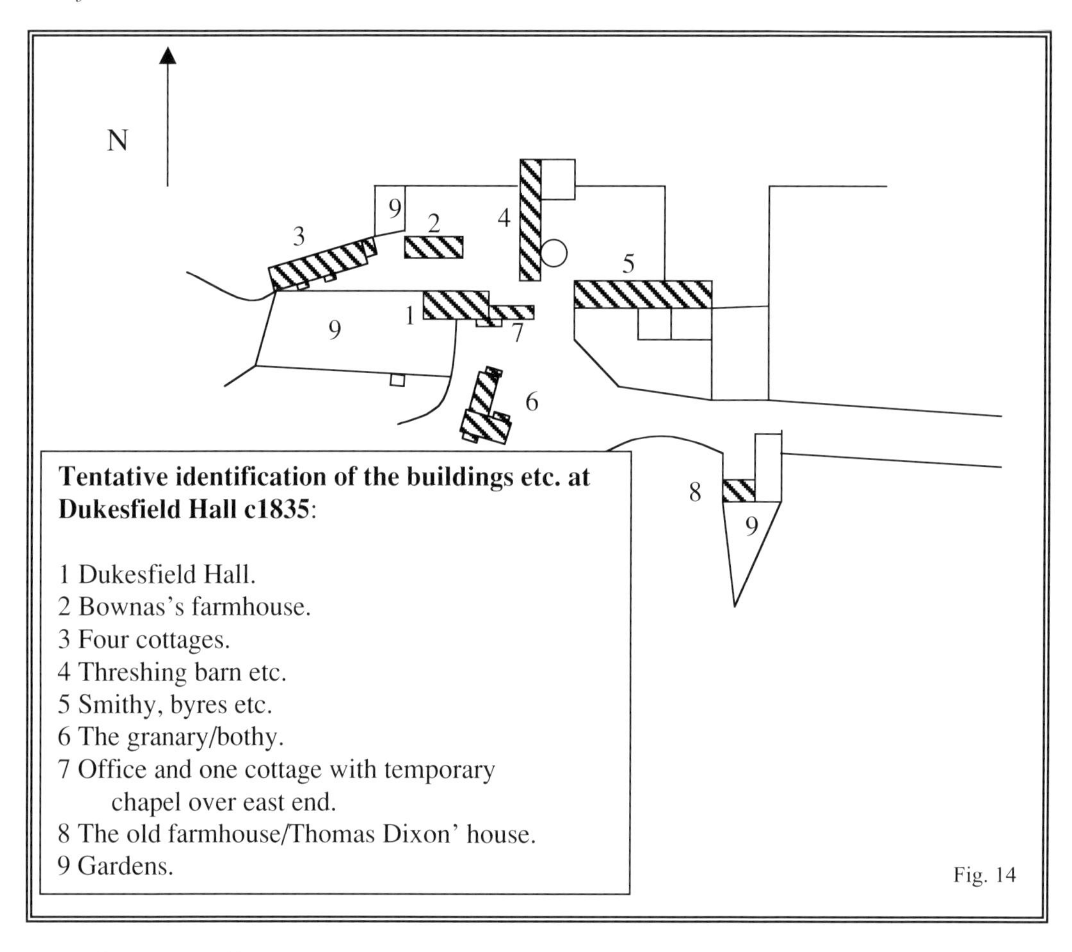

Dukesfield Hall c1835, based on an undated map in the possession of Andrew Swallow of Dukesfield Hall, which is probably a copy of an extract from an estate map.

(See plates 1 - 4 on pages 8 & 9)

The Dixons were clearly literate, and when daughter Elizabeth began to write in November 1836, and then wrote a letter to her grandfather just a year later at the age of 7, Thomas thought these two events worth recording in his diary. Thomas took a weekly newspaper and sometimes recorded items of national and international significance in his diary. It should perhaps be noted that several nineteenth-century visitors to the North Pennine Orefield were impressed by the educational attainments of workers in the lead industry, some suggesting that they were generally better educated, more literate and numerate than, say, the coal miners of County Durham. Indeed, in bargain books as far back as 1720, it is rare to find lead miners who were unable to sign their names, although it was not really until the nineteenth century that school provision was taken seriously by the major lead concerns.

There were no schools other than charity schools in the lead districts before 1800, one such being Slaley School, seemingly erected in the eighteenth century[1] and rebuilt by public subscription in 1849. But the London Lead Company began to provide schools between 1800 and 1840, while a number of Bishop Barrington church schools were built in Weardale. WB Lead then began to provide schools between 1850 and 1860 under the agency of Thomas Sopwith, but these were established in the mining districts and none were built in the Slaley area. There had also been a charity school in Whitley Chapel from the seventeenth century, although its existence thereafter seems not to have been continuous until the early nineteenth century. So if Thomas went to school at all, it would probably have been to one of these two charity schools, and probably that at Whitley Chapel; alternatively he may simply have been taught by his parents at home. When his father became a schoolmaster in 1836 it was probably at Whitley Chapel, for all the available evidence suggest that Milton Carr was schoolmaster at the Slaley school at this time, (and also the architect of the rebuilt Slaley Church), and the Dixon family seem to have had particularly close associations with the established church at Whitley Chapel.

Thomas and Jane made frequent visits to the homes of other family members and friends, who visited them in return, and since they, their parents and several brothers and sisters were all living at Dukesfield, this did not always involve travelling very far. On almost every Sunday they either entertained people to dinner or tea or were themselves entertained by others, especially their parents, often between church or chapel services. A typical Sunday recorded by Thomas in October 1831 reads: 'At Chapel a.m. - Slaley Church afternoon - At Sparks to tea, Jemmy & Liza there - Jane at Fisher's meeting at night'. Whether or not tea was drunk at these teas is a moot point. Thomas did not actually mention drinking tea until February 1833, and in October of that year he noted 'Sparks, Marthas, our folks and Betty Nixons tea drinkings this week', as though the drinking of tea was something of a novelty, and an activity to be performed in good company. It does appear to be the case that the temperance movement had successfully persuaded considerable numbers of people to regard tea as a suitable thirst-quenching substitute for alcoholic drinks by this time, as tea rooms were being opened during the 1830s and tea drinking was becoming increasingly popular.

Ore hearth smelting could be seen as a notoriously unhealthy occupation, especially at smelt mills without horizontal chimneys, and Thomas frequently recorded being 'Sore smoked at the Mill.' It is known that lead poisoning could adversely affect the gums, and Thomas did suffer toothache, but then so did his wife, and who has not. Similarly it may or may not have been the nature of his occupation that made his father 'bad of his chafts'. In reality the

[1] Either in 1729, 1761, or 1780, according to different authors.

Sparke Family Tree

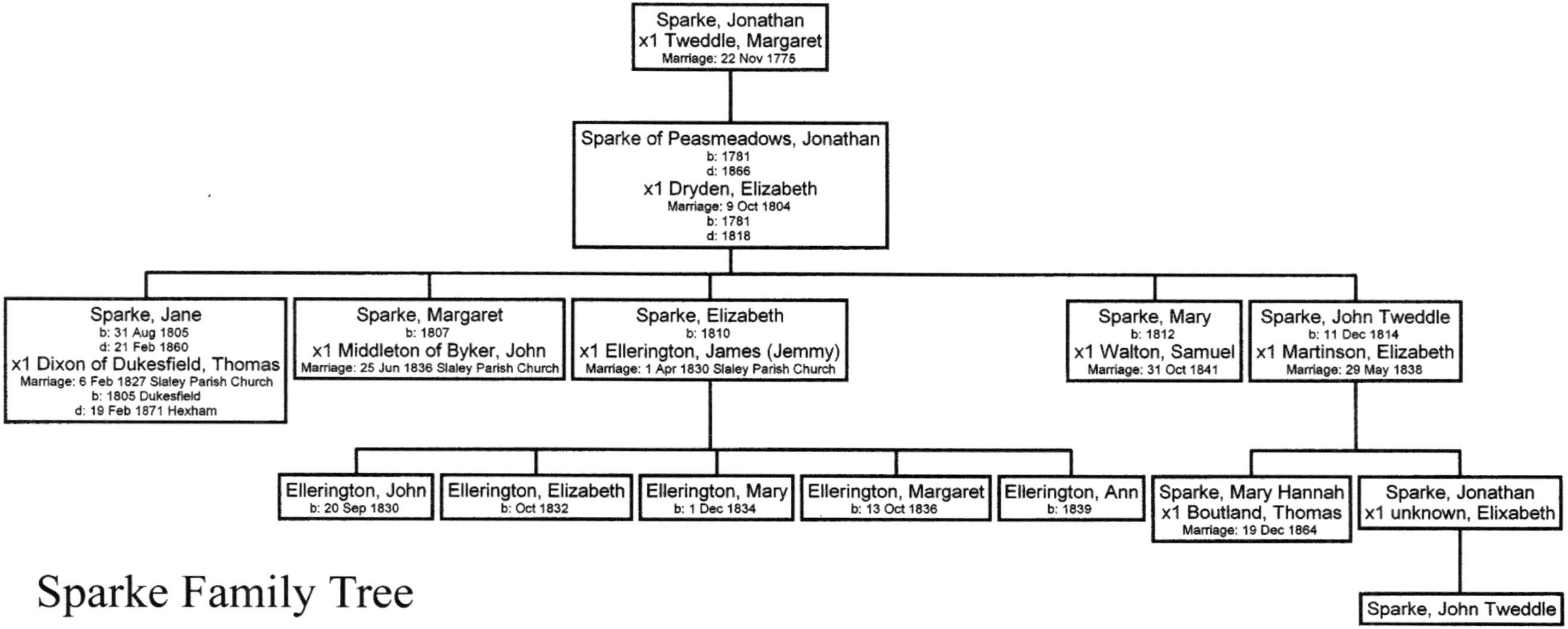

Sparke, Jonathan
x1 Tweddle, Margaret
Marriage: 22 Nov 1775

Sparke of Peasmeadows, Jonathan
b: 1781
d: 1866
x1 Dryden, Elizabeth
Marriage: 9 Oct 1804
b: 1781
d: 1818

Sparke, Jane
b: 31 Aug 1805
d: 21 Feb 1860
x1 Dixon of Dukesfield, Thomas
Marriage: 6 Feb 1827 Slaley Parish Church
b: 1805 Dukesfield
d: 19 Feb 1871 Hexham

Sparke, Margaret
b: 1807
x1 Middleton of Byker, John
Marriage: 25 Jun 1836 Slaley Parish Church

Sparke, Elizabeth
b: 1810
x1 Ellerington, James (Jemmy)
Marriage: 1 Apr 1830 Slaley Parish Church

Ellerington, John
b: 20 Sep 1830

Ellerington, Elizabeth
b: Oct 1832

Ellerington, Mary
b: 1 Dec 1834

Ellerington, Margaret
b: 13 Oct 1836

Ellerington, Ann
b: 1839

Sparke, Mary
b: 1812
x1 Walton, Samuel
Marriage: 31 Oct 1841

Sparke, John Tweddle
b: 11 Dec 1814
x1 Martinson, Elizabeth
Marriage: 29 May 1838

Sparke, Mary Hannah
x1 Boutland, Thomas
Marriage: 19 Dec 1864

Sparke, Jonathan
x1 unknown, Elixabeth

Sparke, John Tweddle

Fig. 15

health dangers in smelting have probably been exaggerated. It was clearly a healthier occupation than lead mining, especially given the smelting shift patterns and the outdoor life which they allowed, and both occupations were infinitely safer than coal mining or deep sea fishing. A witness to the 1842 Commission observed that two men working at his smelt mill were upwards of 80 years old, and if this seems unlikely, the 1841 census confirms his testimony.[1]

In fact there was only one occasion in the period of Thomas's diaries when a potentially serious illness struck his family, but that was quite unrelated to the nature of his employment. While cholera raged all around, Thomas, Jane and brother Joe all went down with small pox in the last days of 1832 and the first weeks of 1833. A Dr Jefferson attended them, probably bleeding each in turn, and it was to be almost a month before Thomas felt able to return to work, other smelters having deputised for him during his absence. There had clearly been a serious outbreak of smallpox in the area and at least one person died from it, Joseph Proud on 11 February 1833. There seems to have been another out break later in the year when several people, including John Adamson of Whitley Mill died.

Farming and gardening.

Thomas already had a kitchen garden when he began to keep his diary, growing vegetables alongside gooseberry bushes and apple trees, and his gardening year, which was quite traditional, can be followed from his diary entries for 1830. Peas were sown in February and were trained up pea sticks from late April. Onions were sown in March and lifted in September. Potatoes were set between late March and late April, and lifted in October and November. Spring cabbage was sown at mid August, transplanted in September and harvested from the following May. He also found time during 1830 garden for W Dixon of Juniper, and to prune W^{m}. Hall's bushes.

Thomas's 1831 gardening year was dominated by moving into Teasdale's old farmhouse, but the flit was eased somewhat by his taking over Teasdales' garden some 3 weeks before the move. This enabled some bushes to be removed from the old garden, and cabbages, potatoes, onions and carrots to be set away in the new garden before they moved house. As already noted, Thomas had 'begun making a new garden' soon after moving, with new walls built by stonemasons, the ground thereby enclosed having to be levelled. It seems that he continued to garden Teasdale's old plot while the new one was being created, cropping his potatoes and pulling berries to be preserved. The new garden was sufficiently advanced by November 1831 for Thomas to stock it with bushes, trees, and plants bought at Hexham. Again Thomas found time to do some gardening for others, in sowing onion seed for his father, some unspecified gardening for William Burdus, a farmer at Middle Dukesfield, and in dressing W^{m}. Ridleys bushes. Some gardening details recorded by Thomas, especially those relating to potatoes, suggest that he was keeping a an aide memoir:

---

[1] It should be noted here and elsewhere, that people aged under 15 years were given their correct age in the 1841 census, whereas ages of those over 15 were rounded down to the nearest five or ten. For example someone aged 48 was recorded as being 45, and someone aged 44 was recorded as being 40.

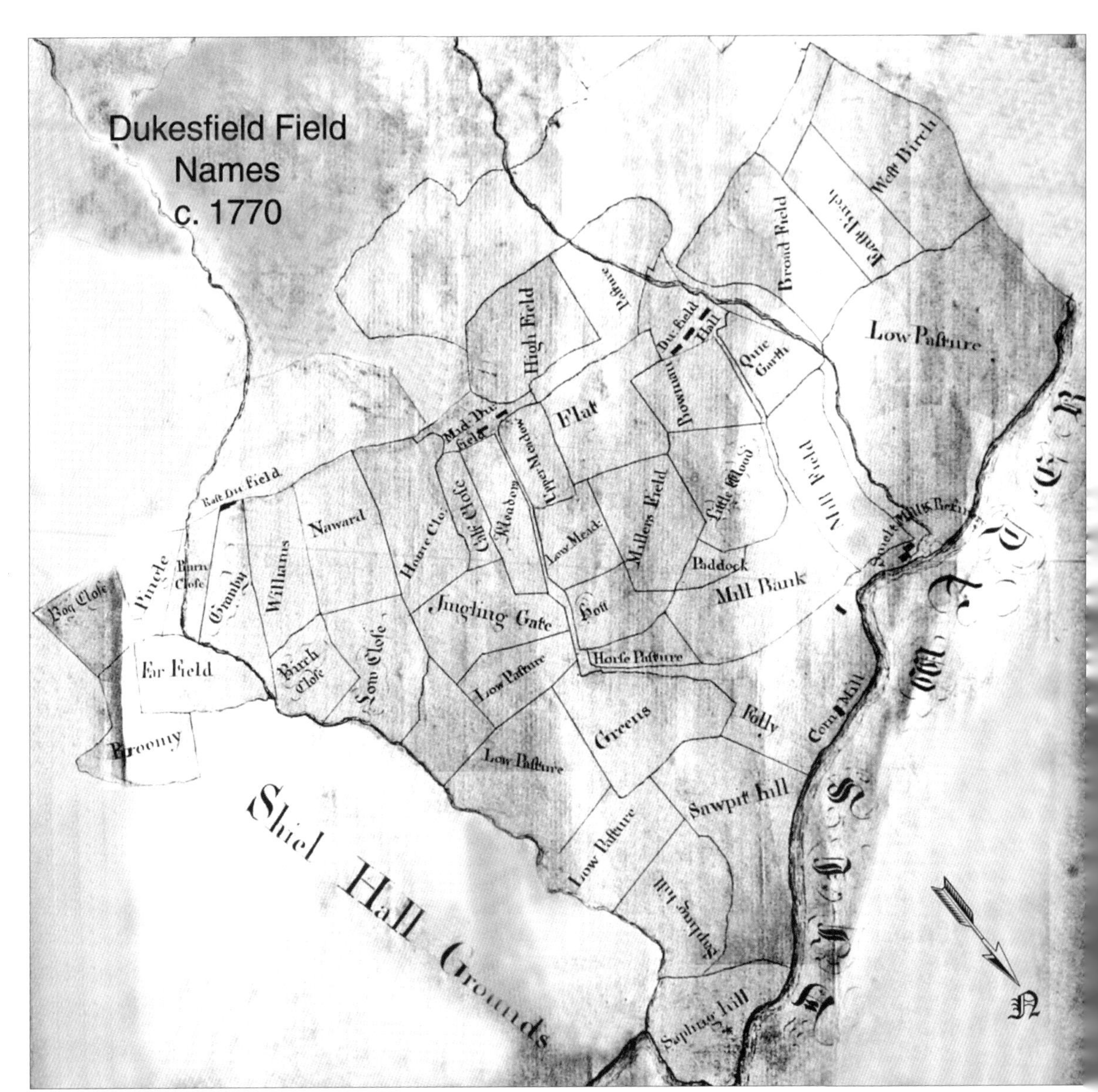
Dukesfield Field Names c. 1770
West Birch
Broad Field
Low Pasture
High Field
Flat
Upper Meadow
Cliff Close
Meadow
Low Mead
Millers Field
Little Wood
Mill Field
Paddock
Mill Bank
Naward
Williams
Granby
Pingle
Barn Close
Bog Close
Far Field
Broomy
Birch Close
Low Close
Jingling Gate
Low Pasture
Horse Pasture
Greens
Folly
Corn Mill
Low Pasture
Sawpit hill
Low Pasture
Shiel Hall Grounds
N

Plate. 66

'19 April 1830: Setting 'tatoes at night - last row of reds, small sets, last row of white large sets'.

The widespread belief, still held by many allotment holders, that it is best to set potatoes during a full moon, is clearly no recent 'organic' fad, although while many of today's vegetable gardeners still aim to set their potatoes on Good Friday, few if any now do it by the light of the moon.[1] Another potato entry is more perplexing, but perhaps Thomas was sowing some potatoes below ground level and some in ridges, as a comparative experiment:

5 April 1831, Setting tatoes at night - 7 rows, 1st below, 2nd above, 3 next below, 2 last above.

A little more development work was needed to finish off the new garden, seemingly located to the rear of the house, the garden doorway being flagged and a garden seat provided in January 1832. Then, in June 1832, Thomas was 'making a garden beside the parlour', presumably at the front of the house, where he planted some rhubarb, an apple tree and some bushes in the following year, and. Rather late in the day some would say, he led some wood for a shed, but this shed may not have been for the garden.

During 1833, shortly after Thomas had recovered from the pox, some negotiations involving his brother-in-law Jemmy Ellerington at Middle Dukesfield and possibly Mr Nixon the Beaumont land agent, resulted in Thomas taking over a piece of land at Middle Dukesfield which was much larger than his garden:

22 April 1833, Parting the field at Middle Dukesfield.
25 April 1833, Mr Nixon here seeing about the ground.
26 April 1833, Measuring the field at night.
29 April 1833, Got settled with Jemmy about the field.

Subsequent diary entries make it clear that Thomas had now added smallholding to his portfolio, his shift pattern, together with help from family and friends, making it possible to carry out small-scale farming alongside his job at the smelt mill. This was in no way unusual, for his father and father-in law did likewise, and Thomas had frequently helped both of them at harvest and other times. Thomas and Jane even undertook some paid farm work in September 1831, receiving 3s. wages for shearing (reaping), and also for 'sheafing corn by the acre', in both cases for a Jack Scott who has not been further identified. Furthermore, they had previously kept a pig for slaughtering, butchering and salting, as most country people did, but now that Thomas had his own patch of land, of unknown acreage, he immediately set about buying a cow, and build a new wooden cowshed (not a garden shed) in June 1833. In fact he had begun searching for a suitable cow some weeks earlier, buying one at Hexham on the day after the field at Middle Dukesfield had been 'parted' in April, and collecting it early in May. This cow calved on 28 May, and Thomas and Jane were now in the business of milking, butter making and the periodic bulling of their cow; Thomas bought some 'milk vessels' at Hexham just 7 days before the calving, and later a barrel churn. They may not always have met with success in this venture, as the subsequent events in 1833-34 seem to illustrate.

Having unsuccessfully put their cow to several bulls between June and August, they had her bled, but then attempted to sell her at Hexham market in November, also perhaps without

---

[1] The custom persists in parts of the USA, perhaps having been taken there by immigrants from north east England.

success but with better luck at Stagshaw Fair in May 1834; Jane bought their next cow in June of that year and by 1835 they had two or three cows at least. Thomas and Jane seem not to have slaughtered any of their cows, unlike their parents who perhaps kept several, and sometimes sought Thomas' assistance in their killing and butchering. Thomas was soon to keep more than one pig, and had a refurbished or new slate-roofed house built for them in July. Their pigs were usually bought around May and June and slaughtered in November. Sometimes Thomas did the killing and butchering, but others did it for him on some occasions, in particular 'Old Tommy Dixon' and a man named Mather who may also have been a lead smelter. Thomas and Jane also kept at least one dog, which produced a litter more readily than some of their cows - '13 November 1830 - Magic puped a week last Thursday' - and they acquired a cat in March 1833.

The farm or field which Thomas had acquired at Middle Dukesfield required some development work when he took it over, and his diaries suggest that he may have subdivided it into three or four smaller enclosures. Certainly much dykeing, railing and quickset hedging took place between May 1833 and March 1834. Thomas even erected a sawpit for the sawing of rails and may have constructed some hurdle fences, for he noted in June 1833 that he had been 'Winding the rails with rice', the latter word meaning brushwood.

1834 was Thomas's first full year of farming his fields, some of which in effect replicated his vegetable garden, for he set cabbages and potatoes 'in the field'. But he also had lime ploughed into part of his land by a neighbour, [1] and then sowed clover and hay seeds for the all-important hay crop. After years of helping out with other people's harvests, he would now have one of his own, and in August he was shearing his own grass and mowing and making his own hay, while his father helped him with his hay stack. This did not of course mean that he was unavailable to help others with the age-old co-operative endeavour of harvesting, for all who could, including other workers at the smelt mill, seemed to join in; even the school for which his father was later to be master seems to have closed for 2 weeks at harvest time. So Thomas and Jane reciprocated in kind for any help which they received, Jane frequently participating in farming and other non-domestic activities, from stacking peats to shearing oats (once alongside Thomas' mother). These gardening and farming activities, and others yet to be described, all had to be interwoven between Thomas's shifts at the mill, and his enthusiasm for recording the local weather no doubt reflects its importance to horticulture and smelting.

Manure collection was important to both smallholding and garden, and much time seems to have been spent filling, leading, spreading and 'brushing' manure onto Thomas's plots, as well as those run by his father, mainly in February and March. The movement and manipulation of 'soil' was also a significant task, usually carried out in autumn and winter, when Thomas might be filling, turning, wheeling, leading, speading, spreading, casting, or finishing soil. It is possible is that these activities all refer to disposal of night-soil by putting it to good agricultural and horticultural use. On one occasion, however, Thomas was 'Casting up soil in the lane', which could mean that he was clearing excessive mud and earth from a road.

Even before they had their smallholding Thomas and Jane were regular attendees at agricultural hirings, fairs and markets, at Hexham and Stagshaw for example, while some members of the family attended fairs at Blanchland, Allendale, Haltwhistle and Durham.

---

[1] There are no indications that Thomas ever possessed either a draught or a riding horse, although his father-in-law owned one or more, and some if not most of the larger farmers had them.

They also went to local 'sales' – perhaps farmstock sales, or selling up sales; Jane got a second-hand feather bed at one such sale. Many of these places were fairly easily accessible by foot and, as Thomas does not appear to have owned a horse, we can assume that he normally travelled by foot before the opening of the Newcastle & Carlisle Railway. When he and his brother Joe travelled the 16 miles or so to the Haltwhistle cattle fair on a Saturday in May 1832, they might have started by walking to Hexham, and then catching the coach to Haltwhistle, but that would have been an uncommon event, and Thomas would surely have recorded it; after visiting Featherstone Castle on the following day and then attending the fair on the next, they returned home via a Tuesday Hexham hiring before Thomas went to smelting work that night. Thomas' mother might also have walked there and back when she visited Haltwhistle in July 1831, but we can probably assume that when she spent a week at Tynemouth in August 1833, she travelled by public coach between Hexham and Newcastle and then by one of the numerous public coaches and gigs which plied the Newcastle to Tynemouth road. The Newcastle & Carlisle Railway along the Tyne valley was to radically alter the family's mode of travel, and to reduce the time that they spent undertaking it.

The Dixons' religious life.

Thomas and Jane frequently joined the congregations at the St Helen's church Whitley Chapel, just over 1 mile from Dukesfield, and at St Mary the Virgin at Slaley at just under 2 miles, and both were, of course, baptised, married and buried at Anglican churches. Curiously one of these churches was extensively modified, and the other completely rebuilt, during the period covered by the diaries. Thomas's parents were clearly Anglican, and Jane's father was probably the same, and the reason that none of the parents were regularly noted in the diaries as going to church can probably be explained by it being too regular an occurrence for Thomas to record; he did however note that his parents had entertained 'Armstrong the Priest' of Slaley Church to tea on at least one occasion and Mr Nanney, the incumbent of Whitley Chapel, at other times.

But Thomas and Jane's attendances at religious services, meetings and events organised by both Wesleyan and Primitive Methodist societies were much more frequent than at Anglican services; neither of their parents appear to have attended Methodist meetings. It should be noted that Thomas almost invariably used 'Chapel' or 'the chapel' in his diaries, to mean St Helen's Church at Whitley Chapel, and the word 'church' to mean the parish church at Slaley; only on one occasion, on Christmas Day 1841, might 'the Chapel' refer to a Methodist meeting. It can probably be fairly assumed that the 'meetings' which he and/or Jane attended were gatherings of Methodists, and it is sometimes possible to distinguish between Wesleyan and Primitive Methodist meetings where information on the preachers can be obtained from other sources or, more obviously, when Thomas uses the word 'Ranters' to mean Primitive Methodists.

The period covered by the diaries witnessed considerable Methodist expansion in the lead dales, and no-one with religious sympathies could fail to be unaware of this development. In particular, the Primitive Methodist break-away from the Wesleyans was catalysing change as the 'Ranters' attracted increasing numbers of adherents, especially from the working classes. The holding of open-air 'Camp Meetings' was the great mode of worship and conversion for the Ranters, and indeed was the main cause of their final separation from the Wesleyans. Camp Meetings often lasted all day, and were attended by visiting preachers and adherents, their assembly no doubt augmented by the curious. One such Camp Meeting was held in June 1832 in the 'Brick Kiln Field' which lay just a few hundred yards north of

Dukesfield Hall, and although Thomas may not have been present, the Primitive Methodist preacher Ralph Ramsay, has left us his account:[1]

> *June 3 1832, Attended a Camp meeting in Hexhamshire, the weather was fine, many attended, there was great liberty in speaking, and in one praying company the power of God came down upon us, some were brought to the ground, and others shook like leaves before the wind.*

Ramsay probably began his ministry in the Hexham circuit of the Primitive Methodists and he was to move on to the Carlisle circuit in 1833, but his 1832 *Journal* provides a graphic, (if not purple), description of early Primitive Methodism in the Hexham area; Thomas was to hear him preach 'at the Ranters' on 24 March 1833, just before he left for the Carlisle circuit. At one Camp Meeting which Thomas and Jane did attend, held at 'Lawslaw' on 5 June 1831, they suffered what must have been a common fate at such meetings - 'got ourselves very wet.'[2] More Camp Meetings were to be held in the Brick Kiln field in subsequent years, and Thomas certainly attended that of 1836.

The first Methodist chapel in the area appears to have been that built by the Wesleyans at Finechambers in c1786; by 1820 the Finechambers society had 28 members. The Wesleyans had also commenced societies (not necessarily with purpose-built chapels) at Slaley and Shirehead by 1810, Dukesfield by 1826, and Mollersteads by 1833, while the Primitive Methodists had societies at Slaley, later called 'Broad Pool', and at Dyehouse by 1832. The Slaley Wesleyans may have operated without a purpose-built chapel until 1842 when one was built at the west end of the village, capable of seating 150 people, a number which suggests either a considerable degree of optimism or, and this seems unlikely, that their congregation might have far exceeded their membership. All of these societies were based within 2 miles of Dukesfield, but not all were particularly buoyant in the 1830s. The membership figures for the Slaley Primitives fluctuated between 6 and 12, the Slaley Wesleyans between 14 and 23, while the Finechambers Wesleyans remained fairly steady at around 22 members.[3] Overall, the aggregate listed membership of the societies in the Dukesfield area varied between 40 and 100 during the 1830s. Straightforward membership numbers, however, are a less than precise guide to attendances at meetings. For example, neither Thomas nor Jane Dixon were registered members of any Methodist society at the time, unlike many of their friends, neighbours and colleagues. There may have been a simple reason for this – their wish to be more ecumenical than membership of any particular society would allow. A Minute of the local preachers meeting for the Hexham Wesleyan Methodist Circuit of June 1836 noted that Bro Wm Smith of Hexham had been found guilty of leaving the society, joining the Ranters, then coming back again 'without any proper understanding', and that his case would be considered at the next preachers meeting. The present writer's great grandfather was stuck off the roll of his local Independent Methodist Society in Monkwearmouth in 1884, for attending meetings of the Salvation Army!

---

[1] Ramsay, Ralph, 'Journal of Ralph Ramsay, 1832', *Primitive Methodist Magazine,* (1834) 191-194. The religious affiliations of some preachers heard by Thomas are given in an appendix, plus any known biographical details.

[2] Camp Meetings were still being held in the north in the 1990s, but one at Newbiggin on Lune in July 1993 was moved indoors on account of the 'cold showery weather', *Cumberland & Westmorland Herald*, (17 July 1993.)

[3] These figures do not include 'members on trial' nor the 'fallen'.

The Dukesfield Wesleyan Society may have been newly formed in 1826, with 18 members in the first class and 8 members in the second class,[1] but a comparison of the members of Finechambers between 1819 and 1823, with those of the Dukesfield Society in 1826, suggests that many former members of the Finechambers society had been embraced by the Dukesfield Society; it seems likely that the Finechambers society had temporarily relocated, perhaps because their chapel was undergoing rebuilding work. The latter possibility is lent credibility by the fact that the two societies appear to have re-grouped by 1828. One person who moved from Finechambers to Dukesfield and back again was Thomas's uncle John Bulman, a Finechambers class leader after 1828. The Dukesfield and Finechambers societies then merged in 1831, and the Dukesfield society ceased to exist as such. One Dukesfield member, Mary Bell of Middle Dukesfield, seems to have switched allegiances at this time and soon became a prominent member of the Dyehouse Primitive Methodists. Her death in June 1860, at the age of 91 years, merited an obituary in the *Primitive Methodist Magazine* of 1861.

Thomas and Jane attended, together or separately, about 38 religious meetings of one sort or another during 1830, but it is not always possible to identify which particular religious body they attended, as a glance at some typical diary entries indicates:[2]

> *Saturday 3 July 1830, At old Hannah's meeting hearing John Bell exhort.*
> *Saturday 7 August 1830, John Hunters here preaching.*
> *Sunday 29 August 1830, At Airdley Meeting at night.*
> *Sunday 26 September 1830, At Chapel - Fishers meeting at night.*

Almost one-half of the services attended in 1830, excluding funerals, baptisms and weddings, can however be clearly identified as Wesleyan Methodist meetings, probably held at the Dukesfield meeting place where preachers came on alternate Sunday mornings. Two preachers shared this function up to late July 1830, each one carrying out one service per month. They were Robert Leake who came to the Hexham Circuit in 1830 and left for Aberdeen during the following year, and P Hardcastle Junr who had come to the circuit during 1829, leaving for Penrith during 1830. Such ministers were known as 'Travelling Preachers', people who were attached to a particular circuit for one or more years but usually less than three, before being moved on to another circuit. While attached to a circuit they were expected to 'travel' to preach to the various societies within the circuit according to a circuit plan and, as John Wesley himself advised, it was better to break a leg than to miss your appointment. These preachers were wholly devoted to ministerial and pastoral duties, and were paid a modest stipend for their troubles by the governing society. 'Local Preachers', on the other hand, lived and worked in whatever was their everyday profession in their home locality, and did not receive a stipend. The fortnightly pattern was interrupted with Hardcastle's departure, and several local preachers such as Watson Forster and Nevison Lorraine filled in. No attendances at Primitive Methodist meetings were recorded as such during the year, and although 12 meetings remain unidentified, it seems likely that the majority of these were Wesleyan. Thomas attended a weekday religious gathering on only one occasion in 1830, being present at 'Old Hannah's Meeting hearing John Bell exhort'. This may have been a 'house meeting', as may the 'Fishers' meetings (26 September 1830 and 23 October 1831) and it may be more than coincidence that Thomas heard a Mr Fisher at two midweek meetings in or near Blaydon in 1841. It is worth noting

[1] The existence of two classes, each with its own leader, was not uncommon when the membership size warranted it.

[2] While the words 'meeting' and 'preaching' in the extracts given are usually associated with the Methodists, that assumption has not been used the summary attendances which follow.

that religious observance could easily be combined with pleasure, as on the Carlin Sundays of 1830 and 1831, when Thomas went to a meeting before moving on to the *Travellers' Rest*, the public house just outside Slaley. Thomas and Jane's attendances at the Anglican churches were relatively infrequent in 1830, only three at Slaley and six at Whitley Chapel.

Their attendance record for 1831 was similar to that of 1830, but demonstrates a much busier religious year, with some seventy-one gatherings attended, including twelve at Slaley church and thirteen at Whitley church, mostly on Sunday mornings when no Methodist meetings were being held; 'singings' held at the churches, of which more later, confuse the picture somewhat, but it can probably be safely asserted that these were religious in tenor. Again attendance at Wesleyan Methodist gatherings predominate, with some twenty-one identifiable meetings at which Thomas or Jane or both were present. The fortnightly meetings of the Wesleyan Methodists continued much as before, probably at Slaley and Dukesfield until the latter society merged with Finechambers, the preachers being Leake and Wright. Leake preached for the last time on Saturday evening 6 August only 2 weeks after presiding at a Love Feast at the 'meeting house'. Wright and Leake were replaced by Samuel Thompson who had first joined the Hexham Circuit in 1824, and 'old' William Norther who had preached in seventeen different circuits before arriving in Hexham. Other, presumably local, preachers were named in the diary, normally for Sunday afternoon and evening meetings. In addition, Thomas noted six Saturday night meetings, mainly held at Dyehouse, two of which had been presided over by the Wesleyan Methodist preacher Robert Leake. Thomas's references to Dyehouse meetings do not necessarily, therefore, imply gatherings of Primitive Methodists, for the Finechambers Wesleyan chapel was, geographically, at Dyehouse, and the Dyehouse Primitive Methodist society may not have come into organised being with a purpose-built chapel until 1832. However, it is the case that Thomas attended four Primitive Methodist meetings during the year, hearing the preachers Bill Adamson and James Bilston for example, and Jane and he attended a Camp Meeting at Lawslaw. Jane also attended four or five religious services without Thomas, one of these being a 'Fisher's meeting'. Music and singing were also recorded for the first time during 1831, when Thomas noted that the 'Methodists [were] here at night singing' in March, and also that he was 'Playing the violin Cello for the first time at the meeting house' in July; likewise he noted 'Chapel afternoon with my fiddle'.

These patterns of varied but regular religious observance continued while Thomas worked at the Dukesfield smelt mill, but two events of some consequence occurred in 1832. Firstly, Thomas and Jane attended the formal opening of a new Primitive Methodist chapel on 27 May 1832, where they heard 'a woman preach'; the Primitives, unlike the Wesleyans, employed women ministers from their very beginning. Thomas frequently noted the name of the preacher at the numerous religious services which he attended, but he failed to name this woman preacher at the Ranters' Chapel. However, it was almost certainly someone already active in the north of England as a paid Primitive Methodist minister, and the obvious candidate is Mary Porteous, who was born in Newcastle upon Tyne in 1783, moved from the Presbyterians to the Wesleyans to the Primitives, and became a travelling preacher for the latter body in 1825. It is known that Mary was attached to the Carlisle circuit in the period 1830-31, and to Hexham in 1833-35, but she may well have visited Dyehouse for this important occasion; she is neither directly nor indirectly referred to again in Thomas's diaries, even though she must often have preached in the area. This 'Ranters' Chapel' was almost certainly that at Dyehouse, although the date usually given for the first Primitive Methodist chapel there, and the date on a tablet of the present chapel building, is 1830, perhaps in error.[1] Be that as it may, the Dyehouse Primitive Methodist society became one of the most successful in the immediate district, with some 42 members in 1832, (evenly divided between men and women), falling to around 26 in 1833-35, but rising again to around 70 in the mid 1840s, one of the highest memberships in the Hexham circuit at that time.

Thomas, perhaps with Jane, both ecumenical as ever, also attended the opening of the rebuilt Slaley Parish Church just 6 months after the opening of the Ranters' Chapel. Thomas had attended a Slaley church service on 11 March 1832, but the church must have been demolished soon after, for he witnessed the foundations of the new church being laid on 25 May. Thomas and Jane may have contributed to its rebuilding fund, ('15 January 1831, Persons seeking money for the church'), and they certainly took an interest in the progress of the work of rebuilding. The church was 'up to the base' by 2 June, the bells were hung on 15 September, and Thomas probably attended a service there on 7 October, hearing the Rev R Heslop, the first vicar after the 1832 rebuild. The 'Slaley school house' may have fulfilled some of the former functions of the church while it was being rebuilt, for Thomas recorded three Sunday attendances there between May and October of 1832.

The restructuring of St Helen's at Whitley Chapel is less well documented, the only details emerging from a locally produced poem, *The Lamentations of Whitley Chapel, in Hexhamshire, in 1836*, which was printed in May 1836 when the work was ongoing. Its lines give the impression that the church was re-roofed in blue slate instead of grey as formerly, and that the pews were repaired, but also that there had been:

> *Such cutting and carving, as they have upon me,*
> *As I'm not deserving, they've nearly undone me;*

The Dixons would also have followed this development with particular interest, although as Thomas was working in Blaydon at the time, he was only an infrequent observer. In fact, Thomas only recorded 10 attendances at Whitley Chapel between 1832 and the start of 1836. But he was to make 9 attendances in the second half of 1836, and 12 in 1837, even though he was based in Blaydon. The reason for this renewed interest in St Helen's can probably be attributed to the simple fact that, just before its reopening on 5 June 1836, his father had been 'elected clerk at the Chapel'. It comes as no surprise, however, that his enthusiasm for a wider range of religious experiences than those offered by the Anglican church remained undiminished, and Thomas was 'At the Camp meeting in Brick Kiln field' within 8 weeks of his father's election. All in all while he remained at Dukesfield, Thomas spent most Sundays in attending religious meetings and enjoying dinner and tea with friends or relations, often going to church, either at Slaley or Whitley Chapel, and also one or two Methodist meetings, a sequence which, in part, remained common in some rural areas until quite recently, and whose origins go back to the early days of Methodism.

It had never been John Wesley's intention that his Methodist Societies would operate outwith the established church. He insisted that members of his Societies should receive the sacraments at the local parish church wherever possible, and that Society meetings should take place at times on Sundays which would not clash with local church services. However, as the number and size of the Societies grew, it became impossible to meet in private houses and the like, and some Societies built 'Meeting Houses' for their own devotional use. Ultimately this led to the split between the established church and the Methodists, so that the

[1] There are examples elsewhere of chapels carrying the date of the formation of the Society rather than that of the building of the chapel, for example at Newbottle in County Durham.

Methodist Church came into being in 1787 with about 80,000 adherents. Soon after this historic event a Methodist Conference allowed its Society's services to be held at the same time as a nearby Anglican Church, but only:

> *... where the minister was notoriously wicked or heretical, where there were not enough churches to contain half the population, or where there was no church within two miles.*

Even so, many Methodist Societies continued to contrive, in their circuit plans, to avoid clashes with the service times of the nearest accessible Anglican church, and evidently some elements of this practice were maintained in the Dukesfield area in the 1830s, but with two Anglican churches and five Methodist societies within a 2 mile radius of Dukesfield, it was clearly impossible to accommodate everyone. Moreover, it seems unlikely that the Dyehouse Primitives would particularly attempt to steer clear of Wesleyan meeting times. Although the absence of circuit plans for that period make it impossible to be certain about the detailed arrangements,[1] Thomas's diaries certainly suggest that attempts to avoid service overlaps were successful, so that he and Jane could attend two or three services on many Sundays:

Sunday 13 February 1831, Jane at church a.m. - At Meeting house at afternoon & Dyehouse at night, myself.
Sunday 8 September 1833, At Slaley Church a.m. Jane and I at meeting hearing Brown.
Sunday 18 September 1831, Hearing Thompson a.m. - Jane & I [at] Slaley church at afternoon - Jane and I at Dye-house at night.
Sunday 23 October 1831, At Chapel a.m. - Slaley Church afternoon - Jane at Fisher's meeting at night.

About once every year Thomas and Jane attended a Love Feast where, by eating of the same bread and drinking water out of the same two-handled 'Loving cup', every participant would be spiritually united. The Love Feast was a feature of early Methodist religious meetings and, like the Camp Meeting, a product of Methodist revivalism. Of the nine Love Feasts mentioned by Thomas, five can be identified as Wesleyan, but they were also a part of the Primitive Methodist preachers' plan. One such plan for the Hexham circuit instructed that only 'Plain Unspiced Bread and Unfermented Wine' were to be used for Love Feasts and Sacraments, but there could be much more to a Love Feasts than that. Ralph Ramsay described a Love Feast held at Slaley in 1832, but not one attended by Thomas Dixon:[2]

> *April 5, Led a lovefeast at Slaley; a powerful time in speaking, many were filled with the glory of the Lord till they sunk to the floor. A shout was heard for mercy; two received pardon of sin, one was cleansed from all sin.*

In spite of what might now appear to be a potentially frightening experience for a child, Thomas and Jane were clearly keen that their children should embrace Methodism at an early age. Their daughter Elizabeth accompanied her parents to her first Wesleyan meeting in January 1832, when aged about 3 years, and to a Love Feast held later in the year; her younger sister, Jane, was attending Methodist meetings with her parents by February 1838, aged nearly 5 years.

---

[1] The walls of Mary Bell's cottage at Middle Dukesfield were said, in her obituary, to be 'covered with preachers' plans some of them twenty-five years old'.
[2] Ramsay, Ralph, 'Journal of Ralph Ramsay, 1832', *Primitive Methodist Magazine,* (1834) 191-194.

Weddings, christenings and funerals were often held on Sundays, and the Dixons frequently attended such events; visiting the sick appears to have been another common Sunday observance. So most Sundays were busy days for the Dixons, but did not include anything which passed as 'work'. With minor exceptions Thomas never worked on Sundays while based at Dukesfield, although he occasionally began work at the smelt mill at midnight on a Sunday. The only exceptions were an occasion when he cut some cabbages, perhaps for Sunday dinner, and another when his cow was bulled, although he may not have personally witnessed that particular event.

Singing and music.

Thomas first mentioned a 'singing school' in March 1830, noting that Robert Smith, perhaps a 'singing master' although there was also a local preacher of that name, had begun such a school somewhere in the Slaley area. Singing masters were usually itinerant teachers of singing who charged those who wished to learn, supplied sheet music and organised the choir practices, the intention being that the choir should subsequently perform at public events. No female members of the singing schools are ever recorded by Thomas, so it may be that these schools were aimed at developing male voice choirs. Hymn singing was just becoming popular at this time, and Thomas probably saw his membership of a singing school simply as an adjunct to his religious life.

But it was in the following year, 1831, that Thomas really became enthusiastic about singing and listening to singing, making some twenty-four references to the one or the other - 'Methodists here at night singing'; 'At Slaley singing school'; 'At uncle John's at night singing'; 'Armstrong begun a singing school at Chapel last night'; and so on. There is little information on the nature of the songs or hymns sung, except for the occasion when the choir sang the *Jubilate*. Thomas's interest in singing continued into 1832, and when Armstrong the singing master ended his school at Whitley Chapel in late January that year, Thomas seems to have taken over his role at the school, writing out tunes for the scholars for example. His readiness to take over the school may have been reinforced by discussions held on the occasions when he and Jane had hosted Armstrong to dinner and tea, 'stoping all night' on one occasion. That school ended in April, and was followed by many public performances, presumably both at Methodist meeting houses in the Slaley area and at the two churches; on two occasions an evening of singing ended at the *Travellers Rest*. There were fewer references to singings in 1833 and 1834, and none at all in the following 2 years. It is possible that this activity simply went on unrecorded by Thomas because, as will be seen, he was certainly to enjoy singing after his move to Blaydon.

As already indicated, Thomas was himself a musician, playing the bass fiddle and the 'violon cello'; he also owned, and possibly played, a clarinet. He must often have played and practised for his own amusement, but he also occasionally played at the 'meeting house' and at Slaley Church, but not, it would seem, at the singing schools. He was not unusual amongst his peers in his interest in performing and listening to music,[1] for his brothers Joe and Peter also had 'fiddles', while his cousin Hugh Armstrong had a violin, and amongst his friends and work colleagues, some had fiddles, bass fiddles, violins, a piano and a dulcimer, (which Thomas tuned).

---

[1] In 1837 Thomas went to Hexham Abbey to see what was still a fairly rare church provision - a recently installed church organ.

Jane is frequently described as going "twilting" – quilting. Plate. 67

"With a common occupational and economic base in lead-mining, communities were close, a network of interwoven family relationships with shared experience and social activity. And what sort of "twilts" were Jane Dixon, her family and friends making? Were they making Framed quilts or stitching the beautiful white Wholecloths of intricate design and pattern? We may simply never know". Dorothy Osler, *North Country Quilts*

Above – Detail from a wedding quilt, c.1825.

Below – Detail from an "Irish chain" quilt, c.1860.

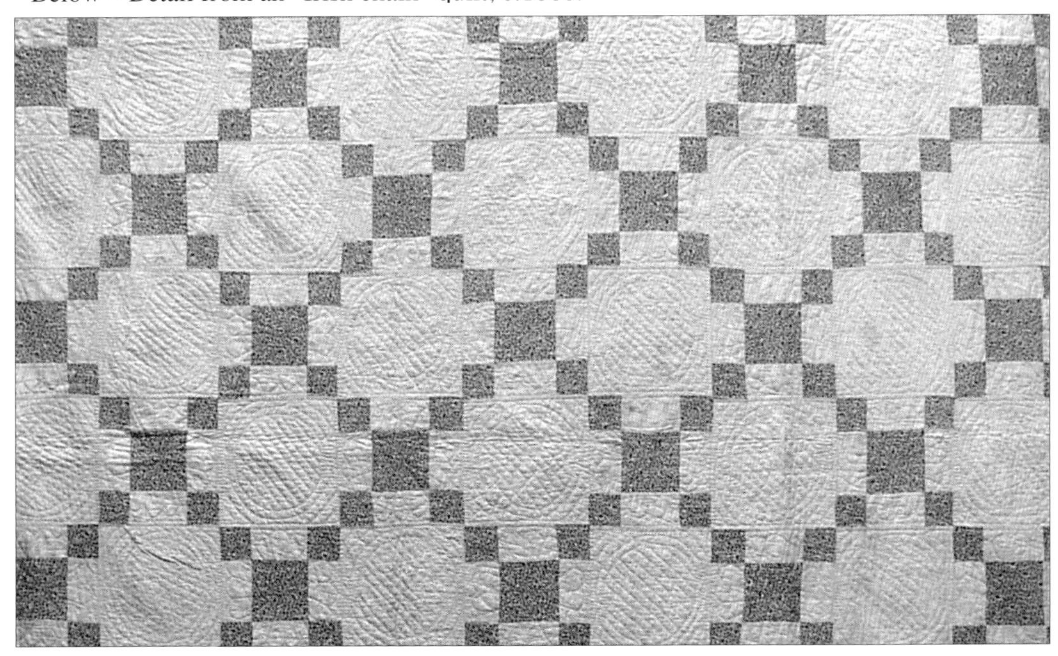

Plate. 68

Social and other events.

The social year around Dukesfield was punctuated by a variety of regular events, something once quite common in rural areas, and the Dixons seem to have made the most of them. They went to 'Lamb Feasts' in August, and to 'Club feasts' and 'Goose feasts' at Christmas time, as well as to dances and parties, when Thomas occasionally provided the music, perhaps along with others. They also went to 'Churns', harvest suppers where Thomas would sometimes play his fiddle while others listened, sang or danced. Elsewhere in the north east this particular celebration was called a 'Kern Supper' or 'Mell Supper', and these get-togethers were often the highlight of the secular social year. They were held on the last day of shearing (reaping) on any particular farm, the churn or kern being the very last cut of corn, competed for by everyone working in the harvest field. According to an account of kern suppers held in the Rothley Shield area of mid-Northumberland in the early twentieth century, whoever got the kern then fashioned it into a figure called the 'Kern Dolly', decorated it with ribbons and mounted it on a pole. The dolly was then carried on high from the field, with everyone present 'shouting the kern', often in rhyme, with a tremendous concerted shout at the end, such as:

> Blessed be the day our saviour was born;
> For Master X's corn's all well shorn,
> And we will have a good supper tonight,
> And a drinking of ale, and a kirn!
> A kirn! Ahoa.

Once the harvest was safely home, the farmer would then entertain his friends and workers to a supper and dance, sometimes held in the farm's granary before the corn was threshed. The music might be provided by fiddles, melodeons, tin whistles, piccolos and whatever else was to hand, and the dancing could go on until six o'clock in the morning when an enormous breakfast was served up in the farmhouse. We may never know whether the churns in the Dukesfield area were as jolly as this, but some of Thomas's diary entries certainly hint in that direction:

> *21 October 1830, At Blackburn's churn.*
> *2 September 1831, Playing at Trygal churn.*
> *16 September 1831, At Young's corn supper at T [Travellers] Rest.*
> *30 October 1833, Had our churn supper.*
> *20 September 1834, Oxley's churn; had a dance at this place.*

The long shifts that Thomas worked meant that Jane and her children potentially spent many hours on their own, but she was readily able to fashion quite a rich social life during Thomas' absences, visiting friends and relatives, helping at 'cakes making', participating in 'Twiltings' (quilt-making social events), going to Hexham market and fair, attending churns, staying with family or friends near Allenheads, and so on. Although she bought some of her clothes at Hexham, friends and relatives seem to have made most of her gowns and dresses - 'Aunt Nancy and Betty Todd here making Jane a gown'; 'Aunt Nancy here making Jane's silk gown right'; 'Nanny Robson here making Jane a cloak'. Thomas and his brothers also bought some clothes from Hexham, but also suiting fabric which a local tailor then made up - 'Henry Wood here on Thursday making a pair of trousers; 'Harry Wood here making me a frigate' (whatever that was!).

It has already been noted that Thomas and Jane made use of the public houses in the area, and the question of alcohol consumption was one of the matters which greatly exercised the mind of the commissioner for the 1842 Report. It frequently arose in his questions to witnesses, and his conclusions were perhaps surprising, but unambiguous:

> *In fact, very little beer is drunk in this country, and many of the teetotallers have long been so in practice before they adopted the principle.*

Nonetheless, it is clear that many people in the industry, including some of those who embraced Methodism and other branches of Christian religion, were partial to a modicum of alcohol in their diet, even if only at times of celebration, dances, etc. The local Wesleyans certainly did not regard the consumption of alcohol as a mortal sin, or anything remotely like that, but were in favour of some limits, as a resolution in the Minutes of the local preachers meetings for the Hexham circuit on 1 October 1832 makes clear:

> *That Bro M Wilson shall abstain entirely from the practise of selling on the Sabbath, what is called dinner beer &c with the exception of those occasions which occur with travellers, & others coming into town to attend Divine Worship. Also, that he shall endeavour to the utmost of his power to keep his house more orderly in future. To this he agrees.*

Another resolution, of 31 December 1838, also seems to have been inspired by a wish for moderation rather than prohibition, requiring that 'Bro Hornsby be censured … for unchristian conduct in … drinking ale in a public house to a late hour on a Saturday evening. And that the Brethren keep an eye to his moral conduct during the next quarter and to report'. Bro M Wilson may well have been the Matt Wilson whom Thomas heard preach on several occasions, while Bro Hornsby could have been Michael Hornsby, the leader of the Slaley Wesleyans in 1835 and 1838.

The absence of any outright proscription of ale drinking by the Wesleyans may explain why Thomas and Jane Dixon happily frequented the *Traveller's Rest*, just 2 miles from Dukesfield Hall, and the *Clickem Inn* ('*Fox and Hounds*') at Whitley Chapel, at just over 1.5 miles;[1] Jane sometimes went to the *Traveller's Rest* without Thomas, (2 June 1834), and occasionally with his mother (22 August 1832). Although mere attendance at a public house does not of itself imply alcohol consumption, Thomas did regularly drink 'Ale', (Sunday 17 October 1830 At Tra^{s}. Rest forenoon, got some 4d. ale), and not only in pubs, for he had ale at a binding for example, and he attended a 'timber drink' at Slaley in July 1832. He also noted the passing of the 1830 Beer Act which simplified the whole business of setting up a beer shop. This Act allowed any rate-paying householder to gain a licence to sell beer from their home simply by paying 2 Guineas per year to the appropriate authority. There was now no need to apply to the JPs for permission to retail beer, nor any need to get character references, and in the 12 months which followed the passing of the Beer Act, some 30,000 new beer houses had been opened up throughout the country. This amounted to a new beer house for every 20 families in the country, and that in addition to the numerous inns and taverns which already existed. A Bob Dixon and a Jem Dodd opened beer houses in the Dukesfield area within 6 weeks of the passing of the Act, and Thomas certainly appears to have made occasional use of these new venues:

---

[1] An 1827-28 Directory names three pubs in Slaley village, viz the *Fox and Hounds,* the *Red Lion,* and the *Board* but these do not seem to figure in the diaries, although one of them might have been 'Johnneys'.

Friday 19 November 1830, Jem Dodd's sporting.
Sunday 24 April 1831, At Jem Dodds afternoon.
Thursday 16 February 1832, At Jem Dodds with P Dixon.
Sunday 9 June 1833, At Jem Dodds with Joe & Hugh.

The Reccabites were formed in 1835 as a teetotal benefit society, becoming particularly strong in Leeds and in the north generally. Thomas attended two temperance meeting during 1835 and, although there is only one subsequent diary entry which may relate to his drinking beer or ale (10 January 1838, Got a Glass with A Hall), his personal financial accounts of 1838 and 1841 do indicate that he occasionally bought small quantities of ale.

Then as now local pubs were the venues for numerous social gatherings. We have already seen that the singers sometimes ended up at the *Travellers*, and that some of the corn suppers and 'feasts' were also held in the local pubs, for example 'a Goose Feast at Clikem'. But probably the largest events associated with the pubs and beer houses were the 'Sportings' and 'Races', usually held in March, April and October. Of the two men who opened beer houses in 1830, Jem Dodds held a sporting just 4 weeks later, while Bob Dixon held one in June 1831 at which Thomas 'played'. Thomas and Jane attended several of these sportings to watch dog racing and wrestling matches. Thomas often noted some of the successful contestants:

12 April 1831, Jane & I at Clickem Sporting - Sim won the tarrier race - Tom Todd the belt.[1]
18 April 1831, At Dalton Sporting - Hugh Nixon won the Hounds, Mather the whelps, Will Armstrong the belt.

Sometimes Thomas swapped shifts with other smelters so that he could attend these events, as when he spent two days away from home enjoy the Allendale races in September 1830. He also noted a couple of professional bare-fist boxing matches, although seems not to have attended them:

24 October 1837, Molyneaux at Newcastle.
31 October 1837, A fight between Renwick of Winlaton and Molyneaux the Black at Cambo.

Molyneaux (or Molineaux) had been a slave on a Virginian' plantation but he became a professional American boxer, (one of the first such), and made his name in England where he arrived in 1809. He first fought Tom Cribb, the English boxing champion in 1810, and it was widely agreed that he had won the match but had been denied an official victory through skulduggery. He was offered a return match in which he suffered a broken jaw in the tenth round, and was knocked out in the eleventh. His quite illegal match with Will Renwick, held at Middleton Bridge near Cambo, was for a purse of £25 each; it lasted for 87 rounds, with a half-minute break between each round, continuing on until dark and ending in defeat for Renwick.

On a more placid level, January 1834 found Thomas 'At Juniper expecting a ventriloquist.' Presumably the entertainer who had failed to turn up was the person whom Westgarth Forster, himself a one-time agent with WB Lead, had heard in August 1833, either at Alston or Garrigill, and enjoyed 'an amusing evening'.[2] Thomas was more fortunate with other

---

[1] Tom Todd was a well known north country wrestler, a native of Knarsdale, Alston, who won his first belt around 1810-11.
[2] Forster's *Strata*, (1883 edn) lvi.

forms of public entertainment, hearing a lecturer on an unspecified topic in Slaley in November 1831 and seing Wombwell's menagerie at Stagshaw fair in 1834.[1]

Clearly Thomas Dixon had a varied and busy life while pursuing his job as an ore hearth smelter at Dukesfield. He most certainly did not need or use his 'week of rest' to recover from his smelting shifts, being especially active at harvest time when the physical nature of the work could be as demanding as smelting. Indeed, he sometimes performed work unconnected with his smelting, such as gardening, on days when he had already put a shift in at the mill. He also took an intelligent interest in events around him and elsewhere, as can be seen in the diary 'Remarks on the Year' which he sometimes made at the year end. Those for 1830 are a good example:

> *The year just ended is remarkable for its wetness, although in this County we had a good harvest. It is also to be noticed for the many Revolutions, in France, Belgium, and other Nations: The overthrow of the Wellington Administration, and the appointment of Earl Grey to the premiership - Also for the disturbed state of the country, the burning of corn, breaking of machines, and the general distress throughout the Kingdom.*

[1] George Wombwell formed his first collection of animals in 1805 and so successful was it with the public that he went on to form another two menageries, all three of them touring throughout Britain. The very last appearance of the menagerie, then known as Bostock and Wombwell's, was at the Old Sheep Market in Newcastle in December 1931.

17

THOMAS DIXON'S WORK AT BLAYDON.

The Blaydon Refinery.

After the LLCo had acquired the Whitfield smelt mill in the West Allen valley in 1706, the Blaydon works was sold to WB Lead who extended its facilities after 1725 and used the works to refine lead produced at the inland smelt mills; there would be later eighteenth-century refineries at the WB mills at Dukesfield and Allen. As the river Tyne was tidal to Blaydon it was therefore navigable to small boats and, after WB's Newburn depot had been discontinued in1832, all of WB's output of lead was despatched from Blaydon; that situation was to change after the development of railways. Some litharge had also been sold direct from the refinery to lead works and to local paint and glass manufacturers from the 1770s.

The refinery was not a particularly grand affair, being much smaller than any of the WB smelt mills, and its arrangement in 1808 was illustrated by the agent John Mulcaster, when he recommended the building of a new quay, as shown below:

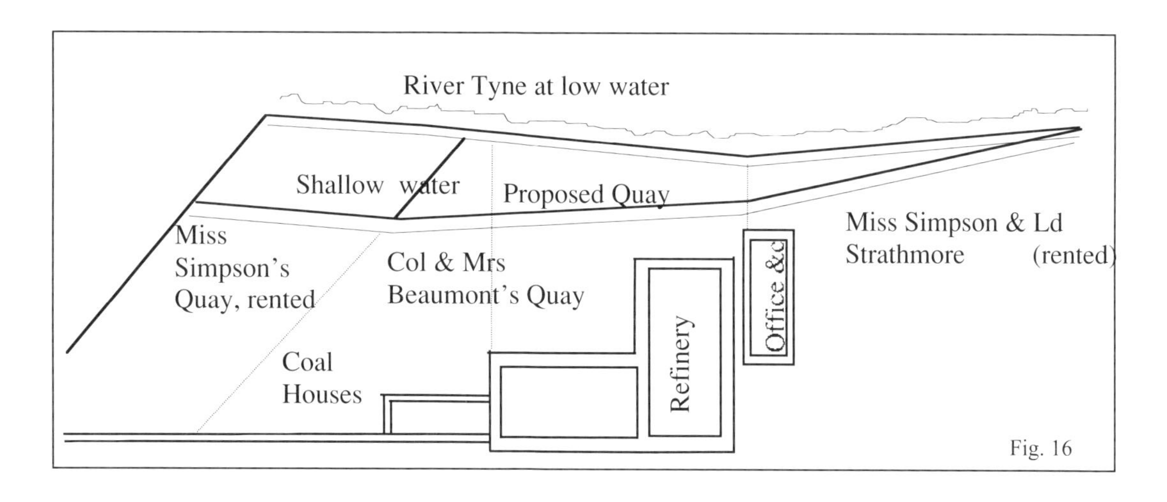

Fig. 16

By 1821 the Blaydon refinery had four refining furnaces, two reducing furnaces and one slag hearth, probably housed in the buildings shown in Mulcaster's sketch, but it is unlikely that more than 20 men were employed on the premises. There was also a windmill within the works, presumably used for the crushing of bones in the manufacture of the bone ash required in the refining furnace but it was removed in April 1837 and probably replaced by a steam-powered mill. The works probably looked much the same when Hugh Lee Pattinson arrived there as chief smelting agent sometime just before July 1832.

Although Pattinson was to bring many changes to the smelting affairs of WB Lead, his most significant innovation was a new method of desilverising lead. Silver had a widespread presence within the Galena of the North Pennine Orefield, averaging about 3.5 ounces per ton of lead ore concentrates. The production of silver and refined lead had therefore always been of considerable importance to WB Lead, and Pattinson was soon experimenting with his new and vastly improved method for refining lead.

In the decades, perhaps centuries leading up to Pattinson's new process, it had only been worth refining lead from ores which produced more than 6 ounces of silver per ton of lead; this calculation took account of the fact that the 'softer' lead produced from the litharge, ('refined lead'), brought a much better price in the market than the ordinary pig lead, ('common lead'), produced directly from the ore hearth. Two associated economic problems faced WB Lead by the early1830s – the reluctance of the market to purchase WB's inferior common lead and its inability to meet the market demands for refined lead. So the economic imperative behind Hugh Lee Pattinson developing his 'desilverising process' at Blaydon on Tyne, was the overriding requirement for WB Lead to produce a better quality common lead, a lead that white-lead manufacturers and plumbers actually wanted. Pattinson was to solve these problems, and in so doing, improve the economic prospects of the entire British lead industry for a generation.[1]

Pattinson tried his new process, still at the pilot stage at Blaydon, with WB Lead's 'worst description of lead', and Benjamin Johnson was able to report in April 1833 that 'I am just returned from Blaydon and am glad to be able to state that I have not the least doubt of its [the process's] success'. So obvious was the worth of the method that Pattinson had decided to patent it by March 1833, and WB Lead promptly introduced it on a commercial scale, possibly at Blagill mill, but more certainly at Allen mill, and continued to use it at Blaydon. However, in the year in which he patented his process and saw it successfully working at Blaydon, Pattinson resigned from WB Lead and, indeed, almost left the lead business entirely. The reasons for this decision are not clear-cut, but they clearly stemmed from Pattinson's belief that he had been inadequately recompensed for his discovery. Although he was later to observe that he had gained £16,000 from his invention, he also noted that:[2]

> *... not long after its introduction [the new process] added £5,000 a year to the income of a certain lead-smelter in the north, who nevertheless grudged the inventor even his comparatively very small share of the profit.*

This was most obviously a reference to Beaumont who, according to Benjamin Johnson, had an agreement with Pattinson to the effect that he should have the benefit of any discoveries of Pattinson's free of any charge. In the event, Beaumont did pay Pattinson £200 p.a. for the privilege of using the new process, while the LLCo gave him £1,050 for permission to use it.[3] .

These momentous events, and their unsavoury outcome, were centred on the Blaydon refinery while Thomas was still working at the Dukesfield mill, but he was transferred there in May 1835, just a year or so after Pattinson's resignation. And it may be that the Pattinson Process and the closure of Dukesfield mill were not totally unconnected for although it is undeniable that the coming of the railways had impacted on the preferred locations for the WB mills, the new desilverising process must also have focused minds on reducing carriage costs. Quite simply, the new process meant that almost all of WB's lead output was now worth refining, and economies of scale could be effected by maximising the use of the railways and reducing the number of the concern's smelt mills and. It seems likely, although no hard evidence has been found in support, that once WB Lead had been

---

[1] The process is well described in Percy (1875).
[2] Lonsdale, 300, quoting Percy.
[3] Raistrick & Jennings, 245.

persuaded of the import of the Pattinson Process, it confirmed its plans to abandon Dukesfield mill, and to take Blagill mill as a stopgap measure while the Allen mill was updated under its agent Thomas Steele; certainly there were considerable capital expenditures at the Allen mill between 1835 and 1840, especially on mill buildings and extended horizontal chimneys. Blagill mill could then be abandoned and Allen would become the concern's main smelt mill, with the Allenheads mill playing a lesser role, perhaps essentially feeding its pig lead down the dale to be refined at Allen mill. Rookhope mill would concentrate on the Weardale ores, and send its products out via the Stanhope & Tyne Railway to South Shields for export shipment. It seems likely, therefore, that the Pattinson Process would have been installed at Rookhope at an early date, for otherwise its refinable lead would have needed to be carried to Allen or Blaydon, both of which options would have negated the benefits of the Stanhope & Tyne Railway.

Dixon the commuter, and his work at the Blaydon Refinery.

Thomas was appointed to work under Mr Emmerson, the chief clerk at Blaydon, and was paid £41 12s. per annum, probably made up of £40 per year salary plus £1 12s. for board and lodgings, and at just over 15s. per week this was perhaps 3s. per week more than he had been earning as a smelter; Emmerson, who had been in his post for some years, was being paid £120 p.a.. It was clearly a step up for Thomas in the sense that he now had a much more congenial occupation, and one which gave him new responsibilities, probably including some of a managerial nature. It may also be the case that he looked forward to the adventure of regular travel by railway, but if so, he was to have an early disappointment.

Thomas, presumably like most people living along the Tyne valley, had taken an acute interest in the building and opening of the Newcastle & Carlisle Railway.

> *27 March 1830, Railway begun [building] this week.*
> *29 December 1834, With Joe and Hugh at Farnley Tunnel.*

The formal opening of the first part of the Newcastle & Carlisle Railway to be completed, that between Blaydon and Hexham, had been held on 9 March 1835, just 5 weeks before Thomas started working at the refinery, and he had been able to join the crowds at the opening celebrations at Hexham station by persuading another smelter to deputise for him at the mill. The morning of that March celebration was said to have been 'uncommonly fine' as the steam locomotives *Rapid* and *Comet* left Blaydon for Hexham just before eleven, with trains full of invited guests. A brass band sat on top of a wagon in each train, one of these bands coming from Allendale, presumably at the suggestion of T W Beaumont. A pumping engine had been mounted on another wagon so that water could be raised from any nearby river should the locomotives run short, which wise precaution was duly vindicated. Reaching their destination early in the afternoon, the travellers were greeted by 'banners, triumphal arches, &c.' before being provided with refreshment at the various inns in Hexham at the expense of the Company directors. According to the local press, the trains then returned to Blaydon, and:

> Throughout the whole of the line, the adjacent country poured forth its inhabitants, and nothing could exceed the interesting spectacle which the villages and cottages presented. Bands of music, flags, the ringing of bells, the firing of cannon, and the hearty cheers of the assembled multitude, gave a joyous welcome to this first and auspicious journey on the Newcastle and Carlisle railway.

It was actually a little more complicated than this suggests, for several faulty wagons had to be removed before the procession commenced, and even so, some of *Comet*'s wagons became derailed.

Thomas cannot have known that he would soon be making that journey on a regular basis, albeit without cheering crowds, brass bands and cannon fire, but the thought would have jumped immediately into his mind when offered the move to the Blaydon refinery. In fact passenger travel on the line was stopped shortly after the official opening, thanks to an injunction against the use of steam locomotives imposed at the behest of Charles Bacon Grey of Styford. That injunction was not lifted until 5 May, some 2 weeks after Thomas had begun his work at Blaydon, and consequently he must have first travelled to his new job by coach or gig. However, having then spent nearly three weeks continuously at Blaydon, he was able to return home for a weekend by taking his very first ride behind a steam locomotive on 9 May; many such trips were to follow. The railway had cut the journey time between Hexham and Blaydon from 3 hours by coach to just under 1 hour by rail, and it became Thomas's preferred mode of travel. Dukesfield was about 6 miles from Stocksfield railway station, and some 4.5 miles from the Hexham and Corbridge stations, all easy walking distances for Thomas. There were only a few trains each way at this time, but enough for Thomas to travel comfortably and, usually, punctually between home and Blaydon. A railway timetable for September 1837 survives and data extracted from it has been summarised below to indicate Thomas's rail travel options.

1837 Timetable	**Going West**		**Going East**	
	Depart Blaydon	**Depart Hexham**	**Depart Hexham**	**Depart Blaydon**
Weekdays	8.0 am	9.30 am	7.45 am	9.0 am
	10.45 am	12 15 pm	11.00 am	12.15 pm
	2.15 pm	3.45 pm	2.00 pm	3.15 pm
	5.00 pm	6.15 pm	5.00 pm	6.15 pm
Sundays	8.15 am	9.45 am	8.15 am	9.15 pm
	5.15 pm	6.45 pm	5.30 pm	6.45 pm

It is apparent that the railway company frequently changed the times of the trains, and indeed Thomas noted a change to the timetable on 11 November 1838; these changes can in part be explained by continued extensions to the line at both east and west ends. Some pencilled notes towards the rear of Thomas's 1838 diary, perhaps made after these changes, probably give the times of those trains heading east from both Corbridge and Hexham which Thomas was most likely to use. These were the 8.27 a.m. and 4.45 p.m. 'mixed trains' from Corbridge on weekdays, and the 9.02 a.m. and 7.02 p.m. trains on Sundays. From Hexham there were the 10.55 a.m. and 6.55 p.m. 'First Class' trains, although Thomas did not make it clear, these were probably Sunday trains. Although Thomas's personal financial accounts sometimes indicate the amounts he paid for his and Jane's rail tickets, we cannot be certain whether he travelled first, second, or third class, partly because he rarely specified either his destination station or whether the amount paid was for a single or a return ticket. However, by way of examples from 1838, his ticket to Stocksfield cost 1s. 6d., & to Corbridge 2s. 0d.

It was, of course, the railway that enabled Thomas to work at Blaydon but retain, for a while, his home at Dukesfield, (usually travelling to Dukesfield on a Saturday and returning to Blaydon on the following Monday morning) and if this presented him with some difficulties, no obvious problems emerge directly from the diaries. He became, therefore, an early railway commuter of a sort perhaps once more common than today, not travelling daily, but at weekends or alternate weekends. Thomas's fascination with the railway was such that he often recorded the name of the locomotive which pulled the train in which he travelled, *Meteor*, *Hercules*, *Eden*, *Lightning*, *Newcastle*, *Tyne*, but sometimes he simply wrote 'took the Steam'. [1] He continued to take an interest in the development of the railway, in the opening of new sections of line, in changes to the timetable, and in unexplained events such as a 'Misfortune at Riding Mill' (11 May 1837).

Initially Thomas lodged at Blaydon with a Matthew Stobbs but, almost from his arrival at Blaydon he regularly returned to Dukesfield, usually on alternate weekends, and sometimes Jane came to stay with him for a few days at Blaydon. Stobbs seems to have had access to a horse and gig, using it occasionally to fetch and carry Thomas between Dukesfield and Blaydon (see 25 July and 16 August 1835). Thomas moved to different lodgings in Blaydon in May 1836, but only after 'Fumigating' and 'Whiting the house'; this house had a garden, and he immediately prepared it to receive potatoes. (An oblique reference suggests that he may have moved again in the following month.) Sometimes, however, he slept at Mr Emmerson's house, presumably when his boss was away on business. (See 22 July 1837 for example.)

He continued to regard Dukesfield as 'home', where Jane had taken on a house servant - 'a girl named Smith' - hired at the annual Hexham Hirings, just 3 weeks after Thomas had begun his work at Blaydon. Another house servant, Rachael Bell, replaced Smith in the following May, again to stay for one year. In fact there is some evidence that the Dixons may have had a house servant in 1833 and 1835, when someone simply referred to as 'Nanny' made trips to Hexham market with onions and butter, and helped in kyleing some hay, but then left the Dixons on Hexham Hiring Day, only, it seems, to be replaced by a Sally on the following day. It may appear unlikely that people in the Thomas's position would engage a house servant, but this may well have been quite common. Thomas and Jane's brother in law, James (Jemmy) Ellerington, doing his ore-hearth smelting at the Allen mill since Dukesfield's closure, had retained his home and smallholding at Dukesfield, probably staying at Allendale when on his smelting shifts. His family certainly had a house servant by 1841, and why not, for he and his wife now had 5 children under the age of 11. It should also be noted that working away from home had been common practice amongst workers in the lead industry for decades if not for centuries. Given the dispersed nature of the industry and its workforce, it was inevitable that many miners and some smelters lived several miles from their workplace, and rudimentary accommodation was usually provided at their place of work – the so-called 'bothies', barracks' or 'mine shops'. [2] Such workers were known as, 'Wallet Men', for they carried sufficient basic provisions to last them for a week in a 'wallet', which resembled a bolster pillow case, slung over their shoulders. Consequently, it is no surprise that Thomas should opt to work in Blaydon for 1 or 2 weeks on end, then return to his Dukesfield home at weekends, for such arrangements were very far from uncommon in the lead industry. Thomas continued to regard Dukesfield as 'home', until Jane and their youngest daughter joined him permanently at Blaydon during May 1837, although this event passed un-noted in his diary: thenceforth Blaydon was 'home' even

---

[1] Details of many of these early Newcastle & Carlisle Railway locomotives are given by MacLean, pp 74-92.

[2] It is interesting in this context, as Mason recorded, that when Dukesfield Hall was advertised to be let in the *Newcastle Courant* in 1807 it was described as having two good sitting rooms on the ground floor with a back kitchen, dairy, pantry and cellar, and five lodging rooms on the first floor.

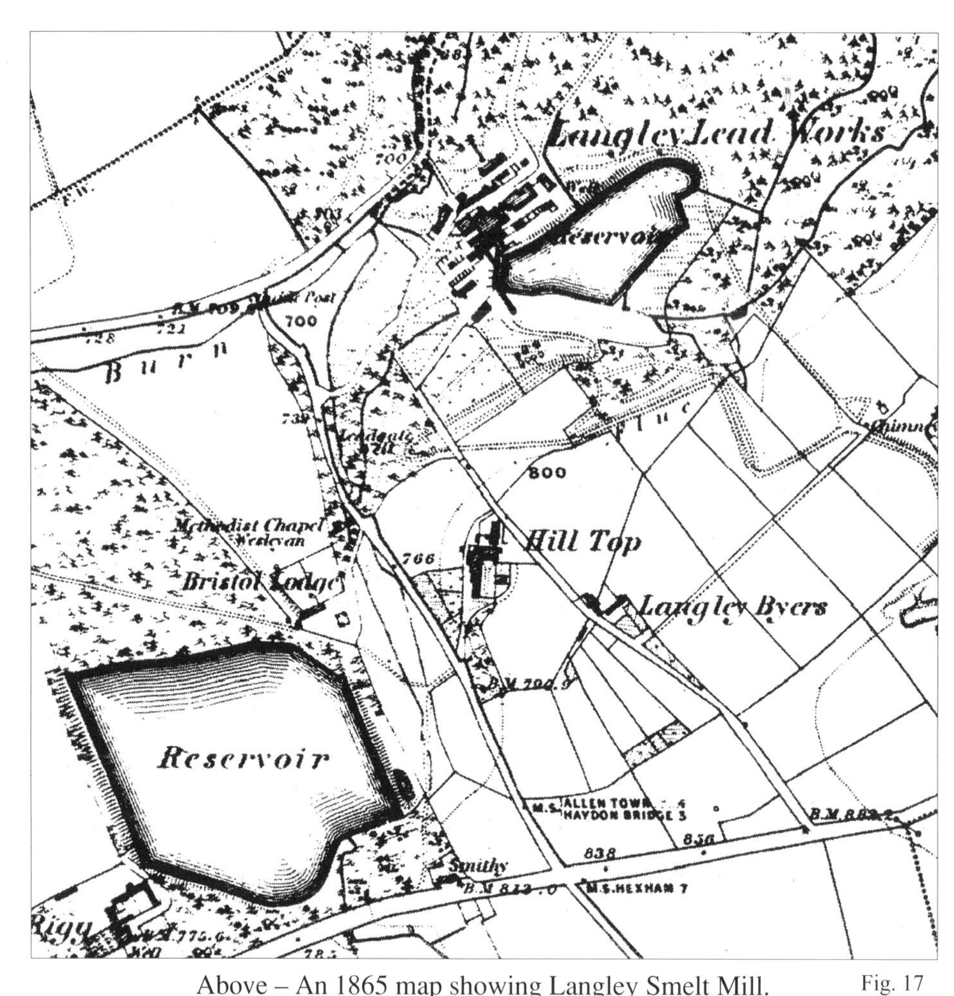

Above – An 1865 map showing Langley Smelt Mill. Fig. 17

Below – Langley Smelt Mill, c.1900, by now deserted.

Plate. 79

though their daughter Elizabeth had remained at Dukesfield, of which more later. Meanwhile there had been some other relocations back home at Dukesfield, notably Jane's father, Jonathan Sparke, who had moved to Langley in 1836, still initially holding some form of agency position with WB Lead; thereafter, Thomas, Jane and the children split their home visits between Dukesfield and Langley.

Thomas neither specified nor indicated directly the nature of his work at the Blaydon refinery, but we can be quite certain that the main activities carried out at Blaydon when Thomas arrived were the desilverising of lead pigs brought in from the west, the selling of some of the litharge produced in that process and the reducing back to metallic lead of the rest of it; the Pattinson process still required the final desilverising process to be carried out in a standard refining furnace, followed by reducing to obtain refined lead. It is unlikely that any of the metallurgical processes would be carried out by Emmerson or Thomas but, as the main depot for the output of the WB Lead mines and mills, much of their time would have been spent in checking the incoming lead pieces, including cooperation with railway personnel and supervision over the export of bullion, lead and litharge in dealing with keelmen. Clearly Thomas would be expected to play a part in all of the clerical and supervisory activities carried out at Blaydon as Emmerson's assistant and understudy, especially when the latter was away on business or was ill, but his varied Dukesfield experiences would also be put to good use. In July 1835, for example, he noted that he had been weighing litharge, but he spent most of that month working on Emmerson's hay harvest: on periodic weekends he also worked on the hay harvest back home at Dukesfield. He occasionally recorded that he had spent time in the Assay Office, where samples of the incoming pigs of lead would be analysed for their silver content, so we must assume that he developed that particular metallurgical skill which while at the refinery. His financial accounts for 1838, which unhelpfully combine his personal expenditures with monies disbursed in his capacity as clerk at the refinery, indicate that he often paid 'Railway Men for Lead loading', but other than these tasks he only hints at a variety of often vaguely described tasks:

> *Went to Hexham seeking lead.*
> *Went to South Shields to weigh lead.*
> *Sent a machine to Langley.*
> *Sent a fan blast away from Blaydon.*
> *Led stones to a new road.*
> *Worked labourage.*
> *Worked at the bone mill.*

Another WB depot was established at South Shields, presumably as a result of the opening of the Stanhope & Tyne Railway in 1835, which line enabled common and refined lead from their Rookhope mill to be shipped direct to the mouth of the Tyne. Thomas was to make frequent visits to the Shields depot, usually for the purpose of 'marking lead', which probably refers to stamping lead pieces to indicate their quality and provenance. Benjamin Johnson had noted in 1833 that:

> The mark (WB) is put on all the lead refined at Blaydon to distinguish it from the refined lead made at Dukesfield and Allen Mills.

The implication seems to be that refined lead pieces from the Dukesfield and Allen mills could be identified by their respective marks, and that when Thomas was marking lead at South Shields, it was with a stamp which identified lead pieces from the Rookhope mill.

There was no railway between Blaydon and the new WB depot at South Shields until 1839 and it is not clear how Thomas travelled between Blaydon and Shields before then, although there would be fairly frequent coach services between Gateshead and South Shields. On one occasion he recorded going to South Shields in Matt Stobb's gig, and on another instance he did the reverse journey, from Tynemouth to Blaydon, by steam boat, although the latter trip was not in connection with his work (23 August 1835).[1] He also recorded on 11 June 1836, that he had come home from South Shields, presumably to Blaydon, 'by Stanhope Railway'; this curious route can only be explained by Thomas's passion for railway travel, for the Stanhope & Tyne Railway headed south-west from Shields towards Stanley in County Durham and beyond to Weardale, and was never any closer than 6 miles from Blaydon as the crow flies. If Thomas did indeed travel up this line from Shields to, say, Stanley, he would have been first hauled by a steam locomotive in whatever passed for a passenger carriage to near Washington, and then by a series of inclined planes, about six in all, worked either by gravity and stationary hauling engines, plus a couple of level stretches where horses took over the traction, all in all quite an exciting trip for the early railway lover.

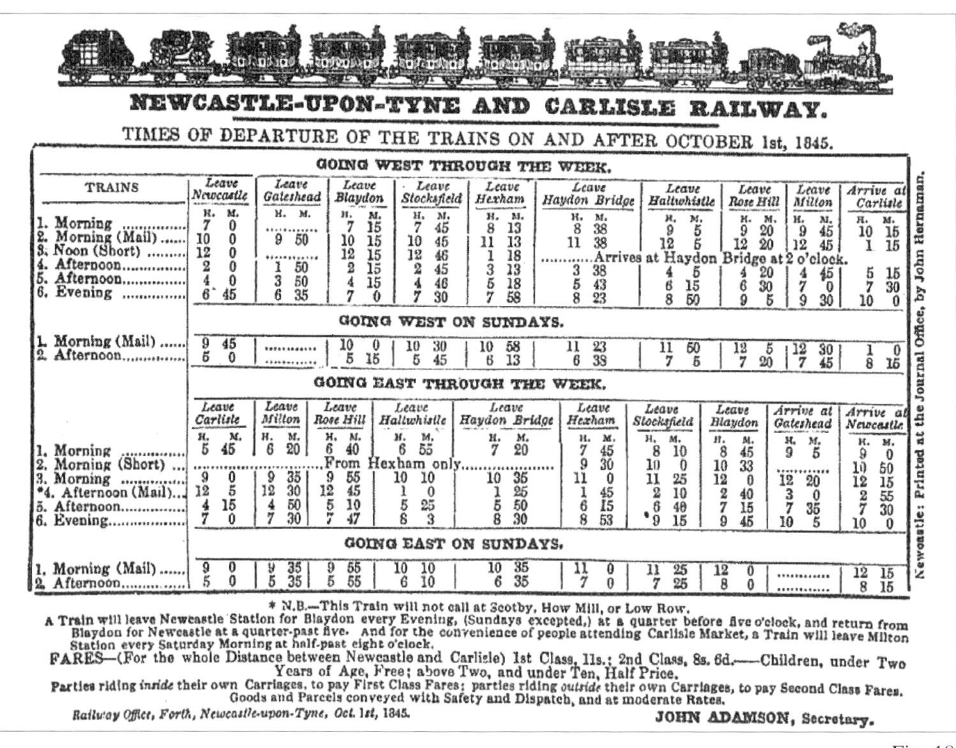

NEWCASTLE-UPON-TYNE AND CARLISLE RAILWAY.

TIMES OF DEPARTURE OF THE TRAINS ON AND AFTER OCTOBER 1st, 1845.

GOING WEST THROUGH THE WEEK.

TRAINS	Leave Newcastle H. M.	Leave Gateshead H. M.	Leave Blaydon H. M.	Leave Stocksfield H. M.	Leave Hexham H. M.	Leave Haydon Bridge H. M.	Leave Haltwhistle H. M.	Leave Rose Hill H. M.	Leave Milton H. M.	Arrive at Carlisle H. M.
1. Morning	7 0	....	7 15	7 45	8 13	8 38	9 5	9 20	9 45	10 15
2. Morning (Mail)	10 0	9 50	10 15	10 45	11 13	11 38	12 5	12 20	12 45	1 15
3. Noon (Short)	12 0	....	12 15	12 46	1 18	............Arrives at Haydon Bridge at 2 o'clock.				
4. Afternoon	2 0	1 50	2 15	2 45	3 13	3 38	4 5	4 20	4 45	5 15
5. Afternoon	4 0	3 50	4 15	4 46	5 18	5 43	6 15	6 30	7 0	7 30
6. Evening	6 45	6 35	7 0	7 30	7 58	8 23	8 50	9 5	9 30	10 0

GOING WEST ON SUNDAYS.

TRAINS	Leave Newcastle	Leave Gateshead	Leave Blaydon	Leave Stocksfield	Leave Hexham	Leave Haydon Bridge	Leave Haltwhistle	Leave Rose Hill	Leave Milton	Arrive at Carlisle
1. Morning (Mail)	9 45	....	10 0	10 30	10 58	11 23	11 50	12 5	12 30	1 0
2. Afternoon	5 0	....	5 15	5 45	6 13	6 38	7 5	7 20	7 45	8 15

GOING EAST THROUGH THE WEEK.

TRAINS	Leave Carlisle H. M.	Leave Milton H. M.	Leave Rose Hill H. M.	Leave Haltwhistle H. M.	Leave Haydon Bridge H. M.	Leave Hexham H. M.	Leave Stocksfield H. M.	Leave Blaydon H. M.	Arrive at Gateshead H. M.	Arrive at Newcastle H. M.
1. Morning	5 45	6 20	6 40	6 55	7 20	7 45	8 10	8 45	9 5	9 0
2. Morning (Short)	............From Hexham only............					9 30	10 0	10 33	....	10 50
3. Morning	9 0	9 35	9 55	10 10	10 35	11 0	11 25	12 0	12 20	12 15
*4. Afternoon (Mail)	12 5	12 30	12 45	1 0	1 25	1 45	2 10	2 40	3 0	2 55
5. Afternoon	4 15	4 50	5 10	5 25	5 50	6 15	6 40	7 15	7 35	7 30
6. Evening	7 0	7 30	7 47	8 3	8 30	8 53	9 15	9 45	10 5	10 0

GOING EAST ON SUNDAYS.

TRAINS	Leave Carlisle	Leave Milton	Leave Rose Hill	Leave Haltwhistle	Leave Haydon Bridge	Leave Hexham	Leave Stocksfield	Leave Blaydon	Arrive at Gateshead	Arrive at Newcastle
1. Morning (Mail)	9 0	9 35	9 55	10 10	10 35	11 0	11 25	12 0	....	12 15
2. Afternoon	5 0	5 35	5 55	6 10	6 35	7 0	7 25	8 0	....	8 15

* N.B.—This Train will not call at Scotby, How Mill, or Low Row.

A Train will leave Newcastle Station for Blaydon every Evening, (Sundays excepted,) at a quarter before five o'clock, and return from Blaydon for Newcastle at a quarter-past five. And for the convenience of people attending Carlisle Market, a Train will leave Milton Station every Saturday Morning at half-past eight o'clock.

FARES—(For the whole Distance between Newcastle and Carlisle) 1st Class, 11s.; 2nd Class, 8s. 6d.—Children, under Two Years of Age, Free; above Two, and under Ten, Half Price.

Parties riding *inside* their own Carriages, to pay First Class Fares; parties riding *outside* their own Carriages, to pay Second Class Fares. Goods and Parcels conveyed with Safety and Dispatch, and at moderate Rates.

Railway Office, Forth, Newcastle-upon-Tyne, Oct. 1st, 1845. JOHN ADAMSON, Secretary.

Newcastle: Printed at the Journal Office, by John Hernaman.

Fig. 18

[1] The first steam ferry on the Tyne was the *Perseverance* of 1814.

18

THOMAS JOINS THE RAILWAY COMPANY.

Thomas's interest in railways continued unabated, and on 18 June 1838, he joined the huge number of people who celebrated the opening of the Newcastle & Carlisle Railway between Redheugh on the south bank of the Tyne in Gateshead, and Carlisle. As usual Thomas had little to say about the event in his diary, merely that he had been to the opening, leaving Redheugh at 1 o'clock in the afternoon and arriving at Carlisle at 6 in the early evening. His train had then left Carlisle at 10 at night and he had arrived home in Blaydon at 5 o'clock on the following morning. He added that it had been a 'Very wet day', but the story of that particular celebration is worthy of a longer telling.

When the tracks were completed between Haydon Bridge and Haltwhistle in June 1838, the whole line, from Redheugh on the south bank of the Tyne in Gateshead to the canal basin at Carlisle, could be formally opened. There had been celebrations of various kinds as each new part of the line had been opened, but the full opening of the line was the most spectacular of these carnivals. The festivities commenced with the departure from Carlisle, at 6.00 a.m. on 18 June, of trains headed by *Eden*, *Goliath*, *Atlas*, *Samson* and *Hercules*, with the mayor and Corporation of Carlisle plus some of the railway directors behind *Eden*, and they arrived at Redheugh at 9.30 a.m. to the sound of cannon. There was, as yet, no rail bridge across the Tyne but the mayor of Newcastle offered his state barges to ferry the more 'distinguished' of *Eden's* passengers to the Newcastle & Carlisle Railway office in the Close, from where they were taken to the Newcastle Assembly Rooms for breakfast. Meanwhile, when the second train arrived at Redheugh, there was such a rush onto a gangplank leading to a steam packet boat that at least a dozen of the passengers took an unanticipated early bath in the murky waters of the Tyne. The trains were intended to leave for Carlisle at 11.00 a.m., but for whatever reason, and we can only guess, the Assembly Rooms' guests were late in arriving back at Redheugh, only to find that the best carriages were now all fully occupied by an un-moveable combination of members of the Gateshead Corporation and a motley assortment of some less-than-distinguished persons; quite where Thomas fitted in is unknown. That little local difficulty apart, it was fairly plain steaming thereafter to Carlisle, as recorded by the local press:

> *The vast number of ladies and gentlemen who had assembled for the purpose of travelling to the other end of the line, the countless spectators and the numerous bands of music, made up a scene of great animation and gaiety. At half-past twelve o'clock the signal was given for the engines to start, when the Rapid was despatched as an advanced guard, without any train, and was followed by thirteen other engines, drawing 120 well-filled carriages. The aggregate number of passengers in all these trains was estimated at nearly 4,000, and the trains, when close together, above half a mile in length. The gay procession was received with enthusiasm along the route, particularly at Corbridge, Hexham, and Haydon Bridge, and the whole party reached Carlisle between five and six o'clock. The shades of night had set in before the trains commenced their homeward journey, and the first did not arrive at Redheugh until between two and three o'clock in the morning, and many of them at a much later hour.*

Not only had the shades of night set in, but a thunderstorm had also broken out on the return journey, and since most passengers were in open carriages, apparently wearing light clothes, they were soon quite saturated. Moreover, one reason for the late arrivals back to

Redheugh, and some trains did not arrive until 6 in the morning, had been one collision near Brampton and another at Greenhead, both of which had resulted in carriage derailments and injuries to a few people. This occasion could have dampened Thomas's obvious enthusiasm for railways but in fact it presaged a considerable change in his life. Some 2 months before the proceedings described above, Thomas wrote some typically enigmatic statements in his diary:

> *7 April 1838, Mr Steel here gave an intimation of a pow-ful nature.*
> *12 April 1838, Got an intimation to stay at Blaydon for some time.*
> *21 April 1838, Mr Emerson gives me know of a change in my situation.*
> *23 April 1838, Mr A here telling me of my change.*

The events of August and September of that year probably offer clarification, for Thomas was interviewed by Benjamin Johnson, WB Lead's chief cashier, on 20 August and again on 10 September,[1] and he completed an application for a job with the Newcastle & Carlisle Railway just 2 days later. It was not until 18 September that he delivered that application, but he was appointed to a job on the very next day by John Challoner, the chief agent to the railway company, and began working for the company on the day after that. He had been made '2nd Clerk' at the Blaydon railway station, surely a position he had long coveted.[2]

Benjamin Johnson's involvement in this affair is interesting, and probably reflects the ongoing influence that T W Beaumont, and therefore WB Lead, had with the railway directors. Beaumont had been a supporter of the railway during the years leading up to its opening. He had bought shares in the company to the tune of £6000 for one simple reason - he hoped to benefit financially, not from interest on his shareholding, but through a reduction in the transport costs of lead ore and lead. The presence of the railway should also allow WB Lead to plan their operations more precisely once they were independent of the troublesome overland carriers. As Benjamin Johnson was to advise some months before the first part of the line opened:

> *I have no hesitation in saying that Mr. Beaumont's mines and Estates will benefit from £1,000 to £1,500 a year when [the railway] is completed to Haydon Bridge, it is expected to be opened from Hexham to Blaydon this year when a very considerable saving in the carriage of lead and materials going to the Mines will take Place – And should it never pay anything to the shareholders, Mr Bt. will be amply paid for his investment.*

In fact, the route taken by the east end of the main line and those of its later branches to Alston and Allendale, seems to have been dictated as much by a wish to serve the lead industry as by constraints of topography or of engineering convenience. Certainly the phased construction programme suited the lead industry well, with, the first section of the line opening between the Hexham and Blaydon stations, the latter being only a few hundred yards from the refinery. The next significant part of the line to open was to Haydon Bridge, just 2.5 miles from the Langley smelt mills, where sidings were constructed at the station specifically to accommodate lead traffic.

---

[1] The 3 week interval between these meetings may have been due to the death of his sister Sarah on 30 August.
[2] There was no 1st Clerk at Blaydon, and indeed most of the intermediate stations only employed a single 'Collector'.

Dixon's work on the railway.

Blaydon railway station had opened with two platforms, and station offices, mainly of wooden construction, on 3 March 1835, to form a temporary eastern terminus of the line. At that time passengers were carried between Newcastle and Blaydon by coach across the 1831 Scotswood Chain Bridge, but the line was extended to Redheugh in Gateshead on 1 March 1837 and passengers could then be ferried between Redheugh and the Close in Newcastle. It was not until after the Scotswood railway bridge had been opened in May 1839 that a regular passenger service could be instituted direct into Newcastle, but still only to a temporary station near the Lead Shot Tower at the Elswick lead works;[1] the Blaydon refinery was so close to the line one of its walls had to be taken down to enable a curve to the new railway bridge to be laid. Thomas was to witness all these railway developments at first hand.

His immediate superior at Blaydon Station was John Scott, believed to have been the first station master at Blaydon, his official title being 'Collector & Station Keeper at Blaydon'. Scott also had previous history with WB Lead, for although he had lost the use of his legs as a boy, he had been employed as a youth in the WB lead yard at Newburn where, with the assistance of an ass, he had been quite able to get from one part of the yard to another. He subsequently moved to the Blaydon wharf, presumably when the Newburn establishment was discontinued in 1832. Scott had been on an annual salary £35 p.a. with WB Lead, but according to an undated Newcastle & Carlisle Railway ledger of c1841, held at the National Archives at Kew, London, he was then being paid £84 p.a. as 'Station Keeper' at Blaydon, where he also had the occupancy of the station house and was supplied with house coals; Thomas was paid £60 p.a. as Scott's clerk (in quarterly instalments), a doubling of his previous salary. The same 1841 ledger listed the other staff at Blaydon station, comprising a yard foreman, 6 labourers, two point keepers, a coke filler, a fixed engineman, a storekeeper & grease keeper, a horse driver, and a watchman, while the company workshops at Blaydon, employed 45 people in all. It is instructive to reflect on the new job opportunities which the railway had brought to the area. The ledger lists some 508 company employees between Newcastle and Carlisle, and although perhaps ten times as many worked in lead mining, washing and smelting in the North Pennine Orefield, the railway nevertheless represented a considerable increase in the areas' employment infrastructure.

As Second Clerk, Thomas was probably essentially a book-keeper, with responsibility for issuing and checking tickets for passenger trains and supervising the reception of goods, in particular the incoming lead deliveries destined for the refinery.[2] The employment of a competent railway clerk who could readily distinguish between refinable and refined lead may have been very important in the eyes of the railway company and of WB Lead. Quite how Scott and Thomas shared responsibilities is not known, for the 1838 and 1841 diaries give few details of the nature of Thomas's work. It seems unlikely that both men worked a 7-day week, although such working was common in many other industries, and there may have been times when Thomas was effectively in charge of the station. Indeed, when Scott was poorly late in 1841 and may have been absent from work for about 26 days, Thomas presumably stood in for him - ideal preparation should he ever seek promotion. The fact that Thomas's 1838 diary after 20 September is remarkably thin on personal activities,

---

[1] Passenger services over this stretch began on 21 October 1839; the Newcastle Central Station was not to open to traffic until 1850.

[2] It is unlikely that any refinery products were despatched via the railway at this time, for river and coastal navigation would still provide the better option.

except on Sundays, may indeed point to a time-consuming working week, although the occasional Monday and Wednesday seem to have been free from work.

Early passenger lines like the Newcastle & Carlisle Railway were not, in fact, particularly busy. In 1839, and perhaps also in 1838 when Thomas joined the railway, there were five through trains in each direction on every weekday, two 'quick' trains and three 'mixed' trains, all stopping at intermediate stations if required; there was also a daily 'short' train from Newcastle to Haydon Bridge. The 1839 timetable is given below:

1839 timetable	**Going West**		**Going East**	
	Depart Blaydon	**Depart Hexham**	**Depart Hexham**	**Depart Blaydon**
Weekdays	5.45 am (Mixed)	6.55 am (Mixed)	8.05 am (Mixed)	9.15 am (Mixed)
	9.12 am (Quick)	10.05 am (Quick)	11.00 am (Quick)	11.45 am (Quick)
	12.45 pm (Mixed)	1.55 pm (Mixed)	3.30 pm (Mixed)	4.45 pm (Mixed)
	2.45 pm (Mixed)	4.15 pm (Mixed)	6.00 pm (Mixed)	7.00 pm (Mixed)
	5.12 pm (Quick)	6.05 pm (Quick)	6.50 pm (Quick)	7.45 pm (Quick)
	6.45 pm (Short)	8.00 pm (Short)		
Sundays	9.15 am (Quick)	10.10 am (Quick)	11.05 am (Quick)	12.00 am (Quick)
	5.15 pm (Quick)	6.10 pm (Quick)	7.05 pm (Quick)	8.00 pm (Quick)

This timetable meant that trains were arriving and departing at Blaydon station from 5.45 in the morning until 7.45 in the evening, implying that the station would need to be staffed from about 5.30 in the morning until 8.00 in the evening, some 14.5 hours per day. Thomas was, of course, quite used to long shifts and, in the absence of any further clarification, it must be assumed that the above timings indicate his weekday hours. On Sundays, however, only two through trains in each direction arrived at Blaydon and Thomas could spend most of the time at home, just turning up at the station at around train times.

If Thomas gives few details of the nature of his work at Blaydon Station, he does at least remark on 'occurrences' which took his fancy, especially those which involved collisions with stray animals – 'The Train run over some sheep'; 'A Horse killed at Ridley Hall by the Train'; 'A Cow killed at Stella' – all in November 1838. But he also continued to note the arrival of new steam locomotives to the line such as *Venus*, and also of accidents which sometimes occurred – 'The *Victoria* off the line at Allerwash'; '*Jupiter* off the line at night'; 'the *Wellington* taken off the line by some cows nr Dilston'.

Travelling on the railway

The Newcastle & Carlisle Railway was clearly popular with those who could afford the fares, and quite large numbers of people fell into that category. Francis Whishaw, a civil engineer who visited the line in 1839 as part of his researches into the railways of Great Britain, noted that 78,687 passengers were carried on the Newcastle & Carlisle Railway in the first 5 months of 1838, and 117,364 in the last 7 months, an average of 548.4 per day; this was said to be eleven times as many persons as had previously travelled along the Tyne valley by coach. The number of passengers carried in 1839 was 236,288, almost as many as on the Liverpool & Manchester Railway during the first 7 months that it was open.

The company operated a mixed fare structure and accordingly provided a range of carriages on the line. The first class carriages, painted yellow but picked out with black livery, had sprung seats and sash windows, and were lined and stuffed throughout; the second class carriages, painted white and picked out in green, had open sides and no plush upholstery; the mixed carriages had a combination of first and second class compartments. The company also ran luggage coaches with seats above, a form of 'third class' provision although that term was not used at the time, goods trucks into which seats could be placed on 'thronged days', cattle trucks, horse boxes, mail vans, and coal wagons; these were all simply painted green.

Although Thomas gives no real indication of a passenger's experience on the railway at this time, other contemporary accounts are instructive and sometimes amusing. Whishaw observed that:

> *No railway in the kingdom is better regulated in point of punctuality of the arrivals, especially in the quick trains, nor is there any upon which fewer accidents have occurred.*

He did, however, complain about the 'snake like motion' and 'frequent jerks' of the trains as, he believed, a consequences of the line's 'curvelinear course'. He assumed that it must have been laid out for horse working (which in a sense it was) for:

> *... no engineer would have ventured to recommend a plan which exhibits ... almost one continuous series of curves from end to end.*

Whishaw was, however, content with the 'neat rustic designs' of the railway stations, and although he believed that they should have been placed a little nearer the lines, he was particularly impressed by presence of intermediate stations such as Blaydon:

> *Besides the terminal stations ... there are no fewer than 19 intermediate stations, at all of which, if necessary, the mixed trains stop to take up or set down passengers.*

This, indeed, was the then unique aspect of the Newcastle & Carlisle Railway, for it was the first line anywhere to provide proper passenger facilities at intermediate stops. Whishaw's praise of the stations was echoed by Dr Granville who also travelled on the line in c1839 during his simultaneous researches into spas and railway travel. Granville suggested that this line was:

> *Unquestionably by far the prettiest railroad in England. It is exceedingly neat and well kept and its station houses, built of freestone, are the perfect specimens of taste and style in architecture.*[1]

But for a more intimate and humorous assessment of travelling on the Newcastle & Carlisle Railway, William Pearson is hard to beat. Pearson much preferred coaching to railway travel but, perhaps from of a thirst for adventure, he used the Newcastle & Carlisle Railway in 1838. The Scotswood railway bridge had not yet opened and so the first part of his journey took him along the Scotswood Road and on to Blaydon station by horse omnibus:

[1] Regrettably, the architect/builder of these stations remains unknown.

> *At 1 o'clock we left Newcastle 'towering in our pride of place' as Shakspeare hath it - i.e. on ye box of an omnibus - the bells did not ring, neither were ye cannon on ye castle fired, w[hich] I presume was an oversight. In due time we entered ye Chain bridge ... & soon found ourselves at ye Railway station [Blaydon] a little beyond ye pretty valley of ye Derwent.*

He set off from Blaydon in a train hauled by *Comet*, but at some point along the way the carriages became detached from the locomotive, and he had to spend some time in a stationary train with some unsavoury characters. Then:

> *After some considerable delay we started on ye outside: for ye carriages on the Newcastle & Carlisle railway are, in part, provided with seats for accommodation of 'outsides'. The Company [in the carriage] was more numerous than select; one poor blind man opposite me had contracted an unfortunate habit of spitting: I bore ye annoyance as patiently as I cd & comforted myself by thinking that if it had been an American carriage they wd all have been spitting.*

> *Unfortunately we were in ye carriage nearest to ye Engine & ye wind was right ahead: so that ye smoke & particles of coal were a great annoyance: & although they did not travel so fast as ye particles of light, according to philosophers, yet they were considerably larger and heavier, they made it very 'sharp work for ye eyes' as ye old woman said, when ye cart-wheel ran over her nose.*

Thomas was very far from the only person who wished to travel on the new-fangled railways, and with good reason, for as Thomas Sopwith noted after a 90 minute train ride from Brighton to London in 1852 'what magic - what annihilation of time & space'. Naturally there were some who believed that the railway companies were pushing things a bit too far. The Newcastle & Carlisle company was heavily attacked by sabbatarians when it was decided to run excursion trains on Sundays, claiming that such provision would violate the scriptures, prevent the Company's servants from enjoying the 'day of rest', and generally encourage a lowering of moral standards.

Indeed, a handbill was issued by the Revd. Kilsyth to dissuade people from taking a Sunday excursion on 29 August 1841, which read:

A REWARD FOR SABBATH BREAKING
PEOPLE TAKEN SAFELY AND SWIFTLY TO HELL!
NEXT LORD'S DAY BY THE NEWCASTLE & CARLISLE RAILWAY FOR 7s 6d.
IT IS A PLEASURE TRIP.

It would appear that Thomas was not at work on that occasion, his diary recording that he attended a child's funeral during the day and went to a religious service in the evening.

19

THOMAS'S LEISURE HOURS AT BLAYDON.

The ways in which Thomas spent his weekend leisure times when working at the Blaydon refinery very much depended on whether he stayed at Blaydon or went to Dukesfield, although his interests in his family, religious observance, music, friendships and the world around him remained unchanged. His wife Jane stayed on at Dukesfield until May of 1837, so that Thomas spent 2 years largely living on his own at Blaydon, and his family life was obviously considerably interrupted while he and Jane lived apart. He first moved to Blaydon on 20 April 1835 and it was not until 9 May that he was able to return to Dukesfield, travelling 'with the steam', of course, for a 2-night weekend visit. During that stay he and Jane went to a meeting, and also met up with some friends who were seemingly about to leave the area. But thereafter he made regular weekend trips to Dukesfield, generally fortnightly, taking the opportunities these visits presented to continue his religious affiliations at meetings, love feasts and camp meetings, also to visit friends or Hexham Fair, and generally to catch up with local news: he must occasionally have backdated his diary on some such occasions. Harvest time still drew him to Dukesfield where his help was still needed, and in any case he still had a house, garden and smallholding there, of which more later.

Life was much quieter when he remained at Blaydon at weekends, for he quite often stayed at home all day, or took a Sunday walk around Swalwell for example, or in the Redheugh Gardens, to 'the Spa Well', or up the waggonway. But Jane came over to Blaydon on a couple of occasions in 1835, and on one such in August, Thomas and Jane joined with their folk in Tynemouth, where they were presumably enjoying a short seaside break; it was, however, 'rather wet' on that weekend. Thomas and Jane caught a 'Steam Boat' back from Tynemouth on the Sunday, and all except Thomas went back to Dukesfield on the following day. In addition, some relatives also lived at Lemington across the river from Blaydon. Thomas's brothers Joseph and Peter had spent a few days with them in 1831 and 1834 respectively, while 'Aunt Mary of Lementon' had visited Dukesfield in the latter year and Jane was to visit Lemington early in 1835. Thomas had spent a day at Lemington after only one week at Blaydon, and he was to make a further seven visits before the year was out. Thomas's brother Joseph was mainly living at or near Shotley Bridge at this time and they were also to meet up occasionally; Thomas left Shotley Bridge on one occasion at 4.30 a.m. to walk the 10 miles or so back to Blaydon. Thomas also established a vegetable garden at Blaydon, and as he made new friends there, and became involved with the local chapels and churches, his weekends at Blaydon gradually became busier.

It seems, therefore, that Thomas soon accommodated to his changed circumstances, and the ease with which he or Jane could travel between Blaydon and Dukesfield by railway made their part-separate lives less divisive that might otherwise have been the case. For example, Jane and daughter Elizabeth, but not daughter Jane, arrived at Blaydon on New Year's Day 1836, staying for four nights, and Thomas spent most of the following week at Dukesfield, perhaps because there was 'very little employment this week at Blaydon'; snowy weather had perhaps halted the lead carriage to the railheads. These cycles of a working week at Blaydon punctuated by at least alternate weekends and harvest time at Dukesfield, plus midweek trips to Hexham Fair, or to Hexham or South Shields on business, continued through 1836 and into 1837, and did not change markedly after Jane and daughter Jane came to live at Blaydon in 1837; their move to Blaydon, was obviously timed to coincide

Blaydon Station, c.1858

Plate. 70

with the end of Rachel Bell's contract as house servant to Jane at Dukesfield, Thomas noting both events on 15 May.

This re-uniting of Thomas with his immediate family was not total however, for daughter Elizabeth, now aged about 7 years, seems to have stayed on with Thomas' parents at Dukesfield, perhaps so that she could attend her grandfather's school.[1] Consequently the comings and goings between Blaydon and Dukesfield continued through 1837. There were other reasons why this should be so, not the least important being that the Dixons seem to have retained their house at Dukesfield Hall, together with its garden and associated smallholding, but also because Thomas's help continued to be valued at harvest time. Although Jane's father had moved to Hill Top, Langley, Thomas's parents, his brother Peter and sisters Sally and Betsy were all still living at Dukesfield Hall, and their assistance in maintaining Thomas and Jane's Dukesfield interests must have been considerable.

Thomas and Jane did not always travel together to visit friends and relations. When Jane's sister Margaret, living at Byker Hill, Newcastle, since her marriage to John Middleton in June 1836, was ill in May 1837, she was first visited by her father, and then by Jane and her brother Tweddle while Thomas went to Dukesfield. But usually they headed west together by train at weekends, visiting Dukesfield or Langley some six or seven times during the remainder of 1837 including, of course, a week at harvest time. The opportunity was usually taken, on these occasions, to go to church at Whitley Chapel, but it would seem that no Methodist meetings were attended.

These visits to the west were occasionally reciprocated by Thomas and Jane's parents and siblings during 1837. Thomas' father had broken up the school for harvest on 23 September, and his granddaughter Elizabeth wrote to him from Blaydon just one week later, perhaps inviting him to come and stay for a few days before taking her back to school at Dukesfield. We will never know, but it is certain that Thomas's father did come to Blaydon for a couple of nights, had a look at the new Scotswood railway bridge, and then went back to Dukesfield with Elizabeth. At the same time the two Janes went to Langley for a night with grandfather Sparke before heading for Dukesfield in Jemmy Ellerington's cart. Grandfather Dixon commenced the school again on 9 October and the two Janes returned to Blaydon 4 days later, where Thomas had remained at work. It is often said that 'the past is a foreign country' and that 'they do things differently there', but anyone reading the above who has or once had young children, with two sets of grandparents, uncles, aunts and cousins living at a distance, (let alone a garden and smallholding needing attention some 16 miles away), will be very familiar with the complex arrangements frequently made in attempting to accommodate everyone's wishes.

Other members of the family and some former work colleagues also visited Thomas and Jane at Blaydon in 1837, his brother Peter for example. Sometimes a Saturday trip was made into Newcastle when guests came to stay, or a Sunday walk was arranged. Jonathan Sparke, as a principal smelting agent, occasionally travelled to Newcastle on business, making it easy for him to call in at Blaydon, or at Byker to see his daughter Margaret. Cousin Hugh actually came to work at Blaydon for a few weeks from the beginning of May, during which time he enjoyed a Sunday walk on 'Summer house Hill' with Thomas and family, but he returned to Dukesfield in June and the Dixons would only see him one more time before he died in November. Thomas's sister Betsy had been at Blaydon in the meantime, staying with Thomas and Jane for 2 weeks, during which time she visited Newcastle and made Jane a gown.

---

[1] See 25 January 1838.

Thomas was still taking a newspaper and several 1837 diary entries refer to events which he had read about rather than attended, the death of King William the fourth, for example, or the Horse Fair in Newcastle, or the boxing match between 'Renwick of Winlaton & Molyneux the black', but he did attend a race meeting in Newcastle in June 1837 when 'the Cup [was] won by *Bees Wing*'. In fact, his leisure activities at Blaydon, other than visiting friends and family and being visited by them in return, remained focused on gardening, the occasional walk and the pursuit of his religious and musical interests; the 1838 and 1841 diaries suggest that this life style remained largely unchanged up to the end of 1841.

The next year, 1838, was to mark a watershed in Thomas's life, although the pattern of the year up to September was to be much like the year just gone. It was obviously a hard winter, so bad that the river Tyne froze and the curious, including Thomas, experienced the novelty of walking across it in mid January. The account of this freeze-up, as given by Fordyce, notes:

> *All passage on the river Tyne was stopped, it being frozen for upwards of five miles below Newcastle, and crowds of skaters appeared upon it. In no year since the celebrated frost of 1814 had one occurred like the present. In proof of this it may be mentioned that loaded carts crossed the Tyne ... and other rivers in the north, upon the ice at various points.*

There was a downside to this of course, for keels could not reach the Blaydon quay, and Thomas's diary entries suggest that it was not until early March that the river was fully opened up. In the mean time Thomas helped out with a Pay at Allendale late in January, combining that trip with a night's stay with Jonathan Sparke at Langley Hill Top, followed by two nights at Dukesfield when he was able to meet up with old friends at Lee & Dyehouse. Jane seems to have remained at Blaydon on that occasion, but went to Dukesfield on her own at mid-February while Thomas looked after daughter Jane, taking her to a Sunday 'meeting' in the Blaydon area. Jane returned with the news that Thomas' mother was poorly, and this was confirmed by letter. Simultaneously Thomas and Jane received news from Byker that 'little Wylam', almost certainly the son of Jane's sister Margaret, was ill. Jane immediately visited Byker, while Thomas visited his mother at Dukesfield. Wylam died a few days later on 11 March, but Thomas' mother soon recovered from her illness. Thomas and Jane continued to make visits to Dukesfield or Langley every 4 weeks or so once winter was over. They were at Dukesfield for the 1838 Easter weekend, taking in a service at Whitley Chapel, and soon after their return Thomas was told of the unspecified 'change in my situation' which probably led to him joining the railway later that year. By the end of June, Thomas's sister Sally was 'very poorly' and she died 8 weeks later on 30 August 'with a full assurance of the blessed Eternity'. Thomas joined the Newcastle & Carlisle Railway just 3 weeks after that, his pleasure at doing so doubtless marred by a difficult personal year to date, culminating in the death of his younger sister.

Thomas's financial accounts in his 1838 diary are rather difficult to unravel, for they combine both personal accounts and expenditures associated with his work at the refinery, but some of the personal expenditures can be unpicked. These include several purchases of railway tickets for the Dukesfield and Langley trips up until the time when he joined the railway, and it must be assumed that a degree of free rail travel was available for some employees of the railway company and perhaps also for their immediate family. Many domestic purchases, such as candles, coffee and treacle, were bought from John Leck and his wife Mary (Mally), whose shop, according to the 1841 census, was probably very close to wherever the Dixon's were living. Meat, sometimes specified as mutton, was bought from a Mr Parker, shoes from George Cox and Mr Fleck, eggs from Mrs Bownas, newspapers (at 1s. 7 1/2 d per quarter) and a hymn book from James Mitford, and so on. Other purchases included coal, ale, liquorice, tobacco, oatmeal, matches, cotton, pans, a fiddle and fiddle strings, and music books; he also recorded an expenditure of 7s. 6d. on 'New Years Gifts' in January. Over the whole year he had received £177. 0s. 4d. and paid out £176 19s. 11d., in both a personal and professional capacity.

The year 1841 again began with the 'Tyne hard frozen. People walking across Tyne', and no regular navigable access to Blaydon for 20 days. Thomas and Jane's daughter Elizabeth may have been mainly resident at Blaydon by now, possibly having a piano lesson in the last month of that year, while daughter Jane was attending a local school, at a cost to Thomas of about 4d. per month. Visits to stay with both sets of grandparents, the Dixons at Dukesfield and the Sparkes at Langley, were now less frequent, but correspondence by post provided some continuity of contact; Thomas recorded five letters received from Dukesfield and one from Langley in 1841. Thomas visited Dukesfield on just nine occasions in that year, two of those being combined with visits to Langley, usually with Jane and the children. Generally they stayed for just two days at Dukesfield, but spent at least three nights away for the combined visits, with Jane often staying a day or two longer at Langley. On one occasion Thomas made a day trip to Dukesfield, an outing only made viable by the railway, although he returned from another Dukesfield visit 'in James' cart'.

Possibly the most harrowing time in Thomas and Jane's life to date occurred to at Blaydon in 1841, with the birth and infant death of their third daughter. Jane seems to have had a difficult pregnancy, Thomas noting on several occasions that she had been unwell in the months leading up to the birth. Indeed, perhaps unwisely it might seem to us now, she had been 'bled' just a few days before the birth, for at best bleeding would have done no harm: the subsequent events are best told directly from the diary:

> *5 June 1841, Jane delivered of a Daughter at 1/2 past 1 this afternoon attended by Dr Simpson.*
> *10 June 1841, The Child taken very ill.*
> *11 June 1841, Mr Wardle Baptizing the child Sarah - Sarah died at 8 o clock p.m.*
> *12 June 1841, At Winlaton this morning. The Infant Sarah buried.*

A melancholy item in his personal financial accounts for 1841 indicate that baby Sarah's coffin had cost 2s. 6d. Thomas' sister Sarah had died at the age of 26 years in August 1838, while his cousin Sarah Skelton had died in December of the same year.

Thomas's 1841 accounts also show that he bought foodstuffs such as potatoes, cabbages, oatmeal, flour, sugar, raisons, liquorice, groceries, and butter seemingly from his mother. As in 1838, he also purchased ale, tobacco, matches, yarn, linen, a waistcoat, cloth for a suit and 1Guinea to a tailor for making it, frocks for the girls, a razor strap, regular newspapers, pills, salve, shoes and the heeling of his shoes, clogs and clog irons for Jane, *Aesop's Fables*, fiddle strings for his brother Peter, and clarinet reeds for himself; amongst the services that he paid for was that of a rat catcher. During that year he made £36 over to Jane and received just over £3 back, but her household and personal expenditures were not itemised. Thomas had also become a member of a 'Loan Society' in which he saved about 3s. per week, but took £4 15s 11d out in October and £4 13s. 8 1/2 d. in November. In addition, he took 3s. 2d. from a 'Money Box' in December 1841, but returned it before the month was out.

Thomas continued to take an interest in the lead business even after he joined the railway, partly no doubt because as clerk at Blaydon station he regularly dealt with lead movements, but also because his father-in-law remained a smelting agent at Langley. Thus he noted the comings and goings of agents, the holding of the Pays, and developments at the Blaydon Refinery ('Beaumonts folk begun making Red lead.'). And although it mattered less to him personally, he persisted in recording the local weather conditions, from very ill days of snow in January, and soft wet days in March, to much thunder & rain in June, fine days in August and very sharp frosts in November. On the other hand the typical north-eastern weather conditions could equally well be fine and fresh in January, the hills could be covered with snow in May, it might be windy and cold in July, and fine days could be common in December.

Gardening and farming

It is clear that Thomas was expected to help with Mr Emmerson's hay harvest at Blaydon, which he did until he joined the railway company, spending a few days at it in each year before then. Moreover, while Jane and the children continued to live at Dukesfield, the garden and smallholding there were kept on by Thomas, with help from his family and friends; for example, Jane and Thomas's mother sheared 'the few oats in our field' in September 1835. In addition, both sets of parents continued to farm even after Joseph Dixon had become a schoolmaster, and Thomas assisted him with the harvests in 1836 and 1837. The vegetable garden at Dukesfield contained much as before, with potatoes, onions, cabbages etc., and likewise the smallholding involved the buying or selling of the occasional cow at Hexham fair, haymaking, and so on. In fact, this aspect of their lives continued even after Jane had moved to Blaydon, for Thomas got his cow bulled, and harvested his hay crop, in August of that year. The help of his father and brother Peter was now crucial to the ongoing viability of the Dukesfield garden and smallholding, both of them helping Thomas to set his potatoes in April 1838; it may indeed be the case that Peter gradually took over the day-to-day running of Thomas's Dukesfield garden and smallholding, for he was still living with his parents in Dukesfield Hall. It seems clear then, that Thomas and Jane retained their house, garden and smallholding at Dukesfield Hall partly as a base for their regular visits, and Thomas certainly paid £8 to Mr Nixon, the Beaumont land agent in January 1838, presumably a rent payment.

It seems likely, however, that Thomas gave up his Dukesfield Hall house and smallholding in 1839 or 1840, possibly at Nixon's behest, for the land agent may have argued either that Thomas's new position with the railway would leave him insufficient time to husband his Dukesfield lands with due care, or that he was bound to discontinue Thomas's tenancies once he had left WB Lead's employ, both of which scenarios might explain Thomas's oblique note of 2 November 1838 – 'Went to Bywell to see Nixon – disappointed'. If it was the case that the smallholding was reserved for Beaumont employees, it is possible that Thomas's brother Peter took it over, for the only diary entry for 1841 which directly related to either gardening or smallholding at Dukesfield simply noted that Thomas had been helping Peter to set potatoes. Although Thomas did pay Nixon £2 10s. rent and was allowed 10s. for lime, in February 1841, this have been a late settlement of rent due in 1840. The general impression gained is that Thomas had given up his Dukesfield house, and both he and his father had given up smallholding, at some time between 1839 and 1840, while Jonathan Sparke's move to Langley in 1836 had probably marked the end of his involvement with farming. If so, Thomas and Jane may have stayed with his parents or with the Elleringtons when visiting Dukesfield during 1841, just as they had stayed with Jonathan Sparke when visiting him at Langley. Thomas still had his garden at Blaydon to look after, although his increased salary on joining the railway must have lessened any economic justification for growing his own vegetables; the only garden vegetables mentioned in 1841were potatoes and cabbages.

Religious observances.

Working, and later having a permanent home at Blaydon, had no long-lasting effect on Thomas's established religious adherences, nor on his leisure pursuits, although he appears to have cut down on both during his first 18 months or so at Blaydon. He continued his church and chapel attendances either at Dukesfield at weekends when he went home, or in and near to Blaydon. In 1836, however, his first full year at the Blaydon refinery, he recorded attendances at only fourteen Sunday services, many fewer than in his earlier years when working at Dukesfield. This probably reflected his new job demands, coupled with absences from Jane and his travels back and forth from Dukesfield, rather than any lapse in his enthusiasm for religious observance. In 1837, the year in which Jane came to live at Blaydon, he recorded some 39 attendances, twelve of which were at St Helens, Whitley Chapel. In the following year he attended some 63 services or meetings, mostly in the Blaydon area, and 75 in 1841, only one of which was identified as being in the Dukesfield area – at Whitley Chapel; again his main affiliation seems to have remained with the Wesleyans, but he attended about 12 Primitive Methodist gatherings in the latter year.

Thomas continued to be ecumenical. When he arrived at Blaydon in 1835 there were several Wesleyan and Primitive Methodist chapels in the area, at Blaydon, Swalwell, and Winlaton. In addition the Presbyterians had a meeting place in Winlaton, as did the Church of England, and the Stella Catholic Chapel, which he attended once, soon after his move to Blaydon, was just along the Hexham road. His attendances at Church of England services in the Blaydon district were rare, although he did attend one service each at the Ebchester, Ryton and Winlaton churches.

Nationally, the first half of the nineteenth century witnessed further schism amongst the ranks of the Methodists following the Primitive Methodist breakaway from the Wesleyans in 1810. However, Thomas seems to have largely confined himself to the Wesleyan 'Old Connexion' - the direct descendents of the Wesley-inspired societies - and to the Primitives, making just one possible visit to a 'New Connexion Chapel'. Several Methodist chapels were mentioned by name in the diaries: the Wesleyan Zion chapel at Winlaton (only fairly recently abandoned), the Brunswick Chapel,[1] the Wesleyan Blenheim Chapel in Newcastle (the opening of which Thomas attended on 28 October 1838), the Nelson St Primitive Methodist Chapel in Newcastle and the Bethesda Chapel.[2] Thomas also chronicled his presence at numerous 'meetings' including a Prayer Meeting, a Love feast, and several 'Sample's meetings'; he may also have attended a Camp Meeting on Gateshead Fell. Joining the railway company did bring a slight change to his Sunday activities, for now Thomas had to attend to the station office on certain Sundays but, with only four trains stopping at Blaydon on a Sunday, Thomas could make himself available for those trains while otherwise spending most of the day in his house or going to chapel services.

At times, as in 1841, his connection with the Primitives seemed to be quite strong, and it is possible that his daughters were going to a Ranters' Sunday School:

> *Sunday 4 April 1841, Hearing Eltringham & Lumley at Ranters Chapel, Winlaton. Hearing Mrs Darly at aft.*

---

[1] Probably the Wesleyan chapel in Newcastle.

[2] Probably the Gateshead Bethesda New Connexion Chapel which had first opened on Good Friday 1836.

Sunday 9 May 1841, In Ranters school at aft.
Tuesday 1 June 1841, Got tea with the Ranters.
Wednesday 21 July 1841, Hearing the Ranters sing at night.
Sunday 24 October 1841, Hearing Wm Kimster - The Sunday Scholars & Eltringham.
Sunday 17 October 1841, At Ranters at aft hearing the Children.

However, it is clear that he was still dividing his allegiances, as for example on 23 May 1841, and 17 October 1841, when he sandwiched a Sunday afternoon Ranters' meeting between morning and evening Wesleyan meetings. He also attended a Bible Society Meeting, whose *raison d'etre* seems to have been the distribution of bibles to people in need of them, but his first foray into the outside world with a collection of 'good books' saw him bitten by a dog at Derwenthaugh.

It is difficult to be certain about Jane's attendances at religious services after Thomas had moved to Blaydon. They went to several meetings together in the Dukesfield area on Thomas's visits home during 1835 and 1836, but there are only three recorded instances of Jane's presence at religious gatherings at Blaydon after she moved there with daughter Jane in May 1837, two in that year and one in 1841 when she was churched. There are two possible explanations for this, assuming that we can discount any notion of her 'losing her faith'. Firstly Jane always accompanied Thomas on his trips back west, but she also visited Dukesfield and Langley without Thomas on about twelve occasions, usually at weekends, during 1837 and 1838. Consequently, she was not often at Blaydon at weekends in those years. The year 1841 was clearly a difficult one for Jane, being often unwell, and bled twice, during the pregnancy which ended in the infant death of her third daughter; she rarely visited Dukesfield or Langley in that year until after her pregnancy. Secondly, daughter Elizabeth was aged about 8 when Jane moved to Blaydon, and daughter Jane was aged 4, and although Elizabeth seems to have initially remained at Dukesfield, baby-sitters would be needed if both Thomas and Jane were to attend religious services in the Blaydon area. As they appear not to have had a female servant living with them at Blaydon, it may well be that Jane felt unable to leave her young child with anyone else.

Music and singing

Thomas did not record any involvement with singing schools in his first 2 years at Blaydon, but made frequent references thereafter – 'At Winlaton singing'; 'At Burdons singing at night'; 'At Swalwell … hearing the singers'; 'Hearing the Ranters sing at night'. The latter quote again indicates a link between singing schools and Methodism, and this notion is reinforced by the occasion when he was at 'Winlaton at aft with the singers hearing [the Primitive Methodist preacher] Mrs Darley'. A slightly ambiguous diary entry, for 28 October 1837 reads 'Begun a school at Blaydon' and while we can be fairly certain that this was a singing school, the word 'begun' could mean that he formed one, or simply that he joined one; his cash account for 1838 suggests that he may at least have acted as treasurer for a singing school.

His interest in fiddle playing remained undiminished. He seems to have bought a fiddle in October 1837, taking it with him to Dukesfield soon after, and also to Shields; he also bought a fiddle and a book of music for his brother Joe in June 1838, at a total cost of £3 17s. 0d. He also had a fiddle repaired or modified in 1841 - 'Tom Henderson taking the fiddle Belly off'; 'Got the fiddle glewed on'; 'Got some Timber for a fiddle belly'; 'Got my fiddle wood glued'. Then, towards the end of 1841, he noted that his wife Jane had come 'from the west', bringing 'a piana with her', and his daughter Elizabeth may have received her first piano lesson just under a month later.

20

THE RETURN TO THE WEST.

Becoming clerk at the Blaydon refinery had increased Thomas's status and his income while his move to the railway raised both still further. Moreover, the move to Blaydon seems to have been quite agreeable once Jane was living there and while they retained a foothold at Dukesfield. The subsequent apparent loss of their Dukesfield base may have been a personal blow to Thomas and Jane, and the loss of their third child was undoubtedly so. But if the stuff of Thomas's dreams was made of the possibility of working on the railway, then that dream had not only come true but would soon surpass itself.

Thomas was still working at Blaydon station at the end of his last known diary and he had been recorded as a 'Clerk' in the Census of 1841, his wife and daughters Elizabeth and Jane, together with their as yet un-named third child aged 2 days, living with him; Mary Spark, aged 25 years, was listed as a female servant but Thomas's diary indicates that this Mary was Jane's sister. Amongst the last entries in the 1841 diary are two of particular interest. The first of these, for 7 December, noted 'The directors here stating the reduction of wages'. This action by the railway company, an attempt to cut operating costs, was probably the outcome of the survey of personnel and their wages as contained in the c1841 ledger held by National Archives. That ledger did indeed suggest cuts to many employees' incomes, recommending for example that the salary of the chief engineer (John Blackmore) be reduced from £600 to £325 p.a., but Thomas's and Scott's salaries were recommended to remain as before. The second entry, made on the last day of the year, noted that 'A great number of men [have been] discharged from the Company's employment'. While these two actions could be related, there may be a more prosaic explanation for the discharge of a 'great number of men', for the company had just completed the major work of doubling the track throughout between Newcastle and Carlisle, and it was perhaps navvies working on that job who had been dismissed.

However, if some members of the permanent railway staff had indeed been dismissed, Thomas was not amongst them, and although little information has been found to indicate his activities after 1841, he had, at some time between then and 1847, been promoted to a position which he must have long coveted, 'Station Keeper' at Hexham; it is hard to avoid the presumption that he relished a return to the west. Thomas probably replaced George Bates who had been 'Collector & Station Keeper at Hexham Station' on a salary of £100 p.a. in c1841, and it is reasonable to suppose that he received at least an equivalent salary. Hexham station was then, and is now, the largest of the intermediate stations on the Newcastle & Carlisle Railway, employing a '2nd Clerk' and a 'Junior Clerk' in c1841, as well as the Station Keeper. Thomas had, therefore, at the age of 42, achieved a position of some local importance, one which bestowed on him considerable status in the town. This new position would also keep him in touch with the lead trade, for he would be responsible for attending to the receipt of any lead delivered by road to the station, as George Bates had been before him.

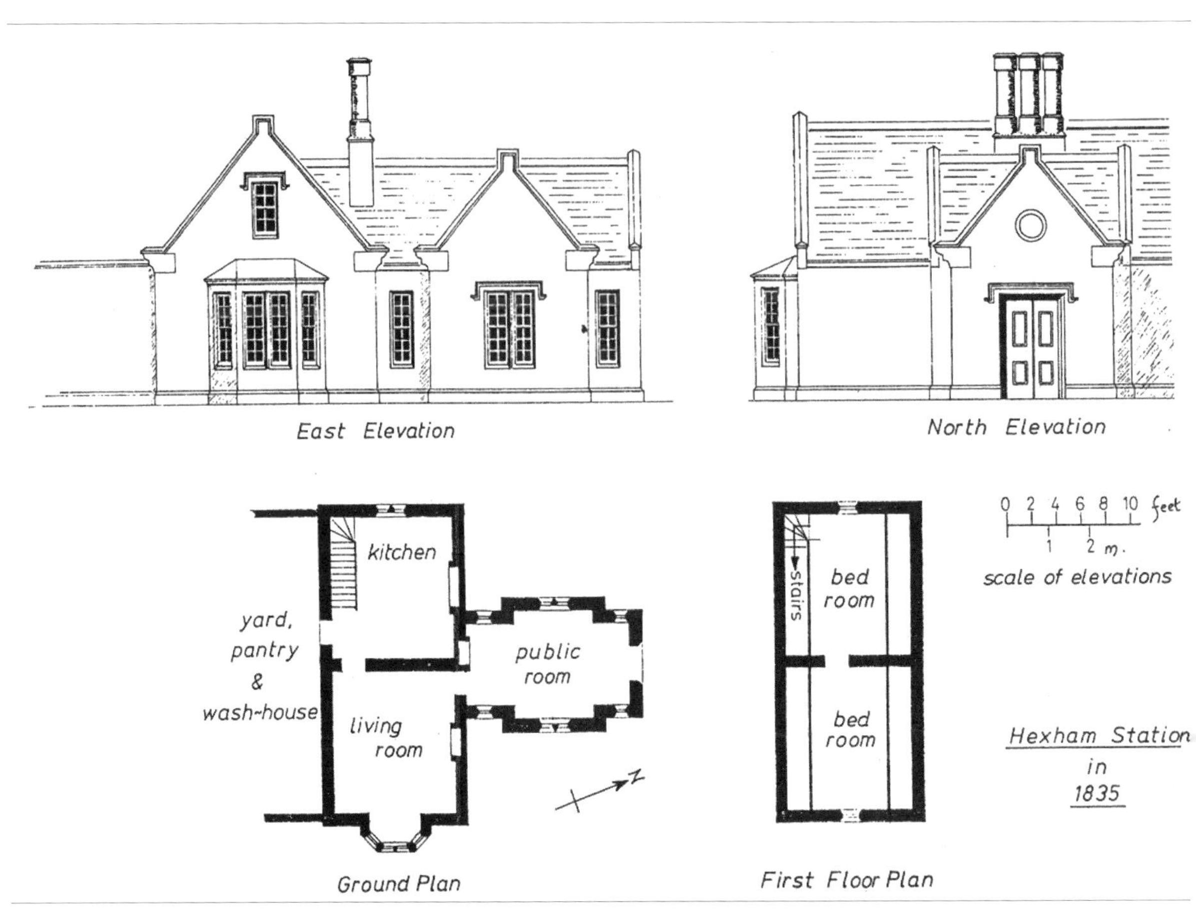

Fig.

Plate. 71

Hexham Railway Station, 1836

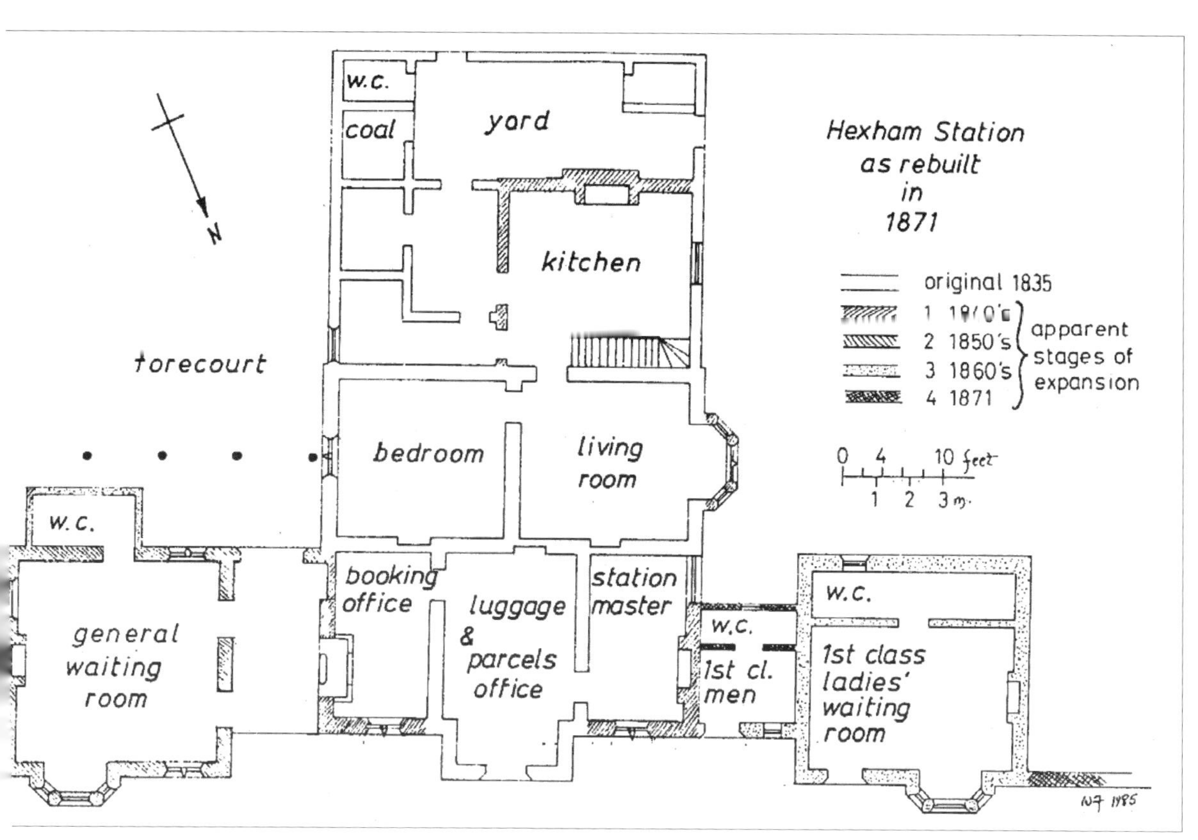

Fig. 20

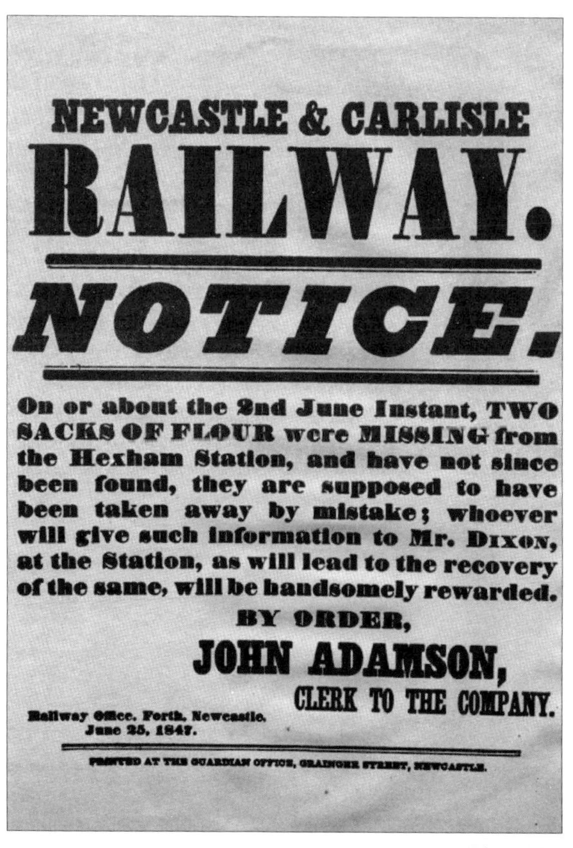

Plate. 72

Other changes had been taking place at Blaydon station at around this time. According to J Maughan, writing for a local newspaper in c1909,[1] when George Hudson, the so-called 'Railway King', gained temporary control of the line, (he leased it in 1848), he instituted a review of the personnel employed by the company which resulted in John Scott being required to leave Blaydon; Scott then became an agent with the London Lead Company. He was succeeded at Blaydon by John Palmer Dalton who had been transferred from Carlisle station on the recommendation of Hudson, and Dalton remained station master from 1848 until 1861, as well as being the local postmaster for at least a part of that time. When Dalton eventually resigned those positions to became the local representative of the London Lead Company in Blaydon, another link was forged in the chain that connected the Newcastle & Carlisle Railway with the local lead concerns.

The Blaydon refinery must also have been in a state of flux. It had been in direct rail connection with South Shields, near the mouth of the Tyne, from 1839, which meant that even the Allendale smelt mill, just 5 miles from a railhead at Haydon Bridge, was quite handily placed for rail connection to deep river quays and large seagoing vessels. Blaydon's shipping wharf, on the other hand, must have been limited to either keel transhipment or small seagoing vessels with striking masts, for only such vessels could pass the small-arched Newcastle road bridge. Consequently, with the building of a new Pattinson-based refinery at the Allen Mill (date unknown), there can have been little justification for continued activity at the Blaydon refinery, except as a depot, and although its buildings remained at least until 1854-55, seemingly still in use but for unknown purposes, and with Thomas Emmerson in charge, it may have been completely closed around 1858.

The 1851 census recorded that Thomas and Jane Dixon were still living at the station house at Hexham, their daughter Jane, now aged 17 years, recorded as 'housekeeper'; they also had a servant, Jane Moor, born at Humshaugh, and aged 18. Interestingly, Thomas' brother Peter had given up lead ore smelting and was now a coal merchant at Hexham station, living there with his wife Margaret (Burdus), and their daughter Elizabeth aged 2 months. It seems likely that the operation of the coal depot, which was integral with the station, was within the patronage of the station master. But Thomas was to experience the loss of more members of his immediate family during the following decade. His sister Sarah had died in 1838 at the age of 26 years, and his daughter Elizabeth in 1847 aged 19, but these were followed by the death of his mother in 1853 aged about 71, his brother Joseph in 1857 aged 48, his father in 1858 aged 77, and his wife Jane in 1860, aged 54. On a brighter note, his daughter Jane seems to have married a Thomas Bulman in 1855. Thus, Thomas was living alone at the station as Station Master at the time of the 1861 census, his daughter Jane possibly living on Tyneside.[2] Brother Peter and family were still nearby however, Peter now being listed as a 'Coal & Lime Agent' while his wife Margaret was listed as a coal merchant; their family had been increased by a son Joseph, and two further daughters, Margaret and Jane.[3]

---

[1] The news cutting is in the author's collection, but it is not dated, nor is the newspaper named.

[2] Jane had a son Jacob Dixon Bulman, born in Newcastle c1857 and a daughter Elizabeth born in Gateshead c1858.

[3] Peter's wife, Margaret, was to die in the following year on 23 July at the age of 42, while Peter lived to be 66, dying at Whitehouse, Slaley, on 2 July 1882: their son Joseph died soon after at the age of 28 on 17 February 1884. All were buried in Slaley churchyard.

Retirement.

Thomas had probably retired from the railway company by 1864 when he was living at Orchard Place in Hexham, (a small group of stone-built houses of 1825, with architectural pretensions), possibly at number 4; he would appear to have been succeeded as station master at Hexham by a Thomas Bulman and, since his father had married a Bulman, it may be that there was a family connection between the two, but it was not his new son-in-law.[1] Thomas may have worked part-time for his brother Peter after retirement from the railway company,[2] but he also became a member of the Hexham Board of Guardians in 1864, and was possibly seen as a radical member of that Board, for he opposed the practice of driving the poor back to the place of their birth when they sought parish relief; he argued, at a public meeting called to unite opposition to this practice, that relief should be given to the poor wherever they happened to be. He clearly continued to maintain his interest in railways, for when the *Hexham Courant* reported on the opening of the Hexham to Langley portion of the Hexham & Allendale Railway on 21 August 1867, it was noted that the invited guests for the special train included 'Mr T. Dixon late station master at Hexham'. Thomas would probably have been able to see Jonathan Sparke's house at Hill Top as the train arrived at Langley, and he must surely have remembered happier times spent there with Jane and the children; Jonathan had died just 11 months earlier. Also present at the celebratory opening of the line was its engineer, Thomas John Bewick, who had been engineer to WB Lead, under its chief agent Thomas Sopwith, for some 20 years.

Thomas died on 19 February 1871, aged 66 years, almost exactly 11 years after his wife had died on 21 February 1860, and almost exactly 44 years after they had been married on 6 February 1827.[3] He was buried in Slaley Church yard, sharing a tombstone with his wife and eldest daughter in the shadow of the church they had watched being built.

---

[1] John Sword, formerly a station clerk at Ryton, was station master, coal merchant and goods agent at Hexham station by 1886, while a Mrs Catherine Dixon was also a 'coal merchant, Railway Station' but living in Orchard Cottage; no connection has yet been found between Thomas Dixon and this Catherine Dixon – see appendix on the provenance of the diaries.

[2] Thomas's death certificate gives his occupation as 'Coal and Lime agent'.

[3] Thomas's death certificate gave 'cirrhosis' and 'exhaustion' as the causes of death; assuming that this referred to a non-alcoholic cirrhosis, it could have been a long-term effect of lead poisoning, although it is possible for cirrhosis to arise through the body reacting to itself; 'exhaustion is a term still used to imply a general decline over a length of time; I am grateful to Dr D C Napier for this information. Thomas left effects valued between £300 and £600; I am grateful to Hilary Kristensen for this information.

Plate. 73

Hexham Railway Station, c. 1970.

21

RETROSPECT

Thomas Dixon was buried only a mile or so away from his birthplace, but his life had encompassed the headlong rush of the Industrial Revolution, and he played a small part in that great upheaval. When he began his diary as an ore hearth smelter at Dukesfield smelt mill, he could reasonably have expected to remain there for the rest of his working life. The closure of the mill when Thomas was aged 30, with the potential loss of some 40 jobs, could have severely damaged the rural community which had operated it and gained financial support from it, were it not for an interesting combination of time-honoured practices, plus the emergence of some new job opportunities. WB Lead's policy of promoting from within must have provided hope of advancement for some Dukesfield workers, as long as the industry remained viable, and Thomas Dixon and William Bownas gained such advancement, the latter, moving from his position as mill foreman at Dukesfield to become mill agent at Rookhope. Other Dukesfield smelters like Thomas's father Joseph, brother Peter, and brother-in-law Jemmy Ellerington, found continuity of employment at other WB mills, Joseph Dixon later becoming a full-time schoolmaster. A few of the Dukesfield smelters moved away from the area, but others were able to find some sort of lodgings at the mills during the week that they were at work, and return home for their week off. This was a familiar, indeed common aspect of working life in the lead dales, where the running of smallholdings by some, if not most smelters and many miners, offered a degree of economic stability which was independent of their main occupation; at the time of the 1841 census, with Dukesfield mill long closed, some 27 men who claimed to be lead ore smelters still lived within a mile or so of the former smelt mill, but presumably worked in the Allen valley.[1]

Perhaps more importantly, new sources of employment were opening up, especially for the skilled, the numerate, the literate, the sober and industrious, for the Industrial Revolution was in full swing as epitomized by the spread of the railway system. The Newcastle & Carlisle Railway was special in many ways. It was the first railway to cross England and, at nearly 65 miles long, it was the longest railway in the world at the time of its building. It was also the first line to be promoted in the North East where coal was not expected to be the sole or major article of traffic, the first important line to use standard rail gauge throughout, the first line in the world to provide passenger facilities at intermediate stations, and to use the once traditional (but now only to be seen on preserved railways) small cardboard railway tickets - from c.1837. A characteristic which it shared with only one or two other lines, was that it operated with trains running on the right-hand side of the track, and did so until 1864. Within 6 years of its opening the line provided direct employment for some 500 people, and was carrying more that 250,000 passengers per year. For all that some people still doubted the wisdom of travelling by rail.

When the MP William Huskisson was accidentally killed at the opening of the Liverpool & Manchester Railway, some believed that this was simply the inevitable start of widespread carnage. *Punch* magazine, c1840, noted caustically: 'A Railway is long, but life is short - and generally the longer the railway, the shorter your life'. Others seemed more concerned about a threat to a way of life, than to life itself. Thus William Wordsworth, a writer of edifying poems for the middle classes, opposed the coming of the railway to the Lake District. Such views were, however, only held by a minority of people, and most seemed to

[1] It has been assumed here that an occupation recorded in the Census implies an active worker.

positively welcome the coming of the railway. Harriet Martineau, the writer of edifying poems for the working classes, believed that railways had the potential to be a liberating influence on country people, and Thomas Dixon would surely have agreed with her on that.

The doubters were not to have their way and nearly 7,000 miles of track had been laid in the country by 1851, carrying some 80M passengers per year. Journeys in Britain which once took several days now only took a few hours, and as Henry Booth, treasurer to the Liverpool & Manchester Railway, had predicted:

> *... perhaps the most striking result produced by ... this railway, is the ... marvellous change which has been effected in our ideas of time and space ... Speed - despatch - distance - are still relative terms, but their meaning has been totally changed ... what was quick is now slow, distant is now near, and this change ... will pervade society at large.*

The relativity of time and space was beyond Henry Booth - we had to wait for Albert Einstein to begin to sort that problem out - but his sentiments and prophesy were reasonably accurate, and would soon be echoed by many. One such was Thomas Sopwith who, as Chief Agent to WB Lead from 1845 to 1871, did his fair share of commuting, but not just the 16 miles or so regularly covered by Thomas Dixon. Based at the Agent's House in Allenheads, but with homes in London where WB Lead now had their main office, and in Newcastle, he also travelled between homes and working places - the railways made that possible, and Sopwith and Dixon's paths must often have crossed at Hexham station. As he noted after a journey from Durham to London by train in1852, 'What a number of events & places may thus be combined in a single day'. Leaving Durham station at noon, he first stopped off at York to admire the Minster and dine at the station, then leaving York at 4.10 p.m., he arrived in London at 10 p.m. 'without the slightest feeling of fatigue after a journey of nearly 300 miles'. Never before in the history of mankind had it been possible to travel so far in so short a time.

Not every railway resulted in economic success however. Although the first section of the Hexham & Allendale Railway had opened in August 1867, and the line had opened for goods traffic as far as Catton Road in January of the following year, this terminus, just short of the Allen smelt mill and nearly a mile north of Allendale Town, was meant to be only temporary, for the plan was to press on to Allenheads. An extension of a few hundred yards was constructed across the East Allen and into the Allen smelt mill yard at an unknown date, providing the mill with direct distribution either to the port of Tyne, or onto the national railway network, but not all was well with the Hexham & Allendale Company. A lack of funds and prospects, together with the closure of Allenheads mill in 1870, ensured that the proposed line up to Allenheads was never begun and, after experiencing constant financial difficulties, the Hexham & Allendale Company happily sold out to a presumably reluctant North Eastern Railway in 1876. In reality the lead industry was by now in unavoidable terminal decline and it suffered a major collapse in the 1880s. The Langley mills closed down in 1887 and Allen mill ceased production in 1896, by which time WB Lead had given up almost all of its local lead interests. If, as seems likely, the Hexham & Allendale railway never made an operating profit, it had nevertheless reduced the cost of lead carriage down the dale for a couple of decades, and was not finally closed down until November 1950.

Thomas Dixon had left an industry that was doomed to virtual extinction before the century was out, although he could have remained with it until his own retirement. But in taking the opportunity to join the Newcastle & Carlisle Railway, he had moved into an industry of the future, as well as one which seems to have captivated him. There was considerable personal grief in his life, but that was not uncommon at the time, and it is undoubtedly true that consolation was often sought and found in religious belief. Even so, it seems undeniable that Thomas had a varied, busy and fulfilling life, while pursuing his jobs as an ore hearth smelter, as a clerk at the refinery and Blaydon railway station, as station master at Hexham and as a poor law guardian. It is self-evidently the case that not all ore hearth smelters could be as successful, or perhaps as lucky as Thomas, their particular skills not being easily transferable. Perhaps if we knew more about the subsequent lives of other people mentioned in Thomas Dixon's diaries, we might conclude that he was not extraordinary, nor especially talented or fortunate, and we would also be even better able to know what it was like to be there at that time.

A brief note appeared in the *Hexham Courant* at the time of Thomas Dixon's death:

> *It is with deep regret that I have to notice the death of one of the most respected and active members of the Hexham Board of Guardians. I allude to Mr Thos Dixon who for seven years was one of the representatives of the ratepayers of Hexham Township. He was chairman of the Finance Committee and was one of the most useful and hardworking members of the board.*

Thomas Dixon, family man, ore hearth smelter, early railwayman, gardener, smallholder, singer, musician, sports enthusiast, church and chapel goer, poor law guardian, and more besides, deserved a better obituary, and it is hoped that this book goes some way to provide just that.

APPENDIX 1 - THE PROVENANCE OF THE DIARIES.

Whilst it was certainly advantageous that Thomas Dixon included his name and the address 'Dukesfield Hall' at the beginning of his 1830 diary, the diarist would have been quite easily identifiable, for example from parish records relating to the birth of his daughter Jane in 1833; the nature and place of his work would also have been self-evident from numerous diary entries. The route by which his diaries came into the possession of Mrs L C White of Hexham, however, remains speculative. The diaries for the years 1830 to 1837 were in Mrs White's ownership in 1975, together with books of early Newcastle & Carlisle Railway tickets, some of which had been partly used as children's scrap books. Two further diaries, for 1838 and 1841, had earlier been loaned to an interested person and never returned to Mrs White, only for them to be subsequently deposited with the Northumberland County Record Office. Mrs White understood that the diaries had been handed down directly from Thomas Dixon though various family members to her late husband James Armstrong Hedley White, but her version of the family's history does not withstand scrutiny.

A significant person in Mrs White's verbal account of the family succession was known as 'Granny Dixon', but contrary to Mrs White supposition, she cannot have been Thomas Dixon's wife. This Granny Dixon, was said to have brought up four of her grandsons in Hexham, and in this respect a household recorded in the 1881 Census is of considerable interest. Living in Orchard Place, Hexham, which short terrace of houses provided Thomas Dixon with his last residence, was the 67 year old widow Catherine Dixon. Catherine had been born in 1814 at Acomb, just to the north of Hexham, and her occupation was given as 'Coal Agent'. With her on the night of the census were four grandsons, Thomas J Dixon, James Dixon, William George Dixon and Thompson Dixon, ranging in age between 7 and 15 years; a niece, Elizabeth Hedley aged 26, was also present. Catherine's occupation is further clarified by Bulmer's *Directory* for 1886 which includes 'Mrs Catherine Dixon, coal merchant, Railway Station; house Orchard Cottage'.[1]

Several pieces of evidence combine to point to this Catherine Dixon having been christened Catherine Hedley at St John Lee near Acomb on 27 March 1814, her parents being John and Ann Hedley. We note that Catherine Dixon's niece was a Hedley, that Mrs White's husband had a Hedley name, and that Catherine Hedley's christening year corresponds with Catherine Dixon's birth year as given in the 1881 Census. But while it can be fairly assumed that 'Granny Dixon' was originally Catherine Hedley of Acomb, it has not been possible to find a marriage record for Catherine, nor to link her directly with Thomas Dixon the diarist, although it remains possible, for example, that she married one of his cousins. Alternatively, Catherine may not have been related to Thomas Dixon in any way, yet it would seem that it was through her descendants that Thomas Dixon's diaries were preserved.

Perhaps Catherine or someone else found the diaries, either in Orchard Place or at the Hexham station coal yard, and as Catherine shared a surname with the diarist, albeit an extremely common one, there may have appeared to be a family connection. If one Catherine's daughters or granddaughters married a White, which family were coal merchants in Hexham in the twentieth century, Thomas Dixon's diaries could then have descended with the Whites. The diaries and other material may then have lain undisturbed through a couple of generations of the Hedley/White families until rediscovered by Mrs L C White's husband.

---

[1] Bulmer also includes a 'Mrs Catherine Dixon, Temperance Hotel, Priestpopple' who, according to the 1881 Census was then aged 46 and had been born in Meldon, Northumberland.

APPENDIX 2 - THE DIXON/BULMAN/SPARKE/DRYDEN FAMILIES.

Joseph Dixon, (1781-1858), Thomas Dixon's father.

Thomas Dixon's father Joseph was born in 1781, possibly a son of Bell Dixon (the father), and christened at Whitley Chapel on 20 May 1781; if so, he had a brother William, baptised at Whitley Chapel on 11 May 1788. (Another less obvious possibility is that he was the son of Joseph Dixon of Peasmeadows, near Allenheads (1752-1800)). He married Elizabeth Bulman on 12 May 1804, probably at Whitley Chapel, and they were to have six children, one of whom died young (see Elizabeth Dixon). Thomas was their eldest child, and they were living at Middle Dukesfield when he was christened on 3 February 1805. Joseph was probably an ore-hearth smelter at Dukesfield mill at that time, although the earliest positive indication dates from 1811. When Joseph and Elizabeth's first daughter Sarah (Sally) was born in 1812, her parents were living at Dukesfield Hall.

Joseph was clearly literate and numerate, and it can probably be assumed that he received the usual education for boys in and around the lead ore field, commencing school at age 6 years and leaving when aged 12 or 14 years. Joseph was still an ore-hearth smelter at the Dukesfield smelt mill when Thomas began his diaries, and it seems probable that Joseph and Thomas worked an ore hearth together, although there is no hard evidence for this until 25 March 1834, when Thomas wrote 'Old Bill Dixon on with me: Father at Hexham fair with the cow'. Joseph was 'bad of his chafts' soon after that, and it took Thomas a few days to locate Stobart the doctor; Joseph did not get back to work until the beginning of July. A measure of Joseph's trustworthiness as a senior smelter at the mill is suggested by an unusual job which he undertook towards the end of 1832, when he was 'at Hexham with a cart taking the silver plate', a product of the mill refining process, the carriage of which was often handled by specialist carriers.

Like many others, Joseph had a vegetable garden and a smallholding where he had a hay meadow and kept a pig and at least one cow, with the usual consequent trips to a Hexham fair or market. Thomas noted that his father was at 'Quartre Bras' in August 1832, and early in the following year Joseph and 'Tommy' (possibly Thomas Oxley) agreed with the Beaumont land agent to take a new farm which, judging by Thomas' end of year remarks, was Quartre Bras. This placename seems to have been forgotten in the Dukesfield area but 'Wester Byres' is shown on a county map of 1828, located near Steel Hall just half a mile from Dukesfield, and one place-name may be a corruption of the other. Further evidence to support this idea derives from a diary comment of 21 October 1837, where it is implied that Thomas's folk were 'done shearing at Steel Hall'. Either way, it was probably at that location that Joseph, Thomas and Tommy were finishing a dyke and dyking a gap in April and May 1833.

With the impending closure of Dukesfield mill, Joseph was transferred to the Allen smelt mill in September 1835, but this situation does not seem to have lasted very long, for just before the church at Whitley Chapel was reopened after extensive refurbishment in June 1836, Joseph was 'elected clerk at the Chapel', and although Thomas did not mention it as such in his diaries, he was also appointed schoolmaster, presumably at Whitley Chapel, either at the same time or soon after. The evidence for this begins with Thomas implying that his father had been away from the school for about 3 weeks in September and October 1836, presumably because it was closed for harvest time.

It would seem that it was not until 1837 that Joseph visited Thomas at Blaydon for the first time, taking advantage of the school harvest holiday in October, but this appears to have been a rare visit, no doubt compensated for by Thomas' regular trips to Dukesfield, and by letters sent between them from 1838; Joseph also seems to have combined visits to Shotley Bridge and Blaydon in September 1841, to enable him to visit his sons Joseph and Thomas.

It seems likely that Joseph had moved into the hall at Dukesfield Hall sometime after becoming a schoolmaster, although no such move is mentioned by Thomas' in the surviving diaries. He was the census enumerator in 1841 for the area south of the road passing through the village of Slaley into Hexhamshire, an area which included Dukesfield; schoolmasters were often chosen for this task. At that time he was most certainly living in Dukesfield Hall, together with his

wife, son Peter and daughter Elizabeth, while another, possibly related family of Dixons were living at Middle Dukesfield.
Joseph would have been aged about 55 when he was appointed schoolmaster, and he probably remained in that position until a new school was opened in 1849, and a new schoolmaster was sought. Kristensen (1999) quoted an advert for the new appointment dated 3 December 1849, which required that the new master should be competent to teach English Grammar, History, Geography and the rudiments of Mathematics, and that 'He must be a member of the Established Church'. Certainly Joseph had retired as schoolmaster by the time of the 1851 census, but was still living at Dukesfield Hall with his wife and daughter. His wife died just 2 years later, and he died aged 77 years on 11 April 1858, both being buried at Slaley.

Elizabeth (Bulman) Dixon, *(1782-1853)*, Thomas Dixon's mother.

Thomas Dixon's mother, Elizabeth Bulman, was born in about 1782, and she married Joseph Dixon on 12 May 1804, probably at Whitley Chapel. Thomas, her first child, was born at Middle Dukesfield, while her second known child, Peter, was baptised on 10 May 1807, but died aged 5 or 6 years. They were to have four further known children, Joseph born in 1809, Sarah in 1812, Peter in 1816, and Elizabeth (Betsy) in 1826.
At the beginning of Thomas's diaries, his mother would be aged 48 years, probably with four of her five surviving children at home, the youngest being 4 years old. Along with the rest of the family, she participated in visiting and hosting family and friends, occasionally went to Hexham to purchase clothes and other items, visited the *Travellers Rest*, made a trip to Haltwhistle in 1831, spent over a week without her husband at Tynemouth in August 1833 and possibly again in August 1837. She also, in common with most everyone else, helped out with the harvest, shearing wheat and oats for example. Thomas made no mention of either his mother or father ever going to church, but this was almost certainly such a regular occurrence that he saw no need to record it.
She did visit Blaydon once after Thomas had moved there, in August 1836, and she may have called in on her way 'to the sea' in August 1837, but seems to have largely confined her travelling to Hexham by then. She died aged about 71 years on 15 March 1853.

Peter Dixon 1, (1807-11), Thomas Dixon's brother.

Peter was baptised at Whitley Chapel on 10 May 1807, and probably died on 1 July 1811, aged 6 years as the parish registers indicate, rather than on 1 July 1812 aged 5 years as the family tombstone at Slaley suggests. [1]

Joseph Dixon Junr., (1809-57), Thomas Dixon's brother.

Joseph Dixon, younger brother of Thomas by 4 years, was born on 12 December 1809, and he would have been aged 21 years at the commencement of Thomas's diaries. Joe participated in many of the events that Thomas enjoyed, attended Methodist meetings and Anglican services, joined in the singing schools, played the fiddle, visited the pubs, and so on. He had been working in Allendale for quite a while by November 1830, and in May and June1832 he seems to have been working at Harwood Shield, some 5 miles south of Dukesfield, seemingly on bridge construction (See 26 May and 8 June 1832.); this bridge, at the west end of a private road to Riddlehamhope and beyond to Baybridge near Blanchland, carries the date 1832.
There is further indirect evidence that he might have been a stonemason, or a mason's labourer. Thomas noted his 'Remarks on the year 1833' that 'Our Joseph left Jacob', and although it is not possible to be certain, it is possible that he had left Jacob Bulman, recorded as a stonemason of Hollinhouse, a *1/2,* mile west of Whitley Chapel, in 1827, and almost certainly 'Uncle Jacob

---

[1] The parish registers have 'Peter Dixon of Dukesfield, son of Joseph Dixon, smelter, and Elisabeth, late Bulman, died 1 July 1811, buried 2 July 1811, aged 6 1/2 years', but the family tombstone in Slaley churchyard suggests that Peter died on July 1st 1812 aged 5 years.

Bulman' (qv). In addition, although again it remains uncertain evidence, when Thomas observed in June 1831 that Joseph had been 'working for Alex last week and this', he could have been referring to Alex Davison, a stonemason of Bywell who did much work for the Beaumonts and may have been directly in their employ. Additionally, and it could be sheer coincidence, Joseph was working in Allendale in 1830 when the Allendale Smelt Mill bridge was being built, and he was in the Shotley Bridge area in 1833 and 1834 when extensive repairs were being made to the nearby Allensford bridge.
Joe did, however, briefly work at the Dukesfield smelt mill, but only in early 1833 when Thomas had the pox and Joe helped to strip and rebuild the ore hearth until he also caught the pox. He later work alongside Thomas at the ore hearth after both had recovered, but perhaps only for a few shifts; it seems likely that whilst two men were needed to work an ore hearth, only one of them needed to be especially knowledgeable and skilled, so that perhaps any vaguely competent and biddable partner would suffice. But Joe does not feature again in the diaries as working at the Dukesfield or any other smelt mill, and indeed he had gone away to work again by the middle of the year, possibly to mason's work. He worked at Satley and Shotley Bridge in County Durham in 1833 and 1834, and at Riding Mill in October 1835. Joe made regular visits home to Dukesfield, but once Thomas had moved to Blaydon, they saw less of each other for a while. As Thomas was to note in July 1835 'About 17 or 18 weeks since I saw Joe'. He seems to have been more or less permanently based at Shotley Bridge from late in 1835, and the brothers now met more often, for at only 10 miles apart, the walking distance between Blaydon and Shotley Bridge would not have daunted either of them; on one occasion, however, Thomas seems to have first caught a train to Stocksfield, before walking some 7.5 miles from there to Shotley Bridge. They also corresponded with each other, several letters passing between them in 1838 for example.
If Joe was indeed a stonemason, then when George Nixon was 'here [Blaydon] seeking a job for Joe' (4, 5 December 1837), this could have been in connection with the construction of Bywell bridge, (1836 to 1838), for which an advert in the *Newcastle Courant* for 11 June 1836 had advised: 'Stone masons and contractors [wanted] for the building of a bridge of 5 arches across the River Tyne. Contact Mr Nixon, W.B. Lead Office, Newcastle.' Joe is rarely mentioned in Thomas's 1841 diary, only a few visits being recorded, and the last entry regarding this brother, in November 1841, noted that he had begun a singing school at Broomley[?]. Nothing more is known of Joseph, except that he died on 19 November 1857 at the age of 48 years, and was buried in a family grave at Slaley.

Sarah ('Sally') Dixon, (1812-1838), Thomas Dixon's sister.

Thomas's sister Sarah was born on 17 July 1812, baptised at Slaley on 27 August 1812, and died at Dukesfield in 1838. She was aged 18 at the beginning of the diaries, and as there is no mention of her marriage, it must be assumed that she was single when she died aged 26. The diaries contain little of note about her, but she participated in twilting, carried out some shearing (reaping), and came to live with Thomas and Jane in 1833 for an unknown period. She was obviously very poorly in June 1838, which might explain why she rode to Whitley Chapel on an ass on the first day of July that year, and she died just 8 weeks later, on 30 August 1838 at the age of 26 years, to be interred at Slaley. Thomas noted her death with an uncharacteristic diary entry – '30 August 1838 Sister Sarah departed this life at 1/2 past nine at night with a full assurance of the blessed Eternity.'

Peter Dixon 2, (1816-82), Thomas Dixon's brother.

Peter was born in 1816, and was therefore some 11 years younger than Thomas. Like his brothers, nothing is known of Peter's schooling with any certainty but it seems likely that it had recently ended, or was about to end, when Thomas began his diary. He was too young then to be a smelter, and indeed it was rare to find boys under 16 years working at the smelt mills, except where fathers found menial jobs for their sons, such as wheeling peat or lime. Once a boy had turned 16 years, he could begin to be trained in smelting operations. Thomas must have undergone some such sort of 'apprenticeship' with his father, and we can see the

beginnings of it in Peter's activities. A few diary entries during 1830 show that Peter helped Thomas with washing at the mill and with 'stacking peats', but then the diaries are silent until August 1832 when, perhaps just turned 16 years, Peter was on smelting, presumably working alongside another ore-hearth smelter; he did occasionally work alongside Thomas at the ore hearth, but only to deputise for their father when he was ill.
Thomas noted, obscurely as usual, on 27 February 1834, that 'Our Peter left the mill', but it remains unclear whether he had pursued another job. He was certainly active during March in helping his father and Thomas with work on the smallholdings, but that would have been expected had he remained at the smelt mill. It is just possible that he tried his hand at corn milling, but the Slaley district is peppered with Peter Dixons at this time, and individual identification is difficult, if not impossible (but see the later appendix on Peter Dixon of Staples). In any case, Peter was certainly back at the mill in April, working alongside Thomas at the ore hearth to stand in for his father when he was unwell, and he remained there until, with Dukesfield smelt mill about to close, he went to work at the Allen mill in September 1835, but retained his home base at Dukesfield. He and Thomas' brother-in-law Jemmy Ellerington, spent a couple of weeks temsing litharge at Blaydon in 1837, for which there is no obvious explanation, but the 1841 census gives his occupation as 'lead ore smelter', living at Dukesfield Hall with his father, mother and sister Elizabeth.
For some time Peter had participated in the usual family activities, visiting friends and family, chapel-going, gardening, farming, haymaking, fiddle-playing, etc. and these were to continue throughout the period of the later diaries. He married Margaret Burdus, at Slaley on 2 December 1849, she being the eldest daughter of William Burdus, a farmer at Middle Dukesfield, and his wife Margaret (Thorborne). Margaret had been christened at Slaley on 16 April 1820, and she and Peter must have known each other since childhood. They were to have at least four children, the first being born in 1851, by which time Peter and his wife were occupied as coal merchants at Hexham station alongside brother Thomas the station master. They were still there in 1861, Peter being classified as a 'Coal & Lime Agent', while Margaret was a 'Coal Merchant', brother Thomas, now widowed, still being the station master.
The 1881 census, however, gives Peter's occupation as 'Farmer', of White House, Slaley, and his marital status was 'widowed', his wife having died at Hexham Station on 23 July 1862 aged 42 years, soon after giving birth to their son William in April. Peter died at Whitehouse on 2 July 1882 aged 66 years, but his son William continued to farm Whitehouse for an unknown period, his wife Polly dying there on 16 October 1915 aged 49 years. William himself died at Maryholme, Hallbankgate in April 1937. The family tombstone in Slaley churchyard reads:

> Margaret, wife of Peter of Hexham Station, died 23 July 1862 aged 42 years
> Peter died at Whitehouse, Slaley, 2 July 1882 aged 66 years
> Joseph, their son, died at Whitehouse, Slaley, 17 February 1884 aged 28 years
> Polly, wife of William of Whitehouse, Slaley, died 16 October 1915 aged 49 years
> William, husband of Polly, born April 1862, died at Maryholme, Hall Bank Gate, April 1937

Elizabeth ('Betsy') Dixon, (1826-?), Thomas Dixon's sister.

Elizabeth was born in 1826 but the date of her death is unknown. She was aged 4 at the commencement of the diaries, and they contain very little unequivocal information about her. She must have been the Betsy who went to Hexham to 'finish her apprenticeship' in July 1837, and that apprenticeship, presumably residential, must have been in dressmaking, for she made a gown for Thomas's wife Jane while staying with them at Blaydon in late August and early September 1837, and made frocks for Thomas' daughters in January 1841. Betsy twice went to stay in Allendale for a few days in October 1835 and late September 1837, and again visited Thomas and Jane at Blaydon in December 1841. She was still living with her parents at Dukesfield Hall at the time of the 1841 and 1851 censuses, her age being given as 26 years in 1851, but nothing more is known of her, although an Elizabeth Dixon married Cuthbert Burdus at Slaley on 10 September 1854 and they appear to have had a son christened Joseph William Burdus at Slaley just under 7 weeks later.[1]

Elizabeth Dixon, (1828-47), Thomas and Jane's daughter.

Elizabeth was christened on 27 December 1828, and there is therefore little of note concerning her in the first years of the diaries; she is only mentioned twice in the diary for each of the years 1833 and 1834, and not at all in 1835. Elizabeth accompanied her mother when visiting friends and relations, or spending time at Hexham, she was occasionally unwell, she seems to have been taken to the *Travellers Rest* when around 3 years of age, and she went to her first religious gathering aged about 4. She made some trips to Blaydon with her mother in 1836, as did her sister Jane but only one of them at a time, and she began to write in November of that year, aged nearly 8 years, sending a letter from Blaydon to her grandfather at Dukesfield in September 1837. It appears that she did not immediately join her mother and sister in moving to Blaydon in 1837, perhaps because, now aged about 8 years, it was seen fit that she should live with Thomas' parents at Dukesfield, and attend her grandfather's school. However, Elizabeth appears to have been mainly resident at Blaydon during 1841. Elizabeth died on 11 November 1847 at the age of 19 years. Enteritis was given as her cause of death.

Jane Dixon, (1833-1906), Thomas and Jane's daughter.

Jane was born on 6 May 1833 and consequently she does not loom large in the diaries. Indeed, she is only mentioned once after her birth before she was weaned on 22 October 1834; the earlier diary reference is rather confusing for it relates to Jane being christened on 16 February 1834, a Sunday, whereas the Whitley Chapel Parish Records indicate that the christening was on 22 May 1833, a Wednesday. It is not until after Thomas' move to Blaydon that daughter Jane appears more frequently in the diaries, for she accompanied her mother on two trips to Blaydon in 1836, moved there with her mother in 1837, and subsequently made trips back to Dukesfield and Langley. Thomas took 'little Jane' to a religious meeting in February 1838, when his wife had gone home to Dukesfield for a weekend, and took her to see the Scotswood Chain Bridge in July 1838. Jane would be just 8 years of age at the end of the last known diary, and other than her attendance at a school in the Blaydon area in 1841, and her inclusion along with the rest of her immediate family in the 1841 and 1851 census returns, nothing more is known of her until 1855 when, it would seem, she married her cousin Thomas Bulman, the son of Uncle Jacob and Aunt Betty Bulman (qv), at St John Lee on 2 May 1855; Thomas's residence was given as West Oakwood and his occupation as 'Agent'.[2]

By the time of the 1871 census, Jane and Thomas (now a 'Commission Agent') were living at 19 Hallgate, Hexham, together with a son, Jacob Dixon Bulman, who had been born in Newcastle and was now aged 14, while their daughter Elizabeth, born at Carrs Hill in Gateshead and aged 13, was with a next-door neighbour on the evening of the census. The family had moved to the city of Durham before the next census in 1881, which recorded Thomas, Jane and Jacob as living at 10 Mowbray St, Crossgate, both men being commercial travellers; daughter Elizabeth was not present on the evening of the census.[3] Jacob would marry Harriette Hannah Colpitts on 12 June in the following year, she being the 24 year old daughter of George Colpitts, publican of Colpitts Terrace.[4] Harriette and Jacob, now described as a corn merchant, were living at 16 Flass Street, Durham, (a street parallel to Mowbray St), when their daughter Jane Carol Bulman was born on 8 January 1888, but Harriette was not to survive until the 1891 census, by which time Thomas, now described as an 'Agent, Insurance', and Jane had moved to 44 Claypath, Durham, on the north east side of the city;

---

[1] William Burdus, the farmer of Middle Dukesfield, and his wife Margaret, had a son Cuthbert aged around 15 at the time of the 1841 census as did Thomas Burdus, a land agent of Coalpits, and his wife Mary.

[2] I am grateful to Hilary Kristensen for this and the following information relating to Jane Dixon.

[3] Mowbray St still exists, a terrace of modest houses, probably built in the 1870s, in the shadow of the railway viaduct.

[4] Mowbray St was only a few hundred yards from Colpitts Terrace where the *Colpitts Hotel* still serves alcohol.

Jacob was living with them, as was their daughter Elizabeth, she being described as a 'Lodging Housekeeper'. The lodging house probably occupied part of 44 Claypath, for there were two 23 year old male lodgers living with them, a student from Breconshire who was attending Durham university, and a South Devon born schoolmaster. Jacob's daughter, Jane Carol Bulman, was visiting a coal-mining family in Gilesgate Moor on the night of the census. At the age of 42, Elizabeth Bulman married James Armstrong Haswell, born in Sunderland and aged 37, the artist son of an engineer, on 16 July 1900, and they lived then or soon after at 38 Old Street, Durham. At the time of the 1901 census, Thomas and Jane Bulman, aged 70 and 67 respectively and 'living on [their] own means', may have moved to live with Elizabeth and James at Old Street, for they and their granddaughter Jane Carol were all there on the night of that census.

Jonathan Sparke (1781-1866), Thomas Dixon's father-in-law.

Jonathan Sparke appears to have been born in the Allendale area in1781,[1] probably the son of the Jonathan Sparke who married Margaret Tweddle, in the parish of Hexham on 22 November 1775. He married Elizabeth Dryden in the parish of Warden, Northumberland, on 9 October 1804, and there is nothing to suggest that he re-married after her death in 1818, when their five children were aged between 4 and 13 years.
Given their policy of promoting from within, it could be that Jonathan had worked as a smelter for WB Lead, firstly at the Allen Mill, and then at Allenheads mill, moving to Dukesfield mill sometime between 1814, when his son John was born, and 1826 when he was listed in a Northumberland Poll Book as being resident at Dukesfield, with a freehold called Stoney Law; he voted for the reactionary Matthew Bell at the 1826 by-election. Curiously, it is possible that he replaced a Thomas Dixon as agent at Dukesfield mill, although the only evidence for this is a tombstone at Whitley Chapel engraved 'Thomas Dixon of Dukesfield Hall died December 6th 1823 aged 33 years, and an associated tombstone to his wife which notes that he had been an agent. Of Jonathan Sparke's daughters, Jane married Thomas Dixon the diarist; Elizabeth (Liza) married James (Jemmy) Ellerington, a Dukesfield lead smelter; Margaret married John Middleton of Byker Hill, Newcastle; Mary married a smelt mill agent. Jonathan's son, referred to as 'Tweddle' in the diaries, became an agent with WB Lead as outlined later.
Quite what hours Jonathan was expected to work as mill agent is unknown, and may never have been specified, but they clearly left him sufficient time to keep a garden and run a farm-holding; Thomas hand-threshed an unspecified cereal for him in February 1830. Jonathan then took over another farm in the following month, together with a Henry Oxley, presumably to be farmed in addition to whatever holding he already occupied. He grew oats, wheat, turnips and hay, kept cows and pigs, and also had horses, perhaps a riding horse as well as a farm horse. Thomas, and sometimes his parents, assisted Jonathan with his farming and gardening activities, especially at harvest time.
Although Thomas never mentions his father in law's attendance at church or chapel, we can probably assume that he was a church goer; certainly many Sunday dinners and teas were provided for Thomas and Jane at the hall, and Sparke obviously enjoyed social gatherings:

> 4 January 1832, At Mr. Sparke's to dinner & tea; a great party there.
> 21 September 1832, Sparks churn today.
> Sunday 7 July 1833, A great deal of company at Sparks.

In December 1834, the last full year of operation at Dukesfield mill, Jonathan made the Pays at the mill, totalling almost £6,200, half to the smelters, and the rest for the carriage of ore to the mill and of lead to Blaydon. His situation during and after the closure of Dukesfield smelt mill is rather difficult to unravel, for there were to be many comings and goings. William Bownas, the Dukesfield mill foreman, was to spend 6 weeks working at the Allen mill and 7 at Blagill mill in the latter half of 1834, before becoming mill agent at Rookhope on an annual salary of £120. Meanwhile, Jonathan remained at Dukesfield, still on his £100 p.a. salary. He made a

[1] Two Jonathan Spark(e)s were christened at Allendale, in 1781, one the son of Jonathan, the other the son of 'Jno'.

much reduced smelter's pay in November 1835 (£581 6s. 2d.), but no ore carriage pay, both indications that Dukesfield mill was about to be largely abandoned; the size of the yearly Pays at Dukesfield then fell markedly as the mill was rapidly wound down. Perhaps as a response to Jonathan's reduced responsibilities, his salary seems to have been lowered to £50 p.a. plus house rent together with expenses of £12 0s. 6d. Probably the only full-time worker at Dukesfield by the middle of 1835 was John Clemitson, who had been kept on at £7 per month to wash any remaining stocks of ore or slags. Some, 427 pieces of lead were smelted during 1836, and Jonathan made a half-year Pay in July 1836 of £67 7s. 10d., and an August Pay of £89 7s. 10d.
Jonathan held a sale in April 1836, and gave up his Dukesfield farm in the following month to move to Langley, where he must, at least initially, have held some sort of agency position with WB Lead. Clemitson continued to work at Dukesfield mill during 1837 and 1838, now being paid around £8 per month, but Thomas Steel, the Allen mill agent, made the Dukesfield pay at December 1838, totalling just £63 1s. 11d. WB Lead abandoned the Dukesfield and Blagill mills were during 1840 and it is uncertain what then happened to Jonathan Sparke. The 1841 census listed him as a 'Smelting Agent' living at Hill Top, Langley, with a female servant aged about 15 years, probably living in an adjacent cottage. It was a very short walk from there to the Langley and Blagill smelt mills and it may be that Jonathan had become an agent for the firm of Wilson & Co, who had bought Blagill mill and presumably kept it going after WB Lead pulled out.

A tombstone at St Peters probably refers to the Dukesfield mill agent and his wife:

> Elizabeth Sparke, wife of Jonathan of Peasmeadows died 7 May 1818 aged 37
> Jonathan Sparke died 1 July 1866 aged 85

Elizabeth (Dryden) Sparke (c1781-1818), Thomas Dixon's mother-in-law

The first two children born to Elizabeth Dryden, Jane and Margaret, were christened at Allendale in 1805 and 1807 respectively, while the next three, Elizabeth, Mary and John Tweddle, were christened at St Peters, further up the valley in 1810, 1812 and 1814 respectively. Elizabeth died in 1818, probably aged 37 years, when the five children were aged between 4 and 13 years. Thomas Dixon almost certainly never knew her.

Elizabeth (Liza/Eliza) Sparke, (1810-) & James (Jemmy), Ellerington,(1806-63), Thomas Dixon's sister- and brother-in-law.

Elizabeth Sparke, the third daughter of Jonathan Sparke and Elizabeth Dryden, was christened at St Peter's, Allenheads, or at Allenheads itself, on 21 October 1810. She moved to live in Dukesfield Hall with the rest of her family sometime before 1827. Early in his 1830 diary, Thomas Dixon noted that he had accompanied James (Jemmy) Ellerington to Bywell where they obtained a licence for Jemmy and Liza Sparke to marry. Jemmy was a son of a John Ellerington of Juniper, (probably the yeoman farmer of High Juniper who was listed in a directory of 1827), and was christened at Whitley Chapel on 1 June 1806. One of Jemmy's brothers was almost certainly John Ellerington, a shoemaker at High Juniper, who had married Barbara (Babby) Gilhespie/Gillhespey on 5 May 1827. Jemmy was probably already an ore hearth smelter at Dukesfield mill by this time although the earliest diary confirmation dates from 1832. Jemmy and Liza's courtship was perhaps of at least 3 years standing, for they had acted as witnesses for Thomas and Jane's wedding in 1827. Their own marriage was conducted at Slaley Church on 1 May 1830, the witnesses being a W Colling and Liza's elder sister Margaret. Liza's first child, a boy whom they named John, was born on 20 September 1830, just 4 1/2 months after her marriage, Jane Dixon having been 'with her all night'. Jemmy and Liza were to have at least four more children, Elizabeth (unaccountably not directly recorded in Thomas's diaries but born c.3 October 1832), Mary born 1 December 1834, Margaret born 13 October 1836, and Ann born c1839.

Jemmy and Liza seem to have lived at Juniper immediately after their marriage, but when the farmer Thomas Teasdale moved from Middle Dukesfield to Hexham early in 1832, they moved into his former dwelling, a house which Thomas Dixon referred to as 'Dukesfield old House'. Jemmy seems to have thereby come into a smallholding of around 10 acres in grass and arable land, and almost certainly a garden. Consequently, like several workers at Dukesfield smelt mill, Jemmy took on farm work alongside his smelting job, and bought a 'black cow' in August. He even acquired his own horse, presumably for general draught use. Jemmy seems to have come to an agreement with Thomas during 1833 that the latter should takeover part of his land at Middle Dukesfield, a gesture which enabled Thomas to have his own smallholding. It is not surprising therefore that Jemmy and Thomas regularly helped each other out in matters agricultural and horticultural. For example, Jemmy made some water furrows for Thomas, while Thomas helped Jemmy to lead his corn and to set some plants. Thomas was able to make use of Jemmy's horse in leading his own hay, and also in travelling from Dukesfield to Blaydon in Jemmy's cart in August 1841; Thomas' wife and daughter Jane had travelled from Langley to Dukesfield in the same way in October 1837.

The brothers in law also assisted each other in their smelting work, Thomas being 'on' for Jemmy when the latter was ill in March and October 1832. Jemmy began to work at the Allen smelt mill with the imminent closure of Dukesfield mill, but his main residence remained at Middle Dukesfield where he continued to run his smallholding. It also seems likely that Jemmy and Liza had a house servant from this time on, if not before, Fanny Rodham aged about 15, acting in that capacity in 1841. Jemmy and Thomas' brother Peter did some work at the Blaydon refinery in 1837, but this was clearly not intended to be permanent.

The two couples often hosted each other to Sunday teas, and Jane and Liza also spent other times together, visiting Babby Ellerington, going to Hexham, and spending a week in Allendale in April 1832. Liza also stayed for a short while at Blaydon in June 1841, together with her sister Mary, when Jane was having her third child. Contacts between the couples had obviously become less frequent by 1841, but as Jemmy and Liza were still living at Middle Dukesfield, they were on hand whenever Thomas and Jane visited the area.

An un-marked burial at Whitley Chapel is of James Ellerington of Middle Dukesfield, surely Jemmy, who died in 1863 aged 57, only 3 years before Jane Dixon died. What became of Liza and the children has not been pursued.

Margaret (1807-?), Mary (1812-?), and Martha (?), Sparke, Thomas Dixon's sisters-in-law

Margaret Sparke was christened at Allendale on 29 September 1805, the second daughter of Jonathan and Elizabeth Sparke. She does not feature strongly in Thomas's diaries in spite of being Jane Dixon's sister. Indeed, Margaret is not mentioned at all between 1830 and the beginning of 1833, and just four times between then and the beginning of 1837. The only event of significance during that time was her marriage to John Middleton of Byker Hill, Newcastle, on 25 June 1836, after which she lived with her husband at Byker; the witnesses to the marriage were her brother Tweddle and her sister Mary. Her first child was christened just 7 months later in January 1837, her father travelling from Langley to Byker in order to 'stand' for the child. Sad events of 1838 suggest that the child was named Wylam, for a letter from Byker to Thomas and Jane Dixon on 7 March 1838, informed them of 'Wylam's illness'. Jane promptly went to Byker on the following day, and Wylam died on 11 March; Jonathan Sparke and his daughter Mary visited Byker two days later. Margaret Middleton continued to visit Dukesfield and Blaydon occasionally thereafter.

Mary Sparke was christened at 'Saint Peter and Allenheads' on 8 March 1812, the fourth daughter of Jonathan and Elizabeth Sparke. Like her sister Margaret, she received only occasional mentions in Thomas's diaries. She did call in at Blaydon on her way to Byker a couple of times in 1836, once in 1837, twice in 1838, and with her sister Liza to attend to Jane Dixon at the birth of her short-lived third child in June 1841. She was presumably living with her father at Langley Hill Top at this time, but later that year, on 31 October 1841, she married Samuel Walton, a smelting agent like her father, who also lived at Hill Top; he was a local census enumerator in 1841.

Martha Spark(e), who was probably related to the Sparke sisters, is only really featured twice in the diaries, the first occasion in 1832 when she spent 10 weeks at Dukesfield, probably living either with Thomas and Jane or with Jonathan Sparke, and the second in 1834 when she spent a few days there.

John Tweddle Sparke, (1814-?), Thomas Dixon's brother-in-law

The 'Tweddle' of Thomas Dixon's diaries was John Tweddle Sparke, son of Jonathan Sparke the Dukesfield mill agent and his wife Elizabeth Dryden, born on 11 December 1814 and christened on 20 December 1814 at St Peters, Allenheads. He is not mentioned at all in the first year of Thomas's diary, which is rather surprising given that he was Jane's 15 year old brother, and there are only five references to him in 1832. However, the latter indicate that he was already participating in a singing school and visiting the *Travellers Rest*.
It seems likely that Tweddle was already assisting his father as a junior clerk at Dukesfield mill, for he was offered a similar or more senior position at the Allendale smelt mill in February 1833 when aged just 18. He made the Allen mill ore carriage and smelters' Pays in December 1834, nearly £4,000 in total, and his father assisted him with the Allen mill accounts in January 1835, perhaps in anticipation of Thomas Steel's imminent promotion to the Allen mill agency from his sub-agent position at Rookhope, and of Tweddle's simultaneous transfer to Blagill, seemingly as mill clerk/agent. Tweddle can not have had any direct personal experience of smelting and his move to Allen mill, and then to Blagill, seem to run counter to what is generally assumed to have been WB's policy of promotion from within, of smelt mill agents having once been smelters. Perhaps accountancy skills now counted as being of equal importance to metallurgical ones, and provided that a good mill foreman was on hand, a clerk could run the show.
Tweddle, like the other mill agents, periodically received sums of money from WB Lead throughout 1835, presumably to cover running expenses at Blagill, or perhaps the smelters' subsistence money, and he made the ore carriage and smelters' pay at Blagill at the end of the year, some £3,300 in total. The mill produced 72,349 pieces of lead in 1835 plus £601 worth of bullion, and at the year end Tweddle received his salary of £50 for a good year's work.
Although he continued as agent at Blagill between 1836 and 1839, receiving monies and making the Pays, some of these Pays were actually made at the Allen mill, for Thomas Dixon noted that he had helped Tweddle with the Allen Pays in January 1836 and 1837. Tweddle spent a few days at Edinburgh in July of the latter year, possibly in accordance with WB Lead's (and the Greenwich Hospital's) common practice of sponsoring the sons of mill agents to undergo a short course in chemistry at the university there. But when Tweddle made the Blagill Pay of £530 15s. 10d. at the end of 1839, and there were no remaining stocks of ore or lead remaining at the mill, that marked the end of WB Lead's involvement with Blagill, and possibly of Tweddle's employment by the concern. It may be that he returned to his old position as assistant to his father, but if so, his almost total absence from Thomas Dixon's 1841 diary, (just one uninformative note of 18 January), is somewhat surprising.
Tweddle married Elisabeth (Betsy) Martinson, daughter of William, on 29 May 1838 in the parish of Warden, Northumberland, when both were 23 years old. They clearly remained in the area, and had at least two children. Their daughter Mary Hannah Sparke, then aged 18 years, married Thomas Boutland, aged 23, in the parish of Warden on 19 December 1864; their son Jonathan and his wife Elizabeth, (possibly Elizabeth Forster, married at Brotton, Yorkshire, on 19 November 1864) had their son John Tweddle Spark christened at Simonburn on 7 October 1866. According to Kelly's *Directory* for 1921, a 'Jn. Tweddle Sparke' was living at 2 St George's Road, Hexham.

Cousins Sarah and Hugh Armstrong.

One of Elizabeth (Dryden) Sparke's sisters, Jane, married a Joseph Armstrong in the parish of Warden on 21 October 1807. They were to have at least two children, Sarah christened at Haydon Bridge on 24 April 1808, and Hugh christened at Haydon Bridge on 30 December 1810. Sarah and Hugh were therefore cousins of Jane (Sparke) Dixon.

Sarah Armstrong does not feature strongly in the diaries, possibly because, living at Haydon Bridge, she did not visit Dukesfield very often. However, she did have tea with her uncle Jonathan Sparke in July 1830 and was again at Dukesfield in April 1831. She married Henry Wilson at Simonburn on 20 May 1833 but, oddly, the marriage is not mentioned in Thomas Dixon's diary. Henry had been christened just a few months after Sarah, at St John Lee on 17 July 1808, and he may have lived then, as he certainly did later, at Dunkirk near Chollerton. Sarah's first child, also Henry, was christened at St John Lee on 23 March 1834, and they were to have at least two more sons, Joseph and Hugh, born c1837 and 1840 respectively. Sarah seems not to have visited Dukesfield after her first child was born, but occasional contact was maintained through visits to Chollerton by her brother Hugh, and by Jonathan Sparke and Jane Dixon. Sarah's husband was listed as a farmer in the 1841 Census, but he was also surveyor to the West End Division (Hexham to Rothbury) of the Hexham to Alnmouth turnpike by 1846, a part-time job with a salary of £30 p.a. (raised to £45 p.a. in 1848/49). The family were still living at Dunkirk at this time, a property which fronted the turnpike less than half a mile north-east of the Brunton cross roads, but Henry may have died in 1855, for his son Henry junr., aged only 21 years, succeeded his 'late father' as turnpike surveyor in December 1855. Henry junr. gave his home address as St Oswald Hill Head, Hexham in 1860, and he seems to have added the surveyorship of at least a part of the West Auckland & Elishaw (Otterburn) turnpike to that of the Alnmouth turnpike. However, Henry junr. had resigned his surveyorships by June 1863, perhaps out of frustration with his inability to perform his job properly due to the trusts' acute and apparently inevitable shortage of funds. In fact the turnpike trust for Hexham to Rothbury section was formally expired only 4 years later; the Wilsons had made the mistake of allying themselves with yesterday's transport system, one which was now being overwhelmed by the new railway system.
Hugh Armstrong was much closer to Thomas and Jane Dixon than Sarah had been, especially evident during 1833 when he actually came to live with his cousins at Dukesfield. Thomas and Hugh obviously enjoyed each other's company, sometimes going to church together, or taking walks and visiting the *Clickem Inn*, accompanied occasionally by Thomas' brother Joe. Hugh seems to have fathered an illegitimate child around the time that he was living at Dukesfield, with a Mary Robson (see 6 December 1833). It is not at all clear what occupation Hugh held, although he did make some drawers for Thomas and Jane and he also appears to have made himself a violin, but whatever job he practised seems not to have generated a permanent livelihood, for Thomas often noted 'Hugh gone to seek work'. He came to work at the bone mill at the Blaydon refinery in March 1837, his child drowning shortly after, but his time at the refinery was abruptly cut short when he died after a short illness on 16 November, aged around 27. Hugh was buried near Dunkirk, perhaps in Chollerton churchyard, and Jane Dixon attended the funeral.

Other Uncles, Aunts, and Cousins.

Thomas named twelve uncles and about the same number of aunts in his diaries, some clearly living in the neighbourhood of Dukesfield, and one of whom, Uncle John Bulman, also worked at the Dukesfield smelt mill; some of these relatives were clearly on his side of the family, others will have been on Jane's, and therefore collectively they might be Dixons, Sparkes, Bulmans, or Drydens, or have surnames of men who married family daughters of either side. Not much can be gleaned about most of these relatives from the diaries themselves, and no serious attempt has been made here to determine the precise relationships, whereabouts, occupations or activities of most of them. Uncles John and Jacob Bulman, however, merit further examination, as the uncles most often referred to in the diaries.

Uncle John, Aunt Nancy, and Sally Bulman.

A John Bulman married Ann Bowman in Hexham parish on 9 February 1807. He was probably a brother of Thomas Dixon's mother, and he and his wife are almost certainly the 'Uncle John and Nancy' in the diaries. They lived at Dyehouse, and John worked at the Dukesfield smelt mill, sometimes at the ore hearth, but also at the roasting furnace. John was listed as a lead ore smelter in

the 1841 census, when he and Nancy were both aged around 50, and their dressmaker daughter Sarah, aged about 30 years, was living with them at the time; 'Sally', as she was sometimes referred to in the diary, had been christened at Whitley Chapel on 5 July 1807. Nancy may also have been a dressmaker, for she both made and adjusted clothes and curtains for Jane Dixon during 1831 and 1832, while Sally made a gown for Jane in December 1834, and a cloak in 1838.
Uncle John was also clearly quite a handyman, widening a fold door and repairing a house for Jemmy Ellerington. He also enjoyed singing, and John and Nancy were part of the family tea hosting circle. There is no indication in the diaries of their involvement in smallholding, nor of any specific religious affiliations, but strong evidence from elsewhere points to the likelihood of their close association with Wesleyan Methodism.
A John and Ann Bulman were listed as members of the Finechambers Wesleyan Methodists at least from 1819 and up to 1833, with John acting as a class leader by 1828; a Sarah Bulman was also a member of the Finechambers society in1830, and Thomas Dixon attended several meetings at Finechambers. A John Bulman was a leader for the Dukesfield Wesleyan Methodists in 1826, but that was a year when the Finechambers society seem to have temporarily relocated to Dukesfield, the two societies subsequently combining at Finechambers in 1831. A Mollersteads Wesleyan Methodist Society then seems to have been commenced in 1833, and its nine members in 1836 included a John Bulman as leader, while Finechambers had 24 members in two classes in the same year, the class leaders being a John Bulman and a John Ellerington. The latter was almost certainly the shoemaker of High Juniper who was brother to Jemmy Ellerington, and it is conceivable that the John Bulman who was a class leader for three Methodist societies at different times was one and the same person. There was, however, at least one other John Bulman in the area, for example the one listed as a stonemason of Low Dyehouse in 1827.
Sally Bulman appears to have died unmarried on 4 March 1858 aged 50, being buried in an unmarked grave at Whitley Chapel. (Kristensen). Again the picture is complicated by the fact that there were at least two other Sarah Bulmans in the Hexham area at the time, and both were probably related to Thomas Dixon's mother. Both of these Sarahs, however, did marry – see Uncle Joshua and Uncle Skelton below.

Uncle Jacob and Aunt Betty Bulman.

Uncle Jacob Bulman, a stonemason, must have been another of Thomas Dixon's mother's brothers. He married Elizabeth (Betty) Cliffan in the parish of Hexham on 15 December 1821. They were to have at least six children, Mary christened at Whitley Chapel on 7 December 1822, Sarah also christened at Whitley Chapel on 28 July 1825, Thomas born on 8 October and christened on 1 November 1830, Elizabeth christened 20 April 1833 but died in April 1838, Thomasin born on 2 December 1835 and christened at Hexham on 1 January 1836 but possibly dying pre. 1841, and Thomasin Elizabeth christened on 28 July 1841 in Hexham.
Uncle Jacob was probably the Jacob Bulman listed as a stonemason of Hollinhouse, a mile to the west of Whitley Chapel, in a directory of 1827-28, and as such he may have employed Thomas Dixon's brother Joe for a while, possibly as an apprentice. Jacob and Betty initially lived close enough to Dukesfield to be part of the regular family tea-hosting circle, and they seem to have organised a communal twilting at their home in July 1830. Contacts between the families remained quite strong even after Jacob and Betty moved to Hexham on 14 November 1832 so that, for example, Jacob came to see Thomas when he was ill with the pox early in 1833. They continued to meet after Thomas had moved to Blaydon, either there, at Hexham, or at Dukesfield. The 1841 Census has Jacob and Betty and their family of three daughters and one son, living in Battle Hill in Hexham, with Margaret Cliffan aged around 70 and presumably Betty's mother, living alongside; Jacob was stated to be a mason. Jacob, Betty and family were at the same address in 1851, Jacob now being classed as a builder, but it would seem that they subsequently moved to West Oakwood at Anick, just north of the Tyne opposite Hexham, where Jacob took up farming. Jacob may have died during 1855, the year in which his son Thomas married Thomas Dixon's daughter Jane. The 1861 census for Anick includes Elizabeth Bulman aged 61, head of household and retired farmer's widow, her daughter Sarah acting as housekeeper.

Betty Bulman clearly had a brother Thomas, and he appears occasionally in the diaries, sometimes named simply as 'Cliffan'. He married Mary Taleford on 5 June 1830, and Thomas and Jane entertained 'Jacob, Thos. Cliffan and wives here at tea' a few weeks later.
It should be noted that there was a Jacob, son of Thomas Bulman, christened at Whitley Chapel on 4 November 1792, and seemingly another Jacob, son of Thomas Bulman, christened at the same place just 7 days later! Uncle Jacob may have been one of these.

Other relatives.

Uncle Willy Hall liked singing and may have farmed locally; he died on Sunday 20 June 1841. Uncle Thomas may have been another Thomas Dixon, possibly a brother of Joseph Dixon ('3 October 1834, Father and Betsey gone to Uncle Thomas'). He may have lived at or near Shotley Bridge, but he kept touch with his nephew Thomas, the diarist, throughout the period covered by the diaries. Uncle Joshua could have been the Joshua Smith who married a Sarah Bulman on 23 January 1796 in Hexham parish. Uncle Skelton, sometimes 'Uncle Robert', was probably the Robert Skelton who also married a Sarah Bulman on 28 October 1819 in Hexham parish; he wrote to Thomas Dixon to inform him of their daughter's death in December 1838.

The diaries also refer to uncles Jemmy and George, uncle and aunt Charlton, and to aunts Betty Bulman, Hannah, Hannah R, Mally, Mary, Mary of Lementon, Peggy, Peggy Bulman, Peggy Charlton, Peggy Hall, Peggy Nichol, Peggy of Hexham, and Sally. Five of the six cousins named by Thomas Dixon died during the period covered by his diaries - cousin Skelton died in March 1834, cousin Hugh Armstrong in November 1837, cousin Betsy Bulman in April 1838, cousin Sarah Skelton in December 1838, and cousin Jacob Bulman in January 1841.

APPENDIX 3 - SOME OTHER DIXON FAMILIES IN THE AREA, MILLERS AT HEXHAM AND DUKESFIELD.

Peter Dixon of Staples, his sons Joseph and James, and Hexham Tyne Mills.

This Peter Dixon was a son of Joseph Dixon (c1731-1812) and Mary (Chatt) (c1735/8-1821/24) of Low Staples, who were married at Whitley Chapel on 17 February 1770. Peter was born c1771, and he married (perhaps for the second time) Isabella Teasdale at Whitley Chapel on 24 July 1815, (she died on 26 August 1830 aged 46). They had sons Joseph (1816-86) and James (1819-1869) and daughters Ann (1820-41), Mary (1823-?) and Isabella (1825-59). At some stage, almost certainly before 1823, Peter Dixon owned or tenanted Hexham Tyne Mills, quite a large corn-milling concern located near the Tyne bridge Hexham (Wright, 1823). Peter was listed as 'corn miller, Tyne Mill [Hexham]' in a directory of 1827-28, but a directory of 1834 indicates that Tyne Mills were then being run by a John Dixon. This John may have been brother to Peter, who would now be some 63 years of age and was to die on 27 March 1841 aged 70. The 1841 Census shows Peter's sons Joseph and James and daughters Mary and Isabella, still living at Low Staples, only Joseph, (christened at Whitley Chapel on 2 September 1816), having a recorded occupation, as 'Flour Dealer'; two 1855 directories give this Joseph as owner or tenant of Tyne Mills and he must have been joined by his brother James in the Tyne Mills enterprise for each of them gave their address as Tyne Mills and Dukesfield in 1859.

Joseph had married a Jane, (possibly Margaret Jane Holmes, at Newcastle on 3 March 1863), and the family tombstone in Hexham clearly confirms his relationship with James and the Dukesfield area:

> The infant children of Joseph and Jane Dixon, Tyne Mills, Hexham.
> Thomas died 24 April 1865 aged 5 months.
> James died 4 January 1866.
> Anne died 25 April 1867.
> Michael Elliott died 9 March 1871 aged 3 months.
> The above Joseph died 28 September 1886 aged 70
> Also Peter, the only son of the late James of Dukesfield Hall, nephew of the above Joseph, died 28 March 1902 aged 40
> Also Jane, widow of Joseph, died 26 October 1913 aged 77

James Dixon (?1819-69), was probably the person of that name who married Jane Blackburn at Slaley on 11 August 1855, and who was described as a farmer of 'Duke's Hall' in that year; their son, Peter, was christened at Slaley on 22 April 1861. An Auction to be held on 20 April 1859 at the *White Hart Inn*, Hexham, advertised two lots:

> 1. 'Hill House' in Hexham High Quarter, a freehold property with 31 plus acres, now in occupation of James Dixon.[1]
>
> 2. A copyhold 'Inn or Public House' and garden at Smelting Syke, in the Low Quarter, tenanted by Mr Stephen Harrison.[2]

Further particulars could be obtained from Messrs Joseph and James Dixon, Tyne Mills and Dukesfield, or from Mr John Stokoe, Solicitor, Hexham. James may therefore have given up Hill House to take a farm at Dukesfield Hall. An unmarked grave at Whitley Chapel is that of James Dixon of Dukesfield Hall, who died on 14 February 1869 aged 50, and this is almost

---

[1] Hill House was about 0.25 miles SE of High Lilswood and is shown as in ruins on recent OS maps.

[2] Stephen Harrison had been publican at the *Fox and Hounds*, Slaley, in 1847; a public house is shown at Smelting Syke on the First Edition 6 inch OS map.

certainly James the son of Peter of Staples; an auction sale in May 1870, for the 'farming stock belonging to the representatives of the late Mr James Dixon' must relate to this James. It is also possible that another unmarked grave at Whitley Chapel is that of his wife Jane who died aged 32 years on 10 June 1861, and another of a son John who died aged almost 4 years, on 1 September 1861.

The Dixons of Dukesfield Corn Mill

Just to confuse matters still further, a Peter Dixon 'of Dukesfield mill', and presumably that meant the corn mill rather than the smelt mill at Dukesfield, must have owned or tenanted the corn mill when his son, also Peter, was baptised at Whitley Chapel on 20 January 1788. It is possible that the mill was locally known as Peter's Mill in the 1830s, which might explain Thomas Dixon's diary entries:

> 16 October 1833, The millwrights come to Peter mill this week.
> 22 January 1834, Peter's mill opened out.

Peter junr. may have had a brother, for a Thomas, son of Peter Dixon, was christened at Whitley Chapel on 26 March 1774, while two daughters of a Thomas Dixon, 'of Dukesfield mill', Alice and Sarah, were baptised at Whitley Chapel in 1805 and 1807 respectively. It is unlikely that this was the Thomas Dixon who died in 1823 and whose tombstone at Whitley Chapel describes him as of Dukesfield Hall, while his wife's tombstone describes him as an agent, presumably for Dukesfield smelt mill. It has not been possible to relate Peter Dixon of Dukesfield mill to the Dixons of Staples except for the tenuous occupation link of miller. Nor is there any obvious evidence to support a direct relationship between any of the above Dixons and Thomas Dixon the diarist, who did not refer to a James, Joseph or Peter as either uncle or cousin, although he did mention an Uncle Jemmy. When Peter Dixon of Staples died on 28 March 1841, Thomas simply noted 'Old P Dixon died', and although he was at Dukesfield at the time it is questionable whether he actually attended Peter's funeral.

APPENDIX 4 - KNOWN PREACHERS HEARD OR MENTIONED BY THOMAS DIXON.

In the Dukesfield area.

Adamson, Bill, Primitive Methodist.
William Adamson was born in 1801 at Spittal Shields in Hexhamshire to William and Elizabeth, was 'converted' in the summer of 1830, and was speaking in public just 3 months later. He was listed in a 'Stations of the Travelling Preachers' for the Hexham Primitive Methodist circuit in 1833 and was the leader of the Dyehouse Primitive Methodists in 1835. He subsequently moved to a County Durham pit village in 1844, becoming a class leader and local preacher at the Thornley station, where he died on 1 January 1872 leaving his widow with two sons and three daughters. He had a brother Thomas, also a Primitive Methodist.

Airey, **Mr**, C of E, Whitley Chapel & Slaley.

Armstrong, Rev H.
An account of the reopening of Slaley Church by 'John Bull' has 'Rev H Armstrong, Curate of Wooler (Mason p33) and implies that he was then the 'late curate of Slaley'.

Bearpark, Wesleyan Methodist.
A John Bearpark, aged around 80, was recorded as a 'Staymaker' of Market St, Hexham, in an 1827-28 directory, and in the 1841 census.

Bell, **John**, Wesleyan Methodist.

Bilson, Primitive Methodist.
James Bilston arrived in the Hexham circuit in 1831, having already been at Nottingham 1823; Bradwell 1825; Belper 1826: Thurne 1827; Malton 1828; Brotherton 1829; Silsden 1830;and left for North Shields in 1833.

Bowman, John, Primitive Methodist.

Coghill, Wesleyan Methodist.
Donald M Coghill matriculated at Glasgow University in 1827 and first joined the itinerant ministry in the Hexham Circuit in 1834 before being moved to Aberdeen in 1835, and Wigan [or Wigton] in 1836. He fell ill in 1840, and as he was unable to perform circuit duties, he was appointed a supernumerary. He died on 9 April, 1842 aged 32.

Ellerington, **John**, Wesleyan Methodist.
A John Ellerington was a leader of Finechambers Wesleyan Methodists in 1836. An R. and a J. Ellerington of Corbridge appear as a preachers on a Hexham Wesleyan Circuit plan of 1851, when both were down to speak at Finechambers.

Forster, **Watn**, Wesleyan Methodist.
A Watson Forster was a member of the Blanchland Wesleyan Methodists in 1819.

Hannah, Mr, Wesleyan Methodist
John Hannah junr was moved from Appleby to Hexham in 1833, and then to Morpeth in the following year. Hills Arrangement has him at Ramsey 1829; Appleby 1831; Hexham 1833; Morpeth 1834; Pickering 1835; Preston 1836; Snaith 1837.

Hardcastle, Wesleyan Methodist.
P Hardcastle junr, joined the Hexham circuit in 1829. During 1830, he was moved to the Penrith circuit, then Wigton (1833) and Oldham (1835).

Harrison, **M^{r}**, C of E, Slaley.

Heslop, C of E, Slaley.

Richard Heslop succeeded the Rev Joseph Smith as vicar of Slaley and remained as such from 1831 to 1850.

Hornsby, **W**^{m}, Wesleyan Methodist.
W. Hornsby of Slaley appears as a preacher on a Hexham Wesleyan Circuit plan of 1851.

Leek, Wesleyan Methodist.
Robert Leake joined the Hexham circuit in 1830, but was moved to the Aberdeen circuit during 1831, then to Middleham (1833), Bangor (1834), and Bridlington (1835).

Loraine, Wesleyan Methodist.
A Nevison Lorraine was a leader for the Hexham Wesleyan Methodists in 1831 and 1836.

Lyons, Wesleyan Methodist.
A John Lyons was a leader of the Hexham Wesleyan Methodists in 1826 and 1836. A tombstone in Elswick Cemetery, Newcastle, notes that the Rev Robt Lyon, Wesleyan Minister, died 12 September 1870 aged 55 years.

Mitchell, Wesleyan Methodist.
James Mitchell was moved from Glasgow to the Hexham circuit in 1835. He was then moved to the Gateshead Circuit during 1837.

Nanney, C of E, Whitley Chapel.
H Nanney was the new incumbent at St Helen's, Whitley Chapel, in 1834.

Norther, Wesleyan Methodist.
William Norther had begun his ministry in Rye in 1803, and then served in a further 15 Circuits before arriving in Alston in 1830, then Hexham in 1831. Hills Arrangement has Rye 1803; Colchester 1804; Bedford 1805; St Neots 1806; Worcester 1808; Wednesbury 1809; Cardiff 1810; Scarborough 1811; Ripon 1812; Wetherby 1814; Pateley Bridge 1816; Otley 1819; Addingham 1821; Shipley 1824; Diss 1826; Haslingdon 1828; Alston 1830; Hexham 1831; Horncastle 1833; Ripon – Sup 1834.

Pearson 'Old', Wesleyan Methodist
William Pearson Junr was a Wesleyan Minister in the Hexham circuit in 1836-1837.

Pilcher, Wesleyan Methodist.
Jesse Pilcher began his ministry in the Hexham Circuit in 1832. He moved to Appleby in 1833, then to Antigua in 1834, Dominica in 1835, and back to Antigua in 1837.

Ramsey, Ralph, Primitive Methodist.
Ralph Ramsey came to the Hexham Circuit in1832, followed by Carlisle 1833; *1/2* year at Ripon, *1/2* at Middleham 1834; Whitby 1835; Lincoln 1836; Horncastle 1837; New Mills 1838; Stalybridge 1839.

Scurr, Mr, C of E, Slaley and Whitley Chapel
According to *Northumberland County History* VI (1902), the Rev Jonathan Scurr had been the incumbent at Ninebanks in 1829. He had married Mary Anne Heron who, with her sister, Elizabeth Mason, held the Shield Hall estate. By 1829 a deal had been done between Mary, Elizabeth and Jonathan whereby the latter got Rye Hill plus 173 acres, and Elizabeth got Shield Hall plus 200 acres. Seemingly he was subcurate at Slaley from at least 1830 to 1841.

Short, Wesleyan Methodist.
Thomas Short was moved from Richmond to Hexham in 1833, then to Stokesley in 1836, and North Shields in 1837. Hills Arrangement has: Lane End 1825; Spalding 1826; Patrington 1827; Stamford 1829; Richmond 1831: Hexham 1833; Stokesley 1836, North Shields 1837.

Smith, Joseph, C of E, Slaley.
The Rev Joseph Smith was vicar of Slaley, 1823-31.

Smith ,Robt,' Wesleyan Methodist.
A Robert Smith was leader of the Dukesfield Wesleyan Society in 1826 and 1828. This Society had 17 members and 8 second class members in 1826. The Dukesfield and Finechambers WMs combined in 1831. An R Smith, Thos Smith, and R Smith junr, all of Spring House appear as a preacher on the Hexham Wesleyan Circuit in 1851; none of them were down to preach at Finechambers.

Smith, W^{m}, ?Wesleyan Methodist.
A W. Smith of Haydon Bridge appeared as a preacher on a Wesleyan Circuit plan of 1851, when he was due to preach at Finechambers.

Stobart, 'Old', ?Wesleyan Methodist.
A John Stobart was a leader at Hexham WM, 1823-36. A Matthew Stobart was a primitive Methodist local preacher in the Hexham circuit in 1834 while a J. Stobart of Haydon Bridge, appeared as a preacher in a Hexham Wesleyan Circuit plan of 1851.

Thompson, Wesleyan Methodist.
Samuel Thompson began his Wesleyan ministry in Yell, Shetland in 1823, moving to Hexham in 1824, Dunbar in 1826, Dundee in 1827, Alston in 1828, Berwick in 1830., before returning to Hexham for a year in 1831. Then Ripon 1832; Pocklington 1835; Fourth Manchester 1837.

Wilson, **M^{tt}**, Wesleyan Methodist.

Wright, **'Old'**, Wesleyan Methodist.
John Wright started his ministry in Derbyshire in 1806, and was moved every year thereafter, to arrive in the Hexham circuit in 1830, where he stayed one year, and was then moved to at least a further five circuits. Derbyshire 1806; Chesterfield 1807; Bakewell 1808; Belper 1809; Rochdale 1810; Garstang 1811; Ledbury 1813; S. Petherton 1815; Shaftsbury 1817; Axminster 1819; Holdsworthy 1821; Barnstaple 1823; Hawden 1825; Douglas 1827; Berwick 1829; Hexham 1830; Wokingham 1831; Richmond 1833; Epworth 1834; Grassington 1835; Settle 1837.

In the Blaydon area.

Barker, Wesleyan Methodist.
Joseph Barker, minister of the Gateshead Bethesda New Connexion Methodists in 1839, but then 'discontinued on acct of many dissensions' re. Baptism etc. in 1841.

Bond, Wesleyan Methodist.
William Bond was attached to the Gateshead circuit 1838-39.

Brooks 'Young', Wesleyan Methodist.
Thomas Brookes was attached to the Gateshead circuit 1838-39.

Casson
Possibly Hodgson Casson, and known as 'Cumberland Hodge'.

Darley, **Mrs**, Primitive Methodist.

Eltringham, Primitive Methodist.

Forsyth, ?Wesleyan Methodist.

A Joseph Forsyth was associated with the Gateshead High Street Wesleyan Methodist chapel from at least 1833, but seemingly he was expelled in 1835 and then joined the Gateshead New Connexion, retiring in 1838.

Hillaby, Wesleyan Methodist.
A Samuel Hillaby was associated with the Zion Chapel, Sheriff Hill.

Ingham 'Old', Wesleyan Methodist.
Thomas Ingham was associated with the Gateshead High Street Wesleyan Methodist chapel from at least 1832. His obituary noted that he had been born in Whalley, Lancashire, in 1769, and died at Gateshead 5 March 1843. He was first a Wesleyan Methodist minister in 1793, and he continued as such until 1831, when through 'advanced age and increasing debility' he became a Supernumerary. 'He then fixed his habitation in Gateshead, a place where he had formerly resided' and where he continued to preach when his health allowed, and also administered to the sick and dying. He was a firm Wesleyan Methodist, and a strict believer in its disciplines.

Jennings, Wesleyan Methodist.
An Edward Jennings was attached to the Gateshead circuit in 1840.

John, M^r^, Wesleyan Methodist.
A Benjamin John was attached to the Gateshead circuit in 1840-41.

Lessey, Wesleyan Methodist.
A Thomas Lessey was associated with the Gateshead High Street chapel from at least 1814.

Lightfoot, Primitive Methodist.
A Mr Lightfoot had spent time in the Hexham PM Circuit, and later in Sunderland. A Mr Lightfoot contributed to an obit of the William Adamson (qv) noting that he (Lightfoot) had spent time in the Hexham PM Circuit, later in Sunderland. Lightfoot died c 1872.

Mackintosh, Wesleyan Methodist.
An Andrew Mackintosh was a Minister in the Hexham Wesleyan Circuit 1838-1840, and in the Gateshead Circuit in 1841.

Mitchell, Wesleyan Methodist.
This was probably the James Mitchell who had earlier been attached to the Hexham Circuit. The 'Old Connexion' name was used, particularly in the Tyne/Wear area, to distinguish it from the 'Methodist New Connection' which had gained some popularity after its formation in 1797.

Moxon, Wesleyan Methodist.
Thomas Moxon was associated with the Gateshead High Street chapel from at least 1836.

Niele, ?Wesleyan Methodist.
A Francis Neal was a Wesleyan Minister in Gateshead, 1838-39.

Pierson, Wesleyan Methodist.
John M Pearson was a Wesleyan Minister in Newcastle East, 1836-38.

Snowball, ?Wesleyan Methodist.
A John Snowball of appears as a preacher on a Hexham Wesleyan Circuit plan of 1851.

Sturges, Wesleyan Methodist.
Thomas Sturgess was with the Gateshead New Connexion in 1840, but was 'discontinued, on act [account] of attitude re. baptism' in 1841.

APPENDIX 5 - SMELTING LEAD ORE AT DUKESFIELD

(AND MOST OTHER SMELT MILLS).

The dominant lead ore mined in the North Pennines was the sulphide, called galena and having the chemical symbol PbS. The washing and dressing of mined ores, usually carried out at or near the mines, prepared them for smelting where the main aim was to produce pigs or 'pieces' of lead, with minimum loss in an ore hearth. Although galena can be smelted simply by heating it in air at a fairly low temperature, several other related process would usually be carried out at a nineteenth century smelt mill. Details of these processes can be found in the publication by Hugh Lee Pattinson as noted in 'Sources Consulted'; Pattinson became smelt mills agent for WB Lead in 1832, and his account is contemporary with Thomas Dixon's diaries. An outline of the various processes carried out at a smelt mill such as that at Dukesfield is, however, provided below, together with an account of ore-hearth smelting to indicate the nature of the work carried out by Thomas Dixon.

The basic smelting processes.

Lead ore might first be roasted, ('calcined'), a pre-treatment which made it more easily reducible in advance of ore-hearth smelting, whereby raising it to a red heat, but without it becoming molten, drove off some of the sulphur, plus 'foreign' metals such as antimony. Before roasting furnaces as such were introduced, ore could be roasted in the ore hearth by adding raw ore on top of the part-smelted burden already in the hearth, and allowing it to roast before mixing it with the rest of the hearth contents, but purpose-built roasting furnaces were in use by the 1830s. Smelting of both roasted and raw ores was performed in an ore hearth, a type of furnace which was certainly in evidence by the seventeenth century. As the fuel and burden were intimately mixed in the ore hearth, peat was the preferred fuel when smelting raw ores, for almost inevitably coal contained some sulphur which made reduction of such ores problematic. Most lead contained varying but always small amounts of silver in solid solution, and an assay indicated whether it would be economically worthwhile to extract the silver from the lead by 'refining', a process sometimes also known as 'cupellation'. Lead was refined by converting it to its oxide, ('litharge', PbO), which could be separated from the remnant silver. Some litharge was sold as such, to be converted into 'red lead' for example, but most was converted back (reduced) to 'refined lead' in reducing furnaces. Lead produced in this way was highly prized, for it was softer and therefore easier to work than lead which had not been through the refining processes. All of these processes, roasting, smelting, refining, and reducing, produced slags of one kind or another, some of which contained lead that was worth recovering in a slag hearth.

The Ore Hearth.

The ore hearth can be described, rather loosely, as resembling the once-common blacksmith's hearth, and its form of construction remained fundamentally constant over time and place. The earliest ore hearths may have been constructed entirely of stone, but certainly by the late eighteenth century the central arrangement of the hearth was assembled from slabs and blocks of cast-iron, normally between 3 and 6 inches thick, rather confusingly called 'stones'; these moveable stones enabled the hearth area to be easily dismantled, cleaned and rebuilt. Essentially the ore hearth consisted of a 'hearth piece', or 'pan', about 22 inches square (inside dimensions) by 4, 10, or 12 inches deep[1]. A 'workstone' sloping down from the top front of the hearth piece, contained a shallow gutter leading diagonally down to a heated sumpter pot. Forming the rear of the hearth, and standing above the hearth piece, three further 'stones'

---

[1] Pattinson (1831) noted that 'some intelligent smelters' were now making the pan '10 or 12 inches deep, by this means increasing the quantity of lead retained in the hearth, and proportionately lessening its tendency to get too hot, during the process of smelting'.

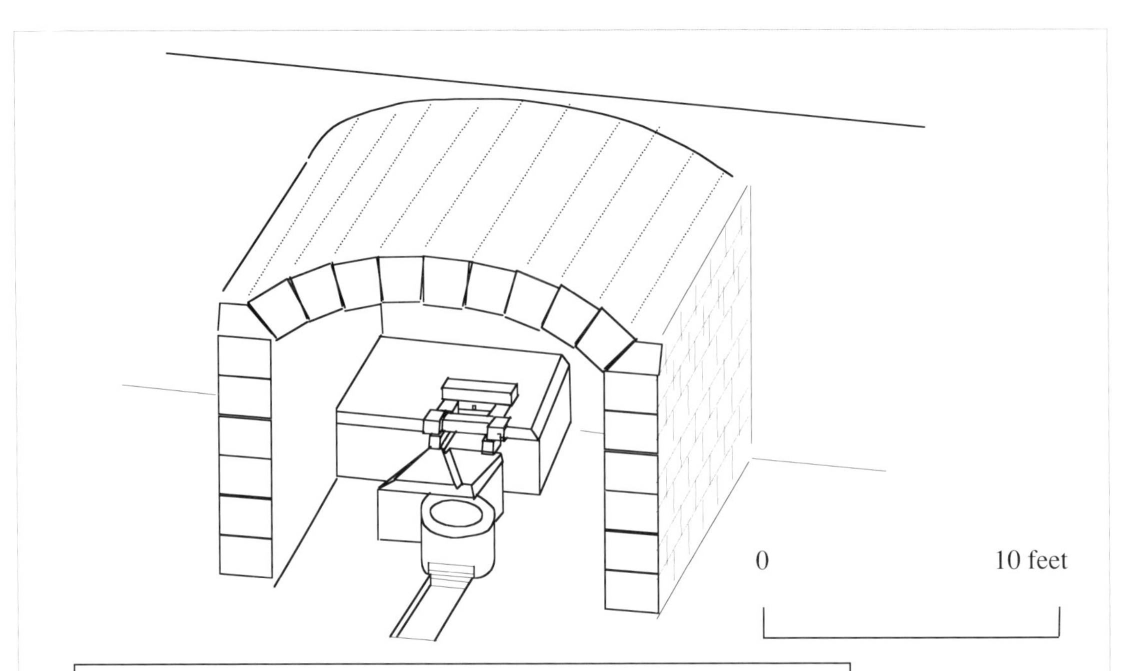

The Ore Hearth, based on Pattinson (1831)

Flues within the arched roof and/or rear wall, were intended to carry off fumes.

Fig. 21

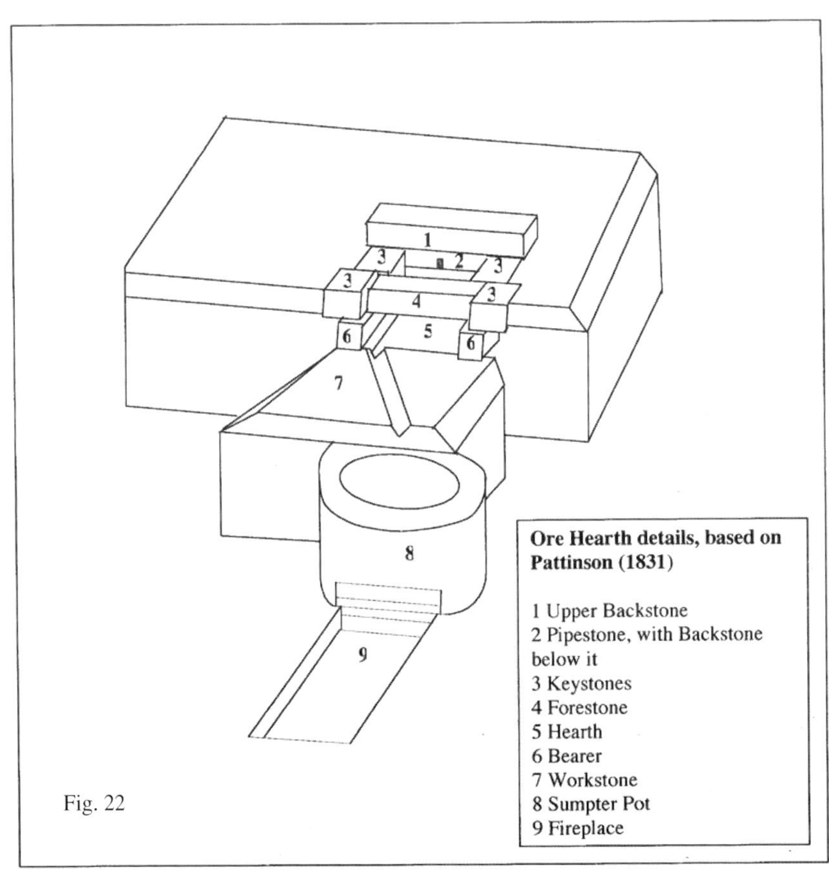

Ore Hearth details, based on Pattinson (1831)

1 Upper Backstone
2 Pipestone, with Backstone below it
3 Keystones
4 Forestone
5 Hearth
6 Bearer
7 Workstone
8 Sumpter Pot
9 Fireplace

Fig. 22

completed the rear of the hearth, and supported the bellows pipe. The sides of the hearth above the pan were enclosed with 'bearers' and 'keystones', and the front of the hearth was completed by a movable 'forestone' which was supported about 12 inches above the workstone, the space between being stoppered with fireclay.

This whole hearth arrangement was secured and sealed with firebricks, the top of the firebricks at the upper level of the hearth stones being finished off with masonry, on which 'hearth-ends' were deposited during smelting. The entire ore hearth was constructed within a house which was accessed by a wide arched opening, while an open space above the hearth led to a chimney for fume dispersal. The bellows and waterwheel were normally located behind the rear wall of the ore hearth house, but this may not have been the case at Dukesfield, judging by the occasions when Thomas Dixon noted that his bellows were on fire.

Two men would normally work at an ore hearth at any one time, and they would usually process about 5-5 bings (1 bing = 8 cwt.) of ore per 14 to 15 hour shift. Pattinson noted in 1831, however, that although it was possible for two men to smelt 20 bings over 3 shifts, a fair rate of working was from 15-17 bings over 3 shifts.

At the start of their shift, a pair of smelters would find the hearth pan full of lead, and some semi-reduced ore, called 'brouse', which had been put on one side by the previous smelters at the termination of their shift. The new shift would then begin by filling the hearth area above the pan and behind the forestone, with peat, wood, cinders, etc., or sometimes just peat. A kindled peat would then be placed immediately in front of the bellows pipe, with the bellows blowing quite hard, to ignite of the fuel charge above the hearth pan area. More fuel would be added when all was well alight, and then the left-over brouse was gradually added above the burning fuel. When good and hot, this pasty brouse was lifted out of the hearth area and onto the workstone. Simultaneously the bellows pipe opening was cleaned, and a fresh peat placed directly in front of it to disperse the blast. The brouse on the workstone was now prodded and pokered, grey slags removed from it, and any fused bits broken up. Slaked lime was thrown on the brouse to thicken it and to enhance slags formation. More fuel was then added above the hearth pan, and the brouse was then returned to the hearth. By now, a trickle of lead would be passing over the front of the hearth pan and running down the workstone gutter and into the heated sumpter pot.

Only now was fresh ore added to the charge, 10 to 12 lbs. at a time, while the whole of the charge above the hearth pan was repeatedly stirred. At 5 to 10 minute intervals, the above processes of removing and returning the brouse, adding lime and fuel etc., were repeated, and molten lead was periodically ladled from the sumpter pot into pig moulds.

As the end of the shift approached, the hearth was made ready for the next shift. No more fuel or ore was added, but the remaining brouse was worked two or three more times between hearth and workstone, any slags being picked out, and then put on one side for the start of the next shift. The air blast was stopped and the ore hearth left for 4 or 5 hours to cool down before the next shift started.

It will be apparent that the ore hearth needed constant attention over the shift. The work of the ore hearth smelter was therefore relentless, and generally unpleasant.

SOURCES CONSULTED.

Books and periodicals

Anon, *Outbye Journey* (Rothley Shield), (W.I., 1950).
Bailey, J., *The Agriculture of County Durham*, (London, 1810).
Bailey, J., & Culley, G., *General View of the Agriculture of Northumberland, Cumberland and Westmorland*, (1st edn. 1794, Frank Graham repr. of 1805 edn., 1972).
Beckerlegge, O. A., *United Methodist Ministers and their Circuits*, (1968).
Bulletin of the North East Branch of the Wesley Historical Society.
Children's Employment Commission (Mines), 1842. BPP 1842, 16 (2).
Fairbairn, R. A., *The Mines of Alston Moor*, (Northern Mine Research Society, Keighley, 1993).
Forster, W., *A Treatise on a Section of the Strata from Newcastle upon Tyne to Cross Fell*, (1st edn. Alston, 1809; 2nd edn. Alston 1821; 3rd edn. Newcastle 1883; repr. Davis Books, Newcastle, 1985).
Granville, A. B., *The Spas of England*, 2 vols., (First pub. 1841; Adams & Dart, 1971).
Hodgson. J. C., *Northumberland County History*, vol. V1 (1902).
Hughes, E., ed., 'The Diaries and Correspondence of James Losh', V. 1 Diary 1811-1823, *Surtees Society*, 171 (1962); V. 2 Diary 1824-1833 and letters, *Surtees Society*, 174 (1963).
Hughes, M., *Lead, Land, and Coal as Sources of Landlord Income in Northumberland, 1700-1850*, (Unpub. PhD thesis, University of Newcastle upon Tyne, 1963).
Hunt, C. J., *The Lead Miners of the Northern Pennines in the Eighteenth and Nineteenth Centuries*, (Manchester University Press, 1970; repr. Davis Books, Newcastle, 1984).
Johnson, A., 'Slaley', *Archaeologia Aeliana*, ns, 16 (1892-3) 339-344.
Kristensen, H., *Memories of Hexhamshire*, (Wagtail Press, 1999).
Kristensen, H., *Whitley St Helen's Churchyard, Hexhamshire,* (Wagtail Press, 2003).
Lonsdale, Henry, *The Worthies of Cumberland*, (1873). (Includes 'Hugh Lee Pattinson', 273-320.)
MacLean, J. S., *The Newcastle & Carlisle Railway* (Newcastle upon Tyne, 1948).
Mason, *A Slaveleia [Slaley] Miscellany*, (Privately published, 1986).
Ministers and Probationers of the Methodist Church …, (1957) [Formerly *Hills Arrangement*]
Pattinson, H. L., 'An Account of the Method of Smelting Lead Ore and Refining Lead, practised in the Mining Districts of Northumberland, Cumberland, and Durham, in the year 1831', [Read 17 October 1831], *Trans. Nat. Hist. Soc. of Northumberland, Durham and Newcastle upon Tyne*, 2 (1838), 152-77.
Pearson, Wm, *A Journal of an Excursion to ye North of England, AD 1838*, Illustrated by R Atkinson Esqr. [Newcastle Central Library, Pearson (1838), L942.8 No. 899618]
Percy, J., *Metallurgy*: Vol. III, (London, 1870; Repr. Eindhoven, c.1989).
Primitive Methodist Magazine.
Proceedings of the Wesley Historical Society.
Raistrick, A., & Jennings, B., *A History of Lead Mining in the Pennines*, (Longmans, 1965; repr. Davis Books, Newcastle, 1989).
Robertson, A, ed, *A Miner's Diary of 1907*, (Hundy Publications, Alston, 2000).
Sopwith, T., *An Account of the Mining Districts of Alston Moor, Weardale, and Teesdale*, (Alnwick, 1833; repr. Davis Books, Newcastle, 1989).
Sykes, J., Latimer, J., & Fordyce, T., *Local Records*, (4 vols., Newcastle upon Tyne, 1833-76).
Tomlinson, W. W., *The North Eastern Railway*, (1915; repr. by David & Charles, 1967).
Turner & Hargreaves, *150 Years of Methodism in Gateshead* [at the Gateshead Bethesda New Connexion Chapel (1986).
Wesleyan Circuits and Ministers, 1765-112, [Known as *Hall's Arrangement.*]
Wesleyan Methodist Magazine.
Whishaw, *Whishaw's Railways of Great Britain & Ireland*, (1842; repr David & Charles, 1969).
Wilkinson, B. Peter, 'Leadmining Families - The Westgarths & the Forsters', in Chambers, B. (Ed.), *Out of the Pennines*, (Friends of Killhope, 1997).
Wright, A. B., *History of Hexham*, (W. Davidson, Alnwick, 1823).

Directories

Bulmer, T. F. (ed.), *History, Topography, and Directory of Northumberland, (Hexham Division) …*, (Newcastle upon Tyne, 1886).
Parson & White, *History, Directory and Gazetteer: Durham and Northumberland*,(vol 1, 1827: vol 2: 1828).
Slater's Royal National Commercial Directory of the Northern Counties, 1 (Manchester, 1864).
Slater's Directory of Cumberland, Durham, Northumberland, Westmoreland and the Cleveland District, (Manchester, 1876).
Ward, R, *North of England Directory* (Newcastle upon Tyne, 1851).

Archives

Tyne and Wear Record Office - Gateshead WM (MC. GA6 (MF1874) 1812-37. RG 1094.
Northumberland County Record Office - Allendale papers, NRO 672, including Jno. Mulcaster's reports on the W B lead smelt mills (NRO 672/2/53); NRO 752/1, 2 (Thomas Dixon's 1838 and 1841 diaries); NRO 2443; NRO EP 68, 163, NRO 894 M5.
National Archives: RAIL 509/96, 58.
Methodist Records at the John Rylands Library, the University of Manchester.
www.familysearch.org.
Author's collection.

Newspapers

Gateshead Observer.
Hexham Courant.
Newcastle Courant.

LIST OF ILLUSTRATIONS

AUTHOR'S COLLECTION: plates 5, 45, 49, 50- 51, 53-54, 59-60, 73.

BEAMISH MUSEUM Regional Resource Centre – The following plates are reproduced by kind permission of Beamish Museum: plate 44 (29327), 61 (18326), 62 (16379), 63 (16762), 64 (16823), 65(15799), 67 (30477), 68 (161458).
© Beamish Museum

KRISTENSEN Collection – plates 1-4, 8, 10-15, 17-18, 20-25, 27, 29-30, 32, 34-37, 39-41, 56-57, 69.
© Wagtail Press

NORTHUMBERLAND ARCHIVES SERVICE, Northumberland Records Office – The following plates are reproduced by kind permission of Northumberland Records Office: plate 43 (1876-C6-197), 6 & 55 (NRO 752/1), 7 & 58 (NRO 752/2).
© Northumberland Records Office

TYNE & WEAR MUSEUMS – The following painting is reproduced by kind permission of Tyne & Wear Museums: plate 28 – "A Border Fair" by John Ritchie (H18251), Laing Art Gallery.
© Tyne & Wear Museums

UNIVERSITY OF NEWCASTLE UPON TYNE, The following illustration is reproduced by kind permission of the Special Collections Librarian, Robinson Library, University of Newcastle upon Tyne: plates 58 & 71 (C582).
© University of Newcastle upon Tyne

The Travellers Rest – plate 9, Mrs M.Christie – plate 16, History of Northumberland Vol VI – plates 19 & 31, Mrs E.Sobell plate 26, Mrs D.Bisset – plate 33, The Green Room Restaurant – plates 41 & 72, Mrs Moore – plate 70, Mrs M.Robson – 47, Mr C.Dallison – plate 48, Mr J.Scott – plate 74. Plates 42 & 66 are from a private collection. Woodcuts by Thomas Bewick. Page 196 – quote from "North Country Quilts" by Dorothy Osler – Reproduced by kind permission of the Bowes Museum and The Friends of Bowes Museu

Figure Numbers

Figs. 1-2, 7-13, 15-16: Stafford M.Linsley.
Figs. 3 & 4: Allendale & Hexhamshire OS map of 1866; Alan Godfrey Maps.
Fig. 5: poem from "Memories of Hexhamshire", published by Wagtail Press 1999.
Figs. 6 & 17: from "The History of Leadmining in the North East of England", published by Ergo Press 2006.
Figs. 19 & 20: by kind permission of Mr W. Fawcett.

Captions for photographs and illustrations by Hilary Kristensen

Halliwell Picnic c.1925 Plate. 74

4th from left – Kathleen Ellerington Extreme right – William Ellerington, of Juniper House

William (1863-1940) and his daughter Kathleen are the only known relatives of Thomas and Jane, the publishers have identified. Jane's sister Elizabeth (Sparke) married James ("Jemmy") Ellerington in 1830 at Slaley church. Their son John was William's father.

Another line investigated is that of Thomas's and Jane's daughter Jane, who married Thomas Bulman in 1855. Their son Jacob Dixon Bulman left a daughter Jane Carol Bulman. Their daughter Elizabeth married James Armstrong Haswell in 1900. We have been unable to find these last three descendents after the 1901 census when they were living in Durham City (see page 237).

If the whereabouts of any descendents and relatives are known the publishers would be extremely interested to know more about the family.

It seems unlikely that these memorandums were the only years that Thomas Dixon recorded his life. If others are known to readers of this book would they please also contact the publishers.

Please contact – Hilary Kristensen,
Wagtail Press,
Gairshield, Steel,
Hexham,
Northumberland,
NE47 0HS
Email – wagtailpress@yahoo.co.uk